Teaching in Post-14 Education & Training

Fifth edition

Andy Armitage, Alison Cogger,
Jane Evershed, Dennis Hayes,
Shirley Lawes and Mandy Renwick

Open University Press

Open University Press
McGraw-Hill Education
McGraw-Hill House
Shoppenhangers Road
Maidenhead
Berkshire
England
SL6 2QL

email: enquiries@openup.co.uk
world wide web: www.openup.co.uk

and
Two Penn Plaza, New York, NY 10121-2289, USA

First published 1999
First published in this fifth edition 2016

A catalogue record of this book is available from the British Library

ISBN 13: 978-0-33-526184-0
ISBN 10: 0-33-526184-1
eISBN: 978-0-3-3526185-7

Library of Congress Cataloging-in-Publication Data
CIP data applied for

Typeset by Aptara Inc., India

Fictitious names of companies, products, people, characters and/or data that may be used
herein (in case studies or in examples) are not intended to represent any real individual,
company, product or event.

Praise for this book

"This fifth edition of what has surely become a classic text on teaching in further education is everything one would expect it to be: packed with practical advice for teachers, underpinned by clear and accessible discussion of relevant theory. Teaching in Post-14 Education and Training encourages the teacher to reflect and to review their own practice. It interrogates current concepts of professionalism and prevalent ideological approaches to vocational education and training. Its exploration of values in relation to recent educational reforms provides the reader with a model of critical analysis essential to the professional educator. This book will prove a valuable resource for teachers and teacher-trainers alike."

Professor Susan Wallace, Emeritus Professor of Education,
Nottingham Trent University, UK

"This revised edition of 'an old favourite' is an important text for student teachers working in or preparing to work in the education and training sector. The new edition provides new teachers with important strategies and theories about how to teach, useful activities to help them think about their practice, and chapters on the sector and what it means to be a teacher in the sector, including links to the Education and Training Foundation's 2014 Professional Standards. Dennis Hayes' chapter documents key policy initiatives and events affecting the sector and should be mandatory reading for all who work in, with and on behalf of the sector; its significance magnified by the recent announcement of the area reviews. The chapter is 'a history lesson' for students teachers, current teachers, managers, principals and politicians, and most importantly it makes visible to the reader the policy hyperactivity since 1976 and evidences the policy amnesia of successive governments."

David Powell, Director, The Education and Training Consortium
and HUDCETT, University of Huddersfield, UK

"In the fifth edition of this respected text Armitage et al have once again provided the sector with a resource which combines academic analysis, theoretical critique and sound practical advice on matters to do with education and teaching. This is a quite an achievement given the pace of change currently underway in the sector. Each chapter is carefully crafted and summarised so that readers can use the text discriminately or as a whole. . Elements of sound practical advice are successfully combined with an extensive critique of the new market economies impacting on the structural organisation of the education system today. The resultant book is both useful and thought provoking."

Dr Liz Keeley-Browne, Oxford Brookes University, UK

Contents

Tables

Figures

Authors

Andy Armitage is an education consultant, Chair of the Universities' Council for the Education of Teachers Post 16 Committee and has led inspections of FE initial teacher education programmes for Ofsted. **Alison Cogger** is Faculty Director of School, College and Learning Setting Partnerships and formerly Programme Director PGCE 14–19, Faculty of Education, Canterbury Christ Church University. **Jane Evershed** was formerly Senior Lecturer in Post-Compulsory Education, Canterbury Christ Church University. **Dennis Hayes** is Professor of Education at the University of Derby and a visiting professor at Oxford Brookes University. **Shirley Lawes** was formerly the Subject Leader for PGCE Languages at the Institute of Education, University of London and works now mainly as an independent educational researcher and writer. **Mandy Renwick** was formerly Principal Lecturer and Head of Department for Professional Development at Cardiff Metropolitan University.

Acknowledgements

The authors and publisher are grateful to the following: the Education and Training Foundation for its permission to use the new professional standards in relation to each chapter (although the selection of these standards was made by the authors); Emily Adkins, Canterbury Christ Church University PGCE 14–19 student for the lesson evaluations in Chapter 2; Mary Garland, Canterbury Christ Church University PGCE student for the extract from her reflective journal in Chapter 2; Catherine Ashdown and Viv Wilson of Canterbury Christ Church University for the section on mentoring and coaching in Chapter 2; Ian Jasper of Canterbury Christ Church University for the section on action research in Chapter 2; Lily-Mae Kew, Gina Winder and Sally Atkinson of Canterbury College, Swale Campus, for the assessment mark sheets in Chapter 6; Anita Goymer of Canterbury College, Swale Campus, for the ILP/tutorial record sheet pro-forma in Chapter 6; Georgina Scott, Canterbury Christ Church University PGCE 14–19 student for the scheme of work in Chapter 8; the following Canterbury Christ Church University PGCE 14–19 students for their contributions to the 14+ reforms section in Chapter 7 – Emily Adkins, Charlotte Burton, Laura Duffy, Jennifer Gavin, Lauren Griffiths, Jenni Jackson, Sarina Loi, Kristina Parker, Camilla Parkinson, Danni Pellowe, Rachel Rickard, Georgina Scott and Ben Stroud.

Individual authors took responsibility for the following: Andy Armitage for overall editorial control and Chapter 6; Andy Armitage and Alison Cogger for Chapters 2, 7 and 8; Jane Evershed for Chapter 5; Dennis Hayes for Chapters 1 and 9; Shirley Lawes for Chapter 3; and Mandy Renwick for Chapter 4.

Abbreviations

ACL	Adult and Community Learning
AE	adult education
AoC	Association of Colleges
AP(E)L	Accreditation of prior (experiential) learning
AQA	Assessment and Qualifications Alliance
AR	action research
AUP	acceptable use policy
AUT	Association of University Teachers
BEC	Business Education Council
BECTA	British Educational Communications and Technology Agency
BTEC	Business and Technology Education Council
C&G	City & Guilds
CAL	computer-aided learning
CAT	college of advanced technology
CBET	competence-based education and training
CBI	Confederation of British Industry
CBL	computer-based learning
CETT	Centre for Excellence in Teacher Training
CLA	Copyright Licensing Authority
CNAA	Council for National Academic Awards
CPD	continuing professional development
CPVE	Certificate of Pre-vocational Education
CSE	Certificate of Secondary Education
CSJ	Commission on Social Justice
DBIS	Department for Business, Innovation and Skills
DCSF	Department for Children, Schools and Families
DES	Department of Education and Science
DfE	Department for Education
DfEE	Department for Education and Employment
DfES	Department for Education and Skills
DoE	Department of Employment

DTLLS	Diploma in Teaching in the Lifelong Learning Sector
DWP	Department of Work and Pensions
EBacc	English Baccalaureate
ECDL	European Computer Driving Licence
ECM	Every Child Matters
EEC	European Economic Community
EHEI	Enterprise in Higher Education Initiative
EHCP	Education Health and Care Plan
EMA	Education Maintenance Allowance
EQ	emotional intelligence quotient
ERA	Education Reform Act
ESOL	English as a second or other language
ETF	Education and Training Foundation
FAQ	frequently asked questions
FE	further education
FEDA	Further Education Development Agency
FEFC	Further Education Funding Council
FENTO	Further Education National Training Organization
FEU	Further Education Unit
FHE	further and higher education
GCE	General Certificate of Education
GCSE	General Certificate of Secondary Education
GNVQ	General National Vocational Qualification
HE	higher education
HEA	Higher Education Academy
HEFCE	Higher Education Funding Council for England
HEI	higher education institution
IAP	Individual Action Plan
ICT	information and communications technology
IfL	Institute for Learning
IiP	Investors in People
ILA	Individual Learning Account
ILP	individual learning plan
ILT	Information and Learning Technology
IPLDP	Initial Police Learning and Development Programme
IPPR	Institute for Public Policy Research
IQ	intelligence quotient
ISP	internet service provider
IT	information technology
ITALS	Initial Teaching Award Learning and Skills
ITB	Industrial Training Board
iWB	Interactive Whiteboard
LA	local authority
LLL	lifelong learning
LLN	literacy, language and numeracy
LLUK	Lifelong Learning UK

LSC	Learning and Skills Council
LSIS	Learning and Skills Improvement Service
LSN	Learning and Skills Network
LSRN	Learning Skills Research Network
MKO	more knowledgeable other
MOOC	massive open online course
MSC	Manpower Services Commission
NAGCELL	National Advisory Group for Continuing Education and Lifelong Learning
NATFHE	National Association of Teachers in Further and Higher Education
NCSL	National College for School Leadership
NCTL	National College for Teaching and Leadership
NCC	National Curriculum Council
NCLB	No Child Left Behind (US)
NCVQ	National Council for Vocational Qualifications
NEDO	National Economic Development Office
NEET	Not in Education, Employment or Training
NETT	National Education and Training Target
NHS	National Health Service
NIACE	National Institute of Adult Continuing Education
NOS	National Occupational Standards
NTI	New Training Initiative
NTO	National Training Organization
NVQ	National Vocational Qualification
OFL	open and flexible learning
Ofqual	Office of Qualifications and Examinations Regulation
Ofsted	Office for Standards in Education
OVAE	Office of Vocational and Adult Education (US)
PCE	post-compulsory education
PCET	post-compulsory education and training
PDP	Professional Development Portfolio
PGCE	Postgraduate Certificate of Education/Professional Graduate Certificate in Education
PTTLS	Preparing to Teach in the Lifelong Learning Sector
QCA	Qualifications and Curriculum Authority
QCDA	Qualification and Curriculum Development Authority
QCF	Qualifications and Credit Framework
QIA	Quality Improvement Agency
QTLS	Qualified Teacher Learning and Skills
PTLLS	Preparing to Teach in the Lifelong Learning Sector
RAE	Research Assessment Exercise
RAM	random access memory
RBL	resource-based learning
REF	Research Excellence Framework
RSA	Royal Society of Arts
RSI	repetitive strain injury

RSS	real simple syndication
SATs	Standard Assessment Tests
SCAA	Schools Curriculum and Assessment Authority
SCETT	Standing Committee for the Education and Training of Teachers
SCOPE	Centre on Skills, Knowledge and Organisational Performance
SEAC	School Examinations and Assessment Council
SENDA	Special Education Needs and Disability Act 2001
SET	Society for Education and Training
SFA	Skills Funding Agency
SSC	Sector Skills Council
SSDA	Sector Skills Development Agency
SSSNB	School Support Staff Negotiating Body
TA	Training Agency
TDA	Training and Development Agency for Schools
TDLB	Training and Development Lead Body
TEC	Training and Enterprise Council/Technician Education Council
TED	Technology Entertainment and Design
TES	Times Educational Supplement
THE	Times Higher Education
THES	Times Higher Education Supplement
TILT	Teaching with Independent Learning Technologies
TOPS	Training Opportunities Scheme
TPIAG	Teenage Pregnancy Independent Advisory Group
TTA	Teacher Training Agency
TTLB	Training and Development Lead Body
TTRB	Teacher Training Resource Bank
TUC	Trades Union Congress
TVEI	Technical and Vocational Education Initiative
T2G	Train to Gain
UCAS	University and College Admissions Service
UCET	Universities' Council for the Education of Teachers
UCU	University and College Union
URL	uniform resource locator
UTC	University technical college
VLE	Virtual learning environment
WEA	Workers' Educational Association
YOP	Youth Opportunities Programme
YPLA	Young People's Learning Agency
YTS	Youth Training Scheme
ZPD	zone of proximal development

Introduction

This book is chiefly a resource for students following courses such as the Award, Certificate or Diploma in Education and Training or in what may variously be termed 'further education' (FE), 'adult and further education' or similar, which all have in common a concern with students Post-14 offered by national awarding bodies or higher education (HE) institutions. While directed primarily at such students, this book will also prove useful for students training to teach in the secondary, FE and HE sectors on Professional or Postgraduate Certificate of Education (PGCE) courses. In addition, those intending to gain and retain Qualified Teacher Learning and Skills status (QTLS) will need to engage annually in appropriate continuing professional development (CPD). CPD will be central to the delivery of the 14–19 curriculum, so that teachers of Post-14 students involved in staff development in schools, sixth-form, tertiary or FE colleges, or in the adult education sector, will find this book a helpful resource. Finally, the book will be useful in relation to a wide range of development activities for those involved in training in industry and commerce, both in the public and private sectors.

Teaching in Post-14 Education and Training is not intended as a textbook to be read from cover to cover. Its purpose is more practical and dynamic. It assumes that its users are engaged in a programme of training or staff development and that they are either teaching/training or engaged in teaching practice. It makes teachers' professional contexts the focus for their development and each section therefore contains a series of practical tasks which, in all cases, are based on those contexts. However, since the emphasis of courses such as the Award and Certificate is on the acquisition of basic teaching skills and we feel the Diploma in Education and Training should build on this foundation by developing the capacities to analyse critically and reflect, the practical tasks are stimulated or complemented by theory, analysis, information, discussion or examples of student work.

Although this book does have a developmental structure (outlined below), users can dip into chapters as they wish. Each chapter is divided into self-contained subsections with their own key issues and can be used separately.

Since Post-14 Education and Training tutors teach in such a range of isolated contexts, often with little experience of the sector as a whole, Chapter 1 looks at the breadth of the sector. It questions whether such teachers are united by a common concept of professionalism, traces the ideas underpinning some key issues to the work of three educational thinkers and ends with a consideration of the current dominance of vocationalism in lifelong learning. This chapter encourages students to take stock of their own professional/ideological stance which we regard as either an implicit or explicit feature of every teacher's work.

Chapter 2 looks at the central learning processes a Post-14 teacher training course is likely to involve. Our experience has been that many students have not been engaged in systematic study for many years and the chapter therefore acts as an introduction to the skills required for using such learning processes. It should be particularly valuable at the beginning of a course when students may be arriving from a variety of course types with a range of curriculum models, as well as for practising teachers engaged in continuing professional development.

In Chapter 3 the major learning theories are examined to see what they can offer to a sector where breaking down learning barriers is a priority and which is very rapidly moving along the road to learning autonomy.

Chapter 4 focuses on the growing range of teaching skills needed in the increasing variety of roles lifelong learning tutors are being required to play: from instructor, lecturer and coach to counsellor, adviser, enabler and facilitator.

At the same time as giving users a very practical guide to the main teaching and learning resources, Chapter 5 develops Chapter 3's concern with learning autonomy by considering the resource implications of the expansion of information technology (IT) and the increasing reliance on open, flexible, resource-based approaches.

Although Chapter 6 looks closely at competence-based assessment, and offers support to those engaged in assessor awards, it recognizes that the expertise of many in Post-14 Education and Training may be limited to such an approach, and so offers a wider view of the basic concepts, principles and practice of assessing students.

Chapters 7 and 8 recognize the increasing importance in Post-14 Education and Training of teachers' capacity not only to reflect on and evaluate the courses they teach but the vital role many may now have to play in designing and developing courses to meet students' changing needs.

Chapter 9 offers a detailed chronology of Post-14 Education and Training as a resource for supporting a research-based project students may wish to undertake into an aspect of the sector, drawing on their work related to previous chapters.

Introduction to the fifth edition

The four years since the publication of the previous fourth edition of this book have seen the extension and development of many of the themes, policies, initiatives and innovations affecting the professional practice of both new and experienced teachers that previous editions attempted to address. In such a rapidly developing sector, however, there are major changes in policy and practice which now require consideration. All of these are noted, explained or discussed in Chapters 1 and 9, which offer an overview of the sector. In addition, specific developments are dealt with as follows. Following Lord Lingfield's report (2012a, 2012b), the government revoked the requirement for those in the sector to have an initial teaching qualification. However, new professional standards were developed in 2014 by the Education and Training Foundation (ETF).

Those standards which we feel are relevant to the content of chapters are set out at the end of each one.

Since 2014, all teachers, trainers and lecturers who successfully complete their initial teacher training have been able to register with the ETF and, after a period of professional formation, apply for Qualified Teacher Learning and Skills (QTLS) status. The Institute for Learning (IfL) ceased operations in 2014. However, the ETF has maintained its commitment to both QTLS and CPD inherited from the IfL and, in 2015, launched the Society for Education and Training as a subsidiary of the Education and Training Foundation, which the ETF describes as 'an aspirational new body for further education and training'.

The impact of changes to initial training and CPD on the profession is considered in Chapter 2. The further changes relating to the role of technology in teaching are considered in Chapter 5, which has been thoroughly revised to take account of these changes. Arguably the most profound changes in the sector relate to the reform of qualifications and assessment practice. There is a re-evaluation of 14+ developments in Chapter 7 which concludes that, following the formation of the Conservative government in May 2015, the process identified in the fourth edition in 2012, the creation of an English Baccalaureate (E-Bacc), the reform of the National Curriculum, GCSEs and A levels will be consolidated and is likely to lead to a sharper focus on key core subjects, all suggesting a greater emphasis on the importance of achievement in traditional academic subjects. This may well result in schools opting out of vocational education and leaving it to specialist institutions such as university technical colleges, studio schools, academies, free schools and FE colleges. In addition, this achievement is likely to be assessed using summative exam-based methods rather than teacher-led course assessment.

1

Working in Post-14 Education and Training

1.1 What is Chapter 1 about?

This chapter sets out a series of problems and choices which face all teachers and trainers in Post-14 Education and Training. Section 1.2 attempts to define what 'Post-14 Education and Training' means and raises the problem of why there is so much talk about teacher professionalism in Post-14 Education and Training. A central theme of this section is how the notion of 'professionalism' is related to quite different discussions of the nature and importance of knowledge. A discussion of the knowledge base of Post-14 Education and Training then leads us to examine the relationship between 'education' and 'training', and 'teaching' and 'training' and their relation to a new professionalism, based on the notions of responsibility, duty and formal membership and regulation by a professional body. Section 1.3 examines the views of three educational philosophers whose ideas are central to thinking about education and training today and invites the Post-14 Education and Training teacher to consider their own philosophical standpoint. Section 1.4 discusses how forms of 'vocationalism' came to dominate thinking in Post-14 Education and Training and the challenges this poses for all teachers and trainers. Section 1.5 looks at what has been called the 'therapeutic turn' in Post-14 Education and Training. Finally, Section 1.6 asks whether education and training policies and proposals under the present Conservative and previous Coalition government constitute a 'revolution' in education.

Task 1.1: Preliminary reading

Our assumption is that you will already know something of the changing nature of further, adult and higher education and informal learning, such as:

- the impact of government policy and that of 'arm's-length' bodies such as the former 'quangos' and those that remain such as Ofsted;

- the range of qualifications from the early National Vocational Qualifications (NVQs) at various levels and the structure of GCSEs and A levels, the Qualification and Credit Framework (QCF) and initiatives such as the ill-fated 14–19 Diploma, foundation degrees, career colleges and university technical schools (UTCs);
- the role of professional bodies such as the University and College Union (UCU), the Association of Colleges (AoC), the Education and Training Foundation (ETF), the Higher Education Academy (HEA), the Universities' Council for the Education of Teachers (UCET) and the Standing Committee for the Education and Training of Teachers (SCETT).

However, if you are unfamiliar with this field, we would particularly recommend the 'chronology of Post-14 Education and Training' in Chapter 9 of this book as a very useful starting point and reference work. Other than this, there are a range of introductory books. For example, Vince Hall's *Further Education in the UK* (1994) is a useful, if now historical, starting point and Prue Huddleston and Lorna Unwin's (2013) *Teaching and Learning in Further Education*, first published in 1997, gives basic information in a straightforward way. With the introduction of mandatory teaching qualifications for lecturers working in further and adult education settings, a range of introductory books came onto the market that provide an introduction to Post-14 Education and Training and what is currently required of teachers (see Hayes et al.'s *A Lecturer's Guide to Further Education*, 2007a, Chapter 8, for a discussion of these). Another useful practical introduction is Peter Scales' *Teaching in the Lifelong Learning Sector* (second edition 2011). The issues discussed throughout this book are of a universal character, dealing with topics such as the nature of professionalism and the conflict between education and practicality.

1.2 Contested concepts of professionalism in Post-14 Education and Training

KEY ISSUES

Professionalism is a notion that is grounded in paid employment although there is a long tradition of informal learning. This is the first and most minimal definition of professionalism.

Professionalism is a broad notion but one which implies subject expertise.

Educational thought of the 1960s and 1970s led to theoretical subjects achieving primacy in the curriculum but this was reversed in subsequent decades (see below and Chapter 9). Does the distinction between the academic and vocational impoverish a great deal of what happens in lifelong learning?

Is there a permanent *deprofessionalization* of teachers and trainers in Post-14 Education and Training or is there a *reprofessionalization* around new concepts of responsibility being promoted and regulated by the government the ETF and HEA?

When this book first appeared in 1999 the title referred to teaching and training in 'post compulsory education' (PCE). The term 'lifelong learning' was discussed in this chapter of that book as faddish and vague (see also Task 9.6 in Chapter 9). Ironically, the title of the fourth edition of this book became teaching and training in 'lifelong learning' but we continued to warn that the term 'lifelong learning' is often a slogan indicating anything from the idea that we live in a technology-driven and empowering 'learning age' to a new view of people as diminished human beings, children for life, needing more and more help with our 'learning' (Ecclestone and Hayes 2008). The recent government-inspired attempts to define aspects of education and training as constituting the 'learning and skills sector' carry with them just this ambiguity between training in skills and infantilization. The term is currently used in reports and in book titles but it will not endure because the idea of a 'learning and skills sector' is top-down or 'policy wonk' speak, taken up by bureaucrats and consultants inside and outside of government (see Chapter 9 for a discussion of the fragility of such ideas).

An equally popular term at the time of the first edition was 'post-compulsory education and training' (PCET). PCE and PCET were often no more than synonyms for further education (FE). All these terms refer for the most part to education that happens outside compulsory schooling, occasionally with reference to the early years, but more often to learning beyond the age of 16 to 99 and beyond. The PCE/PCET/FE field is broad, complex and conceptually confusing. It covers adult education (AE), further and higher education (FHE), higher education (HE), training in industry and commerce, and informal teaching and training situations. We are not alone in finding the language troublesome. Helena Kennedy started her report, *Learning Works: Widening Participation in Further Education* with the throwaway definition: 'Further Education is everything that does not happen in schools or universities' (Kennedy 1997b: 1).

The change in the title of this book to *Post-14 Education and Training* clearly includes more than the Kennedy definition. It refers to some education that is clearly compulsory. If the 14–19 Diploma had continued, the rationale for the change in title could have been based on the existence of that qualification alone. The rationale we will give, despite the demise of the Diploma, is that new developments such as free schools and academies, University technical colleges (UTCs) and career colleges are changing the education and training landscape and will increasingly do so. The boundaries between compulsory and post-compulsory education are breaking down. Coupled with the possibility of post-19 funding vanishing, the future for traditional FE is more uncertain than at any previous time (see section 1.6 of this chapter).

The broadest definitions of PCE or 'lifelong learning' also encompass much that is beyond the scope of this book. We are only talking about education and training in which there is normally a 'cash nexus': someone is paying or being paid for the learning that goes on, or someone is being trained to enter paid employment. There are many marginal cases that might be raised in objection. For example: Percy has retired but still teaches his daughter-in-law German in his home;

Alan provides a group of interested young students with an introduction to Latin outside of their formal programme; Martin shows young people how to do basic plumbing at home. These unpaid or informal learning sessions do not differ in any way that matters from 'paid' sessions. They are simply imitations of them that become less and less recognizable as they become less formal. This distinction is very crude but it has its point. An idealistic colleague recently declared that she would go on teaching even if she wasn't paid, which matches the intention of the volunteering aspect of the so-called 'Big Society'. Advocates of the 'learning society' or 'learning organization' often promote learning, with an evangelical fervour, as the responsibility of all, in a way reminiscent of the 'de-schoolers' and certain adult educationalists. We will return to these views later. What they represent for us here is an elementary attack on *professionalism*. The sort of education and training we are talking about is that brought about by an individual or individuals who see themselves as professional teachers or trainers and who are paid for what they do. In the lifelong learning literature there is a tendency to discuss other sorts of learning than formal learning. This can even include such concepts as 'family learning' which we might think has gone on for centuries (Alexander and Clyne 1995; Alexander 1997). We argue that this is to elevate less important forms of knowledge as equivalent to serious forms of study. Rhetorical talk about 'the information society', the 'knowledge economy' or 'the learning society' often fosters the acceptance of a very wide definition of knowledge that also encourages a lack of discrimination about different sorts of knowledge (Education Forum 2010). This must necessarily diminish the worth of the paid professional. Issues about professionalism, therefore, are closely connected with any teacher's or trainer's view of knowledge and its worth.

Task 1.2: Identifying elements of professionalism

Do you consider yourself to be a professional? Try to identify what makes you a professional. If you do not describe your role as 'professional', how would you describe it?

Apart from being paid, there are other elements to the professional role of a teacher in the sector. The traditional discussion has always looked at two other criteria of professionalism: 'knowledge', which we have already touched on, and 'responsibility' (Langford 1985: 52–3). The debates of the 1970s and 1980s were concerned with whether teaching was a 'profession' or a 'job'. Issues such as status and salary were crucial. The legacy of this historical discussion of professionalism is a focus on the teaching and personal style of individuals. In this light you might have thought of 'professionalism' superficially as a mode of presentation of self or of subject: sharply dressed, perhaps, with a 'PowerPoint' presentation and a study pack for your audience! Alternatively, you might have listed activities in your wider role: serving on committees, undertaking quality audits, designing courses and distance learning packs, recruitment and marketing. Most of this is managerial and administrative work that will often be included as part of a 'wider' or 'less tangible' notion of professionalism that goes beyond the individual (Lingfield 2012a: 25). The requirement to undertake such wider roles is an element of the 'managerialism' that has become part and parcel of teaching today (see the criteria set out in Lingfield 2012b: 22). What we want to examine here is a more narrow 'professionalism' which we could describe as 'subject professionalism'.

It is an assumption throughout this book that there can be both professional teachers and professional trainers. To establish this we need to explore the distinction between the two. This will require further discussion of the sort of knowledge that is being passed on. It might be thought that what 'teaching' and 'training' mean will depend to some extent on what individuals teach and how they go about it. As this book is addressed to a wide audience, we will sketch a general picture to illustrate the problems that this approach would present us with. Consider the following typical teaching and training activities:

- a university lecturer giving lectures based on research critical of the concept of 'learning styles';
- a researcher giving seminar papers on research into boys' learning;
- an AE tutor teaching A level English literature;
- an FE lecturer teaching art and design;
- a practitioner giving talks on an action research project in chiropody teaching;
- a lecturer teaching a motor vehicle National Vocational Qualification (NVQ);
- a hairdresser teaching trainees within a private scheme;
- a police officer teaching crime-scene management;
- a human resources manager disseminating her or his firm's equal opportunities policy;
- an instructor teaching social and life skills to adults with learning difficulties;
- a counsellor teaching basic counselling skills (awareness) to teachers;
- a tutor facilitating a discussion of citizenship with play workers;
- a part-time (sessional) lecturer teaching parenting skills to a group of young mothers;
- a mother talking to her children about their family history and the forms of their extended family;
- students taking emotional quotient (EQ) tests;
- therapeutic arts students discussing transitional lifecourse anxieties;
- a parenting class for ethnic minority mothers.

These teaching and training activities are varieties of 'subject' teaching in a very ordinary sense of the word. But there is another sense in which some are 'theoretical' or knowledge-based subjects, some are 'practical' subjects and others are more difficult to classify but could be important to the college or in a wider social life.

Task 1.3

Review the list of 'subjects' above and divide them into 'practical' and 'theoretical' subjects. Are there any subjects that are difficult to place?

In a paper written in 1965, 'Liberal education and the nature of knowledge', Paul Hirst gave a famous description of liberal education as being 'determined in scope and content by knowledge itself' (Hirst [1965] 1973: 99). He further classified knowledge as follows: '(1) Distinct disciplines or forms of knowledge (subdivisible): mathematics, physical sciences, human sciences, history, religion, literature and the fine arts, philosophy. (2) Fields of knowledge: theoretical, practical (these may or may not include elements of moral knowledge)' (p. 105). In this catalogue, if a subject was 'practical' it was not part of a 'liberal education' as defined. This is not to say that it was not of use – the utility of the practical cannot be denied – but it had no logical connection with the forms of human knowledge. Using this description, very few of the activities above would be part of a liberal education. They might be part of a 'general education' but this means something like 'schooling' or 'the college curriculum'.

Task 1.4

Consider the list of teaching sessions given above in the light of Hirst's distinction between 'forms' and 'fields' of knowledge. Do you now look at it differently?

A parallel distinction to that between liberal education and the practical fields of knowledge is that between teaching and training. Making the latter distinction is straightforward if we base it on the former. But it must not be held to undervalue the role of the trainer in society. This would not be a wise move as the teacher and trainer may be the same person in different contexts. Both the teacher and the trainer aim at getting a student or trainee to think, or act, for themselves. Gilbert Ryle has examined in some depth the differences between teaching and training and notions such as 'drilling' or the formation of 'habits' and 'rote' learning (Ryle 1973: 108–10).When we talk of training we do not mean to reduce it to this limited caricature which, Ryle comments, comes from memories of the nursery. Teaching and training involve teaching and training *how to do something*. They are not 'gate shutting' but 'gate opening' activities (Ryle 1973: 119). We would see the trainer with specialist knowledge and a set of practical skills as equally 'professional' as the teacher of academic subjects. We would add that recent developments, to be discussed below, threaten the professional 'gate opening' activities of both the teacher and the trainer.

Task 1.5

Do you see yourself as primarily a 'teacher' or a 'trainer'? What would you see as the essential difference between the two?

In the 1960s and early 1970s, educational thought was dominated by rationalist principles. Human beings were characterized by their cognitive capacities. A powerful and positive concept of human rationality dominated educational thought. Judgements about objective truth could be made. Human beliefs, actions and emotions could be guided by reason. Hirst has come to see his earlier view to be a 'hard rationalism' (Hirst 1993: 184) and says of his previous position, 'I now consider practical knowledge to be more fundamental than theoretical knowledge, the former being basic to any clear grasp of any proper significance of the latter' (1993: 197). Hirst now sees education as primarily concerned with social practices. More specifically, he prioritizes 'personal development by initiation into a complex of specific, substantive social practices with all the knowledge, attitudes, feelings, virtues, skills, dispositions and relationships that it involves' (1993: 197).

Underpinning the rationalism of the 1960s described above was the thinking of the Enlightenment philosophers of the seventeenth and eighteenth centuries from Descartes to Kant, who established modern intellectual values such as a belief in knowledge, objective truth, reason, science, progress, experimentation and the universal applicability of these to all of mankind's ability to control nature. It has to be said about Hirst's explanation of forms and fields of knowledge that he in some ways merely reflected the current thinking of his time (see Chapter 9 – the 1960s was the decade of the space race and the first moon landing). This does not make his educational epistemology false, but it does mean that as times have changed and people have become less confident about science and knowledge, Hirst has begun to reflect this in his thinking.

There have also been attacks on such confident views of the importance of knowledge by postmodernists (Usher and Edwards 1994) and seemingly radical thinkers (Bloomer 1996, 1997; Harkin et al. 2001). Postmodernists will ask 'Whose knowledge?' and claim there are a variety of truths and distrust reason. They further distrust science and the notion of progress, and question the damage done by attempting to control nature. They seek to emphasize different and particular views rather than universal 'theories' which attempt to explain how the world or society works. It is better to see such views as a reflection of less confident times rather than as a serious contribution to educational thought, although like all extreme and distorted philosophies they are not without their insights. As far as the relativity of knowledge – the notion that there are different 'truths' – is concerned, postmodernists have to answer a devastating critique first made by Socrates in Plato's *Theaetetus* (Burnyeat 1990) over 2000 years ago. A simple formulation of this critique is to express the postmodern viewpoint in a simple statement – 'All truths are relative' – and to ask 'Is this statement true?' The consequences of the question are that either the statement is true or its negation is true. Therefore there is a true statement that is not relative. This simply shows that the more facile forms of relativism that some postmodernists desire are contradictory if they are articulated. Fortunately, postmodernist thought has had little impact on education and training other than, and most worryingly, in some corners of our universities.

Another example of an attack on knowledge is one that comes from the increasing numbers of teacher-educators and trainers influenced by 'critical theory', whether they know it or not! Critical theorists and their followers see the challenge of teaching and training as making 'classrooms more open in language practices', which means that 'Differences of gender, culture and outlook should be celebrated as part of a democratic endeavour' (Harkin et al. 2001: 135). Martin Bloomer's somewhat artificial notion of 'studenthood' comes out of this school of thought. He notes that 'studenthood' conceptualizes the ways in which students can begin to learn independently and recognize 'the problematic nature of knowledge' (Bloomer 1996: 140) through reflection on their own learning experiences. The consequence is that they can begin to 'exert influence over the curriculum' in 'the creation and confirmation of their own personal learning careers' (p. 140). Bloomer's conceptualization of teaching situations might be an example of what is often called 'praxis' or 'practical wisdom'. The result of these individualistic applications of what were originally Marxist ideas is not radical because it leaves students engaging in a critical self-reflection that is a sort of therapy (see Therborn 1978: 125–8). The appeal of this to some teachers and trainers is a false sense of being able to solve social problems through 'the enlightened efforts of critical students and scholars' (p. 139).

This radical view of the potential of teachers, trainers and students has a parallel in a more conservative view of education and training and one that is more widespread. Radical teacher-trainers may see education as transformative for individuals, but managers and government policy-makers are more likely to promote the idea that FE, in particular, can transform and regenerate the economy. We can call this the Bilston College Fallacy as that college did much to promote this view in a series of publications (see Reeves 1997 and, for a critical assessment, Bryan 1998; Wolf 2002). (Ironically, Bilston College went into severe financial difficulties shortly after the publication of its well-known book.) Both the radical and conservative views of FE overestimate the role of education in, respectively, politics and the economy (see Section 1.4).

Task 1.6

Consider the knowledge content in your subject or area of practical expertise and how you present this to students. Do you see yourself as having the traditional role of initiating students into worthwhile forms or fields of knowledge, or areas of practical knowledge; or are you inclined towards the postmodern or relativist school of thought that sees education as something particular and of many varieties; or do you see it in the more radical way as transformative in terms of communication or through 'praxis'? If you see yourself as primarily a trainer, do you consider any of these approaches to be knowledge-relevant?

It can be argued, however, that such challenges to Enlightenment thinking open the door to at least two factors which could seriously undermine the status of knowledge. The first is the introduction of the concept of competence into discussions of education and training. Hyland has made three general criticisms of competence-based education. These are that it is no more than a confused slogan, that it has foundations in behaviourist theories which ignore human understanding, and that there is no coherent account of knowledge in the competence literature (Hyland 1994: Chs 2, 4, 5). Hyland has made some excellent criticisms of various writers on the nature of competence as having a crude understanding of know-how, skill and the complexities of judgements required in making a knowledge claim. All that is held to be required are certain stipulated outcomes that we can pick out. This is linked with a 'tendency to reduce all talk of knowledge, skills, competence, and the like, to talk about "evidence"' (Hyland 1994: 74). This gives some competence statements a spurious and vague meaning. However, it provides us with a very impoverished concept of what it is to 'know' something as relating only to the performance of work functions.

> **Task 1.7**
>
> Competence and knowledge: find examples of competence statements from your own or another subject, or from a teacher training course. Consider what concept of knowledge they embody, and see if it makes sense. Do they refer to narrow skills or dispositions or to broad general capacities? Do they adequately take account of the nature of judgement? You might like to review Hyland's criticisms (1994: Chs 5, 8) and how far the introduction of new vocational qualifications, from General National Vocational Qualifications (GNVQs) to the 14–19 Diplomas attempted to address them.

There is a hint of paradox in that competence-based training schemes are often couched in the empowering 'student-centred' language of progressive or humanistic education. But by emphasizing learning by doing, rather than becoming critical thinkers, competence-based programmes require students to be both intellectually passive and yet very busy. Keeping students working at gathering evidence to establish competence seems to some critics to be merely the introduction of the discipline of the workplace in the interest of any future employer.

> **Task 1.8**
>
> To what extent have you observed the conjunction of competence-based training programmes and humanistic or student-centred philosophies? Try to find a clear example of such a conjunction in a course document or handbook.

The second way in which knowledge could be seen to be devalued concerns the introduction of competence-based programmes of teacher training. The absence of theory and academic knowledge in teacher training programmes is a result of many years of government spokespeople blaming theory, particularly that of the 1960s, for all the problems in education, if not all the ills of society! It is hardly surprising, therefore, that we find competence-based schemes predominating in teacher education. In FE the early 1990s saw the introduction of the competence-based vocational assessor qualifications (D32 and D33) by the Training and Development Lead Body (TDLB), the launch of a competence-based City & Guilds (C&G) Further and Adult Education Teacher's Certificate and the start of many competence-based Certificate in Education (FE) courses. The outcome of many of these courses was already said, in the early 1990s, to be the deprofessionalization of the lifelong learning teacher (Hyland 1994: 93). The replication in teacher training, at all levels, of the competence-based model means that the model of control applied to students also operates with teachers. It provides a work-related, operational form of discipline that is often required but is just as often self-imposed. Many teachers and trainers now have competence-based qualifications. Despite some early cynicism these programmes are now universally accepted and the introduction of the new, but short lived, teacher qualifications, PTLLS, CTLLS and DTLLS in 2007, some believe, was merely the continuation of two decades of development.

The consequence of all these initiatives is that teachers and trainers in Post-14 Education and Training have come to see themselves as assessors, checking portfolios and other productions with their lists of 'learning objectives' or 'learning outcomes' to see if there is evidence that student learning has occurred. It is difficult to find ways of opposing these schemes when not only your own subject knowledge but academic knowledge itself is being challenged. The shift in terminology from 'competences' to 'standards' is an example of a simple change of label and should not be seen as of any importance, except that 'standards' seems to be less obviously work-related. It is, of course, much harder to object to 'standards' than 'competences', which are obviously work-based. There is a danger of this approach to teacher education spreading to HE through the implementation of recommendations from the Dearing Report *Higher Education in the Learning Society* (Dearing 1997). Dearing's report led to the formation of the Institute for Learning and Teaching in Higher Education (ILT), now absorbed into the HEA, that has rapidly expanded teacher training in HE with the specific aim of redressing the balance between teaching and research. The most likely outcome of this development will be a competence-based scheme similar to those found in FE. The crucial difference here is that the primary business of HE is knowledge and research, not developing competence or even skills. It is the ethos created by this focus on advancing knowledge that makes teaching so exciting for many at this level.

Dearing's proposals to make HE teaching more learner-centred will not necessarily help students. The idea is that the student is not to be passive but must actively engage in the learning process. At HE level this is to turn the focus of education away from the knowledge and understanding needed to ultimately engage in research, to playing with methods of learning, something that could turn the academy into a mere centre of 'edutainment'. But, crucially, Dearing's general view of knowledge is as a commodity that can be delivered by teachers or through information technology (IT). His report reveals no clear understanding of what a university is. This failing could reduce all teachers in HE to the position that many FE teachers now find themselves in: as assessors checking off whether they have evidence that learning has occurred. The engagement and interaction with research-based knowledge could become a rare experience outside of the research universities in the 'Russell Group' (see Hayes 2002a). An ironic case study in the dangers of attempting to introduce the assessment or competence model into HE is that of teacher trainers who, at the start of the second decade of the twenty-first century, are once again blamed for all the failings of education and all the ills of society. But the trainers had, some say, been trained to enforce government policy initiatives through a competence- or assessment-driven framework (see SCETT 2011).

Task 1.9: Teaching, assessing or counselling?

The argument we have put forward is that there is a danger that in devaluing knowledge and critical thinking we necessarily turn from being teachers to being assessors. However, the latest shift is for teachers to take upon themselves the role of educational guidance workers or counsellors. Although this may seem to be a welcome shift away from assessing to encouraging transformative personal development, it is a complementary activity that requires teachers and trainers now to assess more and more aspects of a student's private life rather than theoretical or practical learning. The emphasis now being placed on individual guidance is more the formalization of an existing change than something qualitatively different. Many teachers will say that although their formal job is to assess learning, much of their time is taken up with coaching, advising and getting students to reflect upon and explore their ideas, and that therefore the assessment part of their work has become a formality. Consider whether this is true by reflecting upon how much of your own teaching involves imparting knowledge and skills and developing critical thinking, or personal (and emotional) guidance.

It may be thought that the notion of a teacher or trainer as a 'reflective practitioner' could be a way out of the teacher or assessor dilemma. There are problems in understanding what the phrase 'reflective practitioner' means to most people and even of making sense of the most careful expositions (see Gilroy 1993). The term appears to replicate the use of humanistic, student-centred rationales for competence-based programmes for students and trainees. It confines the teacher or trainer to their particular concerns in the classroom and redefines 'theory' to mean the systematic restructuring of the teacher's own experience and ideas. In this way, the model rejects a rationalist model of objective truth (see Elliott 1993). In the context of a general attack on academic knowledge and critical thinking, the term 'reflective practitioner' might not, as we may be tempted to think, allow us to subvert the competence-based curriculum. The theorists of reflective practice could be involved in an implicit attack on just this possibility, however much they dislike the competence-based approach. Some of them would respond that they do offer a sort of theory – critical theory. 'Critical theory', which is the product of former Marxists of the 'Frankfurt School', is essentially a politicization of teaching that works through an emphasis on questioning all assumptions (for an example see Hillier 2005). The aim is a critical consciousness to promote positive or even revolutionary social change but the practical result, in what are far from revolutionary times, is to leave teachers and trainers confused and uncertain, even anxious about what they are doing, as too much has been questioned (Hayes 2005). Others have abandoned any meaningful notion of theory and celebrate a totally subjective 'I Theory' (McNiff and Whitehead 2002; McNiff 2003).

The force of this criticism of reflective practice can be understood by considering the traditional way in which academic studies, such as some of those on any teacher training programme, relate to professional practice. The approach was to pose questions about the relationship of theory to practice. The attempt was sometimes made to link the two perspectives through a notion such as 'praxis' (see above) but, once this becomes more than an attempt to relate theory to practice, and slides into talk about 'practical wisdom' or 'reflective practice', the traditional question has been turned on its head and *practice* is re-presented, however subtly, *as theory*. Tutors and students then begin to systematize and elaborate a description of their practice and call it 'theory'. This is a very special use of the term 'theory' and we would argue that the traditional way of looking at the relationship of theory to practice is still important, if only in that it reminds us of much of the work that has been done in psychology, sociology, philosophy and other disciplines that it is still important for the teacher to know as it is a part of the framework through which we understand the world, whether or not it is of immediate practical use.

The debate about the behaviourist philosophy of competence-based education and training (CBET) and the seeming paradox of humanistic delivery of CBET through the lifelong learning teacher training curriculum is almost historical. This is in part because of the understanding made possible by the recent popularizing in Britain of the work of the French academic and political propagandist Pierre Bourdieu. As a result of Bourdieu's work and his discussion of what he calls 'cultural capital' it is possible to see that a different notion of 'competence' is developing that resolves this seeming paradox. There is also a more important shift in the nature of this seeming paradox which gives more attention to process – the humanistic delivery – and less to content – competence-based or content-based – because of what has been called by Dennis Hayes the 'therapeutic turn' in lifelong learning (see Hayes 2003a, 2004; Hyland 2005, 2006; Ecclestone and Hayes 2008).

However, this needs some contextualizing and we have deferred a discussion of this new notion of competence to Section 1.4 (see p. 24).

At this stage it might be useful to consider the concept of 'guidance' a little further. This is the third of our three criteria of professionalism, in addition to our being paid for what we do and, most importantly, that we possess knowledge of a specialized sort. The notion of guidance we want to consider in the final part of this section is not restricted to the tutorial, personal or career guidance provided by teachers, trainers or personal advisers but 'guidance' related to the concept of making students aware of their *duties*. Increasingly, teachers and trainers find themselves dealing with cross-curricular themes rather than subjects. Key skills have already made inroads into subject-based teaching and it is possible to find whole degree programmes written in terms of the development of key skills, now that these are a required element in all HE programmes. Key skills are content-free. This is not true of other 'neglected' cross-curricular themes such as 'citizenship' and the 'environment'. It is guidance in these issues that is new. These topics are part of a new professional ethic that stresses the importance of 'duties' within an emerging 'global conception' of citizenship and the 'public good' (Bottery 2000: 235).

What is important to note about the new professionalism is how far the idea of being a professional has moved from someone being paid, or having expert knowledge, to the concept of the professional who is the vehicle for giving students a particular (and contestable) set of moral and political ideas.

With the establishment of a professional body, the IfL, there was, on its website and in its publications, evidence of the conscious working out of a notion of professionalism for teachers and trainers that reflects the above discussion. The IfL drew on discussions of professionalism in teacher education and attempted to adopt an external concept of professionalism that requires teachers to commit to certain specified values, including those of environmentalism (IfL 2006a) and to a 'code of professional practice' that was tending towards the paternalistic and authoritarian (IfL 2006b, 2006c). Such externally imposed values are often met with cynicism or indifference because they promote professionalism without autonomy. The IfL adopted a marketing, or public relations, approach to professionalism, often relying on repeating to their members that they were 'professionals, professionals, professionals'. The transfer of their assets and most of their membership to the ETF and the creation of a Society for Education and Training (SET) show no signs of changing the direction of the IfL. This is equally true of the proposed professional body for teachers, the 'College of Teaching'. The only way that these nascent professional bodies can develop a more autonomous and open idea of professionalism that could be grounded in subject knowledge is to create a freer and contested moral space by engaging in serious and public debate around the issues in this chapter.

Task 1.10

Which model(s) of teacher education does your Certificate of Education or other course presuppose? Do you consider any of the dangers of competence-based or reflective practitioner approaches outlined above have the potential to affect you? Do you think that part of a professional role is to ensure that your students have certain sets of values?

1.3 Three educational thinkers

In his inaugural lecture at the University of London Institute of Education in 1963, Richard Peters described educational theory as 'undifferentiated mush' that had 'contributed so much to the low standing of the study of education in this country' (Peters [1963] 1980: 273). For almost three decades after his speech educational thought became more differentiated and several major works were written that remain at the cutting edge of thinking in the field of education today (see McCulloch 2002). Today education as a field of study has reverted to what can only be described as a 'methodological mush' made up of standards and procedures for altering the behaviour of children and young people.

There is a tendency to denigrate what we can learn from the past and past thinkers, as we will see in Chapter 9. Like the People's Front of Judea in Monty Python's *Life of Brian*, the contemporary attitude might be expressed in the answer to the similar question: 'What have the Greeks and Romans to tell us about education?' It turns out to be quite a lot as the now out of print *Ancient Education and Today* admirably shows (Castle 1961). More succinctly, Roy Harris has broadly divided trends in educational thought into the approaches of the three great Greek philosophers: 'The "Socratic" ideal is based on taking the individual mind, the "Platonic" on taking the state, and the "Aristotelian" on taking the universe – as indicating the goals and limits of worthwhile knowledge' (Harris 2009: 123). Aristotle is increasingly popular today as he had a library of information because there was so much knowledge that could not be kept in an individual mind. Aristotle is wrongly appropriated by those who today say 'Why do young people need to memorize anything?' while waving an iPhone (for a critique see Education Forum 2010: 8–11 and Hayes 2014).

We have selected three major educational thinkers to illustrate the historical philosophical basis of contemporary, if theoretically underdeveloped, ways of thinking about education and training. Following our discussion of the 'new professionalism' above, the inclusion of Socrates will be obvious. There are other reasons related to the discussion of professionalism as to why we have picked Rousseau as he is the first significant thinker to stress personal growth as an educational goal and all the problems and difficulties of sustaining such a view are apparent in his work. Our third choice of John Dewey is now a necessity. His thinking dominates all recent work in lifelong learning (see Pring 1995). Every contemporary idea from 'relevance' and 'building on experience' to 'democratic' education and the possibility of a 'vocational education' that is not merely training for a job is to be found in his first major work (see Dewey [1916] 1966 and below). A case could be made for the inclusion of other thinkers. The British empiricist philosopher John Locke has been influential with a commonsensical approach to education that was intended for the English gentleman. Aristotle is in vogue with philosophers and a case could be made for including him because of his historical influence. But our selection is not meant to cover historically or fashionably influential thinkers. Our intention is to stimulate some philosophical thinking about education so that the lifelong learning student can put contemporary thinking into perspective and not be restricted to the eclectic thinking provided in policy documents or, indeed, in books such as this.

We may never think to formulate our educational philosophy, but the terms in which we describe our professional practice will nevertheless indicate a leaning towards some form of articulated philosophy. Our argument is that we all have a 'philosophical style' as much as we have a 'teaching style'.

Task 1.11: Identifying your educational philosophy

Consider the three groups of ideas below and select that which best describes your idea of what education should be about.

1   Critical thinking, the development of knowledge, the search for objective truth, with the teacher having authority about these matters (Socrates).

2   Personal development, autonomy in learning, growth to reach natural potential, the teacher as the facilitator of learning (Rousseau).

3   Knowledge should be useful, socially relevant, involve problem-solving and be taught through practical activities; teaching should be cooperative and democratic (Dewey).

Each of these sets of ideas reflects the views of one of the philosophers we discuss below. You might have found it difficult to choose just one view and this is understandable but, in the end, we argue that they are largely incompatible. Review your choice after reading this section.

Socrates

Socrates (469–399 BC): Athenian philosopher, whose ideas come to us from Plato (429–347 BC). In 387 BC Plato founded a school in a grove in Athens that became known as the 'Academy', which existed for over 900 years. Plato's major educational works are the *Republic* (366 BC) and the *Meno* (387 BC). Another work referred to below, the *Apology*, was written in the decade after Socrates' death.

'The Socratic education begins . . . with the awakening of the mind to the need for criticism, to the uncertainty of the principles by which it supposed itself to be guided' (Anderson 1980a: 69). Criticism is at the heart of the Socratic philosophical method, but it is a criticism that seeks to show that wisdom is 'not thinking that you know what you do not know'. Socrates is wise to the extent that he does not claim to have knowledge but nevertheless seeks knowledge by a ruthless examination of the claims of individuals to have knowledge or wisdom. It is not an empirical method proceeding by reference to facts but a rationalist approach that works through the exposure of contradictions and absurdities in someone's thinking. This method can be irritating for the modern reader of the Platonic dialogues who see their opinions and beliefs subjected to it (Buchanan 1982: 21). Something of the impact of this method on individuals can be gleaned from Socrates' cross-examination of Meletus at his trial, recounted in the *Apology*. Here Meletus is forced into a contradiction by being made to claim that Socrates believes in no gods and yet to see that his charge against Socrates could only be made against someone who believed in gods (Plato 1993: 37–67). This is a method of teaching through which the teacher reveals a person's ignorance to them through the dialectic of discussion and the questioning of answers. Although there is a debate about this, the term 'philosophy' originally meant not 'love of wisdom' but 'love of a wise friend'. It is a wise teacher who shows you your ignorance and education thus requires a teacher to be in an entirely superior position to the pupil. An example of this method is given in the celebrated passages in the *Meno* (Plato 1956: 82a–85e) where Socrates questions a slave boy about geometry. He elicits from him the recollection that the square of the area of a square is equal to its diagonal. The slave boy responds confidently to the early questions but ultimately recognizes his ignorance: 'It's no use Socrates, I just don't know' (p. 84a). This 'numbing' and 'perplexing' part of the Socratic process, or the *elenchus*, does away with false knowledge and instils the desire to learn. We are not concerned here with this proof of the theory of anamnesis, or the remembering of the immortal soul in its contemporary state, but with Socrates' methodology. For Socrates, unlike Plato, there is no end to the process of critical questioning.

It is a common mistake to confuse the views of Plato and Socrates because almost all of what we know of Socrates' teaching comes from Plato's dialogues. Some commentators make excellent distinctions between the two thinkers (Holland 1980: 18; Perkinson 1980: 14–30; Tarrant 1993: xv–xxii). We will only make the broad distinction that for Socrates education was solely about learning to be critical whereas for Plato education led, by the process of criticism, to truth. The view that education is fundamentally about criticism, however, does not require us to accept the Socratic view of wisdom or the metaphysic of Platonism.

Most discussions of the Socratic idea of education in colleges and in educational textbooks look at the system of schooling set out in the *Republic*, ignoring the discussion of the dialectic in Book VII (Plato 1982: 546–84) and in the earlier dialogues. This gives undue emphasis to what Plato would consider the lower processes of education, which are really forms of training and habit formation (see Holland 1980: 18–21). In our short discussion we have tried to give an indication of the power and value of what is now dismissed by the proponents of reflective practice as 'theory-based and impractical' rationalism (Elliott 1993: 1).

In summary, the Socratic education is about the need for criticism. To overcome ignorance it utilizes a certain method: the dialectic of questioning and testing ideas. In turn, this demands that the teacher guides the pupil through a process of learning to be critical which may be perplexing and numbing. Finally, the process may or may not lead to knowledge in the form of objective truth, but that is always the goal.

> **Task 1.12: Education as critical thinking**
>
> Is the development of critical thinking at the heart of your concept of education? If not, what role has criticism in your idea of education? Consider how important the element of critical thinking is in your particular subject area. If you are a trainer, are there ways in which you encourage a critical approach?
>
> *Further reading*: Plato's works are accessible and easy to read. The *Apology* and *Meno* are good starting points. Both are short and relevant to contemporary educational debates about the role of the teacher. There are many editions but it is an advantage to have one with a commentary.

Rousseau

Jean Jacques Rousseau (1712–78): essayist and philosopher of the Enlightenment period. Major educational work: *Émile* (1762).

Rousseau is a thinker of the Enlightenment period but stands in romantic reaction to it. In Section 1.2 we have already considered criticism of the Enlightenment tradition, but it may be helpful to state once again the basic principle of the Enlightenment as: a belief in the universal applicability and value to humanity in overcoming our dependence on nature by means of science, reason, progress and experimentation. Rousseau's work is not aimed at defending the *ancien régime*. He believes in the revolution that is sweeping it away but is concerned at what it is creating, the new enemy, the 'bourgeois'. He is a man who thinks only of himself and whose prime motivation is fear of his own death (Bloom 1991: 3–28). Rousseau's model of the bourgeois is based upon the pre-revolutionary bourgeois he saw growing up around him in France but also on the English gentleman whose education is described in John Locke's ([1693] 1989) *Some Thoughts Concerning Education*.

It is surprising that Rousseau has not been adopted as the educational thinker of the so-called 'postmodern age' or of 'new age thinking'. *Émile* begins with the declaration: 'Everything is good as it leaves the hands of the Author of things; everything degenerates in the hands of man' (Rousseau [1762] 1991: 37). Society, even living in small groups, corrupts man's nature. It is to nature that we must turn to save us from disfiguring everything. Rousseau describes the child as a plant, and organic and growth metaphors abound. 'Plants are shaped by cultivation, and men by education' (p. 38).

Rousseau uses a wide definition of education to mean any change brought about after our birth. It is, therefore, threefold and comes from nature, men and things. It is only the education by men that we have entire control of so we must use it to ensure that education from nature is the dominant form. Nature is defined as a state in which our dispositions are uncorrupted by opinion (Rousseau [1762] 1991: 39). Rousseau enjoins mothers to 'Observe nature and follow the path it maps out for you' (p. 41). In thinking to correct or change that path we do more harm than good.

Man in his natural state is entirely for himself. Both Locke and Rousseau held this opinion. In Locke's view the adult knows best and denies the child all his wants while giving reasons that are appropriate to the age of the child (Locke [1693] 1989: Sections 39 and 44). The adult dominates and only looks for the man in the child. But Locke seeks to limit impositions and restrictions on freedom only to those that are absolutely necessary. Rousseau believes that if a child is educated by nature and things as described in the story of Émile's education, he will come to accept restrictions as legitimate rather than necessary. He will then impose them on himself. This is the essence of the good citizen. Of course, adults are active in the education of the child but only to ensure that nature takes its course. The child or young person must find out for themselves but their tutor arranges things so that certain results will follow.

In the natural order, all men are equal (Rousseau [1762] 1991: 41) so Rousseau considers only the education of the individual into man's estate. Although he was a primitivist to a certain extent, he wants men to live in society and not return to the condition of some mythical 'noble savage'. He praises Plato's *Republic* as 'the most beautiful educational treatise ever written' (p. 40). Yet he believes its vision of public education can no longer exist. His concerns are not with any particular educational institution or arrangement. He is setting out the methodology of a new form of education. In Rousseau's work we see that education has a social aim. This is to produce the citizen who will voluntarily act in accordance with the civil or 'general will'. They will do this in the same way that individuals in a state of nature act in their own self-interest (Perkinson 1980: 145). Pupils or students must learn from nature or things. The teacher must facilitate learning so that pupils or students learn for themselves.

Task 1.13: Learning from nature

Is learning best undertaken by learning for oneself? How far is your own practice governed by concepts that might be compatible with Rousseau's idea of not interfering directly in the educational process for fear of corrupting learning?

Further reading: the clearest statement of Rousseau's philosophy is given in Books I–III of *Émile*. Book V which covers the 'last act in the drama of youth' might be of more interest to the teacher in Post-14 Education and Training.

Dewey

John Dewey (1859–1952): Professor of Philosophy at the University of Chicago from 1894. Major educational works: *Democracy and Education* ([1916] 1966) and *Experience and Education* ([1938] 1971). 'If in our own time the distinction between education in the traditional sense and vocational training, as increasingly demanded by a technological society, has become somewhat blurred, this is in part due to the influence of Dewey's work' (Russell [1959] 1989: 296). In the four decades since Russell asserted this balanced judgement, Dewey's work has remained a subject for fierce criticism and passionate praise. For example, journalist Melanie Phillips criticized Dewey's emphasis on process over product (knowledge) and argued that his influence on education has been 'malign, revolutionary and destructive' (Phillips 1996: 210), while Professor Frank Coffield claims that Phillips has misunderstood Dewey and agrees with him that education is the 'fundamental method of social progress' and is about 'the formation of proper social life' (Coffield 1997).

Dewey's writings encourage such different interpretations. They are written with a radical reforming zeal that often masks the kernel of what he is saying. For teachers in lifelong learning the key element of interest in Dewey's work is his concern with vocational education and with using this to make education more relevant to students. It is important to understand what Dewey actually said because he is the most influential and frequently quoted philosopher in lifelong learning, and because his work is subject to various interpretations. (It would also be useful before tackling the discussion of vocationalism in Section 1.4.)

In *Democracy and Education* ([1916] 1966) Dewey warns against the separation in modern society between the capacities of the young and the concerns of the adult. Direct sharing in the pursuits of adults becomes increasingly difficult. Therefore teaching in formal institutions becomes necessary. This teaching is less personal and vital, and formal instruction 'easily becomes remote and dead – abstract and bookish' (Dewey [1916] 1966: 8).

The teaching of subjects is held to be 'specialist' teaching. The 'technical philosopher' could be 'ill advised in his actions and judgement outside of his speciality': 'Isolation of subject matter from a social context is the chief obstruction in current practice to securing a general training of mind. Literature, art, religion, when thus disassociated, are just as narrowing as the technical things which the professional upholders of general education strenuously oppose' (Dewey [1916] 1966: 67). One of the ways of overcoming this is to ensure that the child's native experience is not undervalued and that 'active occupations' form the basis of all teaching. This is the nearest Dewey comes to being 'child-centred'. What his injunction intends is obviously achieved by the introduction of subjects such as gardening, woodwork and cooking, but for mathematics and science: 'Even for older students the social sciences would be less abstract and formal if they were dealt with less as sciences (less as formulated bodies of knowledge) and more in their direct subject-matter as that is found in the daily life of the social groups in which the student shares' (Dewey [1916] 1966: 201).

Dewey criticizes the individualism of Rousseau and sees 'natural development' as an aim of education, but one only partially stated if it refers only to our primitive powers. He sees nurture not as corrupting but as the development of those natural powers ([1916] 1966: 111–18, 123). There is, however, a particularly American form of individualism in Dewey, who accepted the myth of the frontier as something that had elevated American society from the worst features of the development of European capitalism. In this sense, he looks back to a pre-industrial world in which there is a harmony between learning and adult life. This leaves him closer to Rousseau than he thinks. The difference is that he believes that industrialization has created the possibility for a truly democratic society which can be achieved through education.

Ryan is correct to point out, in opposition to Dewey's cruder critics, that he was not arguing that 'the point of industrial training was to produce a docile workforce adapted to the needs of capitalist employers' (Ryan 1995: 177). Dewey thought that capitalism was at best a semi-ambulant corpse but rejected the revolutionary route (Ryan 1995: 178). The central chapter in Dewey's book is Chapter 7, 'The Democratic Conception in Education' (Dewey [1916] 1966: 81–99). He sets out a vision for education in terms of an end to the separation into classes by ending the division between 'mental' and 'manual' labour. This is experienced as the division between those who receive a 'liberal education' and those who receive something poorer, or mere training for work. He envisages an education that reflects the democratic ideal. Democracy is a form of associated living, with numerous and varied points of contact with a plurality of social groups which in itself will per-petuate democracy (Dewey [1916] 1966: 86–8). Education shares these ideals and is therefore essential to democratic society.

Some writers have held Dewey's chapter on vocationalism to be the poorest in the book. It is, however, Dewey's clearest attempt to spell out the implications of his earlier chapters. Dewey defines vocationalism as 'such a direction of life activities as renders them perceptibly significant to a person because of the con-sequences they accomplish, and also useful to his associates' (Dewey [1916] 1966: 307). It is neither 'narrowly practical' nor 'merely pecuniary'. A later summary adds a temporal requirement: 'A vocation is any form of continuous activity which ren-ders service to others and engages personal powers on behalf of the accomplish-ment of results' (Dewey [1916] 1966: 319). There is a clear emphasis here on the utility of what is undertaken to 'others' or society. The definition is also so general it covers activities we would not normally call vocational. For example it includes academic study and scholarship as a vocation, as training for an academic 'career'. But here the question of 'utility', especially to society, makes no sense and can only be destructive of the quest for knowledge by subjecting it to the requirement of producing results or being useful to society (Anderson 1980b: 139–40).

Dewey claims that 'the only adequate training for occupations is in training *through* occupations' (Dewey [1916] 1966: 310, original emphasis). He argues that industrial society has created the necessity and possibility for educational reorgan-ization but 'there is a danger that vocational education will be interpreted in theory and practice as trade education' ([1916] 1966: 316). The only way of avoiding this is the methodological one of producing in schools 'a projection of the type of society we should like to realise, and by forming minds in accord with it gradually modify the larger and more recalcitrant features of adult society' ([1916] 1966: 317).

Dewey sees education as essential to the achievement of a democratic soci-ety. By reflecting that society in its organization it will ensure that democracy comes into being or continues to develop and change. He stresses the importance of the pupil's or student's experience and of socially relevant activities or 'occupations' in the classroom. Dewey recognizes the dangers in how people may take his suggestions and rejects narrow training for work as a definition of 'vocational education'.

Task 1.14: Dewey: for or against?

Dewey sets education the project of building a democratic society. How far are you in sympathy with this aim? Consider how it differs from the aim of education for Socrates and Rousseau.

These three philosophies of education will appear in discussions of curriculum ideology in broad categories such as classical humanism, humanism and social reconstructionism (Chapter 7) and in learning theory (Chapter 3) when cognitive, humanistic and empirical theories are discussed (behaviourism is merely an example of the latter). When working through these discussions, relate them to the philosophical positions outlined here. Remember that they may not always be distinct.

1.4 The 'triumph' of vocationalism

KEY ISSUES

'Vocational education' is understood in a variety of ways.

According to one particular view, questions of value and value judgement are outside its sphere.

Many have sought to reconcile vocational and liberal education.

The essential elements of the new educational initiatives of the 1980s could be said to fit a special needs deficit model of human beings that continues in various forms to the present day.

The potential of technology to transform lives is the subject of a wide range of views from those of a variety of political persuasions.

Task 1.15

Try to describe what you understand by 'vocational education'. Review your statement when you have finished reading this section.

The aim of this section is to examine how 'vocationalism' has come to dominate thinking in lifelong learning. It is related to the general themes we have discussed in the two previous sections: the attack upon 'academic' or subject-based knowledge and Dewey's criticism of the arid and dry nature of formal education. It is our contention that vocationalism has triumphed in the sense that it dominates our thinking and that Tony Blair's three priorities for Britain, 'education, education, education', could refer to an impoverished notion of education dominated by vocationalism.

Vocationalism is a term used to refer to various theories, ideological positions and some simplistic attitudes that have attempted to link the world of work to a greater or lesser degree with education. Such approaches often suggest that, as work is an important part of life, we should find a place for it in schools and colleges (Lewis 1997). But the variety of these theories and the unanalysed popular usage of terms can seem confusing or, worse still, simply unproblematic. The situation is so chronic that one set of academics has been led to declare that 'No single characteristic defines this new vocationalism. It is marked by a variety of policies and programmes and diversity of action and actors. But it is guided, if not propelled, by a determination to establish closer and better interrelationships between the experience of both formative education and preparatory training and the working world' (Skilbeck et al. 1994: 2).

A general trend we can identify at the outset is for vocationalist initiatives to be presented as part of a package of a supposedly radical rethinking of the aims of education, or providing the basis for reforms leading to a more relevant or modern, technologically based education. They often claim to be more democratic, offering a better education for the masses rather than a pale shadow of the elitist education offered to the better-off or to specific social groups. The terminology of the theorists of vocationalism can be particularly confusing. For example, we come across one theorist arguing for a 'critical vocationalism' (Donald 1992). Intellectual acrobatics are required even to attempt to understand what this could possibly mean. On a more everyday level, we find teachers using the phrase 'vocational education' in relation to a variety of courses, which may have some educational element, or may simply be training courses. Either way, there is no doubt that the advocates of the priority of practice over knowledge have triumphed. Frequent references to the 'vocational element in education' are seen as unremarkable. It is, however, possible to argue for an education that is entirely theoretical and to see it as a duty to combat those who would promote an education that is in any way practical. This would be the traditional position of the liberal educator. However extreme this view may seem, it is coherent and deserves attention (Anderson 1980c: 157).

There does seem to be a consistent refusal by participants in debates about vocationalism to recognize important conceptual distinctions. The Kennedy Report, *Learning Works* (Kennedy 1997b) talks throughout in an undiscriminating way about 'learning'. Kennedy makes no attempt to analyse what we mean by 'learning' in different contexts. Thus learning to use a lathe, to chop vegetables, learning citizenship, mathematics and ancient languages are given a spurious equality. The treatment of complex philosophical distinctions and debates as easily resolved or as semantic questions reaches its apogee in the introduction to the third Dearing Report (Dearing 1997). Here we find Dearing declaring with unmasked enthusiasm that the near future will see the '*historic boundaries between vocational and academic education breaking down*, with increasingly active partnerships between higher education institutions and the worlds of industry, commerce and public service' (1997: 8, emphasis added). Dearing writes as if the 'academic' and 'vocational' divide was something totally unproblematic to be resolved through the mutual respect of the partners as they work together.

The recognition of an academic and vocational divide has been part of the debate about the nature of education for over 2000 years. Aristotle in the *Politics* notes that in his own day 'nobody knows' whether the young should be trained in studies that are useful 'as a means of livelihood' or to 'promote virtue' or in the 'higher studies' (discussed in Lester Smith 1957: 11). The point is not that nothing changes; this would be ahistorical, as ancient Greek society and Britain today bear no comparison. But at least it is apparent from Aristotle that the Greeks felt that there was a real and important problem here. Contemporary discussions are simply trivial and sanguine by comparison.

It is the intention in this section to provide an introduction to what should be a real debate by providing a critical guide to the discussions of the various types of vocationalism that have manifested themselves since James Callaghan (the Labour prime minister 1976–9) launched the 'Great Debate'. We deliberately restrict our use of the label 'new' vocationalism because, if it has any meaning, it applies only to one very particular postwar period.

The way we think now

To understand the sense in which vocationalism is triumphant, it is worth while locating it within a more general intellectual malaise. This has been well described by writer and critic Richard Hoggart, who sees contemporary Britain as being swamped by a tidal wave of relativism, which he defines as 'the obsessive avoidance of judgements of quality or moral judgement' (Hoggart 1996: 3). One element of this dominant mood is the acceptance of vocationalism at all levels of the educational system. Arguments about improving the quality of life, or turning around Britain's economic performance, are often supported by talk of the need for skills training, or of the promotion of some form of vocational education or training. This is apparently a 'classless impulse' (Hoggart 1996: 220), but, Hoggart argues, only to those who oppose the traditional notion of education being a good in itself, whatever its practical benefits. It does seem to be true that vocationalism, as a standpoint which avoids debate and discussion about important differences of value, is widespread. A glimpse of the extent of the obsession with the vocational is apparent from the following passage from *The Economist* (1996):

On the face of it, the case for generous public support for training is strong. Unskilled people are much more likely to be out of work than skilled ones; if only their qualifications could be improved, they might find jobs more readily. Not only would they benefit, but so would the economy as a whole. A better-trained productive workforce would be a more productive one; so more training ought to mean not just lower unemployment but faster growth and higher living standards. Unions like training programmes because they can use them to push up wages. Academics like them because they increase demand for education. Parents like them because they give out-of-work, out-of-school youths something to do. Prophets of a postmodern society praise them as part of an ethic of lifelong learning. And employers don't mind because the public pays the bill.

Everyone is in favour of training. A recent study showed that a massive 66 per cent of workers thought that education and training were the means of progressing their careers (Hudson et al. 1996). There is constant discussion in the media about a 'skills gap' (IRDAC 1990) to be filled by training. But *The Economist* simply refers to training for work rather than vocational education. This is sometimes referred to as 'vocationalism' in its old or traditional sense of training to do a job. The argument of the article is that the most successful training takes place in the workplace and is provided by employers, as opposed to training provided by the state or its quangos. This may be true but it is dynamic economies which are referred to to illustrate the argument. There is a chicken and egg question to be resolved here. Is the problem identified as a 'skills gap' a result of relative economic decline or its cause? Any skills gap which does exist must surely be resolved at the political or economic level and not by scapegoating the employed and unemployed as unskilled. It could, indeed, be seen as a 'jobs gap'. In fact the debate about a 'skills gap' is one-sided, being largely promoted by employers' organizations. When asked to specify skills needed, most employers provide answers in terms of moral or personal qualities that have little to do with 'skills' in the sense that most people understand the term. We think of a skill in a traditional way as relating to, say, carpentry, engineering or IT. However, the skills needed at work are usually those that can be learned in a few weeks with minimal difficulty. The dynamic of industry is to reduce, diminish or replace such skills (Marx [1867] 1974: 407–8, 457–8; Korndörffer 1991: 222–3). Even in the case of IT, it is far from certain that we are at the dawn of a 'new era' or 'knowledge age' (Woudhuysen 1997). It is important to recognize that there is a debate here that is closely related to our assumptions about whether we face a 'skills gap' or a 'jobs gap'.

Task 1.16

Looking at your own area of expertise, identify any 'skills' that are in short supply. Are the skills you identified technical, educational or personal?

Liberal education (early twentieth century)

There have been many attempts to analyse various forms of vocationalism, and most of these attempt to reconcile 'vocational' and 'liberal' education (e.g. Williams 1994: 97–8). In Britain, the traditional or 'narrow view' of vocationalism as 'training for a job' was mostly rejected by educational reformers. R.H. Tawney was perhaps the best-known writer whom we associate with this line of thinking (Tawney 1922). Not only conservatives or traditionalists but also most socialists and radicals sought a decent liberal education in traditional and modern subjects for everyone. Access to the whole of humanity's cultural inheritance was the demand that was made. What was good enough for the sons of the masters was good enough for the workers. Vocational training was held to be entirely a matter for employers. This does not mean that individuals did not seek vocational training, but the traditional position was against vocationalism. This must be stressed as it is now almost forgotten, particularly by proponents of a 'democratic' education. According to this view, there is simply no connection between 'education' and 'training'. It could be argued that work-related training does go on in schools and colleges, but this does not establish anything other than an organizational connection between the two.

Training for jobs (the 1960s)

In the 1960s, employers relied upon the state to provide training in technical colleges but the employer was responsible for the day release of young employees. The lack of system in this method of training led to its being called 'stop gap' or 'gap filling' by many critics (Hall 1994: 43–5), but whatever its faults it was clearly related to training for jobs. When Harold Wilson spoke to the 1962 Labour Party conference of forging a new Britain in the 'white heat of the technological revolution' there was no other conception in anyone's mind but real training for real jobs. The main debates were about 'upskilling' the workforce. This is a reminder that talk of technological revolution is not new and in the 1960s the technological revolution put man on the moon (compare Ainley 1988: 143, who argues 'technological change is developing exponentially'). We can consider vocationalism as training for jobs as the major form of training up to the mid-1970s.

Training without jobs (the 1970s)

In the 1970s, economic crisis and rising youth unemployment changed things. One clear consequence of James Callaghan's 'Great Debate' was the systematic involvement of industry in the planning of the educational process. There were other elements too. The increasing role of the state in directing vocational training in a time of financial cutback has been well discussed (Benn and Fairley 1986; Finn 1987; Ainley 1988, 1990). The training on offer was still largely related to jobs. It is important to remember the general antagonism and resistance there was to the various adult and youth training initiatives. There were youth protests and opposition from the trade unions, trade councils and political groups. The main criticisms were of 'slave labour' schemes or the use of 'cheap labour' to replace existing jobs. Out of this grew an emphasis on pre-vocational and basic skills training. This transitional period is one in which the concept of 'vocationalism' starts to shift in meaning from 'day release' or 'stop gap' provision towards 'pre-vocational provision'. We could date it as beginning in 1976 but its fullest flowering is in the period of the Youth Training Scheme (YTS) from 1983 to 1989. Most analyses focus on the increasing or changed form of state involvement with the training of young people (see Hickox 1995). While these discussions are important it is our argument that the curriculum developments proposed help us to understand the long-term impact of these changes rather than simply seeing them as a matter of the state crudely forcing young people into years of slave labour.

The 'new' vocationalism (the 1980s)

Employers in this crisis situation were asking: Why should we be training young workers who cannot benefit from work because of their attitudes, lack of basic skills or poor discipline? Although this attitude ran counter to the facts, it became the basis of the Manpower Services Commission's (MSC) development of a range of training initiatives, culminating in the YTS, which were available to all unemployed young people. This pre-vocationalism is the basis of what came to be called the 'new' vocationalism. What was on offer was a curriculum derived from special needs programmes based on the sort of personal and social training necessary to prepare youngsters with learning difficulties for the world of work. The limitations of these pre-vocational courses and initiatives did not stop them being successful as a stage in the development of vocationalism.

The YTS can be seen as a failure if judged by comparison with earlier vocational training in the narrow sense, and as a pre-vocational scheme. It provided employment for only two-thirds of the trainees who completed the courses and this employment was often short term. The only vocational element in these courses was an increasingly tenuous belief on the part of the providers that young people could get a job. However, there were wider forces influencing young people and their teachers. This was the decade in which the Further Education Unit (FEU) produced its influential documents winning over the newer college lecturer with curriculum-based papers. Lower-level technical college courses and private training courses sprang up all over the country funded by the MSC. The Technical and Vocational Education Initiative (TVEI) gave educational developments and experiment a free rein. The labour market reality of the time was that there was no work in the traditional sense of a job for life. Employment was going to be intermittent and temporary, and life at college was better than unemployment. A traditional life pattern of the time was for young people to move from a YTS to employment, then on to a college course or evening class, then into a period of unemployment and then back into another, adult, training scheme. Many of those who worked in colleges or were real or potential trainees were totally sceptical about the value of these courses. But a lumpen scepticism is entirely passive: the pragmatic lessons of unemployment had been learned, and youth rebellion did not materialize. The unions and the Trade Union Congress (TUC) came back on-side to discuss training. A credit-led boom brought the yuppie into temporary being, and in this climate there was the expectation that you could make it and find a job but you were on your own.

The new vocationalism is often seen as a Thatcherite victory in creating an employer dominated training scheme for young people. The early opposition to the Youth Opportunities Programme (YOP) and YTS faded away leaving only a few radical educationalists arguing for something better. However, many of those opposing YTS schemes did not see them as a betrayal of the ideal of a liberal education for all, but the failure to provide something different. These writers were influenced by Marx and Engels' occasional comments on education (Marx 1974: 453–4, [1875] 1968: 329; Engels [1878] 1975: 378–82) and generally promote technological education. For example, Willis (1987) and Ainley (1990, 1993) argue that the working classes need to improve their skills for sale on the market and radical thinkers do them a disservice by not arguing for a form of vocational education that will meet their needs as a class. Willis (1987: xvii) puts this case well: 'how is it, and is it, possible to reconcile the tensions between training as class reproduction and training as working-class interest more in the favour of the working class?' Ainley (1993: 93) sees technological advance as the answer: 'In a modernising economy, education and training must raise the skills of all workers from the bottom up . . . Education and training will then integrate rather than separate mental and manual labour . . . New technology provides the potential to enable all working people to become multiskilled and flexible in a true sense . . .'. Precursors of these views include Harold Wilson's populist technological revolution in the 1960s and the 'post-Fordist' utopian visions of the 1980s. Such arguments have been savagely attacked as being unrelated to the reality of contemporary capitalism (Roberts et al. 1994), as this level of training would simply make employment too expensive. With an eye on profits there is no possibility that employers or the state would promote such training and the result would be redundancy for the mass of workers who would be too expensive to employ (see Yaffe 1978: 12–13). The illusion lies in a belief in the power of technology to transform people's lives rather than a political movement doing so, which has been a popular view since the end of the cold war. But such views are not necessarily implied by a Marxist analysis as Brian Simon proved in his defence of liberal education in response to the 'Great Debate' (Simon 1985). The consequence of arguments about the possibility of a new industrial revolution which will benefit workers is a convergence of the views of the 'left' and of the 'right', represented by employers. There is therefore no real opposition to vocationalism, only opposition to its crudest forms.

Education without jobs (the 1990s)

The period from 1989 to the present can be seen as one of containment. The number of young people staying on in FE increased dramatically to 89 per cent of all 16-year-olds, and led Nick Tate, the head of the School Curriculum and Assessment

Authority (SCAA), to comment in the summer of 1997 that the effective school leaving age was now 18. With 30 per cent of all young people going on to HE and many into other training schemes, we might make the effective leaving age 21 or even higher. The mass expansion of FE and HE has few critics, and even they see some basis to be positive about aspects of the work of the new universities (Ainley 1994). This period of containment is also the period of the qualification explosion. Demand for NVQs, GNVQs, GCSEs, A levels, degrees, credit-bearing courses and in-service qualifications seems never ending. The expansion of qualifications available and the apparent improvement in their attainment by young people has been questioned, and one writer is notorious for calling the whole thing a sham (Phillips 1996). Certainly, qualifications are now required for jobs that were previously thought to be unskilled, such as classroom assistants. We need to ask if there is any element of vocationalism here. Perhaps only in the residual sense of 'employability' which was a theme that grew out of government papers and reports in the mid-1990s (DfEE 1995a) and is highlighted in the report of the Commission on Social Justice (CSJ 1994: 175–6). Employability is divorced from vocational skills or even from pre-vocational skills, so why even refer to 'employability' as having to do with jobs at all? Why not just talk of 'learning' and 'education'? This is certainly a popular move with politicians, and educationalists are also seeking a move away from vocationalism: 'Serious attention now needs to be given to educating as opposed to training a majority of the population hitherto denied access to further and higher education' (Avis et al. 1996: 180).

So, is vocationalism defeated? The answer is 'no'. Mainstream education was, before 2011, dominated by the vocational themes of a work-related, often competence-based curriculum, the introduction of pre-vocational or personal and social development under the guise of 'employability' and above all by the supposed need to adapt to a life in a new 'communication' or 'technological' age. Education as a whole has become vocationalized in the sense that the connection between the world of work and education is seen as necessary rather than contingent. What this means is that, whereas people once thought that the knowledge gained in getting an education was not irrelevant to the workplace, now the sort of knowledge that is on offer seems to be only that which is relevant to work. One aspect of this is the use of the term 'learner' and expressions like 'we are all learners'. Rather than hinting at what might be called traditional 'lifelong learning' this reflects more the idealization of the flexible worker always adapting to (technologically driven) change. Even to teachers in vocational areas this must be seen as a complete debasement of knowledge and learning. As mentioned above, the Dearing Report (Dearing 1997) sets out exactly this model for the development of HE. Even if we call for a return to 'educating' rather than 'training', what is likely to be provided is not a liberal education but a poor vocationalized replacement. The same can be said of the Kennedy Report (Kennedy 1997b) with its promotion of lifelong learning. What Kennedy offered was an 'education' that amounts to learning up to NVQ Level 3 – a vocational standard, and one that is set *very* low. This has parallels with the 'back to basics' drives promoted by some ministers that make Britain sound like a Third World country. Standards are being set but set much lower than they were at the time of the Robbins Report (Robbins 1963). Vocationalism is triumphant but it appears disguised as education – 'education' of a debased kind.

There is a major difficulty with this new focus on education, although it is almost self-contradictory for educationalists, professionally and philosophi- cally, to oppose 'education'. There are also other difficulties in making education a political priority. Education is a personal or individual matter. But individual aspirations and achievements cannot be a replacement for the vision of a society actually going somewhere. Even the narrowly, work-related vocationalism that Dewey objected to and the socially divisive 'new vocationalism' had some sort of economic or political vision behind them. The new individualized educational curriculum that begins with key skills initiatives extends through Curriculum 2000 and may become a reality with the introduction of personal advisers and the new Matriculation Diploma may leave people isolated and socially disconnected (see Chapter 9 for an introduction to these developments). A lifelong learning world made up of isolated individuals, like a society of isolated individuals, can easily become fractious and discontented. This will not be the sort of discontent pre- dicted by some writers (Bloomer 1996; Harkin et al. 2001; Tomlinson 2001) but a much more personal affair based on individual rather than social conflict. What explains this state of affairs – which reminds us of Margaret Thatcher's assertion that 'there is no such thing as society only individuals and their families' – is the unpredicted and huge expansion of service industries (see Poynter 2000).

1.5 The 'therapeutic turn' in Post-14 Education and Training

The key asset that individuals now have in the labour market is not their specific vocational (or even academic) knowledge and skills but what Bourdieu (1986) calls their 'cultural capital'. Cultural capital takes three forms: 'connected to individuals in their general educated character – accent, dispositions, learning, etc.; connected to objects – books, qualifications, machines, dictionaries, etc.; and connected to institutions – places of learning, universities, libraries, etc.' (Grenfell and James 1998: 21). Having cultural capital ensures success in edu- cation and at work, particularly in gaining access to employment. It was once thought that the more qualifications people had the more productive they would be (sometimes called an increase in human capital), but at a time of credential inflation when qualifications are universal (there are even those which recog- nize common sense or forms of unskilled work such as many forms of domestic or caring work), other factors come into play in the job market (compare Young 1998: 152). From the period of the economic recession of the late 1980s the sit- uation was unclear as to what was the major factor at play (see Bills 1988), but now it is fairly clear that the crucial factor is 'cultural capital'. It is the cultural capital that you have that makes you 'competent' in the modern work environ- ment and this is a new interpretation of 'competence'. This sense of competence cannot be acquired in the way that NVQ competences can. It would be wrong to consider this as the ever-present 'networking' or 'it depends on who you are or know' emphasized by cynics and theorists of 'social capital'. It is something qualitatively different. If Post-14 Education and Training provision is to keep a nexus between the curriculum on offer and the new service work it will – consciously or unconsciously – have to adapt to develop cultural capital. This is already happening in what is called 'emotion work', the 'Have a nice day!' training for McDonald's and call centres.

There has been a growing debate as to whether the new work requires a different workforce more oriented around 'emotion work' or 'aesthetic labour' which requires a different sort of training that is shifting towards a concern with 'emotional literacy' and 'emotional intelligence' (Mortiboys 2005). The obsessive concern with young people's self-esteem is well known and there is a growing concern with 'emotional well-being' and even 'happiness' as educational goals (Ecclestone and Hayes 2008). There are sociological explanations as to why this has happened. The argument is that there is a general loss of confidence in the possibility of human progress that has led to a downplaying of the intellectual in favour of the emotional (Füredi 2004; Hayes 2006). In lifelong learning the humanistic aspect of training is now dominant but has taken on a specific aspect which ignores the normal content of humanistic approaches, a liberal education or real skills involving the training of judgement, whether or not in the distorted form of CBET, and concentrates instead on ways of approaching the inner emotional life (Hayes 2003a, 2003b, 2003c, 2004). This is a contested view, and Hyland (2005, 2006), for example, still argues that it is the commodified form of CBET that is the major threat to proper education and training and that any therapeutic elements are marginal. The debate will continue.

The illusion that this provision of cultural capital, in therapeutic forms or not, will be 'education' rather than a different sort of preparation for work is contestable. The abstract notion of 'cultural capital', adopted by policy-makers and academics, often merely reflects the views of what government and employers think people need to be employable in a changing world (Hayes 2003b). Thinking of 'education' as merely a preparation for work is now an almost universal assumption, as is thinking that education is all about the acquisition of 'skills'. This functional view of education restricts and limits students from achieving their potential. This criticism is also found in the Wolf Review (2011) which noted that there were too many low-level qualifications of dubious value to individuals or employers. Wolf, it should be noted, does not refer to the therapeutic element in vocational education or the therapeutic elements in general education that make it vocational. The difficulty for all those interested in the direction of education and training is what sort of education and training to propose in its place? A return to subject-based teaching and to training grounded in knowledge seems impossible to argue for, either pragmatically or (for some) philosophically (Ainley 1999; Waugh 2000). Earlier editions of this book considered there was this alternative but the possibility of arguing for it seemed slight. It might appear that we were wrong and a window has opened up.

Are we teachers or therapists?

With the formation of a coalition government in 2010 with a new focus on traditional subject-based education and the celebration of the 'craftsman' it may seem that the there is no longer a therapeutic turn in lifelong learning. This would seem to be the case but if you contrast Michael Gove's Royal Society of Arts (RSA) speech (Gove 2009) with his speech to the Westminster academy you find the statement that: 'Of course academic success at university doesn't automatically make you a good teacher. You need emotional intelligence as well as the more traditional kind' (Gove 2010a). This taken with the government's commitment to a happiness index with which to measure its citizens suggests that the therapeutic culture cannot be easily escaped by a simple commitment to traditional education (see Education Forum 2010).

Task 1.17

We have looked at vocationalism in several forms: as narrow training; as pre-vocational training; as being concerned with employability; and in a 'back to basics' or 'educational' manifestation. We have also seen how the contemporary obsession with 'education, education and education' meets changing workplace needs. We have outlined our belief that this new curriculum does not unlock human potential but restricts it to the needs of the workplace. What role do you consider that education and training has in unlocking human potential and do you think that, if there is an increasingly therapeutic aspect to it, that this hinders or fosters learning?

1.6 A new education revolution?

Writing on the hundredth anniversary of the launch of the *Times Educational Supplement* (*TES*) its editor, Gerard Kelly (2010), commented:

> The *TES* was launched in 1910 to assess and articulate the proposals for educational reform sweeping the country. One hundred years later, we are on the verge of another educational revolution, although this time the radicals are in government, not outside urging it on. The changes Michael Gove is proposing will alter the system fundamentally.

Kelly uses the term 'revolution' loosely but he has a point. The developing philosophy of the 'Big Society' meant an emphasis on localism and volunteering, reversing the regulatory nanny state, and freeing people to engage in traditional informal adult education activities mentioned earlier, such as teaching Latin in your home. However, is this rhetoric a veiled authoritarianism for an 'age of austerity'? In 2010 it was too early to say (compare Cameron 2010 and Williams 2010). The 'Big Society' was soon abandoned as a philosophy and other initiatives such as the extension of academies and the introduction of free schools on the Swedish model created controversy (Cowen 2008; DfE 2010a, 2011). The period of the coalition government (2010–15) was one of hesitation, a lack of confidence in its education policies.

The bonfire of the quangos

The most notable feature of the coalition government's new educational approach was not to initiate but to do away with 'arms-length' bodies in the 'the bonfire of the quangos.' One by one the so-called 'non-governmental' organizations that had dominated educational life were axed or brought back into the government department (see the blueprint in Burkard and Talbot Rice 2009). The General Teaching Council for England (GTCE), TDA, British Educational Communications and Technology Agency (BECTA), QCDA, Teachers TV, and LLUK were among the education quangos reformed or abolished; only Ofsted remained. The abolition of the Learning and Skills Council (LSC) was already a fact and the youth and adult guidance world was once again in crisis with the abolition of the Connexions service and other provision (Hayes 2010b, 2010c).

The age of the subject?

Less obvious, but more important, was a radical change to the curriculum. Over the last two decades educational expansion took a particular form that became both familiar and unchallenged. Schools and FE, and, to a lesser extent, universities, became the site of a social engineering project, covering everything from citizenship behaviour to diet. When children's behaviours were not changing enough, the project turned to manipulating their emotions. History may come to view this period, when politics simply became synonymous with education, as one of the most deplorable in the history of education. The tragedy was that most teachers were compliant with this political onslaught. If they voiced criticisms, it was not usually for educational reasons; it was because they favoured a more radical form of social engineering. They wanted more inclusion, stronger community cohesion and deeper environmental awareness. The most telling and far from trivial instance in this shift under New Labour was when the term 'education' disappeared from the name of the department responsible for schools. The coalition's resumption of this term, when it created the Department for Education (DfE), was a small but welcome step.

But the coalition did more than this. In conversations, consultations and speeches, Michael Gove signalled a desire to return to something like a traditional subject-centred education. He put forward clear arguments for his educational stance (Gove 2010a, 2010b). Some people were pleased with this move because education is in essence a conservative endeavour. The potential impact on Post-14 Education and Training lay in the creation of alternatives to traditional 'feeder' provision in the form of free schools and UTCs.

In another move welcomed by some, the coalition commissioned a review of 14–19 vocational education led by Professor Alison Wolf who was a long-term critic of the previous government's initiatives for being neither educational nor vocational (see Wolf 2002, 2005, 2009, 2011). The review found that 'many low-level courses have little or no labour-market value' and that 'between a quarter and a third of 16 to 19-year-olds are on courses which score well under league tables but don't lead to higher education or paid employment'. Wolf, as expected, endorsed more apprenticeships and backed the idea of UTCs that students could enter at 14. However, she proposed a common academic core curriculum for all up to the age of 16 (Wolf 2011). The review endorsed parity between QTLS and Qualified Teacher Status (QTS), but the future for both compulsory and post-compulsory education and training entered a period of uncertainty under the coalition.

The end of teacher education?

The good news was that the coalition and the subsequent Conservative government seemed to be creating a space for much needed debate about academic and vocational education. The Secretary of State, Michael Gove, had thought seriously about the subjects pupils should study (Gove 2009, 2010a, 2010b). Nicky Morgan, who replaced him as Secretary of State in July 2014, continued his approach. Neither had given equivalent thought to educating teachers. In this, they continued the process of turning teacher education into skill-based training. They had forgotten or did not believe that we need an educated and not just a trained workforce (DfE 2010c, 2010d; Education Forum 2010; SCETT 2011).

As the FE minister celebrated the idea of craft skills, Gove celebrated the idea that teaching was a craft (Hayes 2010a; Gove 2010a; DfE 2010c; see also Sennett 2008). He could have learned from the Greeks 'why the education as distinct from the training of teachers is so important' (Castle 1961: 199).

Both the Coalition government and the current Conservative government blame teacher trainers, and what they call 'pedagogy', for the poor state of British education and vocational training. In turn those trainers and their representative bodies denounce what they see as a return to sitting-by-Nellie forms of on-the-job training – but everyone sees a need for change (SCETT 2011; Hayes and Marshall 2015). Gove denounced many teachers and teacher trainers as 'The Blob' referring to the jelly-like 1950s B movie monster and in response they caricatured Gove as 'Pob', an irritating 1980s children's cartoon character (see Young 2014). Although formal partnership between universities and schools is recommended by the *Carter Review of Initial Teacher Training* (2015) there is a clear emphasis on school-based routes. Free schools and academies do not have to employ qualified teachers. Employers now have more freedom about what teacher training they want in FE. In these and other ways a quiet attack on 'The Blob' continues. Perhaps what has been lost in this debate is that important distinction between teacher *education* and teacher *training*.

We need to begin to discuss it again. If we do not, there may be no teacher education in the future, and we may return to a situation where there is minimal or no training for teachers.

Task 1.18

Consider how this education 'revolution' has affected your professional work as the developments outlined here begin to have an impact. Ask yourself:

- Has the sector become less bureaucratic since the quangocracy disappeared?
- Do future learners in the sector seem to have more knowledge and craft skills?
- Are free schools, including UTCs, changing education and training in the sector?
- Has teacher training altered with equity between QTLS and QTS?
- Is the 'craftsman' approach to teacher training effective?

Coda: the end of FE colleges?

As we were preparing this fifth edition there was a Department for Business, Innovation & Skills (DBIS) 'leak' in October 2014, and in 2015 two very substantial papers were produced, that brought into question the future of FE colleges. FE has always been resilient and responsive but the next five years may see the final dance of this institution.

The reasons are not just those mentioned in the two papers. Both Professor Ewart Keep and Professor Baroness Alison Wolf made the case that funding cuts will possibly put an end to skills training at post-19 (see Keep 2015 and Wolf 2015). The earlier 'leak' by then Business Secretary, Vince Cable, suggesting that government officials had wanted to axe FE colleges because no one would notice may or may not have been true (Wheeler 2014).

The current and forthcoming cuts amount to almost 50 per cent of the DBIS budget, much of which would target post-19 FE and skills training. Wolf feared that young people may head for university rather than seeking training in the technical skills the country needs. Three million new and often employer-based or employer-led apprenticeships were announced in the run up to the 2015 general election and they may not be partly or fully based in FE colleges. Another election pledge to increase the numbers of free schools and UTCs, taking their total number to something like 1000 by 2020, can only impact adversely on traditional FE colleges and partnerships may not save them. A view of their history shows that there have been many crises affecting FE colleges (see Chapter 9). Vince Cable's 'leak' about back-room advice may have been true. Whether it was or not, Keep and Wolf have given Post-14 Education and Training a wake-up call. FE must not go gentle into that good night.

Links to the Professional Standards for Teachers and Trainers in Education and Training

Professional values and attributes

2 Evaluate and challenge your practice, values and beliefs

5 Value and promote social and cultural diversity, equality of opportunity and inclusion

Professional knowledge and understanding

7 Maintain and update knowledge of your subject and/or vocational area

8 Maintain and update your knowledge of educational research to develop evidence-based practice

9 Apply theoretical understanding of effective practice in teaching, learning and assessment drawing on research and other evidence

12 Understand the teaching and professional role and your responsibilities

Professional skills

20 Contribute to organisational development and quality improvement through collaboration with others

2

The Post-14 Education and Training professional: learning and development

2.1 What is Chapter 2 about?

It is assumed that readers of this book will be engaged in a programme of training or continuous personal development and be teaching or on teaching practice. Chapter 2 therefore considers ways in which teachers or trainers can build on their professional profile and support their development. It reflects upon the various mechanisms available to teachers and trainers in ensuring their learning is effective, giving an introduction to skills that many practitioners, while knowledgeable and expert in their own fields, may need to cultivate in order to develop practices that embody their own professional values and principles and focus on their professional context.

From September 2013, the government revoked the legislation requiring new teachers in the sector to obtain a teaching qualification. However, new teachers, trainers and lecturers who successfully complete their initial teacher training may register with the Society of Education and Training (part of the Education and Training Foundation) and, after a period of professional formation, apply for Qualified Teacher Learning and Skills (QTLS) status. In order to maintain this status, each teacher must complete suitable continuing professional development (CPD) each year. It is essential that the CPD is appropriate to the individual practitioner and therefore this chapter is designed to encourage you to reflect upon staff development and how it can be used to enhance your practice and improve your performance.

Section 2.2 considers different notions of 'the effective teacher'. You should be clear about what you understand by this as a basis for your development, as well as examining how your professional context may help or hinder this. Section 2.3 will concentrate on CPD and its importance to you as a practitioner in enhancing pedagogic practice, while Section 2.4 outlines some initiatives implemented to support CPD in Post-14 Education Section 2.5 offers a range of strategies that can be used in planning and meeting your learning and development needs.

2.2 Professional learning and development

KEY ISSUES

Effective teacher development assumes a model of 'the effective teacher'.

Notions of the effective teacher vary in what features they emphasize.

Professional development cannot take place unless learning is applied to the teacher's own professional context.

Your ideas about how you can best learn and develop must be connected with your notion of what makes an effective teacher.

Task 2.1: Our own experience

Consider your experiences as a learner when at school and since then. What qualities did effective teachers have? What qualities did poor teachers lack?

Figure 2.1 shows the responses of a group of adult education (AE) teachers to Task 2.1. Responses such as those shown in Figure 2.1 tend to focus on three aspects of teaching and these are defined in Figure 2.2. You may notice that the three aspects broadly correspond with Bloom's (1964) classification of educational objectives into cognitive, psychomotor and affective domains. The kind of learning that you feel would make you a better teacher will depend on the value you place on each aspect. Nationally policy has swung between all three aspects. In the 1960s

Figure 2.1 AE teachers' responses to Task 2.1

'I remember getting interested in history for the first time when I did an evening course. The tutor had a passion for it.'

'He was clearly a brilliant physicist but he couldn't get his ideas over.'

'However frustrated you became, this teacher had limitless patience.'

'She seemed to be able to help you because she'd experienced the same difficulties herself.'

'We never learned anything because we didn't listen to him. And we didn't listen to him because we didn't respect him.'

'She seemed to make learning even the most routine things fun.'

'He had the ability to bring the subject to life.'

'He couldn't control our class. We soon found he couldn't control any class.'

'She could always explain even the most difficult things in terms you could understand.'

'He didn't seem to enjoy being with students.'

Figure 2.2 Three key aspects of teaching

Subject knowledge and expertise
Those thought of as good teachers tend to know their subjects, either through study or experience or both. But this is no guarantee of effectiveness: a very common experience is of the knowledgeable teacher who cannot communicate.

Skills and abilities
Whether controlling a class, communicating or understanding learning difficulties, the good teacher is seen as one who demonstrates skills and abilities to a high degree.

Commitment and emotions
This third aspect is wide-ranging but includes references to 'enthusiasm', 'passion', 'caring' and 'patience' – all qualities to do with emotions, attitudes and dispositions.

---

there was a move away from 'teacher training' to 'teacher education', a desire to emphasize the knowledge-based academic content of the then new BEd degree in contrast to previous skill-oriented programmes. In the 1990s, teacher education, along with training across many vocational areas, moved towards learning in the second and third aspects, which can be broadly termed a 'competence-based approach'. In the 2000s and post 2010, the subject knowledge of potential teachers has been emphasized once more in addition to the second and third aspects.

Task 2.2: Your own priorities

(a)   Looking at the three aspects in Figure 2.2, which aspects of teaching do you feel you need to focus on to make you a better teacher?

(b)   Share your thoughts with the group. Where the emphasis differs, how do you account for this? Contrasting subjects taught? Differing institutions? Variety in personal and professional background and experience?

You should now have a clearer notion of your own learning priorities and will need to consider how you wish to develop them. However, before doing so, you will need to reflect upon the current context within which you teach. It will have a number of important features, as shown in Figure 2.3.

Task 2.3: Your professional context

(a)   Describe your own professional context in the light of the features in Figure 2.3.

(b)   Given your context, what aspects of it might help or hinder your professional development? Share this with the group. How might common barriers to development be overcome?

Figure 2.3 Contexts in which teaching takes place

Your institution
Is it a large college, a small adult centre, the training section of a public service or industrial/commercial organization? How do you fit into it? What resources and support are available to you?

The extent to which you work with others
Do you work closely with colleagues as part of a course team for example, or do you attend an evening centre once a week, meeting only your students? Do you have a line manager? If not, to whom are you accountable?

Degree of professional autonomy
Who decides what you teach? Is there a detailed syllabus? Can you determine content and sequence?

Student targeting and recruitment
Do you control this or does the institution?

2.3 Continuing professional development

KEY ISSUES

A commitment to CPD is an essential part of being a professional.

The aim of CPD is to raise student achievement.

CPD must be considered on an individual basis as experience and circumstances dictate.

The acquisition of an initial teaching training qualification is just the first step towards becoming a 'professional' teacher or trainer (There is a wide ranging discussion of professionalism in Chapter 1.) It is important to understand that belonging to a 'profession' does not simply mean membership of a 'club'; it means embracing the criteria that ensure a particular job is seen as a profession rather than an occupation, even though the term 'professional' is contestable. The definition proposed by the functional sociologists (Millerson 1964) is broadly useful because, while recognizing the necessity for a profession to insist that a certain standard of skill be demonstrated by means of some kind of examination, it also acknowledges that 'professionalism' goes beyond an initial body of knowledge and skills. It demands that those practising within the profession be given education and training in relevant skills, and that good practice should be promoted; in other words, a commitment to CPD is an essential part of being a 'professional'.

The purpose of CPD, for those in the Post-14 Education and Training sector, is to improve student achievement. This might include building on your skills and supporting career progression, but it must remain focused on raising standards and improving student learning. CPD demands that you keep learning in order to enable you to play an informed role in the delivery of a curriculum and influence developments inside and outside your own institution. The sector is playing a crucial role in the development of Post-14 Education and Training, and therefore it is essential that sector institutions be seen as active learning organizations themselves.

There are no 'hard and fast' identified 'routes' laid down for this professional development; the complexity of roles and responsibilities of the Post-14 Education and Training practitioner means that any continuing education must take account of individual experience and circumstances. However, professional standards have been identified (described as the professional values and attributes, professional knowledge and understanding and professional skills required by teachers, trainers and lecturers in the lifelong learning sector) and these standards are a good place to start when considering your own CPD.

Task 2.4: Professional needs analysis

Think about your professional practice and identify what you consider to be your strengths and your areas of weakness. Do not simply reflect on your performance in the classroom, but look at your wider responsibilities (e.g. course planning and development or contributions to meetings). You might like to discuss this with a colleague.

2.4 Initiatives supporting CPD

KEY ISSUES

Nationally recognized standards are being used to raise the quality of Post-14 Education and Training provision.

There are various initiatives that are designed to support CPD.

Education and Training Foundation professional standards for teachers and trainers

Professional values and attributes

1   Reflect on what works best in your teaching and learning to meet the diverse needs of learners.

2   Evaluate and challenge your practice, values and beliefs.

3   Inspire, motivate and raise aspirations of learners through your enthusiasm and knowledge.

4   Be creative and innovative in selecting and adapting strategies to help learners to learn.

5   Value and promote social and cultural diversity, equality of opportunity and inclusion.

6   Build positive and collaborative relationships with colleagues and learners.

Professional knowledge and understanding

7   Maintain and update knowledge of your subject and/or vocational area.

8   Maintain and update your knowledge of educational research to develop evidence-based practice.

9   Apply theoretical understanding of effective practice in teaching, learning and assessment, drawing on research and other evidence.

10 Evaluate your practice with others and assess its impact on learning.

11 Manage and promote positive learner behaviour.

12 Understand the teaching and professional role and your responsibilities.

Professional skills

13 Motivate and inspire learners to promote achievement and develop their skills to enable progression.

14 Plan and deliver effective learning programmes for diverse groups or individuals in a safe and inclusive environment.

15 Promote the benefits of technology and support learners in its use.

16 Address the mathematics and English needs of learners and work creatively to overcome individual barriers to learning.

17 Enable learners to share responsibility for their own learning and assessment, setting goals that stretch and challenge.

18 Apply appropriate and fair methods of assessment and provide constructive and timely feedback to support progression and achievement.

19 Maintain and update your teaching and training expertise and vocational skills through collaboration with employers.

20 Contribute to organizational development and quality improvement through collaboration with others.

The Education and Training Foundation (ETF) published the new professional standards for teachers, tutors and trainers in the Post-14 Education and Training sector in April 2014 and it is likely that you are familiar with them (ETF 2014). Ofsted is committed to using these standards for the judgements it makes in its inspection of initial teacher education provision. If you are following an initial teaching qualification, it is likely your institution has incorporated the standards into your programme.

Centres for Excellence in Teacher Training

In 2007 Centres for Excellence in Teacher Training (CETTS) were established across England to raise standards in teaching and learning and to help recruit the best teachers into the Post-14 Education and Training sector. These partnership organizations provided not only initial teacher training for those entering the profession, but CPD for those already teaching or training and who wished to enhance their professional practice. The CETTs are invaluable in supporting staff training needs. They were funded until March 2010 but the indications are that all the CETTs are continuing to operate.

Subject enhancement

The Institute for Learning's (IfL) first review of CPD, published in 2009, highlighted the following CPD activities for enhancing your subject or vocational specialism:

- gaining skills for life qualifications to train in supporting and embedding literacy, numeracy and English for speakers of other languages (ESOL);
- gaining further qualifications in your subject or industrial expertise through accredited courses;
- industrial updating through visits, placements, secondments or shadowing;
- being a member of a special interest group or another professional body;
- taking on examiner, verifier or assessor responsibilities;
- attending briefings by awarding bodies and colleagues;
- presenting at a conference in your subject area;
- supervising research;
- leading project development in your subject area;
- writing reports and papers to inform your colleagues;
- planning or running a staff development activity;
- organizing trips, residentials and work placements;
- reading the latest journal articles for colleagues;
- updating knowledge through the internet, television and other media;
- public service and voluntary work.

(ETF 2014)

Task 2.5

Write a brief account of the role and activities of special interest groups or other professional bodies in your subject area. Now compare these with those in other subject areas. Is there a variety of roles and activities these groups/organizations play?

Transition to employment and ongoing CPD

Since September 2012, Ofsted, in its inspections of providers of initial teacher education, has been paying attention to the experience of newly qualified teachers or

former trainees and how well they have been prepared for employment both during the training programme and beyond in their first year of employment. For this
reason, and because of their concerns for their trainees in the early stages of their
careers, providers have been offering support for former trainees subsequent to
their training by offering, for example:

- invitations to provider conferences;
- faster routes through masters programmes;
- drop-in sessions;
- virtual learning environments dedicated to former trainees;
- subject specific support;
- one-to-one coaching.

Task 2.6

If currently on a training programme, discuss what needs fellow trainees believe they
will have when they are in employment and what expectations they have of your
training provider as a result

Task 2.7: Planning for CPD

In relation to your ongoing CPD:

(a)   Share with a colleague your responses to the following questions:
- What professional development activities have you undertaken this year?
- Have you reflected on the learning you have gained from these activities?
- Have the activities and the reflection made a difference to how you teach or train?
- Can you show evidence of what the difference is and the impact it has made to learners, colleagues or the organization in which you work?

(b)   Now specify what professional activities might help you update:
- your teaching and learning skills;
- your subject specialism;
- you on national policy initiatives and the context in which you work.

(c)   Using the IfL's six-step approach:
1   Use the model of dual professionalism to think about the context in which you work.
2   Analyse your needs and goals for development.
3   Draw up an individual development plan.
4   Create a professional development log of activities you have completed.
5   Select the most significant activities that have made the most impact on your practice and set them out in a professional development record.
6   Try to measure the impact each aspect of your CPD has had on your practice.

The following section suggests some strategies that may be of use to you in planning your programme of CPD.

2.5 Strategies for CPD

KEY ISSUES

Self-evaluation and reflective practice are useful strategies for identifying areas for CPD.

Observation offers a more objective evaluation technique than self-evaluation.

The roles of mentoring and coaching are becoming more important as part of the continuing development of teachers.

Appraisal procedures are an effective way to identify CPD needs.

Collaboration with colleagues provides less formal support for CPD.

The process of research can develop the necessary skills and self-awareness that underpin successful evaluation.

Self-evaluation and reflective practice

Self-evaluation and reflective practice are crucial components of all initial teaching training and can be invaluable in the development of professional practice. An evaluative or self-reflective cycle can ensure that you are undertaking a meaningful programme of CPD tailored to your individual needs as an ongoing process.

The concept of 'reflective practitioner' was first introduced by Schön as a way of introducing a new model of professional knowledge (Schön 1983). The theory has been developed into many different models that encourage reflective thinking, but the underlying principles are the same: that is, to challenge assumptions, to develop practical and theoretical knowledge and improve practice. Hillier (2005: 17) summarizes the process neatly:

> We should look at real practical situations which are problematic, complex and open to a variety of interpretations from differing points of view. This provides opportunities to develop capacities which are fundamental to competent professional practice. Thus our acquisition of knowledge proceeds interactively with reflecting about practical situations.

Which model you choose to undertake this process is one of personal choice. Brookfield (1995) refers to 'four critically reflective lenses': that of our own point of view, that of our colleagues, that of our students and the theoretical literature that is available. He maintains that by looking at your practice through these different lenses you will be able to identify any incongruence within your assumptions that needs further investigation. You might prefer to use Smyth's (1989) reflective cycle, whereby the practitioner begins by identifying a significant event, reflects on the significance, enters into a dialogue with colleagues regarding the practice and relevant theories and finally develops new practice based upon the analysis. Many trainees and teachers find recording reflection on practice difficult and have found Part 3 of Jenny Moon's book *Reflection in Learning and Practice* (Moon 2004) a helpful and practical guide to doing this.

Whichever model you choose you will need to begin this process to help you decide on an area of your practice that you wish to focus upon further. Self-evaluation may be of use here as it has an important place in determining your strengths and weaknesses and can be used to identify a relevant focus.

Perhaps the major tool which will be of use to you in your professional development is that of self-evaluation. This has an important place in determining your strengths and weaknesses and can be used with any focus you wish to give it. It could have a wide focus where you consider several or all aspects of the learning session involved, or a more narrow focus, such as the evaluation focusing on assessment shown in Example 2.1. Other objects of a narrow-focus evaluation might be:

- planning and preparation;
- teaching and learning strategies;
- communication skills and techniques;
- group management;
- managing a variety of student behavioural characteristics;
- learning resources;
- management of the learning environment;
- learning needs.

However widely or narrowly focused your evaluation, it should attempt to measure how far your aims and objectives have been met. Of course, you may have realized as the lesson progressed that particular aims and objectives were paramount and you wished to concentrate on related activities, or that unplanned learning, a frequent and often very pleasing outcome of a learning session, had taken place. However, overall, the process of evaluation is an estimation of how far the aims and objectives have been met in terms of student learning. The level of your success will indicate areas for further possible development.

Task 2.8: Self-evaluation

Look at the learning objectives and self-evaluations in Example 2.1 of three AS psychology classes taught by a PGCE 14–19 student. How successful is she in her evaluation at considering the lesson's effectiveness in realizing the objectives specified?

Example 2.1

LESSON EVALUATION

Learning objectives

- Must be able to identify types of conformity in given case study examples.
- Should be able to apply knowledge to answer exam questions related to social influence.
- Could be able to use theory, evaluation and research to answer an essay-based exam question.

How successful were the learning activities in achieving learning objectives? How do you know/what is your evidence?

Learners were required to complete past exam questions relating to the topic of social influence. This was an effective learning activity to assess whether students could apply their knowledge in the context of an exam. In a whole-class feedback, the mark scheme criteria were clarified, which would have ensured that learners understood how to articulate their knowledge so as to adhere to the demands of the exam. The task successfully allowed learners to demonstrate their understanding of social influence and apply their knowledge to novel examples and questions.

LESSON EVALUATION

Learning objectives

- Must be able to identify different kinds of body language.
- Should be able to describe and evaluate studies of posture.
- Could be able to apply practical implications of studies.

How successful were the learning activities in achieving learning objectives? How do you know/what is your evidence?

The 'must' learning objective was addressed by a bubble map creation, and whole-class feedback, encouraging collaborative learning. The 'should' learning objective was achieved by students recording a key study from the textbook: they were encouraged to paraphrase the content, strengthening their interaction with the information, as opposed to just copying. Formative assessment, through questioning students about key aspects of the study, gave evidence for learners' comprehension of the study. It was also addressed by providing students with prompts, and asking them to suggest how they could be employed to evaluate the study. The 'could' learning objective was met by learners being stretched to hypothesize practical implications and applications of body posture (e.g. counselling and business meetings).

Example 2.1 (*Continued*)

LESSON EVALUATION

Learning objectives

- Must be able to describe the biological, cognitive and sociocultural explanations of depression.
- Should be able to discuss research and effectiveness of the explanations of depression.
- Could be able to apply knowledge to an essay-style exam question.

How successful were the learning activities in achieving learning objectives? How do you know/what is your evidence?

The presentation activity allowed for collaborative learning to achieve the learning objectives. Clear criteria helped structure the presentations so that they directly related to the learning objective. Each student presented information to the class, demonstrating their knowledge of the topic and achievement of at least one learning objective. However, it was not possible to tell whether all students had contributed to the presentation poster, therefore circulation and monitoring would be needed to assess whether all students were engaged.

The trainee teacher is clear and precise about how far lesson objectives were met. But the limitation of in-action and on-action reflection by teachers is their inevitable subjectivity: it is very difficult to reflect objectively while teaching or after teaching. The first of two possibly more objective strategies is considered in Figure 2.4.

Task 2.7

Which points in the lesson below might have been missed had the student teacher not had a visual record?

Figure 2.4 Strategy 1: visual recording

The following entry was made in a student teacher's Individual Development Planner:

While I did not want to watch the recording of my micro teaching session as I thought it would confirm how bad I really was, it was stressed that it is an important part of our development so I decided that I would have to. It was nowhere as bad as I thought and I was surprised at how different it was from my original perception of the session. The beginning was hesitant and I will try to start more confidently (by practising starting a lesson at home), but I thought I improved during it. It's interesting that I thought I was really rushing the last few minutes as I was running out of time, but it doesn't sound like that on the DVD at all. I wished I had spent more time on student activities as they did seem to be quite engaged with the activity I used and with the topic itself. The time did not really lend itself to long discussions though and I will make more use of group activities when I teach next month.

Student questionnaires

The second strategy is the student questionnaire. On the face of it, it seems odd to distribute a questionnaire to students you see on a regular basis, but a questionnaire is a more objective evaluation of your performance than others, and has the following main advantages:

- students are more likely to be open and honest than when directly questioned;
- the questions can elicit more specific responses, enabling you to focus on a particular aspect of your performance;
- individual anonymous completion reduces the possibility of conformity of response.

The major drawback is that it is not as easy as it appears to construct even the simplest questionnaire; one difficulty being composing questions of the appropriate type and wording to produce clear, useful information that will be of assistance in identifying areas for professional development.

Judith Bell, in her excellent *Doing Your Research Project* (2014), refers to Youngman's (1994) question types. The following will be of particular use in self-evaluation:

- *Verbal or open:* for example, 'What did you feel about the discussion session?' The answer expected is a word, phrase or comment, and this can make these responses difficult to analyse. However, they can also provide some interesting responses for reflection.
- *Scale:* various kinds of scale or continuum give students the opportunity to choose the appropriate point on the scale as in the example below.

		Strongly agree	Agree	Neither agree or disagree	Disagree	Strongly disagree
1	Academic support was effective					
2	Tutors marked and returned work promptly					
3	Accommodation was suitable					
4	Teaching was of high quality					

Bell (2014) also draws attention to the potential dangers inherent in question wording, and these are shown in Figure 2.5.

Figure 2.5 Dangers inherent in question wording

Ambiguity, imprecision, assumption	Could your question mean different things to different students (e.g. 'Would you describe yourself as able, average or not very good?'), be unclear about the kind of answer required, or already contain an answer within it?
Memory	Does the question rely too heavily on students' memories, which may be unreliable? (e.g. 'What level of basic skills did you achieve at school?')
Knowledge	Does the question presuppose the possession of information the students don't have? (e.g. 'Who sets the fee levels in your local education authority?')
Double questions	Are there two questions present in one? (e.g. 'Did you feel the role play and interview were worthwhile?')
Leading questions	Does the question lead you to a particular response? (e.g. 'Don't you think communication is the most important part of your job?')
Hypothetical questions	'If you could change this lesson, how would you do it?' A pointless question, if it is clear to the students they won't have that power.

Source: Bell (2014: 142–7).

Task 2.8: Devising a questionnaire

(a)   Devise a short questionnaire focusing on a lesson or series of lessons.

(b)   Exchange this with a partner's and comment on question type and wording. Discuss common problems with the group.

(c)   Administer the questionnaire to the relevant students.

(d)   Analyse the results, question by question.

(e)   Once you have analysed the results, summarize them for the rest of your group. Consider how useful the information is to you. Does any of it confirm or conflict with that gained through other evaluation methods? How might you change practice as a result of this exercise?

Observation

Teaching observation provides excellent opportunities for CPD, and yet it can still be seen as a threatening experience. Traditionally, teachers have enjoyed a degree of professional autonomy and there is still a strong proprietorial feeling among many about teaching students in their own classroom. So, however experienced and professionally confident teachers are, being observed by others, whether they be colleagues, line managers or supervising tutors, is often a stressful experience. Nevertheless, such observation of and by others can be the basis of some of the most useful professional reflection you can undertake in order to improve performance.

As with evaluation strategies, like the videotaping and questionnaire considered in Section 2.5, feedback from observation offers a more objective viewpoint on your work. The difference here is that the feedback is 'live', given immediately in an interactive context. However, there are complications that need to be discussed.

The presence of a stranger in a classroom is bound to affect the behaviour of the teacher and the students. Many teachers argue that this makes the observed session unnatural and artificial, therefore reducing the value of the feedback given. In fact, there are many factors that will affect how both the teachers and students behave when a visitor is present: how used they are to visitors; whether the students know the visitor or not; whether the visitor is from inside or outside the institution; how the teacher presents the visitor. More importantly, however, is the role the observer takes in the session. Supervising tutors, for example, may insist on a non-participatory role to increase their objectivity, or a participatory one to diminish the effect of the scrutinizing assessor at the back of the classroom everyone is trying to pretend does not exist! Inspectors, on the other hand, may question students and walk around the class looking at student work. The important thing is for both the observer and observed teacher to be clear about their respective roles and the relationship between them. This will be predetermined to some extent; a line manager or supervising tutor will, however they may wish to play it down, have a supervisory evaluative dimension to their role that a peer will not. A mentor will have yet another role within the observation process.

Task 2.9

(a)   List those who have already and may in future be observing you teach: colleague, line manager, course tutor, mentor. Try to describe how you think they see their role as an observer.

(b)   If possible, present this view to them and ask them if this is, in fact, the way they do see their role. Were there discrepancies? If so, how do you account for these? How can they be minimized?

In order to ensure an effective relationship, it is essential that the observer and the observed be clear about the focus of the observation (in the same way as you are aware of your evaluation focus – see Task 2.4). This is particularly true if you wish to reflect on a specific area of your teaching for development. Below are some examples of communication skills and techniques that an observer of a teaching session might choose to focus on:

- giving instructions, checking understanding;
- supporting pair work: keeping a balance between enabling and spoon-feeding;
- managing attending to individuals while monitoring the group;
- effective explanation of complex points;
- appropriate use of information and communications technology (ICT).

Task 2.10

(a) Describe to your partner a lesson you have recently given or soon will give, detailing both student and teacher activities.

(b) Your partner should then select a focus that they would have chosen for an observation of that lesson, spelling out the features they would have concentrated on. They should share these with you. How far did you or would you emphasize these features in your own self-evaluation?

In considering observation, Wragg (1999) distinguishes between quantitative and qualitative methods. The former represent an attempt to quantify aspects of lessons such as verbal interaction, the use of teaching aids and classroom management as a basis for evaluation. As Wragg points out, there are many ways in which such methods can be useful and he gives examples such as an observer wanting to know how many students get to use computer equipment or the length of answers students give to questions. But such systematic analysis, as we have seen, is more suited to the competence model of mentoring. And, although whether a qualitative or quantitative approach is taken will depend on the focus of a lesson observation, it is likely that a qualitative approach with its focus on the nature of the learners' experiences will be more helpful in identifying areas for reflection and CPD.

We noted above that, although observation provides a more objective approach to evaluation than perhaps the teacher's own review, this is complicated by the observer's interpretation of events in the classroom. This interpretation is central to qualitative methods of observation and will be influenced by a number of factors about the observers themselves:

- their background, experience and educational ideology;
- their awareness of and attitude to the lesson's subject/topic;
- their understanding of student responses, interactions and behaviour;
- their knowledge of and attitude to the teacher;
- their perception of their role and purpose as an observer;
- the way(s) in which they have recorded their observations.

Task 2.11

(a) Table 2.1 shows a series of classroom events. On a scale of 1–5, where 5 means 'good practice' and 1 means 'bad practice', rate each event.

(b) Would you give each the same rating if the subject of the session, where given, were different?

Table 2.1 Evaluating classroom events

Classroom event	1	2	3	4	5
1 Students talk frequently in a session when they are working in small groups.					
2 Students are free to move around the room.					
3 The teacher gives a lecture lasting 40 minutes of the hour-long session, leaving 20 minutes for question and answer.					
4 Most basic skills students' work is in small groups around tables.					
5 The whiteboard is the main visual aid in a lecture.					
6 All teaching is one-to-one or pair instruction in a sub-aqua class.					
7 Students extensively assess one another's work in a business studies class.					
8 The session is based exclusively on active learning; in this case games and role play on a management course.					
9 Students are involved mainly in recording information in a biology class.					
10 The second-year degree session is a seminar where one student reads a paper and the lecturer and students discuss it.					

It is possible that there was disagreement over the ratings between the members of your group. It is likely that you needed to know a great deal more about the context of the lesson before making a judgement. Even then, however, it is possible that group members actually sitting through the lesson itself might have reached different conclusions about what was happening and its value. Nevertheless, it is only by observation that real judgements can be made about the process of teaching and learning – therefore it is unsurprising that observation of performance has become a major part of the inspection process.

The purpose of Ofsted is to evaluate the effectiveness and efficiency of an institution in meeting the needs of its students and, during an inspection, inspectors will be 'collecting first-hand evidence, particularly through observations of teaching, training and assessment' (Ofsted 2010). Inspectors will also expect to see staff development plans and details of staff development activities over the preceding two years. Therefore it is in an institution's interests to ensure not only that their staff are used to observation but also engage in appropriate staff development. This is often achieved by making observation the mainstay of the institution's quality assurance processes, using it as a basis for possible staff development, and it is equally likely that observation of performance is part of the appraisal system.

Mentoring and coaching

The development of mentoring as a process in teacher education has grown largely as a result of the increase in school-based training in the last five or six years, as well as becoming widespread in industry and commerce. It is a practice that is now developing widely in Post-14 Education and Training. A number of research studies indicate that being a mentor not only improves student teachers' teaching, but improves that of the mentor too. Similar evidence is starting to appear about the benefits of acting as a coach. Schools also appear to benefit from the establishment of a mentoring and coaching culture, and several Ofsted reports have identified the value of involvement in both mentoring student teachers, and coaching in terms of school improvement.

The clear message is also that being a mentor or coach is a role which continues to grow and develop through both experience and professional development. Good mentors know that being a good teacher and being a good mentor is not the same thing. Developing professional skills in adults through coaching or mentoring requires a range of skills and knowledge that is difficult to acquire in isolation or through a single training course. The evidence suggests that regular opportunities for mentors to meet, and to find out more about issues associated with the practice of mentoring and student teachers' learning, lead to better quality mentoring and greater professional satisfaction for mentors. Coaches can also enhance their skills and extend their repertoire of strategies through further professional development activities.

Undertaking the responsibilities of being a mentor or a coach involves a commitment to the professional learning of others which deserves acknowledgement. In both cases the identification of clear goals is important but the nuances in this target setting help to emphasize the subtle differences in approach. In the case of mentoring, the mentor and mentee identify learning goals whereas in a coaching relationship the coach provides support to the learner to help them to clarify and refine their own goals. In mentoring there is an element of assessment or appraisal whereas in coaching the aim is that the coach helps the learner to think, to work out solutions for themselves. Coaching is non-judgmental and solution focused, it is about 'one person being available to help another's thinking in order to increase their understanding so that they can take confident action' (Pemberton 2006). To this end, a learner needs to approach coaching ready and willing to take part in a professional conversation that facilitates independence and encourages them to work out solutions for themselves.

Appraisal/performance reviews

There are as many appraisal systems as there are Post-14 Education and Training institutions, each tailored to meet its own individual needs. However, every appraisal scheme should include quality assurance mechanisms, not only to ensure improvement in student achievement, but also to assist practitioners in their professional development and career planning.

Whatever particular methods an institution uses to appraise its staff, there are central themes that underpin all appraisal systems. First, appraisal is a non-threatening process that operates on a regular cycle; sometimes annually, sometimes biannually. Second, after an observation of performance, time is set aside to give the individual being appraised an opportunity to review their job description, to record good practice and to identify training (or other) needs. Finally, a confidential document is produced that records the matters discussed. This is used to initiate staff development and any other agreed courses of action. Properly conducted, the appraisal process is the ideal vehicle for self-reflection and CPD.

Peer observation

Another useful strategy for professional development is through the operation of a peer observation system. The chance to view different teaching styles can focus your attention on classroom activities and lead to improvements negotiated with those who are operating in the same environment as yourself. It is a non-threatening way of providing dynamic, ever-developing practices.

There are many peer observation schemes that can be used for CPD purposes. One such system is where a number of teachers from the same discipline can be paired, or even better, organized into groups of four or five, so that they can observe each other and discuss the outcomes in respect of improving their performance. This forms part of a continuous year-round cycle, with meetings held for the 'observation cell' to discuss their observations and produce an action plan – particularly useful for planning personal learning and development. An added bonus is that documentation, unlike that used for appraisal and inspection purposes, can be a great deal less formal and line managers could become part of a 'cell', so that they are observed in turn and the element of hierarchy/power is removed (Brown et al. 1993).

However, peer observation is only one aspect of beneficial collaboration with colleagues. You may be following a course of study on your own or in a small group through distributed learning, but it is more common for teacher training to take place in groups comprising a wide cross-section of practitioners and students. Evaluations from such groups often cite the group that they belong to as being an important (if not the most important) learning resource they have had access to during the programme. Therefore if you are a member of a group, either as a student or as a member of a team within an institution, you need to ensure you make best use of the group for your professional development. There are a number of ways (apart from peer observation) that groups and their professional contexts can be used for developmental purposes, for example:

- developing and planning jointly run courses;
- developing new resources, particularly course materials;
- conducting trials with one another's course materials;
- trying out teaching and learning strategies seen on peer observation sessions;
- team teaching with one another's groups.

Your response to these possibilities may be to throw up your hands in despair at the narrow specialism you teach. Clearly, there are important ways in which teachers sharing a subject can collaborate, but it surprising how much you can learn from areas which at first seemed so different from your own. Indeed, so many of us are isolated in Post-14 Education and Training that if you are undertaking a course of professional training, such experience of diverse contexts is imperative.

Task 2.12: Working with others

(a)   Each group member should give a brief account to the rest of the group of their professional context, as described earlier in Task 2.3.

(b)   Now select three or four individual contexts you feel it might be useful to explore and, with each colleague, specify at least one way you might collaborate.

(c)   Feed this back to the rest of the group (this often sparks even more ideas and possibilities).

Collaboration with colleagues can also be useful if you decide to engage in the research process to enable you to critically and systematically reflect upon your practice.

Action research

Among teachers and other educational practitioners action research (AR) is undoubtedly the most widely practised form of research. Within the American Educational Research Association (AERA) which is almost certainly the largest educational research organization in the world with 25,000 members, the Special Interest Group for AR is itself one of the largest specialist groups (Rowell et al. 2015). Given that small-scale AR projects often form part of the coursework of teaching related qualifications at undergraduate and postgraduate levels and also that many practising teachers carry out (albeit at differing levels of formality) AR projects, the picture begins to emerge of AR being the single most common form of educational research.

Given that so many people are involved in AR, it should not come as a surprise to learn that there is no universally accepted definition of AR. This is in many ways similar to the way in which many other terms used in education are the subject of discussion and dispute. One has only to think of a few examples such as 'curriculum', 'transformative learning' and 'quality' to see how commonly used terms are actually quite hard to define in a way which everyone involved might agree on. Whatever differences there might be between the competing understandings of the meaning of AR, it is possible to trace certain family resemblances common to almost all the interpretations.

The definition given by Wilfred Carr and Stephen Kemmis in their influential book *Becoming Critical* (2003) is quite widely accepted as capturing the main direction of AR, which they describe as being:

> simply a form of self reflective enquiry undertaken by participants in social situations in order to improve the rationality and justice of their own practices, their understanding of these practices, and the situation in which the practices are carried out.

Anyone investigating AR will soon find themselves looking at diagrams which represent the AR cycle. Most of these diagrams are fairly similar and represent what are seen as the usual steps in the process of AR. The diagrams associated with Jean McNiff and Jack Whitehead (2006: 9) have in particular proved popular with many students making an initial approach to AR.

Below a diagram is presented (Figure 2.6) which assumes almost no previous knowledge of AR on the part of the reader. This shows as simply as possible the path of an AR project within what could be called a standard AR cycle. In this diagram it is assumed that the stages depicted would in outline be those which an individual or a small group of teachers might follow if conducting a small-scale AR project.

In Figure 2.6 the cycle begins at the top with the teacher/researcher becoming aware of something which is considered to be problematic in their practice. In the

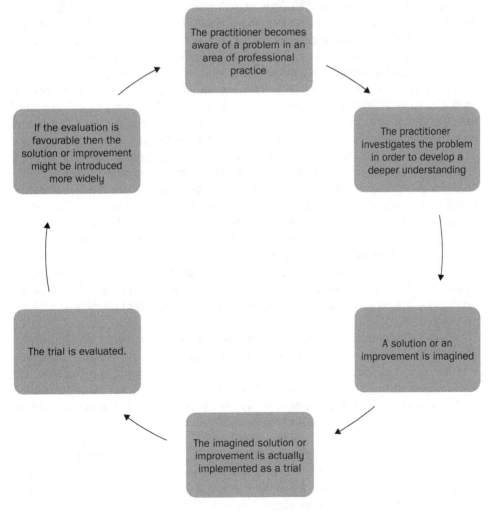

Figure 2.6 The path of an AR project

second stage the problem is investigated. Here we could very usefully think of Stephen Brookfield's four lenses (1995: 28–39) as offering the most easily accessible and contextually relevant way to develop an understanding of the problem. Brookfield suggests looking at problems with a critical understanding drawing on four viewpoints: the teacher's own biography, the student's viewpoint, the experiences of colleagues and the theoretical literature. On this basis, possible solutions to the problem are considered. These are then trialled and evaluated. In this evaluation, Brookfield's four lenses might again be deployed. If the 'solution' is judged to be an improvement, it might then be more widely implemented. Here it is important to stress that the effect of this process on the researcher is important. AR helps the practitioner to develop a deeper understanding of the processes involved in their profession.

A theme common to all forms of AR is that real practical emphasis must be placed on the 'action' part of AR. Without an 'action' a project cannot be described as AR. The purpose of AR is to effect change. At different times and under differing circumstances the interpretation of AR can be shown to have changed but the idea of 'action' is ever present and has been since AR was first discussed.

It is generally agreed that the first person to use the term AR was the psychologist Kurt Lewin (1890–1947). Throughout his life, Lewin was concerned with the ways in which knowledge and research could be used to improve and develop democratic practices. An example of this was the scientific work Lewin was engaged in to try to find ways in which knowledge of psychology might be of societal use (Chaiklin 2011). Lewin, who was Jewish and a left-wing activist, had himself been forced to leave Germany when the Nazis came to power. Some of Lewin's last psychological work was aimed at trying to develop more effective forms of anti-racist community-based work. It was in this context that Lewin spoke of 'action research' and made his often quoted remark that in a social context 'Research which produces nothing but books will not suffice' (Lewin 1946: 35). Sometimes this remark is used in such a way as to portray AR itself as being opposed to academic research. However, when studied in the wider context of Lewin's work, it is clear that the point he was making was that to effect change, practical steps must be taken. Academic reflection is important but, self-evidently, no positive change of practice is possible without action.

From the outset in Lewin's work, AR was closely linked to ideas of 'positive change'. This needs to be considered when thinking about what might be the ethical dimension of AR. Lewin believed that when confronted with problems which had definite ethical dimensions, a purely academic approach which did not seek a solution or at least an improvement was at the very best useless and quite probably immoral. In education, AR is often linked to ideas of change leading to greater 'fairness', improved student opportunities and widened participation. When considering problems and opportunities in education, most people would probably agree that when we discover a problem which constitutes a barrier to student learning and development, or when we can imagine a potential innovation which might improve educational experiences, then we have an ethical responsibility to act. AR cannot be adequately understood if it is seen only as a set of steps to be mechanically completed in a particular order to carry out a research project. To underplay or ignore ethical questions is to misunderstand AR.

A second feature common to all forms AR is a concern with notions of professionalism. In all AR projects, there is a concern to develop the knowledge of practitioners. Conversely, many people who advocate the practice of AR will also argue that there is an onus on professionals themselves to develop the knowledge base from which they work. In this way, AR is inextricably bound up with what we might call 'participatory' professionalism as the production, evaluation and development of knowledge becomes both a duty and an attribute of being a professional.

AR lends itself more readily than most other forms of research to the production of knowledge within the professional's own practice. In the two examples cited below it can be seen that the AR process has involved the teachers concerned developing their own professional knowledge and understanding while making a strong claim that those who manage them need to take this practitioner knowledge into account.

Example 2.2

A teacher who works in a project to develop the parenting skills of marginalized and impoverished single parents is aware of problems with the registration process of new clients. Many people referred to the service in which she works have mental health problems or problems related to substance abuse. At registration, the entrants to the programme are obliged to declare these problems when they complete the entry forms. For many this is embarrassing or even humiliating. The AR project involves the development of alternatives to this initial declaration which are acceptable to the body which funds the institution in which the teacher works. The funding body insists on the declarations even though they aware of the problems the clients have, not least because this is why the clients have been referred to the project. In this example, the second stage of the AR cycle as illustrated above became particularly important to the teacher as it led to her exploring her own ethical values, and those of the funding body. The work on the registration process opened up many profoundly important questions and conflicting imperatives.

Example 2.3

A teacher at an FE college who teaches young people preparing to work in the area of motor vehicle maintenance is under pressure to recruit, retain and achieve high final completion rates. Among the young people he works with there are many whose behaviour is 'challenging'. This creates a series of problems across a wide range of areas: disrupted classrooms, threats to health and safety in workshop sessions, low student motivation and poor attendance, to name a few. Initially the teacher believes that a possible remedy to these problems might lie in improved training. The AR project was initially set up to identify suitable training, to get it implemented and to evaluate its results. In the initial AR process, the teacher began to form the opinion that in considerable part the problems he and his colleagues faced could be attributed to a misconception of the nature of 'challenging behaviour'. The 'common sense' of his institution sees 'challenging behaviour' as fundamentally one of instilling and enforcing 'discipline'.

As a result of the original AR project the teacher now believes that the problems of 'challenging behaviour' are better viewed as being a particular form of learning difficulty which these young people experience. In the next AR cycle, the teacher sets out to implement a series of training days and workshops in which other teachers and managers are expected to consider the implications of this changed understanding and how it might lead to more appropriate and creative approaches to practice.

Links to the Professional Standards for Teachers and Trainers in Education and Training

Professional values and attributes

1 Reflect on what works best in your teaching and learning to meet the diverse needs of learners

2 Evaluate and challenge your practice, values and beliefs

Professional knowledge and understanding

7 Maintain and update knowledge of your subject and/or vocational area

8 Maintain and update your knowledge of educational research to develop evidence-based practice

9 Apply theoretical understanding of effective practice in teaching, learning and assessment drawing on research and other evidence

10 Evaluate your practice with others and assess its impact on learning

12 Understand the teaching and professional role and your responsibilities

Professional skills

19 Maintain and update your teaching and training expertise and vocational skills through collaboration with employers

3

Student learning in Post-14 Education and Training

3.1 What is Chapter 3 about?

The theories that lie behind classroom practice are rarely explicit and we usually content ourselves with 'what works' in helping our students to learn. Nevertheless, the theoretical frameworks that have been developed over time can give us insights into the learning process that enable us to understand *why* we do what we do in our classrooms and are an important part of our professional knowledge. Theories of learning are interpreted and applied in specific social, political and cultural settings, however, and in this chapter we look at how particular theories are considered more relevant to us at the present time. In recent years we have seen a greater focus on 'outcomes', that is, a more instrumental view of learning, and at the same time a greater emphasis on the learner and 'learner-centredness' that have obscured the distinction between 'skills' and 'knowledge'. Alongside this we have seen a much greater emphasis on the collection and use of data to measure attainment, and this has had an effect on how learning is understood. The collection of large amounts of data on student attainment and progress is now required of all teachers and this has a bearing on what they teach and how they teach it. Does the data reflect quality of learning, or merely the 'coverage' of content? Chapter 1 provided the context for understanding the changes in the Post-14 Education and Training sector and traced historical developments in the sector. This chapter seeks to develop your knowledge and understanding of selected theoretical perspectives and to raise critical questions in relation to current developments.

The chapter explores key features of different learning theories in relation to classroom practice. Section 3.2 examines the factors affecting students' ability to learn. What are the differences and similarities between a class of 17-year-old hairdressers, an adult education (AE) French class and a group of postgraduate student teachers? What affects a student's ability to learn? We look critically at some of the factors that have particular contemporary significance. Section 3.3 introduces some of the theories of learning as a background to our understanding of how our students learn. How have behaviourist, cognitive, humanist and social constructivist ideas about learning affected approaches to teaching and learning? What can we learn from neuroscience? Section 3.4 considers what constitutes effective learning and how barriers to learning can be overcome. Are we concerned with knowledge and understanding, with skills development or a combination of the two? How effective study skills and learner autonomy can be developed provides the focus for Section 3.5. What is the value and role of independent learning both within the classroom and as directed self-study? How is independent learning best managed and organized? How has classroom learning become more oriented to the individual and their *personal* learning needs? These are the questions we reflect upon here.

3.2 Factors affecting student learning

KEY ISSUES

What makes one group of learners distinct from another?

What individual differences can we identify in learners?

How can knowledge of factors which affect learning inform our approach to teaching?

Task 3.1

(a) Choose one of your groups of learners and write a short profile of it giving details of what you know about individuals.

(b) Look at what you have written and identify some general headings for the information you have included; for example, ability, motivation, social background.

(c) Now think about a contrasting group, preferably one that you teach, or alternatively one that you have been a student in recently – perhaps a teacher training group or AE class. Write a similar profile using the headings you identified for your first group. What are the differences? What are the similarities? Note these down to return to later. You may like to discuss your observations with a colleague.

(d) If you have been working in Post-14 Education and Training for several years, consider what changes have taken place in terms of assessment requirements, the range of students, the style of teaching and learning and the content of the curriculum. How have these changes influenced the way you teach?

Strong claims are made for the distinctiveness of particular groups of learners. Indeed, a whole body of theory was developed around the adult learner as distinct from younger learners. But what makes one group of learners distinct from another? Is it a question of age, motivation, ability, the chosen course of study?

Every learning group is obviously different because it is made up of different individuals. Given the diverse nature of the post-14 sector, you no doubt encounter a very wide variety of abilities, personalities, backgrounds and so on among your students. These differences not only affect your approach to teaching, which will be considered in Chapter 4, but also have a marked effect on how students learn.

Task 3.2

(a) Here is a list of factors which are said to affect a student's ability to learn. It is not exhaustive and you may want to add others. In your experience, are any of these factors more important than others? Place them in order of importance.

- ability
- motivation
- personality
- attitude
- age
- previous learning experience
- life experience

(b) Why do you consider some factors more important than others? Do some of them overlap?

(c) Now look at each factor in turn and write down an example of how learning is enhanced and how it is inhibited in each case. For example, an older student may bring to a class a great deal of previous experience and knowledge on which they can build; on the other hand, they may be anxious about having had a long period away from education and because of their age have less confidence in their ability to learn.

The order of importance and examples that one chooses will depend to some extent on who the learners are and what they are learning, but there are commonalities as well as distinctive features. Continuity of educational experience is an important influence on the way people approach learning, although it is undoubtedly the case that the previous educational experience of some individuals may not have been entirely positive and this needs to be taken into account both in curriculum planning and pedagogical approaches. Nevertheless, school students taking vocational courses, 16–19-year-olds in further education (FE) and the traditional higher education (HE) cohort have a continuous experience of education from at least the age of 5. Schooling in one form or another has been a dominant feature of their lives. The routines and expectations of educational establishments are familiar to them. This is not generally the case for the adult learner who may not have been involved in a formal educational experience for some time and whose knowledge and expectations of education may only be based on their own school experience. Equally, the adult re-entering the education system at whatever level has many more outside responsibilities and pressures than the younger FE or HE student. That is not to play down the increased financial burdens that younger students may now face because of tuition fees, or the pressure to earn a living while studying, but these, and other responsibilities, are much more acute for the adult 'returner'. Equally, as an indirect result of the freedom of mobility within the Economic Union, together with, although to a lesser extent, migration by people from all over the world, the student population has become much more diverse. Social and political contexts are important influences on the way teaching and learning are approached and the relative importance given to one theoretical perspective over another. Let us look at three factors in more detail with both a historical and a contemporary focus.

Ability

Ability, and more specifically, intelligence, is one of the most contentious and politicized aspects of learning. Even a commonly accepted definition has been elusive. Nor have approaches to measuring intelligence and establishing the intelligence quotient (IQ) of individuals been consensual. Is intelligence fixed? What are the relative influences of heredity and social circumstances on an individual's intelligence? Does IQ exist at all? Can intelligence be measured? These questions remain unresolved.

Attempts at the description and definition of intelligence have often focused on the differences between individuals. Those perceived differences have then been used for political ends. Take for example the eugenics movement in the early part of the twentieth century whose aim it was to 'improve' the human race. Drawing on Darwin's theories of evolution as they could be applied to society (social Darwinism) and theories of heredity and genetic influences current at that time, eugenicists essentially claimed a scientific basis for white Anglo-Saxon superiority. These theories gave a justification to the sort of 'master race' ideas of Nazi Germany, and had already led to numerous pieces of legislation in the USA between 1911 and 1930. Laws were passed in some states allowing for the sterilization of 'misfits', the 'mentally retarded' and the 'insane' and to restrict marriages between certain racial groups.

Eugenics has since been discredited. And yet its spectre seems to stalk present research into genetics and IQ. Nowadays, there is general unease about aspects of genetic research from an ethical point of view. For example, the search for genes which might influence variations in intelligence is viewed with scepticism not for the scientific data researchers present, but for the implications of their findings and the uses they might be put to. What if it were true, as some scientists claim, that genetic factors account for 50 per cent of IQ variations across the population? What might be the effect of such a claim on the way teachers view their students? Other research claims that genetic make-up as much as the socialization process dictates differences between boys and girls in terms of how they acquire social skills, suggesting that gender differences are largely genetically rather than culturally determined (Skuse 1997).What are the implications of such claims? Currently, there seems to be a certain coyness about research into genes and IQ, perhaps due to the fear of a backlash as well as a disillusionment with social explanations. In a more confident age this was not the case.

Task 3.3

What examples can you draw on (from observation of students, your own children or others around you) that appear to be inherited traits? Can you identify any social influence; that is, aspects of upbringing, peer influences or the wider influences in society that might give an alternative explanation for any of these traits?

The 'nature–nurture' discussion has been the subject of research and debate among scientists and educationalists for over a century. Intelligence testing is an attempt to identify the innate ability of the individual. Intelligence tests were first developed at the turn of the century in France by Binet and Simon. Under contract to the French government, their task was to devise a test to identify children who should benefit from special schooling. This test was adapted in the USA and in 1916 became widely known as the Stanford–Binet test (see Child 2007: 210–12). It was used widely, in modified forms, to measure normal, subnormal and superior intelligence throughout the century. In Britain, the work of Cyril Burt is perhaps the best known in the field. Burt's theories formed the whole basis of accepted wisdom on the nature of intelligence for generations of schoolchildren from the 1950s onward. He established that intelligence was partly innate and partly developed as a result of the social environment. His theories were adopted and resulted in the 11+ examination and IQ testing in schools. In later years Burt was criticized for his deterministic approach, and it has been suggested that he falsified some of his data (Hearnshaw 1979).

Since the 1960s, social and cultural factors have been considered more important determinants of intelligence than heredity. While individual differences in ability are acknowledged, educators have regarded social inequalities as influencing more profoundly an individual's capacity for learning. The abandonment (in most parts of the country) of the 11+ examination in the early 1970s was the ideological expression of an attempt at engineering a more egalitarian society through the education system. The value of IQ tests as they were conceived of in the 1950s and 1960s was called into question on the basis that they were gender and culturally biased, aimed at middle-class children who generally performed better and were not an accurate measure of ability for most people.

The nature–nurture debate usually centres on the relative importance of heredity over social factors, but it is also worth taking a step back and asking the question: does IQ actually exist? From as long ago as the beginning of the nineteenth century it has been argued in some quarters that the nature of intelligence cannot be coded, certainly not genetically coded, and that intelligence by its nature has no limitations and is not parcelled-out in specific amounts. Nor is it a merely abstract potential; rather, it has a real and determinant content. It is well known that concentrated teaching can improve IQ scores and that generation by generation IQ scores are improving. What does this tell us? It might also be argued that IQ has served the role of justifying social inequalities in that we live in a meritocracy where income is distributed according to merit and merit is defined as intelligence plus effort. Could it be that the elevation of intelligence as a defining factor of success or failure in society is a way of endorsing social divisions? As teachers and trainers concerned with helping our students to realize their potential, we might consider that humans are shaped by both nature and nurture, but that what is important is our ability to transcend both, by our capacity to overcome the constraints imposed both by our genetic and our cultural heritage (Malik 2001).

The work of Harvard psychologist, Howard Gardner, and his theory of *multiple intelligences* (1983, 1993) has become very popular with educationalists. This is partly because his view of intelligence reflects a current ethos of promoting self-esteem and individual achievement. Gardner sees the traditional understanding of intelligence as limiting. He suggests that traditional understandings do not recognize the range of talents and abilities that many people have who do not excel in what he describes as 'logical-mathematical intelligence'. Gardner identifies and describes six other forms of intelligence as follows: linguistic intelligence, spatial intelligence, bodily kinaesthetic intelligence, musical intelligence, interpersonal intelligence and intrapersonal intelligence. For Gardner, these distinctive forms of intelligence are genetically based and influenced by culture, but can be enhanced through practice and learning. Very recently, educationalists, particularly those working with disaffected and marginalized young people, have become interested in the idea of emotional intelligence which has been explored by, among others, Daniel Goleman (2005a, 2005b). Emotional intelligence appears to be similar to Gardner's interpersonal and intrapersonal intelligences in that it is concerned with such things as self-awareness and empathy, the ability to manage emotions and relationships and to motivate oneself. Emotional intelligence theory taps into an ethos of victimhood in society (Füredi 1997, 2004), and what has been described as 'therapeutic' by Ecclestone and Hayes (2008), and it is easy to see why it is being used in relation to the socially and educationally excluded. Theories of multiple intelligences are attractive in that they confirm that we 'can all be good at something'. On the other hand, they might also provide what appears to be a scientifically based excuse for setting low expectations of ourselves and others rather than striving to overcome difficulties in particular areas (see Perks 2004). Such presentations of 'intelligence' bear little resemblance to other understandings described above, except in the sense that they also seem to accept the overriding importance of genetic influences. They present the contentious issue of intelligence in a non-contentious way, which might lead us to sidestep or ignore many of the, as yet, unanswered questions about the nature of ability, individual differences and their relationship to educational opportunity and equality. Multiple intelligences theory has at its root a biological explanation for the differences between us and as such may lead in practice to a very deterministic view of individual potential.

Biological explanations of human behaviour continue to gain credence. The most controversial area of current debate in education that relates directly to the 'nature-nuture' discussion and more broadly to intelligence, is the growing influence of neuroscience. Indeed, from reading reports in the media and scholarly works too, one might be forgiven for thinking that neuroscience can offer a theory of everything. Cognitive neuroscience, which seeks to relate the scientific understanding of the brain to education has become very influential in recent years, both in terms of informing policy and areas of practice. There are undoubtedly some very interesting discoveries being made all the time, and there are already a number of generally accepted beliefs about how the brain works which claim to have direct implications for education. The mind-brain debate has been reignited over the last decade and is likely to continue to gain importance. In 2007 the Teaching and Learning Research Programme (TLRP) published a comprehensive report on the application of neuroscientific insights to education. Since then somewhat excessive claims continue to be made for neuroscientific explanations that seem to suggest that cognitive neuroscience can bridge the gap between the mind and brain. Objections revolving around the fundamental questions of free will and biological determinism, human consciousness and reason are forcefully made. For example, Alka Seghal-Cuthbert (2015) provides a recent in-depth critique of neuroscience and education, answering some of the important questions in the debate. David Perks (2007) offers an interesting explanation as to why neuroscience is having such an influence at the present time. This important area of development is one to remain critically informed of in the next few years.

Task 3.4

(a) Individual differences in ability clearly have an impact on our approach to teaching. In what ways do you take the differing abilities of your learners into account in order to ensure that each individual achieves his or her potential?

(b) If possible, compare your ideas with a partner and draw up a list together of how you differentiate your approach to teaching according to students' varying abilities.

(c) Read in more detail about multiple intelligences and emotional intelligence theories and consider whether they do indeed promote a culture of low expectations, victimhood and 'therapy culture' as suggested above.

(d) Do some initial reading on cognitive neuroscience and consider your own position on the impact on educational thinking and practice.

Motivation

Motivation is a key factor in learning and is linked very closely to attitude. It is often now seen as an imperative. Motivation has been described as 'a person's aroused desire for participation in a learning process' (Curzon 2003: 195). How to arouse and maintain that desire is of concern both to the student and the teacher. Our students arrive in our classes with all sorts of motives for attending. Those motives may be positive and lead a student to be well motivated towards learning, or they may be somewhat negative, leading a student to be poorly motivated towards learning.

At the present time the majority of young people continue their education beyond the age of 16. HE has expanded to accommodate a much more diverse student population including a larger proportion of mature students. Unemployed people of all ages are required to attend education and training courses. An increasing number of adults attend adult education centres for more functional reasons than for the pleasure of learning for its own sake. The enormous growth and diversity in the Post-14 Education and Training sector brings with it changes in student motives and motivation.

Task 3.5

(a) Choose one of your teaching groups and find out (if you do not already know) what were their individual motives for attending your course.

(b) Now consider how their initial motives for joining the course relate to their attitudes to learning during the course.

(c) Can you identify any changes in attitudes as the course has progressed? How do you account for these changes?

Perhaps the most well-known theory of motivation is Maslow's hierarchy of needs (Maslow 1970: 56–61). Abraham Maslow, whose work is closely related to humanistic psychology, saw 'self-actualization' as what drives people to learn; that is, the need to make full use of one's talents, become creative and achieve one's potential is what motivates us. Self-actualization is an ultimate human goal and need, but before that need can be fulfilled a set of other needs must be met. These needs are generally presented as a pyramid. At the bottom level are physiological needs such as hunger and thirst. Once these are satisfied the next level is the need for physical and psychological well-being which if met leads on to the need for love and a sense of belonging which involves having warm, friendly relationships. Next come self-esteem needs: to achieve, be successful, have the respect of others. Finally, at the top of the hierarchy is self-actualization, the desire to fulfil one's potential. This, according to Maslow, may only be achieved by some people fleetingly throughout their lives, but the top of the pyramid is left open because human potential is not finite. The important thing to recognize about Maslow's hierarchy is that moving to a higher level is dependent on the level below. It follows therefore, following Maslow, that a self-actualized person can only become so if all the other needs are met. Maslow has been criticized for basing his theories on middle-class USA in the 1960s. Lessons from history as well as our own experience as teachers and learners tell us that it is not necessarily the case that motivation to learn is dependent on the fulfilment of interrelated needs in the hierarchical way that Maslow describes. Equally, the extent to which the teacher can meet certain of those needs may be limited. But are aspects of Maslow's theory relevant to learners in Post-14 Education and Training? Can you identify these characteristics among the students you teach? Is it true, as Maslow seems to imply, that only well-off people in caring relationships and successful in their lives can achieve their full creative potential and self-fulfilment? And if so, what are the implications of this theory in relation to your students?

Task 3.6

(a) Take each stage of Maslow's hierarchy of needs and consider what the practical implications are for your teaching. For example, love and belonging might be interpreted in the classroom as creating a positive, supportive atmosphere.

(b) How will each of these practical considerations enhance student motivation?

While Maslow's notion of a *hierarchy* of needs is now viewed with some scepticism, the psychological well-being and self-esteem of students is now considered as being of primary importance in terms of their disposition towards learning. Humanistic psychological explanations have become more fashionable than cognitive theories, but these should not be ignored. Robert Gagné, a notable cognitive theorist, identified motivation as the first phase of the learning process. The role of the teacher, according to Gagné (1997: 206), is 'to identify the motives of students and channel them into activities that accomplish educational goals'. It is essential to student motivation that the teacher identifies and communicates goals and objectives to students and generates expectations in them. What effect do low expectations on the part of the teacher and the student have on student motivation? Is it more a problem today when students may have limited career prospects and may have chosen to continue in education and training because there was no alternative in a much reduced labour market for the under-25s?

Task 3.7

(a) Note down what strategies you use to promote and maintain the motivation of your students.

(b) Compare your strategies with those of a partner. What are the similarities and differences? How do you account for these?

Intrinsic and *extrinsic* are other descriptions that have been applied to motivation. Intrinsic motivation is said to come from an inner drive and this is related to the human need for self-esteem and self-confidence and a desire to satisfy curiosity. Some activities are a reward in themselves and undertaken purely for the pleasure they give. Extrinsic motivation on the other hand is externally produced. Some external incentive with some sort of promise of reward, threat of punishment or need for competition or cooperation with others characterizes this type of motivation. For extrinsic motivation to be sustained, students must have attainable goals to work towards, be given immediate feedback on their performance and be rewarded for success. However, we might ask ourselves whether there is now an overemphasis on outcomes and assessment that leads both teachers and students to have a very narrow and entirely instrumental view of knowledge and skills that mitigates against recognizing the intrinsic worth and pleasure to be gained from learning and mastering something for its own sake. Moreover, there is an increased emphasis on developing an atmosphere of cooperation among students and eliminating any sort of competitive spirit in the classroom as this is seen as being harmful to students, particularly the low achievers. However, competitiveness is linked with achievement and doing one's best. Is it possible that the effect of discouraging competition is to damage motivation and ultimately the fulfilment of individual aspiration and potential?

Füredi (2009) suggests that attempts to motivate learners must not rely on 'techniques and gimmicks', but should emanate from the authority of the teacher and his or her ability to inspire student through knowledge. Is it the case, as Füredi goes on to claim, that 'the pedagogy of "motivation" . . . encourages a culture where the question of how to keep students interested overrides the issue of what is the content that must be taught' (p. 11)?

Task 3.8

(a)   Can you think of examples of how your learners are motivated intrinsically and extrinsically?

(b)   Discuss in a small group the relative merits of cooperation and competition in enhancing motivation. Are they mutually exclusive? What might be the effects on learning of entirely eradicating the one or the other in the classroom?

(c)   Discuss in small groups whether, contrary to what Füredi asserts above, the use of 'techniques and gimmicks' is a legitimate strategy and in what situations.

Ageing

The continual development of individual potential as a lifelong goal seems a laudable aspiration. No longer is it the case that age, in theory at any rate, is seen as a barrier to access to education. It is now clearly understood that the opportunity to continue learning throughout life is part of what it means to be a mature, healthy adult, although we might view with some suspicion current interpretations of what that means. The present-day understanding of adult learning is partly based on psychological lifespan development theories, which date from the late 1960s. Up to that time it was assumed that once people had achieved biological maturity their ability to learn became 'stable'; that is, reached a plateau, and then began to deteriorate. This is called the *decrement model* of adult development. Research undertaken subsequently by a number of academics has concluded that this is not the case. The *personal growth* model, which now has general currency, presents ageing in a less negative light, stressing positive aspects of human development. Several similar descriptive inventories of 'phases' or 'stages' of the human life cycle are available, notably by Tennant (2002) who suggests that there is a general professional acceptance that adulthood is a period of change and development and that in principle an adult's capacity to learn throughout life is not significantly diminished. However, it may not be widely acknowledged among the general public that this is the case. How often do our adult students use their age as an excuse for some difficulty they have with their learning?

Task 3.9

(a) Discuss in a small group what would be the objections to the above description of adult development. How might such a model be useful to you?

(b) What sort of 'inventory of life' might apply to your students?

Task 3.10

(a) List all the difficulties with learning something that your students (or you!) have attributed to their age.

(b) Which ones have a physical cause and which ones might be caused by other factors (e.g. social)?

(c) Discuss in a group ways of helping your students overcome these difficulties.

The demographic reality of an ageing population has contributed to some extent to changes in attitudes to age and ageing. By 2041 it is predicted that 25 per cent of the UK population will be over the age of 64. If we believe the new cliché that '60 is the new 40' then it follows that most people are living more active and fulfilled lives for longer. In a general sense then the old cliché 'You can't teach an old dog new tricks' is no longer credible, although at an individual level it is the case many people lack confidence in their ability to learn as they get older.

It is not surprising that ageing is a preoccupation in the twenty-first century, since an increasingly ageing population is assumed to be a burden on society. Whether or not this is the case is disputed since there is contesting evidence to support the assertion (see e.g. Mullan 2001). However, it is clearly in the interests of society to keep as much of the population as possible active and healthy for as long as possible in order to reduce the effects of that perceived burden.

Another way of understanding adult development is as a dialectical process; that is, the change and development of the individual is both a product of the change and development of society and an agent of change and development in that society. This approach to understanding adulthood rejects psychological explanations of adult development. Rather, it is argued, the development of the individual is governed by the objective circumstances of their lives. If opportunities to learn, achieve and develop potential are restricted then the potential to learn will eventually become restricted. 'Use it or lose it' is the old adage.

The extent to which society can enable everyone to achieve their potential is a perennial discussion and raises the issue of whether education should be for the benefit of the individual or the greater benefit of society. In the context of our discussion of ageing and learning it is clear that the extent to which people have the opportunity to be physically and mentally active and to fulfil individual potential is important at all ages and is no less of a priority for the elderly.

In practical terms, however, we know that some older learners do experience certain physical difficulties such as hearing, sight and mobility. The important thing to remember is that these difficulties do not necessarily signal an impaired ability to learn. As you identified in Task 3.10, they merely require fairly straightforward changes of approach to learning both on the part of the teacher and the learner.

Task 3.11

Discuss with a partner some of the difficulties you have come across with older students. What strategies have you used or could you use to overcome them?

3.3 Learning theories

KEY ISSUES

What are the main theoretical perspectives that inform our approach to learning?

How does an understanding of theories of learning affect our approach to classroom practice?

It is not the intention here to provide an in-depth study of learning theories, but to present an overview of the main theoretical perspectives and to raise some critical issues related to them. Since the whole chapter is devoted to learning, aspects of theory are presented throughout and relate to the schools of thought discussed in this section. Theories of learning are based on psychological understanding and seek to describe what happens when learning takes place. Learning theory in essence is not about the conditions required for effective learning: it is for the practitioner to extract and interpret elements from theories and apply what is perceived as relevant to his or her own teaching. No one theory can supply a blueprint for how we learn, but each offers insights which are essential to us as teachers if we are to ensure that our students learn effectively.

All too often textbooks on educational psychology and learning theory, while explaining clearly the principles of learning, are less effective in the practical advice they give. As Tight (2003a: 24) suggests, they offer a '"cook book" approach to practical advice'. This is because they do not relate to the content of the learning that is to be undertaken, but to the process of learning. The application of learning theory should therefore proceed on this basis; some insights into how people learn seem more appropriately applied to certain areas of subject matter than others, as we shall examine.

The broad strands of learning theory are: *behavourism, Gestalt theories, cognitive theories* and *social learning theories*. Behaviourist, Gestalt and cognitive theories of learning have tended to centre around how learning occurs in children and date from the latter part of the nineteenth century. Social learning theories, andragogy and related theories, concerned with how adults learn as distinct from young people, are more recent and derive from the humanist school of psychology.

According to behaviourist theories, which formed the basis for all learning theories, all behaviour is learned, thus eliminating any biological influences. Put crudely, behaviourists contended that all learning involves 'an observable change in behaviour' and only what can be measured can be regarded as learning. Behaviourist psychologists did not seek to discover anything about thought processes, but about how learning occurred. Experiments involving salivating dogs (classical conditioning, after Pavlov), cats and monkeys (the law of effect, after Thorndike), rats and pigeons (operant conditioning, after Skinner) are well known and are the basis of stimulus–response (S–R) theory. The earliest behaviourist was Watson who established the principle of trial and error learning which other behaviourists developed. For a full account of individuals' work in this field see Child (2007). The American psychologist, B.F. Skinner, has been perhaps the most influential figure in the field. Skinner (1938) developed some of the main principles by which behaviourist theory is known. His 'Skinner box' involved putting hungry rats into a box and 'training' them to pull a series of levers to release food pellets. At first, pulling the lever was accidental, but after it happened several times the rat began to associate pulling the lever with food and then did so intentionally, thus displaying learned behaviour. Such behaviour he called *operant conditioning* and what differentiates it from classical conditioning is that the individual is required to act on the environment (the rat operated the lever to obtain the food). The need for reinforcement, rewards and punishment, and feedback are all concepts attributable to Skinner's work. Skinner's experiments with teaching pigeons to walk in a figure of eight led to his identifying these elements as key features of learning: correct responses are reinforced by rewards, incorrect responses are ignored (or possibly punished, a negative reinforcement). Skinner subsequently made a major contribution to the development of programmed learning, the early forerunner of computer-assisted learning and mastery learning. Skinner's operant conditioning also forms the basis of behaviour modification, the technique used to bring about a change in behaviour, often used in special needs education.

In a behaviourist approach, learning should progress step by step and build on previously learned material. In the early stages the learner should be regularly rewarded when correct responses are given. This feedback stimulates motivation to continue. Learning is reinforced by rewards and knowledge of success. Skinner's work and the behaviourist method in general is appealing in that they identify components of learning which we can readily understand. Anyone who has trained a dog to sit on command or potty-trained a small child will recognize the features of the behaviourist method. But does all learning occur in this way? Essential to a behavioural view of learning is that any learning can be measured. Can all learning be observed? What about more abstract knowledge such as understanding Plato or appreciating classical music? Is there a danger, therefore, that anything that cannot be measured in behavioural terms gets ignored? Can all learning be demonstrated?

Task 3.12

(a) Think of two examples from your own teaching where you could or do use a behaviourist approach. Describe how the learning takes place step by step.

(b) Discuss your examples with a partner and try to apply the behaviourist terminology to stages in the learning.

(c) Draw up a list with your partner of the types of learning activity that might best be approached through behaviourist methods.

The examples you chose in Task 3.12 may well have been drawn from a vocational or competence-based course. For example, National Vocational Qualifications (NVQs), which are discussed in various contexts elsewhere in this book, offer a clear example of how behaviourist theories of learning are applied in practice. Indeed, many professional qualifications, including the Postgraduate Certificate of Education (PGCE) and the Certificate of Education are based on assessment of competence in a behavioural sense, even though they are presented as holistic 'standards'. If you write a lesson plan or course programme with objectives which state precisely what students will be able to do, you are writing behavioural objectives intending to measure a learning outcome. The competence 'movement' has a very important influence on the post-14 curriculum and pedagogy today, but it is not without its critics (see e.g. early critiques by Hyland 1994 and Wolf 1995) in terms of what is claimed to be the restricted, instrumental view of knowledge that it embodies, the reductive nature of learning and also the limitations of competence-based assessment. However, we now work in an education system that is largely outcomes driven and the legacy of behaviourist learning theory is very much alive and well.

The contribution of Gestalt psychology to learning is particularly important with regard to perception and the role it plays in learning. Wertheimer, Kohler and Koffler founded the Gestalt school of psychology in the 1920s. Unlike behaviourists, who attempted to analyse behaviour, however complex, into S–R units, Gestalt theory looks at how we see patterns as a whole. In fact, *Gestalt* means 'pattern' or 'form' in German. The visual 'trick' silhouette pictures which have two interpretations are well-known examples used to illustrate visual perception. The Gestaltists concluded from experiments such as these that the way we look at things and the ways in which we perceive things depends on our prior experience.

They emphasized closure, which is our ability to process component parts of information and create a whole, and described this as insight. Insight learning applies the laws of perception to learning. It refers to that sudden flash of inspiration that we have when we suddenly see the solution to a problem. To experience what is meant by insight learning, try doing a jigsaw puzzle without the picture to guide you. You will proceed by trial and error, but at some stage, hopefully, you will have that sudden insight as to where to place a crucial piece as you realize what the picture is supposed to be. Insight, according to Gestaltists, is a response to a whole situation, not separate responses to a series of stimuli, as behaviourists would suggest. 'The whole is greater than the sum of its parts' is a description often applied to Gestalt theory, suggesting that something is missing in the behaviourist approach. From a Gestalt perspective, learning is a complex process of interrelationships which occur as a result of engaging with a new problem in the light of previous experiences.

Task 3.13

(a)   What other examples of insight learning can you think of?

(b)   How does insight learning feature in your students' learning? Think of some examples.

Gestalt theories add another dimension to behaviourism in terms of an understanding of learning processes. Insight learning and theories of perception are often described within the cognitive theoretical framework in study texts because they have in common an emphasis on more abstract psychological concepts such as 'understanding', 'reasoning', 'thinking' and 'human consciousness' as opposed to a simplistic attempt to reduce the rich variety of human learning to 'observable behaviour'.

Piaget is the most well known of the cognitive theorists writing and researching over a period of almost 40 years from the late 1920s to the early 1960s (see Child 2007). Although his work was focused on the development of children, he established nevertheless that learning is developmental. This has important implications for adult learning since it suggests that adulthood is a stable period in terms of intellectual development. Through experimentation, observation and research Piaget identified stages of intellectual development in children which are sequential and established that the changing nature of learning and the capacity to think throughout childhood is qualitative rather than quantitative. These developmental stages are known as: sensory motor (0–2 years); pre-operational (2–6 years); concrete operational (7–11 years); and formal operational (12 years +) (see Tennant 2005 for a full account and critique in relation to adult learning). In short, each stage marks the development from practical thought to the abstract thought equated with mature adulthood. Is this an end point? Some theorists argue that it is not. Is the process necessarily age-related or more to do with the range and depth of learning experiences that we undergo at any age? Piaget has been criticized both for a lack of rigour in his methodology and for over-interpretation of his data. Nevertheless his analysis has been the bedrock of learning theory for a vast number of schoolteachers for the past 40 years or more (see Boden 1994 for a concise guide to Piaget's work).

A key feature of cognitive theory is that knowledge is constructed through interaction with the environment. It is a cognitive process, which involves acquiring new information which enables the learner to evolve and transform their existing knowledge and then check out and apply the new state of knowledge to new situations; and so the process goes on. New patterns of meaning and understanding are formed to enable further learning to take place. The process is dynamic. The work of Jerome S. Bruner from the 1960s to the 1980s, following on from and influenced by Piaget, has made a significant contribution to cognitive theory. For Bruner, it is essential that the learner has a fundamental understanding of the underlying principles of a subject. Discovery learning, according to Bruner, is the most effective and authentic method of achieving a real understanding of the principles of a subject and then applying those principles. Discovery learning involves confronting the learner with a problem and allowing them to explore the problem and try out solutions on the basis of inquiry and previous learning under the guidance of a teacher. The newly acquired knowledge is then used to formulate a general principle which can then be applied to other situations. For example, when learning the concept of 'conservation' a young child might be given variously shaped containers, a measuring jug and a bowl of water with which to 'play'. The child is encouraged by the teacher to try pouring water from one container to another. Some of the containers, although differently shaped, contain the same amount. Gradually through experimentation, and prompting and questioning by the teacher, the child arrives at an understanding that the quantity of water remains constant and is able to articulate their understanding. Over a period of time, they would be given further opportunities to demonstrate their knowledge and apply the principle in other situations.

Task 3.14

(a)   Discovery learning has been a popular approach with very young learners for the past 30 years or more. Discuss in a small group examples of how it might be an appropriate approach with learners in lifelong learning.

(b)   Think of some examples from your own experience where you have encouraged discovery learning. Compare these examples with those from Task 3.15 below.

(c)   What would be the role of the teacher in a discovery learning situation?

Bruner's work is associated with what is known broadly as *constructivism*. The central idea is that human learning is constructed, that learners build new knowledge upon previous learning and therefore learning involves constructing one's own knowledge from one's own experiences. Individuals engage in their own knowledge construction by integrating new information into their 'schemes' and negotiate meaning through a shared understanding. The teacher acts as a facilitator who encourages students to discover principles for themselves and to construct knowledge by working to solve realistic problems.

Cognitive theorists relate their theories to subject content, as do behaviourists. The approach of humanist psychologists is more concerned with the process of learning and therefore contrasts sharply with behaviourism and cognitivism. Theories of learning related to humanistic psychology were arrived at as a reaction against behaviourism and provide the intellectual basis for much adult learning theory. According to humanist insights, learning is a total personality process; life is a learning experience; true education is individual and about personal growth. Malcolm Knowles presented *andragogy*, 'the science and art of helping adults to learn' (Knowles 1984: 52) as a theory of adult learning. It was Knowles who developed and popularized the andragogical model, the notion of the adult as a self-directed learner. Knowles based his model on his experiences in teaching in American universities which has been pointed to as an essential weakness of his theories. While the 'assumptions of andragogy' have been challenged and much criticized, nevertheless the notion of the self-directed learner underpins much of adult education practice and remains the keystone of adult learning theory. Knowles identified five elements of the learning process: the concept of the learner; the role of the learner's experience; readiness to learn; orientation to learning; and motivation. He contrasted a characterization of pedagogical assumptions with what he identified as andragogical. Table 3.1 sets out Knowles' 'assumptions'.

Task 3.15

Discuss in a group of four or five the extent to which you would support or reject the assumptions in Table 3.1. Use examples from your own experience of children and adults learning to inform your discussion. Would we now make these distinctions? Or have the distinctions been blurred between the two categories?

Table 3.1 The assumptions of andragogy

	Pedagogical	*Andragogical*
Concept of the learner	Dependent personality	Increasingly self-directed
Role of learner's experience	To be built on, more than used as a resource	A rich resource for learning by self and others
Reading to learn	Uniform by age, level and curriculum	Develops from life tasks and problems
Orientation to learning	Subject-centred	Task- or problem-centred
Motivation	By external rewards and punishment	By internal incentives and curiosity

Source: Knowles (1984: 116).

Humanist psychologists, in particular Carl Rogers, provided a framework of understanding upon which Knowles built, rejecting previous theories of learning as being appropriate only to children. Rogers, a therapist, applied his observations of adults in therapy to learning and conceptualized student-centred learning as a parallel to his client-centred therapy. 'Teaching, in my estimation, is a vastly over-rated function' (Rogers 1983: 119). Rogers considered that the 'facilitation of learning' with a focus on the interpersonal relationship between the learner and the facilitator based on trust, 'empathic understanding' and genuineness on the part of the facilitator is the key to effective learning. 'Changingness, a reliance on *process* rather than upon static knowledge, is the only thing that makes any sense as a goal for education in the modern world' (p. 120, original emphasis). According to Rogers, much significant learning is acquired by doing, and therefore experiential learning is the only true learning, and the antipathy of any sort of memory learning. Like Knowles, Rogers emphasizes the 'self', self-development and self-direction. Unlike Knowles, for whom 'self-direction' involves the learner controlling the content of a course according to their needs while the teacher controls the processes, Rogers leaves the process in the hands of the learner and content appears to have little importance. Rogers, in common with Knowles, has been criticized for offering a partial theory, but both have nevertheless been very influential in the development of contemporary thinking on adult education.

Indeed, many of the ideas relating to andragogy and humanistic psychology have passed into a common-sense understanding of how learning is best 'facilitated' with learners in all sectors of lifelong learning and are actively promoted by many mainstream educationalists. We talk much of 'learner autonomy' and 'personalized learning' in the post-14 sector, both of which are linked to the idea of the 'self-directed' learner and the tenets of theorists like Rogers. However, certain problems arise from the wholesale adoption of such an approach to teaching and learning. Tennant (2005: 23) provides a useful, if partial in itself, summary of his reservations concerning andragogy:

> . . . I have argued that the rationale and empirical support for the humanistic concepts of self-development and self-direction has gaps and weaknesses which need to be acknowledged. There is a need to distinguish the rhetoric of adult education from its rationale and empirical base. The prevailing rhetoric asserts that in everyday life adults are basically self-directed and that this self-direction is rooted in our constitutional make-up, it also asserts that self-development is an inexorable process towards higher levels of existence, and finally it asserts that adult learning is fundamentally (and necessarily) different from child learning. These assertions should not be accepted as articles of faith.

Task 3.16

(a)   Reflect on your classroom practice and consider the ways in which theories of learning based on humanistic psychology have influenced your teaching.

(b)   Consider the issues raised in the paragraph above and discuss with a partner your ideas for dealing with them.

It is also useful to think about the consequences of elevating process over content, by replacing the *what* with the *how* in teaching and learning. Is self-direction the starting point or the goal of education? Does the practice of experiential learning reduce all learning to the instrumental? Is the transmission of knowledge and the pursuit of excellence redundant? What does it mean to be a 'facilitator of learning'?

Social learning theories may be seen as a sort of bridge between behaviourism and cognitive theories of learning and have become very influential, although sometimes criticized for being relativistic in that all knowledge is treated as the same, presented as an expression of social interests (Young 2008). Theorists such as Bandura (1997) focused on the role of observation and modelling in learning – both familiar ideas that have been adopted into current thinking about learning and classroom practice. In social learning theory, unlike behaviourism, behaviour change is not necessarily apparent and cognition plays an important role. Lev Vygotsky is perhaps the best known and popular social learning theorist and his work has provided the foundation for much associated research and theory on cognitive development. Although his work dates back to the 1920s, it was hardly known outside the Soviet Union until much later and, according to some observers, has fallen victim to 'distorted or at least highly selective contemporary interpretations' (Young 2008: 66). That said, terms such as 'scaffolding', 'apprenticeship' and 'zone of proximal development' (ZPD) are now in common use in education, although perhaps less well known in the post-14 sector. Vygotsky emphasizes the effect of social factors in learning and stresses the fundamental role of social interaction in learning. His sociocultural approach to learning and cognitive development was distinctive in the way he emphasized collaborative dialogue between the learner and a more knowledgeable other (MKO) in moving from an existing level of knowledge to acquiring new knowledge. He called the gap between the known and the unknown the ZPD, where knowledge and skills that are too difficult to learn alone, but are nevertheless within the grasp of the learner, are mastered through the guidance and encouragement of an MKO. This MKO could be a teacher, or another learner – someone who has a better understanding or a higher ability level than the learner with respect to a particular task or concept. Vygotsky's theoretical work and insights have greatly informed the collaborative approach to learning that is much favoured in many classrooms and is worthy of further reading and study.

3.4 Effective learning

KEY ISSUES

How do we identify learning needs?

What are the barriers to learning and how can they be overcome?

How do we help students to learn effectively?

Each group of learners is different from the next; each student is an individual with their own goals and expectations. These may or may not coincide with those of the teacher or the externally prescribed goals of a learning programme. A sound starting point for any course is to share those goals and to work out what can be achieved by the group and by individuals in that group. It is often the case that some goals are predetermined by the nature of the course; preparation for achieving a qualification, for example. From the teacher's perspective, it is very useful to know what your students' learning needs are, their motives for joining the course and so on in order to support their learning more effectively. What do students need to know about you and what you are going to teach them?

Task 3.17

(a)   List the information you need to know about your students and their learning needs, aspirations and expectations at the beginning of your course. Discuss your list with a partner and draw up a short questionnaire that you could use with your students.

(b)   Now think about the start of your course from a student's perspective. What information could you provide them with?

(c)   Why is this information exchange important? How can you use the information you obtain?

Of course, not all students have a clear idea what their goals, expectations or aspirations are. Is it always possible or even legitimate within the confines of a prescribed programme of study in a group situation to expect to have all of one's individual, sometimes idiosyncratic needs met? However, by discussing these issues early on, it is possible to set a mutually supportive, cooperative tone to the course conducive to effective learning.

Do all learners approach their learning in the same way? Do individuals have a 'preferred style' of learning? Within the framework of experiential learning, several theorists have evolved models of learning styles. Perhaps the most well known of these and the most frequently used with students is Kolb's (1984) 'learning style inventory'. Based on his model of experiential learning, David Kolb identified four categories of learning which occur in a cycle of concrete experience (CE), followed by observation and reflection on that experience (RO), then by the formulation of some sort of theory or hypothesis which involves abstract conceptualization (AC), and then, finally, by the testing-out of the hypothesis or theory in active experimentation (AE). According to Kolb the truly effective learner has abilities in all these four areas but most people have varying abilities in one area or another. The purpose of the inventory is to measure the relative strengths individuals have in each area by completing a questionnaire and then plotting the results on a quadrant. This purports to enable learners to identify their orientation to learning and discover how, given their natural inclinations, learning can best be approached. How useful is the method in identifying areas of 'weakness' and how might the information be used? Is it helpful to 'label' students in this way or might there be unintended consequences? Is it potentially limiting for students to label themselves? Teachers in in Post-14 Education and Training may be more familiar with the idea that we are all visual, auditory or kinaesthetic learners (VAK); 'VAK' seems to have been absorbed into educational culture and accepted as received wisdom in the way we understand learning, but it is perhaps worth exploring the body of research that suggests that there is no firm scientific evidence to support it. Like multiple intelligences and cognitive neuroscience, learning styles theory draws on biological explanations and again runs the danger of being over-deterministic. 'Learning styles' may have lost credibility among the academic community (see Füredi 2009 for a critique of all aspects of psycho-pedagogy and Coffield et al.'s research report from 2004 on learning styles), but the ideas still seem to have currency with teachers. Is that because they seem to make sense and are simply another way of categorizing learners?

Task 3.18

(a)   Consider what might be the unintended consequences for teachers and students of the use of 'learning styles' in the classroom?

(b)   What other ways might you use to identify needs and support learning?

The philosopher of education, Robin Barrow (1984: 107) comes at the issue from another perspective, suggesting that 'People come to learning in different ways, partly as a result of content, partly as a result of being different people preferring to or finding it easier to acquire understanding in different ways' and points to the importance of the relationship between how people learn and a clear understanding by the teacher of what is to be learned. Barrow is right to emphasize the importance of the teacher's subject knowledge and expertise as well as pedagogic knowledge.

Let us now turn to how effective learning can best be promoted. We have already looked at various theoretical perspectives on learning, and the point has been made that learning is related to content. Any number of claims can be made about how learning is best achieved, but what is learned is the test of how effective the learning has been. Let us consider a typical classroom scenario on a PGCE course. The topic for the session is 'equal opportunities in education'. The sequence of the lesson is as follows:

1   Teacher 'brainstorms' ideas with students about what equal opportunities issues they have come across, either from their own experience or the experience of others.

2   Teacher gives a short talk about legislation and its impact/success/failure and invites the questions/comments/views of students.

3   In groups of four, students discuss various short case studies of practical equal opportunities issues and are asked to offer possible solutions to the problems.

4   Small groups feed back their ideas to the whole group.

5   Teacher leads the group in a discussion of the underlying causes of inequality and draws together key points from the session.

Task 3.19

(a)   What do you think are the strengths and weaknesses of the lesson? Look at each stage, preferably with a partner, and discuss how you would ensure that students learned effectively.

(b)   What is missing? For example, no mention is made of the teacher introducing the topic or stating any learning objectives or outcomes. Does this matter?

(c)   Now draw up a five-point 'recipe for successful learning' from a student's perspective based on your discussions about the above lesson sequence.

This sort of lesson format is probably familiar to you. It begins with the students' own experiences and broadens out by introducing new knowledge and challenging students to think about practical and finally abstract principles. This is one way of approaching learning. How else might the topic have been addressed? It could be argued that a good, informative, challenging lecture would have been as effective. What do you think? Your own lessons provide useful 'real-life' case studies for reflection along these lines and will enable you to consider how effectively your students learn. Chapter 6, on assessment, will also introduce another dimension to the subject of effective learning.

Task 3.20

(a)   Consider in turn the following short 'pen sketches' of typical students. What barriers to learning might they encounter?

Julie is a 17-year-old who left secondary school a year ago with no qualifications. She has been unsuccessful in finding a suitable job although she has done some casual work in a fast-food restaurant. Julie is about to begin, somewhat reluctantly, a vocational course in hospitality and catering at her local FE college.

Amol is at the beginning of a three-year BA course in media studies and sports science at a 'new' university. He is 18 and has just left school with two A levels at grades C and D. Amol tried to get a job in leisure management, but has realized that he needs a degree if he is going to build a good career. His parents are unable to support him financially.

Mary is a 30-year-old mother of two, recently divorced. Her children are both of school age and she has now decided to do an access course at her local FE college with a view to going on to HE. Mary left school at 16 with four GCSEs and did office work before her children were born.

Frank has recently retired at the age of 57. He left school at 14 and had been a shopkeeper all his life, working long hours. He now wants to keep his mind alert by joining a beginner's Spanish course at his local AE centre because he hopes to buy a holiday home in Spain.

Jack is 15 and a pupil in an academy school that is developing a vocational strand for low achievers at Key Stage 4 in partnership with a local FE college. Although he has little enthusiasm for it, Jason has been 'guided' towards a construction course which will take place partly in the FE college where he will join in with students of all ages.

(b)   Try to place the barriers you have identified into the categories of educational, institutional and societal. Do some of them overlap?

Some educational barriers might equally be considered to be institutional problems. For example, a tourism teacher might be ill-equipped to help a student deal with a severe spelling problem. We might expect a learning support workshop to be available to give expert guidance and tuition. However, it is the responsibility of that tourism teacher to ensure that the student is aware of the problem, to mark the student's work carefully and ensure that they get whatever support is available. Many mature students lack confidence in their ability to learn, have low expectations of themselves or have memories of bad educational experiences. These and other barriers to learning may have an educational aspect, but are intrinsically linked with institutional and particularly societal barriers.

Institutional barriers are sometimes harder to overcome. In the past, many battles were fought in colleges and higher education institutions (HEIs) by staff and students alike to facilitate access for disabled students, for example. Those sorts of problem have largely been resolved and there is a far greater awareness of and adherence to the principles of inclusion. While the huge expansion of FE and HE in recent years has eroded some of the barriers to access that existed in the past, others have taken their place. We have already mentioned the greater diversity of the lifelong-learning student population. How have institutions fared in meeting the needs of such a wide range of students? Have new barriers to learning been created within institutions as a result? But perhaps the biggest institutional barrier for students in lifelong learning is the financial one. The issue of the long-term financial burden that tuition fees places on students and the problem of deterring students from less well-off backgrounds from going on to HE are well known and the removal of financial incentives for young people to participate in lifelong learning is taking its toll.

This leads us into a discussion of the societal barriers to learning that people encounter, since education is a key part of social policy and is certainly the service which attracts a great deal of public and political attention and concern in the twenty-first century. Successive governments have expressed a firm commitment to Post-14 Education and Training and a widening of access to education for all sections of society. Numerous studies have confirmed that participation in lifelong learning is predominantly composed of higher socioeconomic groups. Certain groups of people continue to be under-represented: unskilled/semi-skilled manual workers; unemployed people; women with dependent children; older adults (aged 50+); and ethnic minority groups. For people in these groups, there are a wide range of reasons why they do not continue their education beyond school, some of which have already been mentioned. But the overarching barrier may be that education is something that other people do, and is perceived as not something they need. Since the late 1990s a plethora of reports and policy initiatives have focused on these 'excluded' groups and vast sums of money have been channelled into courses and other provision. Widening participation has become the cornerstone of HE policy and has therefore increased the pressure on schools and colleges to prepare a much wider range of young people for university study. Already over 80 per cent of young people stay on in some form of education after 16, but it is uncertain whether the real barriers to learning have been overcome by many of them.

This section has cast the net very widely over practical issues concerned with learning and has aimed to promote discussion about how we can ensure that our students achieve to the best of their ability and have high expectations of themselves. The next section will explore the idea of learner autonomy.

Task 3.21

(a) Consider what changes have taken place in the FE, AE or HE sectors.
(b) What new barriers to learning have emerged and how has participation been widened and improved as a result of these changes?
(c) How do societal barriers to learning link with educational and institutional barriers?

3.5 Learner autonomy

KEY ISSUES

What distinguishes the autonomous learner from learner autonomy?

Is learner autonomy concerned with the process of learning or is it an educational goal?

How do students develop good study skills?

What do we mean by 'personalized learning'?

If we brainstorm the variety of terms used to describe learning that is not teacher-centred, the list seems endless with little apparent distinction in the way labels are used. Tight (2003b) makes a distinction between what he calls 'learning concepts' which 'focus mainly on the perspective of the organisation providing education or training' and 'those which are more concerned with the perspective of the individual learner'. In the first category he places distance, flexible and open learning (which will be discussed in Chapter 5) as distinct from experiential, independent and self-directed learning where the shift from institutional responsibility to the individual leaves the learner in charge of and supposedly in control of their own learning.

The notion of the self-directed learner comes, as we have already seen, from the andragogical theory of adult learning. While a variety of criticisms have been ranged at andragogy, nevertheless many aspects have been incorporated into our understanding and practice in Post-14 Education and Training. Not least, the self-directed, autonomous learner. Moore (1983: 163) suggests that:

> Autonomous learners – and this means most adults, most of the time – sometimes formally, often unconsciously, set objectives and define criteria for their achievement. Autonomous learners know, or find, where and how and from what human and other resources they may gather the information they require, collect ideas, practice skills and achieve their goals. They then judge the appropriateness of their new skills, information and ideas, eventually deciding whether their goals have been achieved or can be abandoned.

To what extent and to which groups of learners in the Post-14 Education and Training sector might this description fit? Perhaps not the average FE student, but what about groups in AE, or HE undergraduates? How many of the characteristics described by Moore do your learners display? Are our students 'naturally' self-directing, or is self-direction and learner autonomy something which the teacher can encourage through a particular style of teaching and which learners develop over a period of time? More importantly, should autonomy be more than knowing how to study and direct your learning or about developing the ability to think critically and independently? Can independent, critical thought be achieved autonomously? What are the implications for the role of the teacher?

It is increasingly the case that learners in all sectors of Post-14 Education and Training need to develop their ability to study independently, to increase their 'learner autonomy'. Whatever the educational justifications that are made for 'learner autonomy', the reality is that cuts in course hours, and the shift away over a period of time from examination to project and assignment work, means that students do spend much more time working alone, in groups or in front of a computer without teacher guidance and supervision. Independent study is now an integral part of all vocational courses and therefore the demands on both students and teachers are different from the teacher/student relationship associated with traditional craft courses. The 'autonomous learner' may seem to be an idealized description of many young people in FE and developing that autonomy is indeed a challenge for all concerned. This curriculum change is coupled with an explosion in the FE student population that dates back to the collapse of the youth labour market in the mid-1990s as well as substantial budget cuts that the sector has suffered.

The shift in the AE curriculum towards more accredited courses puts more pressure on learners and teachers to achieve qualifications. In order to keep fees within affordable limits, course hours are often inadequate to cover the whole syllabus adequately in class time. It is therefore essential that students engage in a significant amount of independent study. In HE the shift is slightly different. Independent research and study has always been a defining feature of academic study and quite rightly so. In some respects the undergraduate epitomizes the autonomous learner described above. However, the recent massive expansion in HE has created several new problems. To begin with, the new expanded HE student population is much more diverse. There is now a greater proportion of mature people, part-time students, a slightly higher social and ethnic mix and, perhaps more importantly, a wider range of ability entering HE. Alongside this, the rise in student numbers has not been accompanied by a parallel increase in funding. Not surprisingly this has led to cuts in course hours and thus a much greater emphasis on independent study.

The possible reasons for these curriculum changes throughout the post-14 sector are discussed elsewhere (see Chapters 1 and 7 in particular). However, it is useful to consider how you would interpret 'learner autonomy' in your work and what emphasis you would place on it. The use of technology has become a fundamental, some would argue, essential feature of everyday life and work and in many ways education has become reliant on information technology (IT). Strong claims are made for IT in relation to the development of learner autonomy, but we should not confuse development of technical abilities with educational endeavour. The use of technology is discussed in depth in Chapter 5 but it is mentioned here since one of the claims made for it is that it promotes learner autonomy. Certainly the availability of information through the world wide web is infinitely greater than what is on offer in the average library, but depth of knowledge is sometimes questionable and making judgements on the quality of information retrieved requires skill. How do we judge one set of information over another if we know nothing about the subject? This is where the teacher plays a crucial role in guiding learning. It is particularly important in relation to learner autonomy and technology that teachers understand the distinction between knowledge, information and understanding and that they are not conflated.

Besides the sort of open internet research that we all engage with, there is now a plethora of web-based learning programmes, and most recently the phenomenon of 'MOOCs' (massive open online courses) that are often very attractive to use, but the question arises, what knowledge can be 'packaged' in this way? The concept of 'autonomy' has taken on a new meaning in that it describes *how* learning takes place and could be seen as a diminished concept. What if, however, we define 'learner autonomy' as the achievement of intellectual freedom and critical thought through the mastery of a subject? Is this still an appropriate goal to aspire to? How far can it be achieved through the process of 'autonomous learning', independent study, workshops, resource-based and 'e-learning'? What of the social aspect of learning?

> **Task 3.22**
>
> Note down some of the arguments for and against autonomous learning.

In Section 3.4 we considered learning needs of our students. What often emerges from such analyses is that many students do require help and support in the way they approach learning. We also considered effective learning in the classroom in Section 3.4. What we shall explore in Task 3.23 are the skills that students need to enable them to learn and how they can be developed by the teacher. As teachers we routinely offer ad hoc guidance on how to approach a piece of work, or perhaps we have a 'study skills' handout that we give to each student with advice on time management and approaches to reading and so on. Alternatively, we might want to build strategies into our teaching so that students develop a systematic approach to their learning.

> **Task 3.23**
>
> (a) Choose one of your typical teaching sessions and write down the sequence of activities in the lesson. Organize the information in three columns. In the first column write down what you do throughout the lesson; in the second column record the parallel student activity. When you have done that, look at each student activity and identify what learning strategies your students need at each stage. For example:
>
> - teacher activity strategy: introductory talk;
> - student activity: listen, take notes;
> - learning: assimilate information, extract key points and write them down.
>
> (b) Now examine the learning strategies you have identified. Are all your students able to apply these strategies effectively? Which ones could you give help with during the lesson? Which ones require a longer-term plan to develop? How can you facilitate and support this?

Whatever subject you are teaching, students need to develop effective learning strategies. It is essential that they are acquired and practised in the classroom if students are going to be able to learn effectively on their own. *Learning to learn*, that is, supporting students to develop appropriate attitudes, strategies and approaches to learning, has become an important focus of professional development for teachers in both the compulsory and post-compulsory sectors. On some courses, *the way* that students approach their learning is given as much time and attention as *what* they are learning. Is that legitimate? Has 'learning to learn' become an end in itself, a process prior to learning?

Personalized learning has recently become a notable concern for policy-makers and academics (see, e.g. Leadbeater 2004; Pollard and James 2004), and also impacts on the work of teachers in Post-14 Education and Training. Although conceptually somewhat obscure, and now attracting some criticism, personalized learning has been promoted as the panacea of the protracted problems of under-achievement, particularly among disadvantaged children and young people. The 'personalization' of learning can be seen partly as developing out of theories of multiple intelligences, emotional literacy and learning styles, and based on the per-ception that education must meet individual needs. As such, it reflects a focus on developing learning behaviours, and on the construction of 'personal understand-ings' redolent of constructivist theories of learning. Pollard and James (2004), who provide a useful examination of personalized learning, note that it 'is not a matter of tailoring the curriculum, teaching and assessment to "fit" the individual, but it is a question of developing social practices that enable people to become all that they are capable of being'. There are now a number of research and policy doc-uments available, notably those published by the TLRP (Teaching and Learning Research Programme), but the key document to consult is *2020 Vision: Report of the Teaching and Learning in 2020 Review Group* (DfES 2007a). It is here that personalization is set out as that which will liberate children and young people from the perceived failures of education. However, critics suggest that far from being a radical step forward in promoting educational achievement, personalized learning reflects a retreat from the idea that education has the capacity to trans-form people's lives. The focus on developing 'learning behaviours' is being substi-tuted for knowledge, and learning to learn is seen to be more important than what is learned. The extent to which personalized learning promotes learner autonomy in the way it has been discussed above is uncertain.

The diversity of learners in Post-14 Education and Training is as wide as the types of courses and programmes on which they enrol. Faced with such diversity, and the pressures on teachers to respond to every individual's learning needs, it is not surprising that we sometimes lose sight of the similarities between learn-ers and their common goals. It is easy to make erroneous assumptions about the individuals before us in the classroom and lower our expectations of them accord-ingly. This chapter has introduced a variety of aspects of learning and has sought to relate theoretical perspectives to contemporary issues and professional practice in order that we may better understand our students and how best to support them.

Links to the Professional Standards for Teachers and Trainers in Education and Training

Professional values and attributes

2 Evaluate and challenge your practice, values and beliefs

3 Inspire, motivate and raise aspirations of learners through your enthusiasm and knowledge

4 Be creative and innovative in selecting and adapting strategies to help learners to learn

Professional knowledge and understanding

8 Maintain and update your knowledge of educational research to develop evidence-based practice

9 Apply theoretical understanding of effective practice in teaching, learning and assessment drawing on research and other evidence

11 Manage and promote positive learner behaviour

Professional skills

13 Motivate and inspire learners to promote achievement and develop their skills to enable progression

4

Teaching and the management of learning

4.1 What is Chapter 4 about?

This chapter deals with the relationship between teaching and learning as two inseparable processes and examines the prerequisites for success in teaching for learning. The phrase *teaching for learning* has become increasingly dominant in recent years as a result of a growing awareness that teaching and learning must be considered as complementary activities. So, in any planning and curriculum development activities, the aims of the teacher must be to ensure that the learner is placed at the core of the structure, content and delivery of the teaching process.

The teacher has two major responsibilities of equal importance which will determine the success of a learning experience for individuals and groups. One responsibility is the planning of well-structured, stimulating and effective lessons, with coherent, appropriate aims and learning outcomes and clear assessment strategies. The other is the management of the learning environment, so that learners can achieve their potential in a safe, efficient and mature environment which is fair and inclusive to all, while recognizing the differences which characterize each individual within a group of adult learners. Thus, planning and managing the learning environment are parallel activities. It is possible to plan a good lesson, with appropriate goals, interesting material, varied teaching and learning experiences and excellent resources. If, however, a teacher is unable to manage the learners, then the planning is wasted, since barriers to learning will arise and these will diminish learning potential. Adults do not learn effectively in an environment in which they feel psychologically or physically uncomfortable. There are many distractions to the learning process, and while not all of these can be eradicated all of the time, the exercise of sound management skills in the learning environment is essential to learner success, not to mention teacher satisfaction.

Section 4.2 deals with the planning of learning at micro and macro levels – lesson plans and schemes of work. These planning processes require coherent thinking at whatever level in order to ensure that there is alignment between aims, outcomes and assessment and this is dealt with in the first part of this section. At the same time it is important to cater for individual achievement, while recognizing that in most groups each individual may present particular learning needs, and it is this that can make planning short- and long-term goals quite a complex process. There are many factors to be taken into consideration. Those looked at in this section include: motivation; inclusion; differentiation; individual learning plans; equality and diversity issues and the embedding of functional skills. The increasing importance of incorporating the SEND Act 2014 into the planning process is also considered.

The focus of Section 4.3 is classroom management and the role of good communication skills within the learning environment to effect this, as well what is entailed in maximizing motivation and achievement at an individual level. Planning must ensure that all individuals within a given group can work cooperatively and effectively in that setting and that the conditions in a classroom to facilitate this are in place. The use of a learning contract can often assist in this endeavour, helping to establish a safe working environment in which trust and respect facilitate a harmonious rapport between individuals.

Finally, in Section 4.4 the issue of managing different types of learning environments is discussed both inside and outside the classroom. Learning nowadays takes place in a wider variety of settings than ever before, each of which presents its own challenges for the teacher in management terms.

4.2 The planning process

KEY ISSUES

How can we plan for the delivery of effective and well-structured lessons, with coherent aims, learning outcomes and a clear assessment strategy?

How can we plan for the *range* of learners we may encounter within a teaching group?

How can we ensure that we plan for individual achievement, so that learners achieve their goals, assume responsibility for their own learning, and are encouraged to become lifelong learners?

In what ways can we plan for 'wider' learning – i.e. that which goes beyond our subject specialism?

Planning teaching lessons and schemes of work

The first stage in planning a teaching lesson is to assemble all the information which is relevant to the needs of the learners. This includes practical information such as the length of the lesson, the environment, and the ages and abilities of the learning group. It also includes the following: the subject or topic to be taught; an understanding of how formal or informal the teaching context is; the balance between teaching knowledge and demonstrating skills and a view of the best strategies for achievement in these areas. Other influences include health and safety considerations, the availability of resources and the actual time which is at our disposal to plan lessons. When gathering this information it is normally essential to liaise with colleagues, especially if we are new to an organization and/or to teaching itself.

This information can then be translated into a lesson plan, which acts as a *planning tool* prior to the lesson and a *guide* to the teacher during that lesson. The lesson plan can be produced in different formats. Provided a plan covers essential detail the format chosen will be determined by personal preference, but a useful test in determining a good lesson plan is to ask whether it is clear and coherent to anyone who might need to teach from it and not just ourselves!

So what detail should a lesson plan contain? The minimum requirements are that it should outline the following: the aims and objectives; the activities undertaken by the teacher and those by the student and how these link to the objectives; the structure and timing of each activity within the lesson; use of resources and the assessment strategy. Later in this section we consider the inclusion on the plan of the non-specialist elements of learning which may form part of the learning process. Lesson plans can follow several formats and it is personal choice which should really dictate the style of plan we write, although many institutions now require their staff to follow an established template in the interests of quality assurance and consistency. Some prefer a 'linear' template, which contains sections for each of the planning elements, such as 'resources' and 'assessment', as well as a step-by-step description of what will be happening during the lesson. Others might prefer a 'read-across' format, which shows what is happening at each stage of the lesson. Petty presents ideas for lesson plan formats (Petty 2014: 413), while Reece and Walker (2007) also discuss other types of formats and examples.

The starting point for the plan is the establishment of aims and objectives. Settling these not only gives confidence to our teaching, but often eases the rest of the planning process. A series of questions which you pose for yourself before you begin writing the plan can be useful in determining the aims which you as a teacher have for your learners and translating these into the learning outcomes; in other words, stating clearly what the learners will be able to do by the end of the lesson as a result of what they have learned. The formulation of coherent aims and learning outcomes requires practice, even if on the surface it may seem straightforward. As a novice it is probably worth collaborating with more experienced practitioners when first establishing these learning *goals*. There are, however, basic guidelines for formulating aims and outcomes.

Aims are statements of *general* intent. Usually aims will be written as long-term statements of intent to cover an entire programme, as well as aims that are specific to each lesson within that programme. The aims spell out for the teacher what she wishes to achieve in the lesson, giving the teaching a structure, direction and helping to break learning down into manageable units. From the aims the objectives are derived, and these are statements of *specific* intent, which give a clear indication of what a student will be able to do as a result of the learning. These are also known as *learning outcomes*. There should always be a 'match' between aims and objectives/learning outcomes, showing how the objectives are achievable *through* the aims. Here are two examples.

Example 4.1

A

Aim:	To instruct the learner to produce a simple diagram which explains how a car engine functions.
Objective:	By the end of the lesson the learner will be able to draw a simple diagram explaining the function of a car engine.

B

Aim:	To demonstrate the safe and hygienic application of a bandage to a cut.
Objective:	The learner will be able to apply a bandage safely and hygienically.

Task 4.1

Choose a topic which you teach and formulate aims and objectives for a teaching lesson. Try to specify conditions and standards for your objectives.

Furthermore, objectives need to be as specific as possible. Sometimes we will want to specify the *level* or *standard* at which a learner is expected to achieve. So, in example B above, standards meeting health and safety requirements were specified. At other times we may wish to outline the *conditions* under which a task might be completed. In example A, we may have specified that the task was to be completed without copying any practice diagrams.

Bloom was an American psychologist who created a *taxonomy* of educational objectives, in which he stated that the design of learning processes should take account of three domains of learning: cognitive, affective and psychomotor (Bloom 1964). Within each of these domains Bloom specified levels of achievement for learners as a result of a learning 'episode'. The most widely applied of these today in relation to the setting of objectives is that of the *cognitive* domain, covering the categories of: knowledge; comprehension; application; analysis; synthesis; and evaluation in ascending order of intellectual challenge, with the idea that *evaluation* is the most demanding intellectual skill, with *knowledge*, or the ability to recall or retrieve facts, at the other end of the scale. Bloom's ideas are useful in the consideration of levels of competence/achievement within unit and module descriptors, in order to ensure that there is a differentiation in the expectations of intellectual achievement, and thus these levels are articulated through the writing of objectives. The taxonomies for the affective and psychomotor domains are also worthy of consideration when designing courses that concern the development of attitudes and skills.

Now that we have a sense of the goals for the lesson we can consider how best to help learners achieve them. For this purpose we need to consider the many teaching and learning strategies at our disposal and make a choice about which are most suited to our purposes. These choices can be determined by a further set of questions which we need to pose in relation to the ages and abilities of our learners, the resources at our disposal and, to some degree, our own confidence in and preferences for using a particular strategy. While being aware of personal reactions to particular strategies, the needs of the learners are key to our choices and this is where our evaluations of what works well with groups in terms of activities are crucial to successful outcomes. There is no doubt that some methods lend themselves more readily to certain types of learning than others. The issue of appropriateness is not usually difficult to determine if we know our learners well and think carefully about the subject matter. Experience will also assist with the selection of methods. Variety is a key factor in sustaining learner interest, and so normally a varied diet of methods will ensure motivation. We also need to be open to new methods and be prepared to experiment.

The development of a clear assessment strategy is an integral part of the planning process and should be thought about at the same time as the objectives or learning outcomes are being formulated, since it is these outcomes that we are assessing. Very often considerable effort is put into deciding what we want our learners to be able to do in their classes, but far less thought is given over to how we can know that they have achieved. Put simply, if we want to know whether learning has taken place we need to be able to check this through assessment techniques. Each learning outcome should be assessed in some form in order to ascertain that learning has taken place. In this way we will also know whether there are gaps in understanding, in which case we will need to revisit particular parts of the learning experience, possibly adopting different strategies. More guidance on establishing assessment criteria to meet learning outcomes is given in Chapters 6 and 8.

As teachers in Post-14 Education and Training, we are no longer simply delivering our subject specialism, and we have to adjust our mindsets to take account of this fact, as for many of us our own experiences as learners have been those of learning one particular subject and only that subject. Along with our subject specialism, we are expected to embed a range of generic skills into our teaching. These are now referred to as *functional* skills and their exact nature is determined by the level and age of learners we are teaching. The skills are derived from government initiatives, supposedly designed to improve employability and raise levels of literacy and numeracy. The skills initiative is the subject of lively debate and the 'embedding' of skills a constant challenge, particularly in vocational programmes, where there is often resistance among learners to any component of the teaching which is not perceived to be strictly relevant to the subject area. The challenge takes two main forms. One is *how* to embed skills – a task which has proved demanding for even experienced practitioners, and the other how to make the skills relevant to the needs of learners. So, during our planning stage, we need to be sure that we are clear on which skills we are embedding and how we can embed them. These are processes which we will undoubtedly need to collaborate with colleagues over.

It is usual for trainee teachers to practise their planning skills initially by writing individual lesson plans. With confidence the transference of these skills into long-term planning should become straightforward. Again, experienced colleagues should be able to offer model schemes of work and often teachers in a new post will find that schemes of work are already in existence. Not always however! A *scheme of work* is a long-term planning document, which will present a view of what is to be learned over a period of several weeks or even months. It is made up therefore of a number of individual plans which link together and when perusing a scheme of work it is this sense of linkage which is a key feature of a good scheme. When looking through the plans it should be possible to see how learning from one lesson is reviewed briefly in the subsequent plan and leads logically into that plan. It is through this process that the scheme of work becomes a coherent and cohesive planning tool and not just a series of lesson plans.

One very important factor to be borne in mind in longer-term planning is the need to review learning on a regular basis. This helps to consolidate this process over a period of time and ensures that learners are given opportunities to revise material which they may have experienced difficulty with on first exposure. Learning is, after all, a cumulative process.

Once the planning stage has been completed it is important to communicate the learning outcomes to learners, so that they understand fully the goals which have been established for them. This will normally happen at the beginning of a programme, but it is an ongoing process, in the sense that learners need to be given short- as well as long-term goals, and the goals need to be monitored on an ongoing basis. We will look in greater detail at the communication of learning goals later in the chapter, but this process is integral to planning as well as managing learning, since we may have to adjust planning if learning goals are not being reached.

Task 4.2

Gather together as many other examples of plans that you can find, either from the group you are studying with or from the organization(s) you work for. Having gathered a number of examples you can make a decision about how best to format your own plans. Remember that you need to evaluate how well a lesson plan format has suited your needs once you have used it, so that you can refine the process of producing the most satisfactory plan for yourself.

Planning for equality and diversity: ensuring an *inclusive* environment

Our second key issue in this section is that of planning for a *range* of learners. Government-led policies in the last two decades governing access, inclusion and widening participation, particularly the Equality Act 2010 and SEND 2014, have signalled a recognition that the learning opportunities that have been opened up to a larger spectrum of the adult population must be fit for purpose. This has produced not only a larger number of participants in formal and less formal adult settings across the UK, but an increased mix of adults within individual learning groups.

Planning for diversity and inclusion are thus crucial factors in managing learning, and showing that we as teachers value diversity and recognize the relationship between diversity and equality as a requirement of our role.

There are two pieces of legislation that are key to a good appreciation of the principles underpinning equality and inclusion. Firstly, you should look at the Equality Act 2010 to gain complete knowledge, understanding and application of the most updated legislation that affects anyone working in the public or private sector. Secondly, the 2014 SEND Act outlines the statutory duties and responsibilities of all educational institutions for embedding principles of fairness and equality into their practice for those with learning difficulties. From 2014, special educational needs (SEN) learners are entitled to an education, health and care plan (EHC plan) that will be reviewed annually to ensure the effectiveness of support. Chapter 7 of the SEND Code of Practice 2014 lays out clear guidelines for the management of an individual's learning, specifying the need for:

*   high quality differentiated teaching;
*   a coherent programme of study with targets and clear progression opportunities;
*   relevant screenings and assessments;
*   establishing the support required through discussions with the student;
*   special educational support (assistive technology, specialist tuition, etc.);
*   regular reviews of the effectiveness of the various support mechanisms

---

Task 4.3

Try to get hold of an EHC plan for a learner with SEN who has been identified as requiring support. Examine the plan in terms of how the student's learning is being managed in relation to the following factors:

*   initial discussion with the student and or parents/guardians/carers;
*   identification of differentiated learning for the student within the group learning process;
*   plans for reviewing the student's progress;
*   the audit of special educational support deemed necessary to ensure her/his learning , including staff with relevant qualifications.

The Office for Standards in Education (Ofsted) and Her Majesty's Inspectorate for Education and Training in Wales (Estyn) are also scrutinizing more closely how equality, diversity and inclusion are being promoted and practised in colleges and other post-14 settings, and expect educational organizations to recognize good practice at every level of their operation.

What does this mean at classroom level? It means that lesson planning should indicate an ability to identify the specific learning needs of individuals at the planning stage and that in the classroom or learning setting you can demonstrate how you would deal with individuals who display discriminatory behaviour towards others, or harass, bully and victimize them. Furthermore, it means that your own behaviour in this respect must be beyond reproach. It is possible that members of a learning group might approach you outside classroom time with allegations of unwanted behaviour of this description that is happening within the group beyond the classroom, and you will need to investigate such claims diplomatically. Clearly, the promotion of equality and diversity principles will be an essential part of the learning contract discussed on page 105.

Few learning groups nowadays are homogenous in terms of their identity, although some uniformity can more commonly be found among groups of 14–19-year-olds in further education (FE) settings who are studying for vocational or academic qualifications. Even within these groups, however, more mature adults, often returning to study after a period away from school or college, will mix with younger learners. Within one class setting, therefore, it is usual to find learners with very different attitudes to and experience of learning and teaching.

The presence of a range of learners within one group can affect planning considerably. In varying degrees, and depending on the teaching context, learners will vary in obvious and less obvious ways. The more obvious differences will be in terms of age and an often related issue of prior learning experience. Gender, personality and social class are other factors which produce differences in attitudes and behaviour among learners.

When we meet a new group the issue of motivation can be hard to determine. Are the members attending the group for social and personal advancement, intellectual satisfaction and career development? Is their attendance mandatory or voluntary? Again these reasons are often clearer, or apparently clearer, with younger adults on college-based vocational programmes, but are less obvious where the choice to attend a programme has been voluntary. As a course progresses, motivations for attending a course will become more obvious, and autobiographical details about each member of the group will begin to emerge. Working with a group is rather like character development in a novel. In the beginning we make guesses as well as assumptions about who the characters are and how they will develop, but, as with a novel, some of these assumptions are naïve, partial or simply wrong!

As time progresses, learners' likes and dislikes in relation to particular styles of learning and teaching strategies will of course become apparent, and such information can be helpful to the tutor in the planning process, although we have to be wary of planning our teaching wholly to satisfy the strategies our students state a preference for, since these may not be the most effective for delivering the learning. Additionally, useful learning can sometimes be gained by a person through moving outside their comfort zone. It is not only teachers who have from time to time to be prepared to move outside their comfort zones!

Planning for a range of learners with different experiences and expectations of learning reinforces the need to have a repertoire of ways to deliver learning. We have already discussed the need for such a varied diet in terms of sustaining interest during a lesson. Meeting the learning preferences of different personalities in a group is another good reason for varying our modes of delivery.

Another very important factor in planning for a range of learners is to plan for *inclusiveness*. In order to promote a climate of inclusiveness and guard against exclusion it is of course essential that we gather as much information about individual students as possible before we begin teaching them, so that we are aware of factors which will affect their ability to perform certain tasks or engage in particular forms of learning. A key to planning activities which are accessible for all is to think about disability, both seen and unseen. Nowadays, learners are usually asked to declare forms of disability on enrolment so that appropriate adjustments can be made to facilitate the learning process prior to commencement of the course, although not all learners venture such information in the case of unseen disabilities, and sometimes, of course, learners are unaware of having a disability. The information we have from learners gives us the opportunity to undertake a review of the learning experience prior to the commencement of a programme. One example would be organizing the classroom in such a manner that a wheelchair user could participate in group activities with the same ease as other learners; another would be preparing PowerPoint presentations and handouts in a larger font for a partially sighted learner. The use of certain coloured paper in handouts may be helpful to somebody who is dyslexic. Encouraging individual learners to be open with us about their needs is crucial if we are to plan for them, and so trust must be built early on in a course if we are to know about the factors we need to take into account when planning learning. We need to promote the idea of a joint responsibility, where the learner feels able to disclose the information we need to plan efficiently for them, and where we make sure that we use this information to make the arrangements necessary to facilitate learning for that person. Finally, as Powell and Tummons (2011: 71) state: 'a definition of inclusion encompasses all of those ways by which the provision of education and training can be made accessible to any groups of potential students who might otherwise face structural, financial, or cultural barriers to participation'.

Task 4.4

Take a group you are currently teaching or observing. Analyse the members of the group individually and identify and discuss with others on your course, where relevant, the specific needs of these individuals that you would need to take into account in the planning process. These might include levels of motivation, learning difficulties, disabilities and learning preferences.

The ultimate goal of our planning, whether we are working with small or large groups or with individuals, should be to enable each learner to achieve their potential during the learning experience. We are, in effect, planning for *achievement* and the achievement of the individual is a much valued aspect of our learning culture today. If we are to plan for everybody in a group to reach their potential we may have to *differentiate* learning. Differentiation is the response to a recognition that not all learners learn in the same way, more especially at the same pace, and the consequent organization of learning activities according to certain needs and abilities. By differentiating learning we can allow a person to learn successfully as part of a group, while achieving different outcomes from a fellow student. To some degree, we will all recognize differentiation from our own learning experiences, in the sense that we have probably all been in learning situations where we have been aware that we have been progressing more quickly or slowly than others in a group. In such a case there is often a sense of pressure, of having to 'keep up', and this in itself can create a barrier to a learning task, as well as feelings of stress, negativity and demotivation. For adults who have already experienced such barriers in previous learning situations, a sense of despondency can descend and adversely affect the attitude to the learning.

Differentiation can be planned in a number of ways. It is possible to set tasks at varying levels for small groups within a whole-group setting, so that individuals can be grouped according to ability. Indeed this kind of differentiated learning is very useful for teaching mixed-ability groups. Alternatively, a teacher might set each group the same basic task, but prescribe different outcomes.

How do we show differentiation in our planning then? It may be that we spell out on the lesson plan our differentiated learning objectives, as this is evidence that differentiation has featured in our planning. Equally, we may have written differentiated goals into the rationale of our scheme of work. Most important of all, of course, is the need to communicate the differentiated learning goals to learners, so that they are aware of what is expected of them. This is crucial to planning for *success*, which is the third issue we need to focus on in this survey of planning learning.

Planning for individual achievement

So far in the chapter we have focused largely on planning for group learning. In the previous section we turned our attention to individual achievement through differentiation of activity and assessment; this is only one example of how we can help adult learners to achieve goals. Part of the responsibility of a teacher in Post-14 Education and Training is to identify and support individual learning needs – a skill which is integral to their professional role, and one which is constantly being developed as new challenges from learners present themselves. The concept of learning as a personalized affair is a dominant force in current educational thinking and Section 3.5 in the previous chapter deals with personalized learning.

In planning terms this involves firstly diagnosing need, a skill for which knowledge and understanding of potential barriers to learning is essential. Sometimes we are able to readily identify such barriers and address them in our planning. At other times we may need to enlist the support and guidance of more experienced practitioners in assisting our understanding of how best to plan for a particular learner's needs and this is where the use of referral systems has a part to play. As a teacher, for example, we may have generic knowledge of a learner's difficulties, but may require assistance from a specialist in knowing how best to plan to meet their needs in a classroom setting. This demonstrates our dependence on a wider network of professionals, assuming one is available, for our planning. There is clearly a link here between planning for inclusiveness and planning for individual need.

Nowadays, planning for individual success and achievement is a purposeful and well-refined activity. There is currently a requirement for all learners in a formal lifelong learning situation to have an individual learning plan (ILP). This is a tool which is negotiated between learner and teacher and which is designed to support and maximize achievement through the establishment of learning targets. While the targets are individual, they should be achievable within the framework of the learner's everyday classroom experiences, so that they link very clearly to the learning objectives that form part of the scheme of work. An important point to remember about ILPs is that they are live documents that will require amendments and ongoing discussions with students. Equally, they offer an opportunity to track and document progress that has been made and are, or should be, an aid to motivation.

The ILP will normally follow a format which has been prescribed by the learning establishment, and newly appointed staff will need to acquaint themselves with the format in use. There are, however, features which are common to all ILPs. These include: clearly communicated short- and long-term learning goals; a record of all forms of assessment which relate to these goals and document their achievement; and evidence of regular review and updating of the plan. This is a basic analysis of a learning plan. The Learning and Skills Network (LSN) has produced a useful 'ILP checklist' which outlines good practice in the creation and use of such plans (see www.lsneducation.org.uk).

It goes without saying that helping learners to plan for individual achievement involves us as teachers in ensuring that we create time for the review of our learners' plans within our scheme of work. This entails building regular review and tutorial time into our teaching schedules in order to avoid an 'ad hoc' approach, which will surely result in a failure to find time to see each learner properly.

Ultimately, of course, success will only occur if the learner, supported by the teacher, has a commitment to the goals which have been established. After all, these goals have been *negotiated* between teacher and learner, rather than imposed by the former. Within a lifelong learning setting there is a clear duty to encourage and support learners of whatever age. When working with those who have recently left school, however, there is an increased responsibility towards preparing them for further study and/or the world of work. Part of this is planning to promote independent learning through involving learners in regular self-evaluation and review of targets, so that they too have a hand in modifying learning plans where necessary. We are, in effect, planning for 'wider' learning – for *lifelong* learning.

Earlier, we discussed the fact that a learning programme often reaches beyond the subject or programme to encompass *functional* skills. The purpose of functional skills is to improve the employability of young people through enhancing their literacy, numeracy and information technology (IT) skills. The *Skills Funding Statement 2012–15* provides information about the embedding of such skills into your curriculum (Department for Business, Innovation and Skills/Skills Funding Agency 2012).

A further way of creating lifelong learners is through promoting learner independence. Such independence can only be acquired through teaching those skills which enable learners to learn effectively on their own as well as in a formal classroom setting. In addition to key skills, therefore, learners need study skills. These include effective reading and writing skills, research techniques, time management and organizational skills. There is not often much time to plan formal study skills components into our everyday teaching, but we can plan to include teaching, learning and assessment strategies which allow learners to practise and hone these skills. Furthermore, we can and should make time to induct learners into the 'learning support' units which exist nowadays in lifelong learning settings to help with the acquisition of these skills.

Task 4.5

Select *two* of your learners and construct for each of them an ILP which takes account of the factors discussed above. Do not forget to negotiate the plan with them!

In this section we have reflected on the centrality of sound planning in the creation of effective learning. We have seen that a teacher needs to be equipped with not only the knowledge and skills to plan varied and purposeful lessons, but also an understanding of the needs of individual learners. We have established that planning is an activity requiring practice and one which must be thought of in both the long and short term. Finally, we are contributing not only to a learner's immediate goals, but to developing them as lifelong, independent learners. Our legacy therefore is one of importance.

4.3 Classroom management: groups and individuals

KEY ISSUES

How do we recognize and manage the attitudes and behaviours of a variety of older and younger adult learners within learning groups?

What is the value of a learning contract?

What do we mean by group dynamics?

In what ways can we help learners to manage their own learning: what factors do we need to be aware of?

Managing group behaviour

As has already been noted in the introduction, we can have planned effectively for learning to take place, but without sound management skills our planning will go to waste. We now consider the knowledge and skills that are necessary to ensure that the learning environments which we manage are indeed conducive to learning. At this point it is important to assert also the role of the teacher as the only person who should be *managing* the environment of the classroom, even though learners will *contribute* to this process. This section looks at techniques for managing older and younger adults, in formal and informal environments. Some of the ideas apply to any group of learners, but firstly there is a consideration of managing younger learners in the Post-14 phase.

Managing classrooms in the Post-14 phase can be especially challenging, especially because the desired intention is to move away from the tightly-prescribed frameworks for imposing and maintaining 'discipline' that prevail in schools, and encourage learners to assume greater self-control and independence in and for the learning process. This transition however is not easy to achieve. As Woods and Hine (2009: 30) observe: 'what is known is that young people in late modern societies are characterized as leading immensely complex and fragmented lives'. Managing a diverse range of expectations, levels of motivation and challenging behaviours in one classroom is daunting. Furthermore it is widely recognized nowadays that even low level disruption in a classroom can impact significantly on effective learning. As Wallace (2013: 9) points out, the reasons for challenging and difficult behaviours are many and complex and the notion that they arise from low levels of motivation is overly-simplistic. It is worthwhile therefore with a new group of younger learners to ascertain both the reasons they are in your classroom – which will offer clues to motivation – but also their prior experience of learning environments, because this will indicate possible reasons for behaving as they do with others and explain their responses to you as a teacher.

Three important concepts in managing classrooms will now be looked at in turn: clarity, consistency and challenge. These three concepts will be revisited throughout this section, but considered initially in relation to working with younger learners. Clarity relates to yourself, as well as your learners, and the messages about why you are in your role that you communicate to them. Reflect carefully on what you communicate to learners about your attitude to them, what you expect from them, and how you yourself will behave when unwanted behaviours manifest themselves. We discuss the importance for self-control among learners. Do we model well with respect to our own behaviour, or do we react in such a way as to escalate disruption? How clearly do we communicate our expectations of behaviour and how consistently do we apply these expectations? Consistency in the way in which we approach and deal with younger learners is key to giving them confidence and trust in us. Are learners secure and confident in the knowledge that we will be vigilant in adhering to the learning contracts discussed further on in this section, for example?

Applying the theories of learning that derive from psychology, such as behaviourism, is important. You may wish to explore the ideas underpinning transactional analysis (TA) to understand how adults in a learning situation operate in different child/adult ego states and your role in being aware of and then managing this. We need to avoid game-playing, (related to TA) and psychological warfare, as well as check that we do not 'buy in' to behaviours that are manipulative. All learning should offer challenge, which will hopefully lead to reward and, with reflection, a valuing of the learning process and desire to undertake more challenges. For many learners, of whatever age, learning brings intrinsic rewards and this will result in achieving goals. For other younger learners, this motivation is less obvious and you will need as a teacher to find out who in your group lacks intrinsic motivation and manage this issue. Communicating expectations as *challenges* is especially vital with younger learners who seek to disrupt your classroom, and these challenges will have to be negotiated on an individual basis, involving the learner and encouraging them to establish small-scale challenges and meet them. You will need to take the lead in helping them to set themselves challenges as much in dealing with their behaviour, as well as their learning, as the two are so closely linked.

We need now to consider therefore how to make the learning environment a place where boundaries are established and channels of communication are clear. Managing these features of the learning process allows learners to feel positive about their commitment to learning and ensures that our planning for inclusion, equal opportunities and fairness to all learners is effective. Creating this type of environment does not just happen of its own accord, however, and needs to be managed; an effective tool for this purpose can often be a learning contract.

A learning contract is a set of what might be loosely termed *rules*, governing the way in which learners behave with respect to each other and the teacher. The contract should be negotiated by the learners themselves, with varying amounts of assistance from the teacher, usually depending on the age of the group of learners. Early on in a course it is worth taking time to establish such a contract with the learners and to make a copy available to all members of the group. The contract may specify a number of ground rules for the way in which individuals within the group interact with each other and with the teacher and often specifies 'rules' concerning their commitment to the learning process. From time to time, and depending on how long the group is to be together for, it may be necessary to revisit the contract and use it as a reminder about boundaries. This can normally be an effective way of reaffirming the principles to which the group signed up – principles of which they have ownership. Moreover, of course, use of the contract is not confined to whole-group management, but can be during personal tutorial time with individual learners who have crossed particular boundaries. It may also be the case that there will be a need to add to the original list of rules in order to take account of changing dynamics within the classroom. Learners should feel free to raise issues of concern to them through evaluation processes and need to know that these will be considered carefully by the teacher and not disappear without trace. This is a way of strengthening the learning environment and making learners feel valued.

Task 4.6

What would you put into a learning contract for a group you are currently a part of?

An essential aspect of managing adult learners is to recognize and deal with the variety of behavioural characteristics they display when learning in groups, and this is the second issue for consideration in this section on managing learning. It is important for us as teachers to understand both how groups function and the roles that individual members of a group play as contributory factors in this process.

Each learning group develops a unique culture, which is one of the reasons why teaching can be such a fascinating profession! So it is possible to have two parallel teaching groups, that is, two groups working on identical programmes, which behave very differently and require different management skills.

How is a group culture created? It is produced by the interaction and interdependence between its members and the beliefs, feelings, attitudes, personalities and life experiences which they bring to the group. Drawing on the ideas of Freire and Rogers, Jarvis (1995: 99) informs us that learning is an 'emancipatory experience which may involve a change in self-organization and perception' and that 'much socially useful learning is learning the process of learning and retaining an openness to experience, so that the process of change may be incorporated into the self'. If we accept this view, it follows that the group is not a static entity, and that it will be constantly reshaping itself according to the way in which its individual members respond to their learning environment. It should not surprise us, therefore, if we find the behaviour of a particular group mercurial and unpredictable and therefore, on occasions, difficult to manage, for their behaviour is the product of a complex network of interactions which are in part to do with the learning process, as described above, but also to do with individual life experiences, of which we have often only partial knowledge. The latter are played out within the group and affect the learning process. What is perhaps important here for us as teachers is to recognize our *limitations* in managing lessons and realize that we cannot always change behaviour, despite our best efforts. This will make us more realistic with ourselves when dealing with groups.

In addition to thinking about group culture, we need also to recognize 'stages' in the life of a learning group. Tuckman (Napier and Gershenfeld 1989) talks of the following stages in group development: forming, informing, storming, norming and performing. In the first stage of *forming*, a collection of individuals come together with a common goal and express their willingness to interact and signal a common bond. Following this is the *informing* stage, during which individual members set and explore goals, aligning individual goals with the agreed goal. During this stage, members interact because they see that others are looking towards the same or similar goals. They express their mutual dependence and begin to explore other bonds they may share, such as common interests, concerns or acquaintances. Next, the group begins to structure itself and its members begin to adopt roles, roles which – after a period of experimentation, jostling and even conflict (the *storming* stage) – stabilize into the formation of agreed role identities and the acceptance of common roles for all members of the group. Finally, the individuals become a working group: dynamic and not static, with interlocking roles, specializations and division of functions. At this stage the group has become in effect a team, ready to commit to the achievement of commonly agreed goals.

Bearing in mind what has already been said about our limitations in managing the functioning of a group, and if we accept Tuckman's ideas, we need to reflect carefully on the manner in which we handle the stages of the group. First of all, it can be a useful exercise to actually share with the group the idea that, as a group, they will experience highs and lows, although this is debatably a more risky strategy with younger learners. In this way the group shares an understanding of the notion that they are a dynamic entity and will need to accept the positive with the less positive in terms of their experience of being part of that group. Second, it seems clear that the trickiest stage to handle will be the *storming* phase, for it is a safe passage through this that will allow the group to function well in the long term. During this phase there can be a number of sources of conflict: personality clashes, manifestations of dislike for others in the group, including the teacher, concerns about achievement of the goals and/or the amount of work needed in pursuit of this. Managing the storming phase requires a blend of strategies to minimize personality issues, offer reassurance about the goals and sometimes engage the learners in open and frank discussions, allowing them to air grievances and then setting an agenda for 'recovery'. The skills required for this will develop with experience and trial and error, and teachers must be realistic in their expectations of themselves in this regard.

Task 4.7

Take *two* learning groups you are or have been familiar with. How did those groups develop in terms of Tuckman's ideas? Were all the stages apparent in both groups? How long did each stage take? You may find some surprising differences!

Managing individual behaviour

Turning our attention away from the notion of the group per se, we need to think about the very obvious issue of individual behaviours which can limit the effectiveness of a group and which require our attention. Some individuals within a group setting, and this is not confined just to learning situations (as we will know from life experiences generally), are inclined to play out particular roles.

The roles that they play are determined by a plethora of factors including: roles they have played in previous groups; perceptions of how they wish to be seen by others; a natural predisposition towards certain behaviours; and emotional and intellectual needs. In a learning situation some behaviours are shaped by the nature of a school experience, such as memories of inadequacy and the subsequent strategies an individual employed to counteract such feelings. Conversely, if the school experience and parental pressure focused on high achievement, then it is possible that such standards will still be fixed as the norm and that any failure to reach these in a new learning situation will have a detrimental effect on the learner's motivation and behaviour within the group. Roles can be adopted for a range of reasons, some of which may be conscious, others less so. Some individuals may wish to court popularity and others may wish to be the group leaders. Other roles which are recognizable are: the 'smoother'; the aggressor; the distractor; the joker; the rescuer; and the person who tries to monopolize all of these!

It is difficult to eradicate role-playing in learning groups and some roles are of course healthy for the well-being of a group in any case. To a certain degree adults will tolerate 'otherness', particularly during the *forming* stages of the group. At the same time they will be interested, albeit covertly at times, in how we as teachers deal with these emerging patterns of behaviour. It is only when the behaviour which follows from the role becomes problematic that we need to act. For example, it is sometimes useful to have a 'joker' in the group. If, however, there is an attempt to sabotage the group dynamics through the overuse of unwanted wisecracks, then the behaviour needs to be dealt with, for such behaviour has now reached the point of being difficult.

And it is up to us, as managers of our groups, to decide on that point of intervention; a point normally reached when particular behavioural patterns are beginning to threaten the effectiveness of the group in terms of cooperative learning. We will normally be aware of this phenomenon through the body language of those in the group who are upset or distracted by such behaviour. Having watched us for a while to see how we have reacted, they will often suddenly tell us either verbally or through their body language that they have had enough. Sometimes a group reaches a point where they feel that the rules of respect have been flouted; normally, we as teachers will have intervened before this stage has been reached.

One-to-one interventionist strategies can often be the most effective, whereby we address the issue personally with the learner in question. This has the advantage of allowing us to probe possible root causes of the behaviour and enables us to offer the learner an opportunity to reflect on the effect they are having on their own learning and that of others. Again, this is where the learning contract can have its uses. We should not forget the use of referral systems either, needing to recognize where our ability to deal effectively with difficult and challenging behaviour is limited.

In addition to talking through behavioural issues with individuals there are general classroom management techniques that we can learn about and practise and which will be advantageous to us throughout our teaching careers. Sadly, these are sometimes ignored on teacher training programmes. They involve the use of our own body language to transmit messages to those who are undermining the well-being of both the group they are in and possibly our own authority as manager of that group. We can often minimize unwanted behaviour through simple gestures, such as where we stand in the classroom and the use of eye contact. A full discussion of such techniques can be found in John Robertson's *Effective Classroom Control* (1989). *Understanding Behaviour 14+* (Duckworth et al. 2012) also offers useful, workable and practical strategies and *Teaching Young Adults* by Dawn et al. (2000) is useful in its treatment of the role of the teacher in effective learning.

Finally, in this section on the management of behaviours which are detrimental to the group's well-being, we need to address the issue of *discrimatory* behaviour. This type of behaviour must be dealt with quickly and effectively. We need also, of course, to include ourselves in this challenge, ensuring that we are non-discriminatory in our treatment of others. Discriminatory behaviour and attitudes emanating from one individual or individual(s) towards another or others should be challenged directly and discussed openly, if this is appropriate, before it escalates out of control. A zero-tolerance attitude on the part of the teacher towards such behaviour is vital.

It is in this way that we can actively promote equal opportunities and deal with prejudice. For younger adults this is an important part of their social as well as intellectual development. If we have created the safe environment discussed earlier in this chapter and established a learning contract, then it should not be too difficult to facilitate open discussions on key issues such as gender and race.

To summarize the first two sections of this second section of the chapter, our role as teachers in Post-14 Education and Training is to manage the learning environment in such a way that learners can work effectively in an atmosphere of safety, mutual respect and tolerance, in which communication channels among themselves and between themselves and the teacher are open. In this way a purposeful learning environment has been established.

Task 4.8

Specify two learners you have encountered whose behaviour has been problematic. With a partner, or in a group, consider the following:

- What were the underlying causes of the behaviour and how were you able to identify these?
- How did you manage the situation?
- How successful were your strategies and how might you manage a similar situation differently if it were to arise again?

4.4 Managing different learning environments

KEY ISSUES

What is involved in managing a learning environment?

What about learning inside and outside the classroom?

How do teachers manage blended and distance learning?

Health and safety considerations

In the final section of this chapter we consider the management of different learning *environments* – traditional and less traditional. We begin with the traditional, looking at how we can create a safe and pleasant working environment within a classroom. Health and safety considerations nowadays are given much prominence and in a learning setting making sure that learners are physically 'safe' is just as important as guaranteeing their psychological safety or well-being. Again safety is measurable by bodies such as Ofsted, and it is quite likely that your organization will offer you training in health and safety issues. Make sure you find out who is responsible for health and safety issues in the buildings(s) you work in, and talk to that representative about anything you are unsure about. You need to know also the relevant phone numbers in case of emergency and what the protocol for such situations is. This is very important indeed at times when you might be the only person teaching in a building, at night, for example.

An examination of a teaching room should alert us to general issues such as whether furniture is laid out to allow sufficient room for the traffic that will be in the room and if wires are arranged in such a way that learners are likely to trip over them. In the event of an emergency, it is important that all members of a group can exit a room swiftly and that they are aware of the meeting point. Fire, accident and emergency procedures are essential information for all students and should be clarified when you first meet a new group. This is part of your professional responsibility and in the litigious climate in which we operate it is worth remembering this. In addition to these general safety points we need to be aware of potential health hazards in relation to particular students and use the information we have about our learners to avoid problems.

An increasingly growing proportion of students nowadays are sensitive to substances we find in seemingly harmless tools such as felt pens, dyes and plastics. To these we can add pollutants such as fumes from chemicals, particularly where ventilation is not good. Solvents are another issue, the effects of which have been widely publicized. A suggested approach to managing safety in the particular environment in which you teach is to consider carefully the substances, equipment, tools and/or furniture which form part of the essential working conditions for delivering your subject and to create an inventory of any part of this paraphernalia which you consider could be risky for an individual. In this way you can 'tailor' your safety checks and thus avoid wasting time checking details which are not relevant to the delivery of your subject. If you are unsure about any of these issues, there will be a health and safety representative that you can talk to in your organization.

There are a few generic aspects of the learning environment to which all teachers should pay attention and these are heating, lighting and ventilation. Ventilation is a much ignored feature of good classroom practice and yet is often a simple technique for keeping learners alert! Without adequate ventilation students become sluggish and their performance is impaired. Even in winter, windows need to be opened for a few minutes several times a day, particularly between classes in a room which is going to be filled with people for much of the day. If not, the environment will become stuffy and increasingly unpleasant as the day wears on. Attention should also be paid to lighting. The widespread use of PowerPoint means sometimes that classrooms are dark places and while this may be good for illuminating the slides themselves, it is not good for note-taking. It is good to try to strike a balance. Finally, there are few teachers who have not experienced problems with heating. Often the issue of heating is outside our control, but we need to take any sensible measures to ensure that reasonable temperatures are maintained at different times of the year by reporting extremes of heating. There are a few simple and practical tips to remember as well. Sitting for a long time in a cold classroom makes people unhappy, so find some pretext for getting them moving from time to time. In periods of hot and cold weather you will need to think of strategies for re-energizing learners if you want to get the best out of them and this is part of managing an efficient environment. An efficient environment is one in which the opportunities for learning are maximized not only by good planning but by attending to the welfare of the learners. Your classroom might be very safe in terms of some of the issues already discussed here, but if your learners are tired, cold or lethargic then learning will be minimized. Classroom management is the axis on which planning turns.

Task 4.9

Do you know the answers to the following questions? If not make sure you find out!

1   Where is the health and safety policy for my organization?
2   Where are the evacuation points in the building(s) I teach in?
3   What is the procedure for the evacuation of disabled students in the event of fire?
4   What kind of signage is there on the premises relating to health and safety?

What about learning that takes place outside the classroom, often in an open-air environment? Clearly, the same basic health and safety principles apply, with additional areas for scrutiny and planning. As a result of a number of accidents and incidents that have been recorded in the press in the past few years, mainly in what we would term as 'field trip' type activities, very stringent guidelines are now available to inform planning from its earliest stages. The management of outdoor education has become an industry in itself; if you look on the internet you will find a number of companies offering to remove this element of stress from you, some even using scaremongering tactics! Use the guidelines your institution provides: there will be a policy. Putting aside health and safety issues, you will need to be able to demonstrate in your planning processes that all learners are engaged in activity at all times, albeit different activities. All of these need to be monitored all of the time if you have learners under the age of 16 and this can be more resource-heavy in terms of staffing than activities based in a classroom.

Managing blended and distance learning

The availability of technology and economic considerations are driving an acceleration in blended and distance learning. This type of learning also offers a number of advantages to adults whose lives are busy, and for whom regular attendance at classes is difficult. For teachers it requires a review of the respective responsibilities of learners and themselves in managing the learning process. Clearly, the successful management of this type of learning is no less challenging than regular face-to-face contact with students, but are the management skills different? The answer lies in a detailed consideration of how the essence of the learning situation is in itself different. Self-directed learning relies heavily on three factors. One is that the learner is motivated to engage in learning on their own, without constant group support, and another is that they possess the study skills necessary to be able to work efficiently on their own. A third is how reliable and student-friendly the supporting technology is. If any one of these factors becomes a problem the efficacy of this type of learning is severely limited and learners can become demotivated quickly.

Even though the teacher can be on hand for email and telephone communication, for some learners this is more difficult to handle in actuality than face-to-face contact. This may account for the formal and anecdotal evidence that suggests that dropout rates on such programmes can be high. So what can be done to ensure that learners who elect to work in this mode are supported, yet made aware of their own obligations in the process? We are back to the learning contract! Such a contract might establish important patterns of communication between ourselves and the learner, so that the latter feels secure in terms of a regularity of contact, and the teacher confident that boundaries have been set around those patterns. The idea of flexible learning patterns is attractive to many learners for reasons already outlined, but boundaries can often be transgressed and then neediness can take over. We need to preserve our sanity as teachers in being firm about our own boundaries. We also need to be highly organized in managing this type of learning, ensuring that we give the learners that we do not meet on a regular basis the same support as those we see daily or weekly. We need, for example, to be careful with deadlines for distance learners, ensuring that we adhere to both those we set for learners as well as our own marking deadlines.

In addition to good lines of communication, we need to get learners to realize that they can acquire the all-important study skills which will facilitate their success outside the classroom as well. If the learner is part of an educational establishment then often they will have access to study support mechanisms, either on a 'drop-in' basis or by appointment. There is also a good selection of literature on this subject, such as Stella Cottrell's *The Study Skills Handbook* (2013). This is a user-friendly text which offers invaluable assistance to learners on a range of skills, including time management, research skills and learning styles.

Dealing with technology problems can be harder for the teacher, as often we are dependent on support systems in our institutions for the smooth running of this aspect of learning. In this respect the teacher becomes a kind of go-between – between the student and the organization – trying to reassure the student that they will communicate with those responsible for the virtual learning environments (VLEs) and then nervously tackling an often overworked team who are providing increasing levels of technical support as well trying to develop better systems. It is advisable to be sure that you can get adequate support from your institution before you embark on ambitious blended learning projects. Innovation needs to be tempered with caution!

Encouraging learners to develop autonomy is a theme which has run throughout this chapter. Ultimately, it is the best gift we can offer our learners, for it is a truly transferable skill which will serve a lifetime of learning. Many of the skills discussed so far in the chapter favour the development of active and reflective learners, from taking responsibility in negotiating a learning contract to agreeing to ground rules which commit an individual to patterns of study. There are a number of absolute 'basic' skills which learners need to acquire in order to begin the road to autonomy and which we should be able to teach them through working with them in the classroom. First, learners should be able to plan and prioritize; in other words, manage their time efficiently. These and other organizational skills, such as meeting learning targets, can be covered in an individual learning plan. Other skills relating to reading, writing and critical thinking can be developed as part of classroom and assessment activity with the teacher helping to increase confidence, through praise, and identifying with students through feedback on areas for development. As already mentioned, there are usually a number of support mechanisms within an educational establishment to which we can refer learners for further advice on study skills and we have a role to play in referring learners to the appropriate unit for them. Our role, while our learners are with us, is to *help* them manage learning, particularly if they are not used to this. Their goal is to gradually become less dependent on us and manage learning for themselves. This is the essence of independent learning.

Teaching and the management of learning are vast subject areas. It has been shown that you cannot teach effectively without paying attention to how learning is managed, both for individuals and groups. The management of the learning process requires a good knowledge of learners, insight into group dynamics and a responsiveness to different types of learning environments.

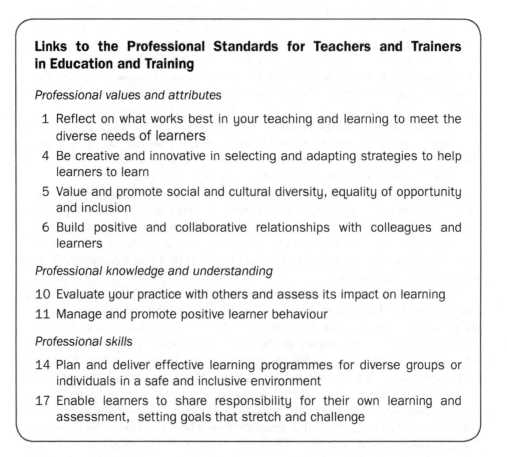

Links to the Professional Standards for Teachers and Trainers in Education and Training

Professional values and attributes

1 Reflect on what works best in your teaching and learning to meet the diverse needs of learners

4 Be creative and innovative in selecting and adapting strategies to help learners to learn

5 Value and promote social and cultural diversity, equality of opportunity and inclusion

6 Build positive and collaborative relationships with colleagues and learners

Professional knowledge and understanding

10 Evaluate your practice with others and assess its impact on learning

11 Manage and promote positive learner behaviour

Professional skills

14 Plan and deliver effective learning programmes for diverse groups or individuals in a safe and inclusive environment

17 Enable learners to share responsibility for their own learning and assessment, setting goals that stretch and challenge

5

Resources for teaching and learning

5.1 What is Chapter 5 about?

This chapter examines how teachers and trainers in the Post-14 Education and Training sector can effectively deploy resources to aid learning. It is not primarily concerned with the technicalities of the production of teaching and learning resources, although it does contain some straightforward advice in this area, which can be used as 'revision' material, as a stimulus for new ideas or, in the case of the new teacher or trainer, as a list of starting points for further reading. Therefore, this chapter reviews a selection of 'traditional' teaching and learning resources that continue to be significant in teaching.

However, these are also exciting times in the field of teaching and learning resources, with the introduction of new technologies in particular playing an increasingly important part. For many tutors and trainers in the sector these developments have become essential against the backdrop of a 'more for less' ideology where reusable and shared resources can be deployed for increasing numbers of students and trainees. The majority of teachers have begun the process of embedding technology into their practice and it promises much for the future of learning. It is for this reason that a considerable part of this chapter is also devoted to the use of these technologies as resources for teaching and learning.

Section 5.2 considers the nature of teaching and learning resources and how these may be linked to both ideologies of the curriculum and the management of learning. Aspects of equality and diversity and the impacts these have on the choice of differentiated resources and multi-sensory aids that have a broad appeal are also discussed.

The production and development of learning resources can be one of the most creative and satisfying aspects of our professional lives. However, in many cases there is no formal or organized attempt to assess the effectiveness or even the appropriateness of these resources. Section 5.3 attempts to redress this and examines the implications of published reports on the use of learning resources in the sector. Section 5.4 looks at four models for the organization of learning resources in a typical educational establishment and the implications such structures have on teaching and learning.

A range of traditional learning resources including whiteboards, handouts, flashcards and photocopied materials are described and assessed in Section 5.5. Practical advice on their use and ideas to encourage active learning are also provided. Section 5.6 covers a broad range of information learning technology (ILT) resources and their pedagogic impacts on technology enhanced and technology enabled learning. The impact of these resources on ideas for best practice is described when using data projectors, audio and video files, virtual learning environments (VLEs), webquests, digital scrapbooking and video conferencing. Relevant methods of teaching through e-learning are then discussed in Section 5.7, investigating the advantages and disadvantages of different models including blended and massively open online courses (MOOCs). The sustainability of digital resources and aspects of e-safety are also described and discussed. Finally, in Section 5.8 the role of the library and its changing role in teaching and learning is considered as is the development of student skills in using learning resources and aspects of copyright and continuing professional development (CPD) that are of importance for all teachers in the sector.

5.2 What is a learning resource?

Appropriate teaching and learning resources assist in opening and extending communication channels in teaching and can be a powerful means of motivating learners, and conversely demotivating students if we get them wrong. Careful consideration of how resources assist the learning process is therefore necessary to optimize learning benefits. There are many examples of resources: some commercially available, some freely accessible, some directly linked to a specific examination board or curriculum and many more designed and created by teachers themselves.

Task 5.1

List three learning resources that you currently use in the classroom or that you have seen used by other teachers.

How do these resources promote and enhance student learning?

Examples that you might have identified may include flashcards, gapped handouts, slide shows, case studies, video clips and various forms of realia (e.g. a potted plant to show leaf structure, a skeleton to teach anatomy or a wall to demonstrate various methods of bonding bricks).

As Thorndike (1912) contends, teaching and learning resources should complement or extend the work of a tutor:

> A human being should not be wasted in doing what forty sheets of paper or two phonographs can do. Just because personal teaching is precious and can

do what books and apparatus cannot, it should be saved for its peculiar work. The best teacher uses books and appliances as well as his [*sic*] own insight, sympathy and magnetism.

Resources should be used to promote and enhance student learning rather than replace a teacher, to act as stimuli to facilitate the demanding and often challenging environment of Post-14 Education and Training. However, some analysis of resources is required to direct their use towards maximizing their effectiveness for student learning.

Historically, much debate has focused on the differences between what constitutes a 'teaching' resource and a 'learning' resource, but today the boundaries between such definitions have become so blurred and the terms so interchangeable that any distinctions have become largely meaningless. For example, a teacher may use a set of photographs to illustrate their lecture to assist them in recalling their next point (teaching resource), but they could equally be used as the starting point for a class debate (learning resource). In practice, any teaching resource used in a different manner or context can become a learning resource and vice versa.

Resources and learning styles

Learning theorists have demonstrated how students differ in the way that they assimilate, process and remember information. According to Reece and Walker (2003), 75 per cent of the general population learn through seeing and it is important to recognize this and to incorporate visual resources, such as colour photographs, video clips and handouts with colour pictures, charts and diagrams into our teaching. Indeed, the Office for Standards in Education (Ofsted) inspection reports often highlight the need for more engaging visual resources in teaching and less reliance upon textbooks and poor quality photocopies. However, it is also important to incorporate resources that create opportunities for learning through auditory and kinaesthetic (hands-on) means such as listening to a tape or podcast on a particular subject or by providing opportunities for students to feel what it is like to mix pastry or to touch and 'play' with equipment or artefacts. However, the distinction between visual, auditory and kinaesthetic learners is often very blurred and a variety of approaches within a lesson or the use of multi-sensory resources is highly effective. An example of a multi-sensory resource might be a questionnaire to conduct a class survey on food likes and dislikes (kinaesthetic and auditory) from which students can then create a graph to represent the results (kinaesthetic and visual) which are then discussed (auditory).

Task 5.2

Think of another example of a multi-sensory activity.

(a)   Identify what resource/s you would require.

(b)   How will the resource be used – kinaesthetically, auditorily or visually?

Resources and learning domains

Just as it is important to match teaching and learning strategies to outcomes and individual learning styles within a group of learners, it is also essential to adapt learning resources to fit the learning process. For example, in many models of curriculum design (see Chapter 7), the consideration of appropriate teaching and learning resources arises as a direct or indirect consequence of the desired learning outcomes, the teaching and learning styles and the subject matter. Definitions of what constitutes a learning resource often depend on the curriculum design adopted and more specifically its underlying ideology (see Chapter 7) and implicit theories concerning the acquisition of learning (see Chapter 3). In adult teaching in the twenty-first century, prevalent pedagogical ideologies encourage the use of student-centred learning where the teacher facilitates the learner in discovering new knowledge. In this way, the selection of a resource is determined by its potential to aid students to connect, or scaffold, previous experiences with any new knowledge. Hence, resources can be viewed as 'advance organizers' (Ausubel as cited by Curzon 2003) or 'scene setters' to provide context and tone to the learning process.

Furthermore, resources can support learning in all three of Bloom's (1964) learning domains (see Chapter 2). First, in the cognitive domain they can, for example, help to explain the curriculum content with PowerPoint presentations, handouts and diagrams to demonstrate the aims and objectives of the lesson. Second, models and equipment provide opportunities for learning in the psychomotor domain to demonstrate and practise activities, such as changing a print cartridge or using a real timetable of local buses to plan a journey. Finally, in the affective domain, realia, such as paintings, provide learners with opportunities to examine and discuss how they were made, what the artist's intentions were and how they make the viewer feel. Some resources, such as magnets, offer the opportunity to touch and experiment with them. Resources therefore play an important role in the construction of knowledge, by specifically linking new knowledge to prior knowledge, learning and experience.

Task 5.3

Construct an inventory of the learning resources you have used recently (e.g. handouts, software, etc.).

(a) How many of these resources provide opportunities for kinaesthetic, visual and auditory learning?

(b) In which of Bloom's learning domains does each resource operate?

(c) Compare your list with a colleague in the same broad area of work. How do they compare?

Differentiated resources

To meet the needs of individual learners within a group it may be necessary to tailor resources for individual students to ensure equality of access to the learning process. The following case study from an information technology (IT) lesson indicates how an activity can be individualized using differentiated resources (Evershed and Roper 2010).

Case study 5.1

An IT teacher wishes to create some resources for a lesson on the component parts of a computer. One of the learning objectives is that by the end of the lesson students will be able to recognize at least three component parts and explain their functions. The learners have a mix of experience and competence in working with computer hardware. The teacher has created vocabulary handouts and a diagram displaying and labelling six constituent parts of a computer and a list of the units of measurement associated with random access memory (RAM), processor speed and hard disk capacity. The teacher has also planned to use a short video that demonstrates how a hardware technician can upgrade the RAM to make it work more quickly and a worksheet for students to complete during the lesson.

Task 5.4

In Case study 5.1 the teacher organized multiple resources for the learners.

(a) Identify the resources.
(b) How could the selection be improved and why?
(c) What forms of differentiation might have been provided?

We would suggest that one way of improving the kinaesthetic/psychomotor resources would be to include some actual computer parts so that students can see their size, feel their weight and manipulate them so they can discover how they might fit together within the computer base unit. As students successfully locate the appropriate parts of the computer within the base unit, learning in the affective domain will also be engaged as they become more confident in handling the component parts. In addition, the worksheet could be tailored to meet both the learning outcome described in the case study, and also extend the learning for those that already have some experience in this subject or to provide additional assistance for those students who have very limited experience. This would involve creating three slightly different versions of the worksheet shown below, but will enhance opportunities for active learning of the subject material.

- **Worksheet A (for those with limited experience)** might contain multiple choice questions with alternatives to choose from such as:

  The processing unit (CPU)/hard disk/RAM is the part of the computer that stores the data. Its capacity is measured in Megahertz (MHz)/Gigabytes (Gb).

- **Worksheet B (for those with some experience)** might contain gapped questions such as:

  The _____ is the part of the computer that stores the data. Its capacity is measured in _____ (units).

- **Worksheet C (for those with** more **experience)** might ask:

  Write a short description of three of the six component parts that you have investigated today. Ensure that you include a description of their function, appropriate unit of measurement and list any health and safety procedures used by the technician in the video.

A second example of utilizing differentiated resources might be in a media studies class where a teacher is attempting to encourage critical analysis of a storyline and characterization using film clips. Rather than providing students with the same film clip, those with little confidence and experience may be tasked to critique a film with fewer main characters and a simpler plot than those with more experience.

Task 5.5

Revisit your inventory of resources from Task 5.3. How do you differentiate to meet the different needs of students?

Differentiated resources provide a communication of the teacher's high expectations for their students. They may also reinforce the perception that the teacher has taken time to prepare resources, which motivates individual students to persevere with their learning, as it indicates the teacher's belief in the students' abilities, and provides a role model of dedication to learning. Teachers should consider the need to plan differentiated resources to ensure equality of access to the learning process for all students, including those who require support due to a disability. The preparation of flexible resources is made much easier and quicker by the use of computer technology especially if they are available on a VLE (see Section 5.7). Resources also help learning to continue after the initial contact, in the student's own time, or in subsequent structured learning sessions. It is an advantage if the aid can promote learning over a period of time and if the preparation time is reduced as this will increase the input-to-learning ratio, the cost-effectiveness, of a resource.

5.3 The effective use of learning resources

In September 2013 the government withdrew the mandatory requirement for teachers in the Post-14 Education and Training sector to gain a teaching qualification, following the recommendations of the Lingfield Report. However, the White Paper that led to the introduction of the Qualified Teacher Learning and Skills (QTLS) qualification for teachers in the sector states that 'teaching and training will be inspiring [and] based on imaginative resources' (DfES 2006a: 17). The emphasis on information and communications technology (ICT) to provide effective resources as a means of improving teaching and learning is also made clear (Golden et al. 2006). Indeed, the effective use of resources continues to be central to Ofsted policy which promotes high quality resources including 'the use of ILT so that it complements and enhances learning as well as giving learners wider access to learning resources' (Ofsted 2014: 9). The evaluation of resources to determine their effectiveness continues therefore to be of fundamental importance.

Learning resources should be used to bring variety into learning, to take the focus away from the tutor and help to make essential learning points clear. However, it is easy to fall into the trap of using something 'because it is there' and one way of avoiding that problem is to evaluate resources. Before you use a resource, ask yourself:

- Why do I want to introduce this resource?
- How does it match the learning objective?
- How will it help students to learn?
- Is it simple/relevant/clear?
- Is it appropriate to the group and size of room?
- Does it need a lot of organizing and rely on certain equipment being available?
- Is it adaptable and sustainable so I can use it again and modify it?
- Can all the learners in the group use it or do I need to differentiate it?
- Does it meet equality and diversity principles?
- Is it acceptable to copy or use the resource without infringing copyright?
- Does it use unnecessarily complex language?

Once you have used the resource, determine its worth by careful reflection. Evaluate it by asking yourself:

- How well did the resource work?
- What was the student reaction?
- Would you use it again?
- Did it work the way you thought it would?
- Would a different resource be more appropriate?
- What would you change?

ICT skills were incorporated into the minimum core requirements for trainees seeking a teaching qualification in the sector from 2007 in addition to those of literacy and numeracy. They are seen as key to the development of 'a range of practices to personalise learning, including the effective use of e-learning and new technology [with the] aim to make the system as a whole more capable of responding to individual needs and aspirations' (DfES 2006a: 48). Others, such as Cuban (2001), question the amount spent on these resources in relation to their effectiveness as a tool for improving learning and, indeed, teaching. The problem, it appears, lies with the general inability to conclusively evidence significant improvements in learning through the use of ICT (Livingstone 2012; Rodriguez et al. 2012) and this is discussed further in Section 5.6. However, we believe that there is a good argument for both these positions: what matters most is that the resources are of good quality and differentiated to make the learning as accessible as possible.

The use of ICT learning platforms is now firmly embedded in the sector, reflecting the ubiquity of technology in everyday life and the recognition by the House of Lords Digital Skills Committee (2015) that digital skills are as important as lessons in numeracy and literacy. The number of VLEs through which resources are distributed to students rose significantly from 58 per cent in 2004 to 92 per cent in 2009 (BECTA 2009a). E-maturity of students, teachers and institutions is also rising rapidly, but the effective use of ICT, through technology enhanced learning or technology enabled learning, remains patchy with some further education (FE) colleges taking little advantage of the efficiency and effectiveness benefits for students, teachers and the institutions themselves. Where ICT is most successful, it is often the attitude of the tutor towards the use of technology in teaching that is the key factor (Hennessy et al. 2005; Hammond et al. 2009). While 77 per cent of tutors feel competent or advanced in the use of ICT, 65 per cent feel able to use it with their learners in the classroom as well as for preparing, planning and researching teaching resources to enhance learning (BECTA 2009a). Student-to-computer ratios in the sector are also improving with the majority of institutions in the FE sector having one computer available for every four students, though this ratio is substantially worse in adult and community teaching (LSN 2008). The effective use of learning resources using ICT is clearly improving but there are still some inherent structural difficulties within organizations and general anxiety and inexperience of some staff in such learning resources. Section 5.6 continues the discussion on the use of ICT in technology enhanced and enabled learning and pedagogy further.

Task 5.6

(a) How satisfied are you with your own understanding and use of teaching and learning resources, including the use of digital technologies in their development and deployment of learning resources?

(b) To what extent do you feel that your ability to create effective resources is affected by institutional organization or by your own experience and skills?

(c) Within your organization, identify where you would be able to access support and/or training to enhance your use of learning and teaching resources.

5.4 The organization of learning resources

It has been suggested (e.g., Davies 1975) that there are four main models for the organization of learning resources within an institution, and these are outlined below.

All resources centralized

In this model most of the teaching and learning resources tend to be under the direct control of a central group, sometimes accountable to a committee or 'user groups'. Typically, requests for equipment loan, the purchase of new software or even an increase in the photocopying allowance are made to this controlling body. 'Technicians' tend to be deployed and controlled by the centre.

Only commonly used resources centralized

In this model the 'centre' retains control of those teaching and learning resources that tend to be used by most staff or students and often those which are particularly expensive to purchase, because of considerations for the security of the equipment. However, departments or units are permitted to control some learning resources that may well be specifically related to their own function or curriculum area. For example, a typical police training centre in England would place responsibility for its reprographic services, books and periodicals on general policing matters but its firearms simulator would be under the control of the appropriate training branch.

All resources localized but staff retain control

All resources are placed where teachers and trainers have the easiest access to them, often on a departmental, section or unit basis. Budgets are devolved as closely as possible to the level of use. However, particular staff may have an important role as gatekeepers to these resources, controlling their use by teaching staff and students. 'Technicians' may also be employed by the departments to help develop and maintain the resources.

All resources localized allowing near-open access

'Localized' here means that there is the greatest possible devolution of access to learning resources. In practice, this may mean that learning resources are placed in a central position (such as a college open learning centre or library) and staff and students have unrestricted use of them.

In more recent years, this model of open access to shared digital resources, often via a VLE, has increased. Here, students can access and interact with resources whenever they wish and increasingly from wherever they are located (see also Section 5.7). The use of VLEs and blended approaches to learning resources, where some are localized and others centralized, has gathered considerable impetus in the last few years. Smith et al. (2008) reported that the use of VLEs in many Post-14 Education and Training establishments as their main platform has now risen to 46 per cent, though within these establishments only 35 per cent of staff and students use them frequently, suggesting that full maturity of this approach still has some way to go in some establishments. In others, VLEs form the backbone of much of the learning which is integrated into management systems to generate reports and data on achievement and attendance, etc. For yet others, the use of e-learning and MOOCs has greatly extended the range of qualifications available (see Section 5.7).

Task 5.7

(a) Does your organization have a strategy or policy for the use of learning resources (including digital technology)? If so, what is it?

(b) Can you locate your own institution within the list of organizational models above or does it have a mixed approach?

(c) List the advantages and an individual or unit/section that you could approach for assistance with creating resources.

5.5 Commonly used resources

The best learning resources provide students with the optimal number of communication channels using sight, hearing, touch, taste and smell. Those that combine these senses give more opportunities to learn to a wider range of students. They assist in promoting learning, reinforce ideas and concepts and aid students to recall and memorize learning, prolong attention spans and act as motivators. In addition, it is essential that any resources are able to be used repeatedly and can be adapted easily to make them as cost-effective as possible. The concept of an audio-visual aid has dramatically broadened with the advent of digital technology, and has largely become interchangeable with a multi-media resource. The following section describes and analyses some of the more readily available digital resources for teaching today.

Whiteboards

It is acknowledged that whiteboards are not the most exciting of teaching and learning resources. However, we offer no apology for beginning a section on learning resources with the humble yet ubiquitous whiteboard.

The whiteboard is essentially a democratic resource. It is usually blank at the start of the lesson and student contributions are added and changed as the session progresses. In this way, it is used collaboratively with the students, providing the opportunity for students 'to do' as well as 'be told'.

It is a useful aid to capture impromptu student contributions, summarize unexpected conclusions, highlight key information and terms, and serves as a written cue, all of which can aid memory retention and recall. Mini-whiteboards are also becoming increasingly popular for individual students to note responses to questions on and are useful for individual, formative assessments. They can be made very cheaply by laminating a piece of white A4 paper or card and can be reused many times using a whiteboard pen.

Practical advice for using whiteboards

- Always use drywipe pens! One of the rites of passage that most teachers or trainers undergo at some point in their career is 'trial by permanent marker pen' with all-too-visible results! Proprietary, spirit-based cleaners will remove any mistakes.

- Use a range of colour pens to add interest, but do not use too many at any one time and make sure the colours you have chosen are clearly visible.

- Check the board can be clearly read from all parts of the room before you start the lesson by writing some sample text and moving around the room.

- Write on the whiteboard using upper- and lower-case letters rather than all capitals as this aids students, especially those who have restricted sight or those with some forms of dyslexia, to access the material.

- Reduce whiteboard 'glare' by dimming lights or adjusting window blinds if at all possible.

- Remind yourself not to stand with your back squarely to the class when writing on the board. This not only helps to maintain clear communication, but also allows the teacher to assess visual cues to understanding.

- Remember to clean the board regularly during the session when the information is no longer needed. However, check with the students and, if your teaching establishment allows, offer them the opportunity to take a photo of it using their mobile devices. A clear board helps to focus attention away from it when required but it is sometimes helpful to leave the information on display to refer back to.

- A whiteboard used as a form of class notebook can sometimes be misleading after a section of teaching has finished. For example, arrows are often used by teachers and trainers to explain and link the concepts discussed (Figure 5.1). At the time it might be clear what an arrow signifies but this clarity may be lost when next encountered by students in their notes. For example, when encountering the following notation, is it meant that A led to B, or that A and B are connected, or that A *becomes* B, or something else entirely?

Figure 5.1 Example of whiteboard notation

Task 5.8

Leave the whiteboard uncleaned at the end of a teaching session when you have used it.

(a) Look at the board again 30 minutes later. How much of it now makes sense and is a clear representation of the ideas or material covered?

(b) What strategies do you use to ensure that the information is unambiguous, useful and can be revisited?

Flipcharts

One of the main advantages of using individual flipchart sheets over whiteboards is that they can 'capture' the thoughts and ideas of small groups or individual students and give control of what is written to the students. Students can present their ideas using the flipcharts as prompts. Flipchart paper can also be a useful means of displaying diagrams prepared in advance of the lesson by the tutor or students, which allows more time for careful preparation. However, the paper is often of poor quality and it is difficult to reuse them successfully.

Practical advice for using flipcharts

- Use flipchart pens. Pens designed for writing on whiteboards will work but they tend to dry out more quickly than proprietary ones designed for flipchart paper.
- Remember to carry some Blu-Tack or similar non-marking, removable fixing medium so students can easily refer to them when presenting.
- Use a range of colour pens to add interest, making sure that the colours are visible.
- It is often useful to give each group a different colour pen so that it is clear which presentation the 'red' group produced, for example.
- Encourage students to record their ideas in whichever way they feel most comfortable including as posters, diagrams and mind maps as well as list formats.

Handouts and worksheets

Handouts are predominantly pre-prepared written notes used to reinforce or summarize learning. They are a useful and popular learning resource commonly used throughout the sector as a means of explaining lesson content, demonstrating complex diagrams and formulae, as an aide-memoire or as a reference list to further reading sources. Worksheets are also pre-prepared and most often contain instructions and relevant information concerning a particular activity that students are asked to complete. Both handouts and worksheets can be rela-tively expensive to produce in large quantities so it is vital that they are useful to the student and/or save time in class.

At its simplest, a handout can be a straightforward record or summary of the teaching that has taken place such as a set of lecture notes. However, anecdotal evidence at least indicates that handouts used solely in this manner, although a useful record, rarely lead to sustained learning. Instead, it would appear likely that successful handouts, like worksheets, have the additional capability to *engage* students with the material by making them active rather than passive. This is achieved, for example, by using gapped handouts or by leaving spaces for students to make their own notes. In addition, most handouts are now produced electronically, so hyperlinks to relevant multi-media resources can be added and editing and updating is made easy. This is especially useful for incorporating extension tasks and for differentiating learning.

Practical advice for using handouts and worksheets

- 'Gapped' handouts are a popular way of involving students in the active learning of subject material. Essentially, gaps or lines are placed in the text which replace single words, whole phrases, mathematical formulae or parts of a diagram. Students then complete the handout using their own understanding and other resources, attention to the lecture and so on.

- Differentiated worksheets can be created for individual learners that have different text or omissions depending on individual learning goals (see Section 5.2 and Case study 5.1).

- Think carefully about how you wish to present information. Tutors often produce handouts that reflect their own learning preferences, for example, information presented in linear format as a series of points, and which reflects their own personal ideologies about how we learn.

- 'Skeleton' handouts are often used, particularly in higher education (HE). As the name suggests, a skeleton handout gives the bare bones of the session with space where students are encouraged to make their own notes, comments and so on. An example is the handout printed from a PowerPoint presentation (Figure 5.2). However, this requires that students have a relatively advanced set of study skills.

- Ensure that any visuals used do not contain stereotypical images and that you have provided references for any material under copyright (see Section 5.9).

- Coloured paper can emphasize the importance of a particular handout, for example if an important summary is produced, and can help some students with dyslexia or visual impairment.

- Resist the temptation to place too much information on a single page and try to use at least a 12 point, preferably 14 point, sans serif font such as Century Gothic, Comic Sans or Arial, all of which have a clean, uncluttered appearance, especially important for visually impaired and dyslexic students (Figure 5.3).

Information Technology
1. In pairs or small groups discuss the following questions.
Spaces have been provided for you to make your own notes.

A.   What is meant by the term IT?

B.   What (if any) is the difference between IT and ICT?

C.   What is ILT and how does it differ from IT and ICT?

In this area make any notes from our class discussion of this question.

Barriers to Technology
2. Watch the video on the social impact of using IT in teaching
and then answer the following questions.

A. What potential barriers to using IT are discussed?

B. Can you think of any other barriers?

Figure 5.2 Typical 'skeleton' handouts in outline form indicating areas for students to make their own notes

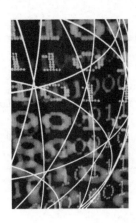

Information Technology

- What is IT?
- What is ICT?
- What is ILT?

- Can you give examples of each?

Barriers to Technology

In small groups discuss possible barriers to learning

- Identify your own barriers to ICT
- List 3 possible barriers to ICT for other students

Figure 5.2 *(Continued)*

This is in Times New Roman typeface and is a serif font

This is in Century Gothic typeface and is a sans serif font

This is in Comic Sans typeface and is a sans serif font

This is in Arial typeface and is a sans serif font

Figure 5.3 Text comparison of sans serif and serif fonts

Task 5.9

Conduct an audit of the handouts you produced or used for your last course or topic.

(a)   Is there a pattern in terms of how the information is presented?

(b)   Do they promote active thinking and enhance learning?

(c)   Do they contain any stereotypical attitudes in terms of race, gender, religion, age, disability and so on?

(d)   Produce a new handout using a different presentational technique than you might usually use and try it out with your students.

Flashcards

Flashcards are resources that aid memorization, can be used to assess student learning and develop cognitive skills by assisting students to make connections and scaffold knowledge. In their simplest form, they are slips of paper, which are moved around to match, for example, questions with answers. Students can also use them to rank ideas or group words, numbers or pictures in a variety of different ways, which encourages kinaesthetic learners to engage in the learning process.

An example of using flashcards in a class is when developing understanding of the haiku form of poetry. The rules of haiku vary between traditional and non-traditional forms, but in English the form often includes dividing three lines of verse into five, seven and then five syllables and includes a 'season' word or *kigo* (such as blossom equating to spring). Chains of verse are then linked together. To start the cognitive process it is important for learners to understand what a syllable is, how to count them, how to identify the seasonal word and how to place the lines in order.

Task 5.10

Create three flashcards using either the lines given below or some of your own, bearing in mind the practical advice given on font size and so on. Count the number of syllables on each line and move them into order (five, seven, five syllables), before and after laminating them. Are they easier to manipulate with or without laminating? Use a whiteboard pen to circle the seasonal word in the poem and note how easily this can be removed on the laminated card so they can be reused.

Dances on the air

Knowing cherry trees

Blossom whispers on a sigh

Practical advice for using flashcards

- Laminate them so that they are reusable and easier to slide over the surface of a desk or attach them to a board using Blu-Tack.
- Use different coloured paper or fonts to distinguish questions from answers.
- Use upper- and lower-case letters and at least a 14 point sans serif font (see 'Handouts').
- Print sets in different colours to quickly enable you to return them into sets at the end of your teaching.
- Perhaps include some blank cards for students to write their own ideas on.

Task 5.11

Do this activity with a colleague if you can. You might choose a resource that you both use.

(a) Select a written learning resource currently in use on one of your courses; for example, an instruction booklet, some flashcards, a handout, an introduction to a topic, a written briefing for a task or assignment or a list of legal definitions.
(b) Examine your chosen material for readability, clarity, layout and tone.
(c) Briefly comment on how you might improve the chosen resource to enhance the communication with the learner.

Photocopiers and photocopying

Photocopiers occur in a bewildering variety of types and sophistication and it is doubtful that we use anything like the full potential of the facilities available. In teaching, they are extensively used to copy resources such as handouts, activities, reading materials and so on, but with the growing need to reduce budgets and carbon footprints, alternatives such as VLEs are increasingly becoming the norm. In the meantime, it is still good practice for all teachers to be able to perform the following tasks:

- copy a single page of A4 size;
- copy multiple pages of a single page of A4 paper;
- enlarge and reduce;
- change the tone (lighter/darker);
- produce double-sided copies;
- collate;
- collate and staple.

5.6 Information learning technology (ILT)

ILT is a generic term which describes any teaching or learning process where technology is involved in its conception, delivery, deployment and educational resources. For employers, the use of ILT promotes the appropriate aptitudes and competencies necessary for many occupations. From a teaching perspective ILT has revolutionized the way that resources can be created, edited, individualized, disseminated and employed, both within and beyond the physical world of the classroom. From a student's perspective, the use of technology as a learning resource helps many to embed their IT skills and to motivate them in the learning process. Research indicates that good use of technological resources in teaching renders the learning experience interactive, more student-centred, increases the effectiveness and efficiency of the learning process and improves learner engagement and student attitudes to education (BECTA 2009a). Research by Hammond et al. (2009) identified that teachers felt that ILT gains student attention, matches student expectations, encourages more independent learning, allows access to more up-to-date information, assists students in collaborative and peer learning and allows teachers to create, edit and share resources more effectively.

Other research advocates caution. Higgins (2009) questions whether such claims can be solely attributed to the use of digital technologies, indicating that the complexity of education may obscure improvements made by other pedagogical changes. There have been many attempts to conclusively demonstrate significant and direct improvements to learning outcomes via ILT without success. Recent studies indicate that 'a simple increase in ICT provision does not guarantee enhanced educational performance' (Livingstone 2012) and that much relies on the pedagogic approach and beliefs of teachers (Higgins 2009), teacher attitudes and skills (Hammond et al. 2009) and ICT infrastructure and deployment skills (Hennessy et al. 2005). However, Selwyn (2011) identifies that using ILT can be credited with improving a range of 'soft skills' including motivation, improvisation, creativity, experimentation, multitasking and the ability to select and analyse diverse information sources. This tension makes 'schooling in the digital age a complex, compromised and often contradictory affair . . . [but] this is not to say technology cannot act as a focus for improvement' (Selwyn 2011: 136).

It is indeed important to note that, as with any other resource, teachers need to be clear about what digital resources can add to the learning process. However, technology in the classroom has undoubtedly revolutionized the way in which many students learn. Even if technology is not used in the classroom, it is still the case that the majority of resources will have been created initially using computers, printers and photocopiers and much teaching relies on digital technology for the production, distribution and location of resources. We argue, therefore, that the reluctance of some teachers in the sector to use digital resources in learning should be challenged. As with any resource, it is important that teachers feel confident in using digital technologies and it is often a general anxiety about trying something new or the fear that it is not reliable that prevents teachers from using it. However, in our experience, most digital technologies used in teaching have matured significantly in recent years and they are more reliable, more intuitive and easier to use than ever before. Indeed, the use of digital technologies as learning resources is key to the new teaching qualification standards for the sector (ETF 2014).

More recently, ILT appears to have diverged into distinctive, though closely associated and often interchangeable, camps, both confusingly termed 'TEL'. On the one hand is technology *enhanced* learning where ICT is used to support teaching and learning activities and to develop resources *enhanced* by technology (Dillenbourg 2008). Here, students learn *through or by* technology and teachers design, create or present suitable learning resources using technology. For example, teachers (and increasingly students themselves) may create a slide show to project through an interactive whiteboard. The presentation can be passive or more active where students can interact during the presentation by means of, for example, electronic voting, or completing an associated worksheet or quiz while watching a video clip embedded in the presentation. TEL in this sense can therefore be considered as enhancing course design and delivery by providing a degree of flexibility within largely existent modes of learning and requires a degree of pedagogical adaptability to be successful. Hence, curriculum design based on the principles of content and end product is shifted slightly to allow for a more process derived ideology where the learner can begin to have more input into their learning experiences.

On the other hand, there is technology *enabled* learning, which implies that learning occurs with technology. Here students are encouraged to use the resources, information, software or processing abilities of available technology to scaffold their own knowledge and understanding from a variety of digital sources rather than reproducing those provided directly by the teacher. It requires a significant degree of pedagogical adaptability to be successful and can encompass a broad range of programme designs. Students 'relish their new-found expertise and status in the digital world . . . we are witnessing some genuinely new learning opportunities, centring on the possibilities of student-orientated digital creativity and on collaborative communication' (Livingstone 2012: 21).

This extends from elements of e-learning through blended learning and MOOCs (see Section 5.7), often associated with CPD, which generally involve limited direct teacher/student contact to ideas of 'flipped classroom' approaches. Here, teachers with in-depth and broad subject knowledge are able to facilitate a wide range of different outcomes and processes, tailored to individualized learning preferences. In a flipped classroom, learning in class is spent on project collaboration, presentation of findings, design and problem-solving with the help of peers and the teacher to research and actively acquire and construct knowledge. Home study involves initial research and investigation and requires a high degree of self-motivation, cognitive development and processing ability, and curriculum design is shifted significantly towards a more process derived ideology where learners have significant input to their own learning experiences. However, enabled learning also relies on all students having equality of access to resources away from the classroom.

The following section examines some of the more readily available digital resources used in the sector today to *enhance* and/or *enable* the learning process. This is followed by some examples of how both can be incorporated into course design to demonstrate the different pedagogic processes involved.

Data projectors

The availability of the data projector is now widespread with 83 per cent of colleges reporting that their teachers have access to data projectors (BECTA 2009b). 'However, there is still some way to go until a tutor can expect to find them in every teaching room' (BECTA 2006: 23). The advantages of using a data projector in a lesson is that high-quality material can be prepared in advance and complicated graphics can be displayed with clarity. When the associated laptop or computer is linked to the internet, it also means that presentations can include 'real-time' information and 'live' demonstration of interactive software. If speakers are available then video and audio playback can make presentations very attractive to the majority of learners. This capability is obviously very useful when trying to teach how to use a particular piece of software, or when bringing specific subject matter to life – for example, the use of film footage from the Second World War.

Data projectors are often permanently fixed in a particular room, usually to the ceiling and connected to an interactive whiteboard. They can also be portable devices that are used in combination with a laptop computer and it is this arrangement that often causes the most anxiety for teachers. However, the set-up procedure is very straightforward: a single data cable is required to link the laptop and data projector together via two visibly different 'ports' (see Figure 5.4).

After connection, it is simply a matter of powering up the projector followed by the laptop. The majority of software on the laptop will automatically find the projector and display whatever is on the laptop monitor after a short warming-up period. Do not forget to remove the lens cap from the data projector if there is one. One of the function keys (usually F5) toggles the display between laptop screen only, both laptop screen and projected image displayed

**Laptop Monitor   Data Projector
Input Port   Input port**

Figure 5.4 Examples of the data projector and laptop ports connected by the data cable

simultaneously and projected image only. It is then a case of adjusting the image size by moving the projector towards the projection area (making the image smaller) or away from it (making the image larger). This is not usually a problem with fixed data projectors as the optimum viewing distance is pre-set. The image can be focused using the remote control or the controls located on the projector if required.

Practical advice for using data projectors

- Be aware of health and safety issues such as trailing wires when using portable data projectors and laptops.

- Adding (wireless) internet access and speakers and then using video clips and internet sites can create opportunities for multi-media presentations.

- It is essential to allow the data projector to cool down after powering it off. The cooling fan will continue to function until it has completed the cooling period.

- Projecting onto whiteboards can produce glare so it is sometimes better to project onto a blank wall if a screen is not available.

- Data projectors can be noisy, and leaving information displayed when completing a group activity can be distracting for some students. Turning off the projector for short periods of time is not recommended as it takes approximately 5–10 minutes to cool down and be ready to restart again. Instead, most projectors have a 'blank' or 'display off' button either on the remote or on the projector itself. This option will toggle between the screen displaying and not displaying information.

Interactive whiteboards (iWB)

Interactive whiteboards rely on the presence of a fixed data projector so the connections are on the whole already made. Some boards have now been developed that are projected onto from the rear so the projector is not as apparent, but it will still be part of the system. At their simplest, they can be used as a teaching resource to provide a surface onto which an image can be displayed from a data projector, but this denies their main purpose as an interactive learning resource for students to use as the name suggests (Golden et al. 2006). When blended with traditional methods of teaching, the electronic whiteboard can enrich learning experiences by bringing subject matter directly into a teaching room through interactive resources including music, images, online collaboration and web conferencing.

According to BECTA (2009b), 81 per cent of FE colleges and 54 per cent of work-based learning establishments have electronic whiteboards installed in classrooms. Market share varies between the different manufacturers, but the boards commonly found in the sector are Smartboards, Promethians and Starboards. Each comes with its own software that can display a huge variety of pre-prepared and highly detailed resources including maps, paintings, geological structures, diagrams of bone and muscle and architectural plans. There is also software that facilitates the creation of animated electronic flashcards that students can move around on the whiteboard using their fingers, and online assessments designed for classroom use. Discussions can be captured on the board using 'light pens' rather than conventional dry wipe pens and screen shots can be printed or saved and distributed electronically either through a VLE or by email.

The use of additional software such as Active Vote allows students to participate in interactive learning quizzes and to display the results of their own learning to other members of the class, which encourages peer learning. The following websites are free interactive resource banks that can be used in conjunction with an interactive whiteboard to make lessons more interesting:

- BBC learning resources: www.bbc.co.uk/learning;
- Times Educational Supplement (TES): www.tes.co.uk/teaching-resources;
- Learning and Skills Improvement Service (LSIS): www.excellencegateway. org.uk.

Research suggests that enhancing teaching through learning technologies in terms of presentational tools has 'a strong impact on *engagement* factors' (Finlayson et al. 2006: 10).

Task 5.12

(a) Write on an interactive whiteboard using a light pen. It will feel different from writing on a conventional board. Notice that on most boards you should only pick up one pen at a time from the tray, though newer versions recognize more than one colour.

(b) Use the electronic eraser to remove the writing.

(c) Connect to the internet and download some of the free resources from www.bbc.co.uk/learning/ or one of the other sites listed.

(d) Listen to a podcast from the BBC or other website (if you have external speakers installed).

(e) Locate the board's specialist software and create a new resource for use in your own teaching that will encourage students to interact with it, such as a matching exercise.

(f) If you have access to a VLE or intranet, upload this new resource and test what it will look like when projected. Are there any changes you need to make?

Presentation software

Presentation software such as PowerPoint, Prezi or FreeMind, combined with a communications package such as email or a VLE has revolutionized possibilities for both enhancing and enabling learning beyond the classroom. Presentations can be used in class, emailed or accessed by learners outside the class, shared with colleagues, posted on the internet, are cost-effective to produce and distribute, do not degrade with reuse and can engage students with the learning process in a wide variety of ways. In student surveys, Frey and Birnbaum (2002) determined that PowerPoint presentations were considered useful tools in developing cognitive skills and helpful when reviewing learning content. However, it is also important to remember that student attention spans can waver if the presentation is dull and uninteresting just as easily as when faced with any other form of communication. Indeed, Tufte (2003) argues that content in presentations can even be almost entirely lost in the drive to make the slides too full of gimmicks. Adams (2006) argues that teachers need to tailor presentations to match students' needs rather than using the default options in the software and to think creatively about its use, adding pauses for interaction and combining it with other resources.

Practical advice for using presentation software

- To retain student attention limit slide presentations to a maximum of 20 minutes before changing activity. Even better, make them interactive by posing questions interspersed throughout and soliciting student discussion to engage them in the process.
- Include pictures and graphics on slides as much as possible, keeping to no more than six bullet points on each slide. Resist the temptation to use too many words on a single slide and to have too many slides. As a rule of thumb, 10 slides are more than enough to provoke 20 minutes of discussion, but obviously it depends on the content and your teaching style.
- Always double-check content, spelling and the use of apostrophes (errors enlarged to the size of the teacher's head when projected tend to get noticed).
- As with handouts, use upper- and lower-case letters *otherwise it looks like you are shouting*. It also assists students to read the slides more easily.
- Add images and colour as long as the slide does not become too busy.
- The size of font that you use is important. The minimum font size recommended for bullet points is 28 point.

about this size

- Consider your audience and any corporate image. Do you need the college logo at all? If so, is it needed on every page or just the first and final slides?
- Always leave time for questions and discussion.
- As with whiteboards, do not block the audience's view and never read the slides out word for word or you will soon find that audience attention wanders.
- Learn how to add interest to your presentation by embedding video clips, music, pictures and audio files into the presentation (beware of copyright) so you can

access them seamlessly without having to leave the presentation and open additional software.

- Consider using the animations option in software that allows progressive disclosure of the bullet points, but do not overdo it. The technique can reinforce the notion of 'teacher as giver' and with adult students in particular we try to encourage greater learner autonomy. Therefore, it might be more appropriate to think about a design that allows information to be added rather than revealed. Examples of this are slides that contain open questions, or strategies that encourage students to write on the whiteboard at the same time as the projection of a slide, to overlay the slide with discussions and thoughts.

- Most projectors have a 'blank' option (see 'Data projectors') so you can check for yourself what the next slide is, or log in to software without user IDs being projected.

- Emailing presentations to students or uploading copies to VLEs leaves a much lighter carbon footprint.

- Memory sticks are a superb portable method of transporting presentations to different sites. However, this is also one way that computer viruses spread, so ensure that you install and use virus checker software routinely.

Task 5.13

(a) Prepare a short slide show with different fonts, images and colours. Project it using the data projector and view it from the learner's position. Are there any changes you would make?
(b) How could you embed ICT in your teaching by involving the learners in creating their own presentations?

Video cameras and video clips

As discussed previously, it is likely that different students will have different combinations of preferred learning styles. Video clips are likely to engage the majority of learners and will interest more auditory learners with the accompanying soundtrack. If the teacher also creates an activity such as completing a quiz at the same time or an activity such as identifying particular features found in the video clip, more kinaesthetic learners are also likely to react positively to the resource.

An alternative method for utilizing the video medium as an interactive resource is to involve students in creating their own. Video cameras, such as the Flip and Jazz, are portable, cost-effective, robust and easy to use. They embed ICT skills, make learning interesting and motivational, and can revolutionize teaching pedagogy in subjects such as English spoken as a foreign language, drama, dance, art, music and many vocational subjects such as hairdressing and construction. Recording learning is invaluable in terms of evidencing assessment and can be the preferred method for many students. The use of video as a resource for learning is only limited by the imagination of the teacher. However, a word of caution: it is imperative that guidelines and rules are discussed with the group as part of the safeguarding policies of the institution. This should pre-empt some of the e-safety problems arising, such as students exploiting recorded material through social and mobile phone networks (see e-safety).

Practical advice for using video resources

- Select videos carefully with specific learning goals in mind.
- Keep them relatively short, approximately 15 minutes.
- Be selective about showing particular parts of a video.
- If you are concerned about internet connectivity or firewalls that will prevent videos from being displayed, many sites, including those listed in the 'Interactive whiteboard' section will allow you to download the files to a memory stick.
- Create accompanying activities for the videos, perhaps asking different groups of students to comment on different aspects of the video or presenting a quiz that focuses on the learning outcomes.
- Make sure you know the content of the video clip and have checked that it does not contain inappropriate images or language, nor contravenes equality and diversity principles.
- When students use recording equipment themselves, ensure that they know how to use it, what the purpose of the activity is, the time period in which it should be achieved and set out strict rules on the equipment's appropriate use (see e-safety). Better still, involve the students in setting the ground rules on what is appropriate practice.

Task 5.14

Watch a 10-minute video clip from the internet and then try to convey everything you have seen through either written or spoken words. It is very likely that it will take substantially longer to convey the same information.

Digital recording and podcasts (audio files)

Audio files can be downloaded from the internet or created by teachers and students using low-cost and reliable digital recording devices. They can then be accessed via devices such as computers, mobile phones, iPads and iPods. Podcasts are pre-recorded audio files that are produced either on a regular basis, as a series of short summaries on specific topics, or as one-off recordings. They are often created for a specific purpose such as revision but students could also be encouraged to create their own to evidence learning or to share with peers.

The main advantages of audio files are that students can listen at a time and place convenient to them and that files can be stored and replayed when revising. The audio medium suits the learning preferences of some students and can have other advantages such as the development of speaking and listening skills for students whose first language is not English. The audio medium is often associated with passive learning so care should be taken to include the use of linked questions or quizzes to promote active thinking and to broaden their appeal. Students can also be encouraged to make their own audio files using digital recorders and very simple, free to download, software such as Audacity. An example activity might be to ask learners to research a topic and prepare a small-scale radio-style interview. This has immediate applications to business studies, media studies and the arts. However, the potential is much broader: roving reporters could interview students and use the results to create statistical data, for example. Some lecturers in HE have used podcasting to replace traditional lectures, suggesting that it frees up time for smaller group activities and promotes widening participation (Stothart 2006). Podcasts can be used as study materials prior to a lesson or as a recap following it.

Commercial podcasts are also produced and are often accessed as real simple syndication (RSS) feeds via an aggregator that collects the audio files from multiple websites and allows teachers and students to select 'favourite' sites. This means that individuals can subscribe to a service that 'alerts' them when new material is available via a very easy-to-use interface. The presence of the RSS icon (Figure 5.5) indicates that the podcast is available to feed to multiple devices and a teacher can ask students to access podcasts as homework, for example.

Figure 5.5 The RSS icon indicating that a feed is available to download

Practical advice on using digital recorders

- Audio files should be no more than 15 minutes in length to maintain interest.
- Focus the resource on a very specific topic.
- Record using a digital device that records using either an MP3 or MP4 format for easy compatibility with most playback technology.
- Audio files are easy to upload to your VLE but they can be too large to be emailed to your students as an attachment. Place them on the VLE instead.

Task 5.15

(a) Record a short (five-minute) interview with a colleague on a subject of your choice using a digital recorder. Upload it to your VLE with an accompanying question for students to discuss.

(b) Set a task that incorporates students interviewing each other based on a specific question. This type of activity fits well with informal assessment strategies.

Internet searches and webquests

The internet should not be confused with the world wide web. The former is a collection of interconnected computer networks and the latter comprises the documents and other resources accessible via hyperlinks and uniform resource locators (URLs) known as addresses. This collection of resources and information is arguably one of the key changes to the way in which tutors and students research and find information. The internet combines an incredible array of resources from many sources that tutors and students can locate and use in teaching and learning quickly, cost-effectively and at almost any time. Indeed, another frequently cited problem with using the internet is that there is too much information available.

In 2007, a search of the internet using the Google search engine and the phrase *learning and teaching resources* elicited 1,090,000 responses from the UK only. In 2011 the same search criteria produced 12,400,000 results in only 0.13 seconds. By 2015 the number of responses rose to 382,000,000 results in 0.25 seconds. By refining the search to locate sites containing the phrase *'learning and teaching resources'* within double quotes, the number of websites reported back in 2011 from the UK dropped to 230,000, perhaps not quite as extraordinary, but still impressive. Interestingly, in 2015 this exercise responded with almost similar results at 228,000. In filtering the search results it is sensible to recognize that with anyone being able to publish material, some information accessed may be inaccurate, misleading and outdated, so caution is always essential to cross-check its validity.

One of the issues faced by teachers when asking students to use the internet as a resource is that students can be tempted to simply cut and paste information from a variety of sites, creating potential allegations of plagiarism and a feeling by teachers that students are not engaging enough with the material provided. One example of a resource that could improve the situation is a webquest, similar to a treasure or scavenger hunt, where all the answers are online. Many webquests are freely available including those from museums and art galleries and ask specific questions, which the student has to engage with in order to locate the information required. Students can bookmark the websites they visit and the inquiry-oriented resource encourages them to research the topics thoroughly before, for example, writing a short essay, recording an interview or creating a presentation. In their simplest form, they can be a set of questions created by the teacher that are investigated by the student and can usually be explored in any order, but this depends on the ability of learners to analyse the material they find. The teacher can stipulate appropriate websites where information is located to ensure that the students access accurate information if this is a concern. Webquests support problem-based discovery learning, motivate learners, encourage independent learning and improve general research skills and analysis. If students create webquest resources for others in the group, they can learn and teach simultaneously which provides opportunities for learning in the higher cognitive domain.

Task 5.16

Create an interactive webquest resource for your students. This might include:

- links to other relevant websites;
- links to appropriate documents;
- links to a relevant e-journal or book;
- links to a multi-media file (e.g., a video clip).

Digital scrapbooking and bookmarking

These are web-based technologies and are becoming increasingly popular to collect and share multiple ideas and themes into a single place. It is not permissible to use such sites to teach from, but students can be shown how to use them for themselves to create a central point to which they can upload resources and ideas. They may also help you as a tutor to centralize information from a variety of sources to aid your preparation of lessons and your own CPD.

One free example is Pinterest (www.pinterest.com) which digitally re-imagines the traditional noticeboard. Instead of pinning bits of paper to a physical board, this software allows you to keep links to websites and digital images. Then it allows you to create multiple noticeboards on different themes or topics and access them via the internet on your mobile phone or laptop. Others also have their boards too, which can either be shared or kept private. Images that are pinned to individual boards link back to their original source. Another is Delicious (www.delicious.com), which allows sites to be bookmarked and stacked to make libraries of information. Instead of cutting and pasting links from your internet searches they can be bookmarked or pinned to your own boards wherever you see the relevant icons.

Task 5.17

If you are unfamiliar with scrapbooking or bookmarking;

(a) Create an account and start to investigate and experiment. They are meant to be intuitive and have the look and feel of other social media. Online help and mini-tutorials are readily available.
(b) Talk to others who use them. How do they use them and what for?
(c) If appropriate, ask your own students whether they use them and then determine whether they are a useful resource for your own students to use.

Webinars, webcasts and voice-over internet technology

The use of voice-over internet technology (VoIP) application or video-conferencing software (e.g. Skype) as a learning technology has gained considerable popularity, specializing as it does in facilitating real-time audio-video transmission between different locations via computers, tablets and other mobile devices via the internet. It makes conference calls possible using a webcam and can connect individuals or groups of students and/or teachers to specialists, other groups of students/teachers and other learning environments without incurring travel costs. It requires only some advance arrangement so that both parties are available at a pre-set time and perhaps the use of an interactive whiteboard to project the audio-video feed in the classroom for group discussions. It has been used very successfully in the teaching of languages, geography, history, engineering and science to gain useful insights into subject content and relevance. Webinars also use VoIP technology and allow interested parties to watch live lectures, presentations, seminars or science experiments in real time (e.g. Royal Institution Christmas Lecture series). A key feature is the ability to interact in question and answer sessions.

These contrast with webcasts where data transmission is one-way and interaction is not available. Webcasts generally involve the steaming of media over the internet from a single content source to many audiences simultaneously, often live but also available on demand. Source media are often copyrighted and cannot be re-cast without a licence but make it possible to watch a live performance of perhaps a ballet, opera or play (e.g. Royal Shakespeare Company), without the difficulties of arranging travel and the cost of tickets.

Task 5.18

Arrange a video conference between yourself and a colleague broadcasting from a different room. One person will need a tablet, laptop or PC with Skype, speakers, microphone and a webcam installed. The other person might like to try using a PC linked to an interactive whiteboard. Both will need access to the internet.

(a) How easy is it?

(b) How do you alter the sound on the speakers?

(c) What is the best place or angle for the webcam?

(d) Swop over and let your colleague see the results.

(e) Is this something that you could use in your lessons or as an alternative to a meeting?

Other useful software

Many free software products and websites can be used as interesting learning resources, but it is up to you and your imagination to research them and decide if they can enhance the learning experience for your students. Some examples are given below and Figure 5.6 demonstrates how some of these and those discussed previously might be included in lessons.

- Audacity, free audio file editing software: http://audacityfreedownload.org.
- Hotpotatoes, free puzzle creation site (crosswords, matching tasks, gapped handouts): www.hotpot.uvic.ca.
- FreeMind, free mind-mapping software: www.sourceforge.net/projects/freemind.
- Podbean, free podcasting site: www.podbean.com.
- Survey Monkey, free survey software for generating online questionnaires: www.surveymonkey.com.
- Prezi. for simple but stylish and fun-looking presentations, free for education establishments: www.prezi.com.
- Election Buddy, online voting for polling answers to questions or collecting responses and displaying them as pie charts etc.: www.electionbuddy.com.

Subject	Environmental science	Topic	Carbon footprints
<ul><li>Investigate the potential impacts of carbon footprints on climate change using advanced web searches</li><li>Communicate findings by creating a short video (3 mins max.)</li><li>Argue both for and against the concept of carbon footprints by questioning the validity of information located on the selected internet sites</li></ul>		Students should already understand concepts of acid rain, climate change and ozone layer	Project perhaps over a half-term period, but depends on your timetable. Select parts that you think might be useful if you have fewer hours available

Teaching objectives – to understand:	Learning objectives – students will:
1 how carbon dioxide can damage the ozone layer (recap from previous learning and assessment)	1 recap on the implications of carbon dioxide for the environment
2 the concept of a carbon footprint and how it may be calculated	2 research what carbon footprints are and how they can be calculated
3 how different businesses and corporations view the idea of a carbon footprint	3 discover how different organizations view and manage carbon footprints within their own business
4 how they might alleviate or ignore impacts of carbon dioxide	4 practise communication skills by producing either a 2-minute video or podcast to be uploaded to the VLE and peer assessed
5 planning and undertaking independent and collaborative research	5 work collaboratively to develop advanced internet search skills and make informed judgements by evaluating evidence from different internet sources
6 the use of a number of sources to widen knowledge and inform different views on carbon footprints selecting and using (personal, learning and thinking skills)	

1	Students recap, discuss and map key points on acid rain and the ozone layer using FreeMind mapping software in small groups. Upload mindmaps to VLE for later assessment by tutor.
2	Introduce topic and assessment video.

Figure 5.6 Pedagogic examples for integrating technology enhanced learning into the teaching of carbon footprints

3   Introduce concept of carbon footprints: What are they? How are they created? Compare with video (e.g. www.youtube.com/watch?v=YB9TCxhjVHo Group discussion). Storyboard ideas in small groups using Prezzi or similar presentation software.

4   What are implications of not reducing carbon footprints? Independent research using internet and other resources. Perhaps use Pinterest to scrapbook, collate and share ideas with other team members – continue for home study.

5   Add homework from Pinterest to storyboards.

6   What does the Carbon Trust do? Look at some of their work at www.youtube.com/user/TheCarbonTrust.

7   Students research independently and decide what questions they would like to ask of the Trust. (Teacher can previously arrange this with the Carbon Trust, a local wildlife trust education officer or other business or council that looks after recycling, for example.) Arrange to Skype or use Live Chat and ask questions.

8   Watch short video on emissions. Complete worksheet on the amount of CO_2 produced by in different ways (e.g. www.youtube.com/watch?v=AGRIo87oAUg).

9   Calculate your own carbon footprint. As home study keep a log of the time you spend watching TV, travelling by car, on the computer, listening to music, having the heating on, cooking, having a shower etc. for a week. Enter the log on a spreadsheet.

10   Use the logs to calculate carbon footprints using either a ready-made online planner (e.g. www.carbonfootprint.com/calculator.aspx) or edit the calculator to suit your students and use the spreadsheets. Create a pie chart and compare with other students. Add information to storyboard.

11   What can we do to mitigate carbon emissions? Perhaps split groups into teams to investigate renewable technologies (e.g. wind, wave, solar, geothermal, hydro), carbon offset, re-greening ideas, recycling etc. Present findings to peers and upload onto the VLE. Add relevant information to storyboard.

12   Each team investigates a business to see how they approach their carbon footprint (e.g. congestion charge in London and other cities – polluter pays principle – Innocent Fruit drinks, Tesco etc.: all are keen to show their green credentials. Add information to storyboard.

13   Reflect on your mind-map storyboard – select some of the main points you have learned. Is there anything that you will change to reduce your own carbon footprint? Make a short video for each group. Upload to the VLE.

14   Peer group watch other videos and vote on the best video using voting software (e.g. Election Buddy or Survey Monkey). Students are assessed on their storyboard, collaboration and video. Students keep the storyboard and scrapbooks as ready-made revision primers.

Figure 5.6 *(Continued)*

The examples in Figure 5.6 compliment teacher input via presentations, discussions, collating of resources etc., and suggest some elements of flipped classroom pedagogy. However, it must be stressed that some of these elements rely on students being able to access the resources once outside the main institution.

Virtual learning environments

VLEs in their purest form are software systems that are used to organize and disseminate learning resources. However, they are often combined with a managed learning environment (MLE) which facilitates course management, administration and information (such as grading, maintaining registers, fees information, automatic enrolment and so on), but these two areas can and often do operate independently. You may already be familiar with Blackboard, Moodle or Virtual Campus products. In terms of TEL a VLE can both enhance and enable learning depending on how it is structured. Often its use is limited to the sharing and dissemination of resources and as a tool for uploading student work for assessment purposes. However, in a much broader sense, VLEs can enhance learning where students use the resources, information, software or processing abilities of available technology as a starting point from which to expand their own knowledge through webinars, discussion boards, social media links and video conferencing (see Section 5.7). However, to use VLEs successfully in this way requires a high degree of customization and a stable infrastructure.

A learning platform most often features:

- Static learning resources, such as copies of presentation notes, uploaded by the teacher for access by students both within and outside the classroom.
- An announcement facility, often on the first page of the VLE, to provide a general communications area.
- Interactive learning resources such as activities, tasks and video clips.
- An email function so that tutors can send messages to individual students or groups of students.
- Online discussion areas where students can leave messages for each other and work collaboratively on projects and tasks.
- Online discussion groups to demonstrate subject knowledge and also support peer learning, collaboration and student-generated research. They can be accessed synchronously, whereby all the students are timetabled to be online simultaneously, or asynchronously, where students can add and respond to ideas as they occur. Larger groups can be divided into specialist interest groups or subject specialism areas (Salmon 2002).
- The facility for a teacher to moderate comments and content before being published.
- Facilities for students to upload completed tasks and assignments, sometimes as individual pieces of work and sometimes as e-portfolios (see 'E-portfolios').
- The ability for tutors to record and send feedback to students on uploaded assignments.
- Gradebooks or report cards for students and teachers to track and record progress.

VLEs are now available in most of the sector and their use is becoming more wide-spread and mature. They are often justified in terms of cost and flexibility and this is discussed further in Section 5.7. However, it should also be remembered that, while it is a valuable aid in organizing learning resources in many subjects and can aid cross-curricular learning in particular, a VLE is not always the most appro-priate method of distributing and organizing resources. The message with using IT-based resources is similar to any other learning aid: appropriateness should be measured by how effectively it helps our students achieve their learning objec-tives. Inaccessibility to appropriate IT equipment can place some learners at a dis-advantage and it is important to investigate this matter before using any teaching strategy that relies solely upon access to an IT resource for its success. For this reason, many courses use blended learning strategies that combine both face to face and e-learning to allow for the benefits of each to be utilized.

Task 5.19

(a) Do you have access to a VLE in your organization? If you do and have not used it before, ask someone to show you how they use it. Then design and upload a resource to incorporate into your own teaching.

(b) If you already use a VLE, make a list of which functions you use and which you have yet to explore. Design a resource for your learners using one of the functions that you do not currently use.

(c) If you have no access to a VLE in your organization, make contact with a colleague who does. What do they consider are the advantages and disadvantages of using a VLE?

E-portfolios

An e-portfolio is a collection of digitalized evidence which can be used to col-lect and record learner achievement, and is often closely associated to a VLE. At its most limited, it can be used as a digital equivalent of a student's paper-based portfolio. The electronic nature of the resource allows students to create and sub-mit assignments and tutors to provide assessment feedback electronically and as a record of progression through a qualification route. The more imaginative e-portfolios allow for uploading of not only word-processed documents, but also, for example, video and audio files, web pages, images and copies of discussions and debates between students. At its most ambitious, an e-portfolio can contain a host of digitally created evidence that represents an individual's learning jour-ney, rather than as a means of achieving a single qualification. It can be used to provide evidence of progression to another educational award, but also evidence of wider abilities such as effective communication, IT proficiency, organizational skills and CPD to prospective employers and professional organizations, espe-cially for the purposes of moderation and quality assurance.

5.7 E-learning and sustainability

We are focusing on e-learning in this chapter for two reasons:

- E-learning appears to be an increasingly important dimension in the work of many Post-14 Education and Training establishments. Many colleges have invested in open learning centres, partly as a sound economic development and partly because they may also sense a growing popularity for this type of approach among individual students and businesses approaching colleges for training.
- E-learning relies on good quality resources. The choice and design of these resources plays a vital part in helping students achieve their learning objectives.

Recent years have witnessed a dramatic increase in the impact of ICT on both the production of teaching and learning resources and in the nature of the resources themselves. This is no doubt partly because of the potential ICT possesses for improving the quality and effectiveness of learning resources as well as the obvious virtues of automation, capacity, interactivity and 'provisionality' (the relative ease of changing a learning resource). However, there must surely also be a case for ICT being seen as a means of delivering learning to yet greater numbers of students in a more flexible and cost-efficient manner, and this ideology is at the heart of e-learning pedagogies, which are increasingly accessed by students through a VLE. Some contend that digital learning is empowering and democratizing in the way that it challenges traditional teaching pedagogy and assumptions of traditional knowledge formation. However, for others, the extension of digital learning outside traditional institutions 'curricularizes' leisure and enters learning into the field of 'edutainment' rather than creating genuine new knowledge (Buckingham et al. 2001).

E-learning takes many forms and the literature utilizes a host of terms to describe broadly similar concepts which quite often overlap in meaning. It is often described as any application of digital technology that aids the core business of learning establishments, *including* their management, such as enrolments and course fee management, whereas BECTA defines the concept of e-learning as only 'those parts of ILT which directly support effective learning and teaching' (Hill 2008: 9).

Our definition of e-learning includes:

- *Distance learning*: students are taught and assessed solely through online resources and means, where tutors and students rarely, if ever, meet each other. Courses are flexibly designed to meet individual requirements by removing barriers that prevent attendance on more traditional courses and therefore usually include arrangements for people to learn at the time, place and pace that suits their circumstances.
- *Blended learning*: students are taught and assessed using a mix of both online and non-electronic resources, usually blending distance learning with face-to-face methodologies. Blended learning pedagogies themselves vary

enormously in the extent to which online resources are used, perhaps just for occasional homework through to courses where students meet up on perhaps only three study days a year and then complete the remainder of their course online. The quality of tutorial support and guidance is vital to the success of any such model.

- MOOCs: freely available universal access to educational courses that anyone can follow online. They have been available in different guises for some time, notably the Open University's OpenLearn programme, rebadged in 2012 as 'Futurelearn'. However, the availability of MOOCs is rising exponentially following the launch of three major US providers: Coursera, edX and Udacity. In 2015 the Coursera learning platform had over 1,000 different courses available and almost 14 million students compared with 4.5 million in 2013. Programmes are created and designed by universities and organizations across the globe and uploaded to the host site. They are available in an array of subjects including android programming, forensic science, cataract surgery, human rights and psychology, and some have the option to purchase a verified certificate on completion. A list of some of the latest MOOCs on offer can be found at www.mooc-list.com.

- 'xMOOCS' also exist. These follow the same idea as MOOCs but are not open-licensed and are copyrighted for in-house use only. They are usually structured to increase the scalability of learning within a specific environment and tend to resemble a traditional pedagogy, but through a different medium. As such they are considered as technology *enhanced* resources as many of the courses on offer tend to follow a strictly prescribed path which reproduces the knowledge of the course designer.

- 'cMOOCS' centre around attempts to connect communities of learners to answer and discuss each other's questions or to collaborate on ideas and may be considered more technology *enabled* as they alter the pedagogic structure of learning considerably and can encourage learners to access and develop their interests and knowledge from multiple sources. However, a blended approach of technology *enabled* and *enhanced* learning can be identified in many programmes.

Task 5.20

(a) List three advantages of using e-learning resources to the learner, tutor or the learning organization.

(b) List three disadvantages of using e-learning resources to the learner, tutor or the learning organization.

(c) Now review Table 5.1. How far do you agree with the advantages/disadvantages listed?

Table 5.1 Some advantages and disadvantages of incorporating e-learning resources into curriculum programmes for learners, teachers and/or organizations

Advantages	Disadvantages
Accessibility to learning – portable devices improve coverage and access to programmes Intuitive interesting design incorporating multi-media can make learning accessible and fun	Potentially deepens divide between those with and without IT and appropriate skills
Busy adults prefer flexible learning arrangements which fit round their lives and they like to work at their own pace – e-learning can make it easy to revisit parts of a course whenever necessary	Learners need reasonably up-to-date, reliable and appropriate IT equipment and skills to access programmes
Wider choices of assessment strategies can be integrated into courses – for example, video, audio, discussions, presentations	Deadlines for qualifications can limit flexibility. Any online discussions with other learners and availability of tutors often means that in practice there is still a timetable
IT accessibility options can be used to widen inclusivity in learning. Embeds IT skills	Learners need to be self-motivated to keep working largely on their own with distance support
E-learning is more cost-effective for larger cohorts of students	Tutor is unlikely to be able to 'get to know' students individually and wider experience of 'campus learning' is lost
Reduced overheads in terms of buildings and administrative procedures. Learning can be designed to be differentiated	Strategy requires flexible, supportive and highly motivated teachers and both broad and deep subject knowledge to ensure resources are adapted and updated
Timely feedback and automatic grading can occur	Assessment can tend towards multiple-choice and peer assessment rather than longer answers to perhaps test more depth of knowledge
For employers, causes less disruption of work schedules, training funds are better utilize. It can target specific training needs as employees can tackle only those modules they need without having to take an entire course	Courses are often non-credit-bearing and practical subjects lack opportunities for direct experience. Retention rates on MOOCs are low at about 10 per cent according to Coursera (Koller 2012)

Task 5.21

It has been suggested that elements of one of the courses you teach could be redesigned as an e-learning module. Students would be expected to use self-study packages, work at their own pace, and use a range of resources in addition to tutorial support as part of a blended learning programme. Consider the following.

(a)   Which elements might it be possible to deliver through e-learning? Why have you chosen these elements as the most appropriate for e-learning?
(b)   What would be the major advantages and disadvantages of using e-learning for parts of the course you have chosen?
(c)   In order for e-learning to be integrated successfully into your course, what organizational elements would need to change in your establishment (e.g. timetabling)?
(d)   What training would you and your colleagues need to enhance your skills and to enable you to support e-learning most effectively?

Selecting e-learning resources

Great care must be taken when choosing and preparing resources for e-learning and when writing the instructions or guides that explain to the learners how to achieve the most from them. The best e-learning resources use high-quality, carefully designed and researched resources such as interactive video links to online journals, audio files, matching activities, quizzes, webquests, discussion boards and web conferences; in fact, anything that can be accessed online. E-learning materials cannot be written like an ordinary textbook.

Just as with teaching resources used in the classroom, it is essential to evaluate and review online resources to ensure that they are not just 'one-way' but are interactive. You do not get the same instant feedback of the classroom where, if the resource is ineffective, learners will soon let you know. A final point to remember is that when preparing online resources a teacher must be aware of the reading level and IT skills within the group. If resources are written in an abstract, technical or complex manner, or if they rely on complicated or expensive technology, they are unlikely to be accessed and utilized to their full potential.

Sustainability of e-learning resources

Resources take a great deal of time, thought and effort to produce, individualize and tailor to learning outcomes and individuals, and it is only when teachers believe that innovation offers value beyond current practice that new practices are adopted (Deaney and Hennessy 2007). Furthermore, there are many and various practical constraints in using new technologies in the learning process that cause considerable barriers to this perception. Given these challenges it makes sense to reuse, update, adapt and share resources and best practice with other teachers. Using existing resources as a base and adapting them for your own teaching saves time and acts as a stimulus for you to try out new ideas. You will probably already be familiar with the TES resource bank as well as others which encourage sharing as part of best practice. However, it is also worth considering how this might be done within your own learning environment using your networked computer systems, VLEs or cloud-based technologies which can all be harnessed to store resources in digital libraries or web-based repositories. Thinking through the depth of changes will considerably add to the sustainability and scalability of any resource reforms. Here, sustainability refers to how changes can be maintained and scalability refers to the ease with which change can be replicated throughout an establishment (Batchelor and Norrish 2005).

Task 5.22

Think about the resources you used this week in your teaching.

(a)   Where did they originate?

(b)   How have you adapted them?

(c)   Ask a teacher who teaches a similar subject what resources they find useful and why.

(d)   How do they compare with yours?

(e)   Ask another teacher, perhaps who teaches a different subject, what their favourite resource is and why.

(f)   Have you found this useful? Has it inspired you to adapt any resources for your own teaching?

(g)   Does your establishment have a resource bank? If not, is it something you could start, perhaps even within your own department?

The following are some ideas to consider to support resource sustainability when considering the development of a common, centrally-held resource bank:

- *Compatibility*: we tend to use readily available software to create our resources such as MS Office, Apple OpenOffice or Adobe, etc. On the whole they are compatible, but some are created using specialist software (e.g. CAD) that will only run on systems with identical software, so a standard suite of packages may need to be determined from the outset. Furthermore, if a VLE is being used to host resources it is likely that a mixture of both formal (e.g. articles, notes) and informal 'work in progress' documents (e.g. notes, sketches, essays, reports) will need to be catered for.

- *Storage*: will resources be stored on the web, on a network or as part of a VLE? Web-based storage means that you will need consistent access to the cloud or the network in most of your classrooms as well as at home, so you can access them when you need to. Is this possible?

- *Multiple copies*: it is almost guaranteed that at present there will be multiple versions of the same resource held on computer networks and VLEs which take up valuable and expensive storage space. Having a single repository for all commonly used resources (e.g. on e-safety) which all teachers can access means that when they are updated there is only one version to alter and teachers will always be accessing the most up-to-date version. Other areas can then be added for subject-specific resources, perhaps by year group. A standardized, but flexible, learning technology approach will help here.

- *Control and manage*: standards will need to be set to ensure that resources are saved in a particular way so they are accessible and easily identifiable. It may be the case that only certain people (e.g. an assigned information specialist) can upload resources for a particular department or subject, or that strict protocols are set out so that duplication is prevented or tracked.

- *Access*: if using a VLE, will students be able to interact with the resources dynamically or will they be using them in a read-only style format? In the former case you will need to make sure that the students have access to a COPY of the original resource rather than the original itself. This is best achieved by dividing access to resources between teachers and students.

- *Back it up*: make sure that wherever your resource bank is stored, it is backed up regularly. All that hard work could easily be lost if there is a server failure.

- *Organizational change*: if your establishment wishes to implement and sustain the flexibility to initiate discussions with tutors and peers using both electronic (mobile phone, email, chat rooms, texts, instant messaging) and face-to-face methods it is likely that managers, administrative staff, teachers and students will all need support and training to manage a significant change in organization and culture. Transformational change underpins effective use of a VLE, but it is possible to start, for example, by auditing all the resources each department or tutor uses and collating them in a repository based on your organization (e.g. by subject, by year, by department etc.) and removing all the duplicate, out of date and ineffective resources.

- *Cultural change*: for any change in practice to be sustained, a range of stakeholders must be involved in the process. The risks and benefits of change can be viewed in terms of the wider benefits to your institution but, in particular, how resource banks can improve content, delivery and administration to improve learning and teaching. Any change in working practices is complex as many are interconnected, but clear guidance and incorporating them into policies will help the process. Whatever the perceived barrier, it is vital that you have senior management support.

- *Recognition and scope*: undertaking change will require time and effort and it is essential that this is recognized and supported by senior staff and colleagues. Make sure you keep them in the communication loop before implementing any major changes, but be prepared to lead by example if necessary. If appropriate, why not ask students how they would prefer to use resources, in what format, when and where? This could be a project for a whole school to get involved in or a college department to investigate.

• *Staff training*: implementing these novel learning and teaching practices will require changes in institutional attitudes and practices and also a degree of staff training dependent on the scale and depth of the changes. It is imperative that appropriate time and resources are allocated for teacher training and to encourage them to not only discover existing resources but to be creative and innovative too.

E-safety

While e-safety is not a specific teaching resource, a teacher must be aware of the potential threats to learners associated with online resources, reinforce best practice and deal with any breaches of e-safety with appropriate reference to institutional policy. These policies will vary according to age group and the degree of vulnerability of students to potential issues. Resource banks for raising e-safety awareness in schools can be found at:

• http://digizen.org: backed by the Childnet International this website contains many resources including short films and quizzes about how to make informed choices and decisions;

• http://chatdanger.com: this interactive, quiz-based site has thought-provoking advice on how to keep safe and cope with day-to-day issues that learners might meet online including bullying, unsolicited contacts and the implications of posting messages, images and videos;

• http://safety.ask.fm/resources: is specifically tailored to a teacher perspective and has many up-to-date and interesting ideas for raising your own e-safety awareness and for teaching it.

E-safety can be taught as a separate subject but it should also be continually reinforced and incorporated into other subjects whenever appropriate. In particular, a common thread woven throughout the use of digital information and contacts mirrors one from the real world – that you should question how much you can trust the person, organization or information that you find.

Prior to planning any activity that uses digital technology as a resource, such as the internet, digital cameras or voice recorders, students should be made aware of any potential risks to their safety. The internet has significantly changed the way in which we communicate and seek information, including personal use of a much greater range of applications beyond the basics of word processing or email. The development of wi-fi technologies has enabled the use of portable technologies such as smartphones, netbooks, tablet PCs and e-readers to help us keep in touch while on the move and these, along with the explosion in social networking, have revolutionized the way that learning can be accessed. However, this also means that teachers need to be ever vigilant for potential security threats and proactively help students to become aware of the risks and pitfalls of using digital resources to create a safe learning environment. According to Evershed and Roper (2010: 77) 'safeguarding adults from inappropriate and or/inaccurate content and making undesirable contacts through, for example, social networking sites is everyone's responsibility'.

The Byron Review on digital safety (DCSF 2008) focuses on managing the risks associated with e-learning rather than attempting to prevent access to digital resources. The recommended safeguards include restricting access to certain websites, educating learners about the potential pitfalls of trusting material published on the internet, using virus checkers to detect malicious software and being circumspect with personal information. It also involves setting conventions and acceptable ground rules for using discussion boards and social networking sites, and sending emails. The approach to e-safety varies according to each educational establishment, but most often it will be available in the form of an acceptable use policy (AUP) formulated as an element of a much wider range of policies on appropriate behaviour.

Digital footprint

Almost daily there are revelations surrounding moments of ill judged 'over-sharing' being exposed through social media sites. Both students and teachers need to understand the impact that their digital footprint has on both their immediate and future privacy, employment prospects and security. It needs to be understood that even 'deleted posts' are only hidden and can re-emerge later from redistributed sites outside the original user's control. The following list are some examples of what to consider when using such sites.

- Never leave posts open to the public. Limit your sharing options so they are only visible to friends to reduce the risks of cyberbullying.
- Trading photos always carries risks and software can easily identify people and locations from the tags assigned to them.
- Using messaging apps such as Snapchat and WhatsApp which 'self-delete' are not as safe as some believe. Permanent screenshots can be made of messages before they are deleted.
- Don't believe everything you read. Anyone can place anything on the internet and it is important that this is understood when evaluating material from the web.
- Don't use passwords that bear any relationship to you or your loved ones. Mix it up with numbers and symbols.
- Never share personal information with anyone you don't personally know or trust.

Task 5.23

(a) How do you make your students aware of e-safety policy at your establishment?

(b) How do you encourage students to develop the necessary cognitive skills needed to validate internet sources and cross-check information before using it in their learning?

(c) What is your own digital footprint? Try searching for your own name on the internet. You may be surprised as to how much information is available.

(d) Look at the ask.fm website for teachers at http://safety.ask.fm.

If you have any suspicions about the misuse of digital resources you should inform the appropriate person in your institution. E-safety policy should be regularly discussed as part of your CPD and become central to any learner's educational practice.

5.8 Other resources

The role of library resources in supporting learning

Inspection reports and research into the use of libraries have drawn attention to a valuable but expensive learning resource frequently underused and undervalued. One of the main issues with library resources is that they are often mistakenly viewed as a 'warehouse' for books of marginal relevance to many of the practical subjects taught in the Post-14 Education and Training sector. However, in the last decade, this idea has changed significantly. E-journals and books can be easily accessed at any time, are cost-effective, require less paper and can be easy to file and locate. They are also increasingly available for downloading to e-readers and some online retailers allow a reader to browse inside books to judge their suitability before purchasing. It is a good idea to encourage students to access these to enhance knowledge and understanding before and after taught sessions. Some journals are also readily available online and many larger organizations provide students with a wide range of online databases from which to choose via their e-library.

Libraries have become much more than just about the written word. The growth of more assignment-driven courses, assessment criteria that include research skills and processing information, and an increase in the number of part-time adult learners who work independently, have brought radical changes to the 'old college library', turning it, in many cases, into a learning resource centre. In such centres, the range of resources available is obviously important but the atmosphere, the provision of spaces for different types of work, and the skills support available are equally important. The JISC report (2006) emphasizes the need for particular attention in the design of new learning spaces. Awareness of the learning environment and its effect on learning and motivation has long been recognized. It is clear that the lines between learning and social environments are becoming blurred. The role of the library, for example, has changed dramatically over the last decade. Libraries are now considered to be key elements of the community where access to resources should be available to all. These spaces have become much more people-centred, interactive hubs, rather than hideouts and places of isolation. However, some learners still prefer to work in quiet areas that are set aside for reading and thinking.

The emergence of the internet café illustrates the benefits of open access spaces where individual activity coexists in mutually supportive and collaborative surroundings. The opportunities for peer support to enhance less structured or informal learning atmospheres are optimized. A fundamental difference to the design of learning spaces is the change in attitude to that of 'enabling, rather than controlling, access to learning' (JISC 2006: 8). Learning spaces that are designed to encourage and foster the coexistence of informal and formal learning are a feature of modern design, as is mobile technology and greater use of audio-visual resources such as webcams and video conferencing/streaming. Innovative 'e-borrow' schemes in many libraries have become mainstream, where laptops and digital equipment can be borrowed in the same way as books, and 'group breakout' areas allow students to borrow a room in which to practise their presentation skills.

Task 5.24

(a) What role(s) does the library resource centre play in your institution?

(b) How important is your library resource centre in the development of your students' skills and abilities? How, if at all, would your students' learning suffer if you did not have a learning resource centre?

(c) What changes would you like to see to the learning resource centre in your institution to make it better able to support learning? Think broadly: for example, range of resources, layout, staffing, access and so on.

(d) Design a creative learning environment – what digital technologies would you include?

(e) What are the implications for enabling as opposed to controlling learning spaces?

Development of student skills in using learning resources

While it may be accurate to say that students now have access to more data and a wider range of resources than ever before, this is of little consequence unless they also have the relevant IT, information and media literacy skills to research and critically interrogate the resources available. Such skills are developed through investigating, analysing, synthesizing and evaluating data to create information from which opinions can be formed. According to Evershed and Roper (2010: 66):

> such learners will be more likely to develop appropriate criticality and thinking skills, recognize more easily the consequences of actions and constructively question the actions of others. These 'higher' [cognitive] skills form the scaffolding required to create learners with abilities to problem-solve, innovate and create new knowledge.

The question of how best to facilitate this process of thinking and learning has become more pressing in recent years because of the changing patterns in the sector which demand students to undertake complex assignments that frequently require research. Without the necessary information-handling skills, many adult learners who may not have studied since school can find the array of resources facing them very daunting. Many professions, including the police, nursing and teaching, are required to demonstrate critical reflection as part of their training and the emphasis is on teachers facilitating learning through appropriate and effective resources so that learners feel empowered and critical reflection becomes an intrinsic part of how students learn to learn.

Resources and copyright

When creating resources or directing students to the array of online resources, it is important to understand the limitations that copyright legislation imposes. Most educational institutions or centres hold a licence administered by the Copyright Licensing Authority (CLA) and this varies between HE, FE, schools, adult education (AE) establishments and language schools and depends on whether your establishment is situated in England and Wales or Scotland. However, according to the CLA (2011), education licences generally allow teachers to:

- copy and share extracts or articles from millions of UK and international books, journals and magazines;
- make digital copies by scanning or retyping for distribution to pupils, parents and teachers who have access to an institution's secure network;
- use copies with digital whiteboards, VLEs and in presentations for teaching or training purposes;
- allow digital copies to be made (certain licences) from e-books or e-journals to be downloaded, printed out and stored by students or stored on a VLE or course-restricted intranet.

Task 5.25

Find out what the CLA licence in your own establishment allows you to copy by accessing the CLA website (www.cla.co.uk/Licencesforeducation) and following the links to your own type of establishment.

Continuing professional development

In 2013 it became no longer mandatory for teachers in the sector to gain QTLS and training budgets were relinquished directly to schools and other teaching establishments. However, the ability to utilize digital resources and technology in teaching remains spiky and uneven. The Digital Skills Committee report (2015: 49–50) states that there is a need for increased investment in CPD, as 'new teachers develop the required skills, knowledge and understanding but quickly become out of date as technologies move quickly'. It goes on to state that the future of a digital workforce is 'being let down by inconsistent training for teachers' and that central leadership and coordination is essential.

The *Harnessing Technology Review* (BECTA 2009b) aimed at narrowing the gap between those with and those without home access to digital technologies. The main aims of the resultant policy were to transform the delivery of teaching and learning, take learning to hard-to-reach students and improve the efficiency and effectiveness of teaching using strategies such as e-learning. It is clear that teachers are expected to model effective practice in using digital technologies. However, to do so, teachers themselves must keep up to date not only in their own specialist teaching subject but also in using technology to enhance learning opportunities for their students.

Most teachers feel confident with the basics such as word processing and email, but many remain uncertain of the wider implications and benefits of using technologies in their own teaching. Discussions with colleagues suggest that this is not because staff are resistant to technology and change, but rather they feel unsupported and, more importantly, uninformed. Indeed 'lack of confidence or competence with ICT was cited by 38 per cent [of college staff] as reasons for low use' (BECTA 2007: 7). For example, if you do not know what a podcast is you are unlikely to use one as a vehicle for updating your own CPD or in your own teaching; CPD for teachers is crucial to boost confidence and to maximize the potential of using any new resource whether it is digital or not.

For CPD on using digital resources, there are many excellent free online tutorials and videos. You could investigate the many free resource banks available online or try some of the techniques suggested in some of the many books available on e-learning skills, such as Clarke (2008), which give tutorials and practical advice on creating IT resources. There are also many private companies that offer courses and it might be something that you need to look into for your next appraisal or review. From experience, it will increase your chances of attending these courses if you are willing to cascade your new knowledge to others. Alternatively, like many teachers employed in the Post-14 Education and Training sector, you could simply sit down at a computer and experiment.

An important aspect of teacher training in any sector is that of the placement, any peer observations and the role of the mentor. Evidence suggests that a key factor in determining the contribution of the mentor appears to be the level of confidence in their ability to use ICT, both personally and in the classroom, which in turn has an effect on both the nature and range of the support given to the trainee teacher (Muttona et al. 2006: 1). In the light of the standards and guidance for the training of tutors in the Post-14 Education and Training sector (DfES 2004c) where there is a clear emphasis on the centrality of the mentoring role, this has implications in terms of the training and upskilling of mentors as well as tutors.

Links to the Professional Standards for Teachers and Trainers in Education and Training

Professional values and attributes

1 Reflect on what works best in your teaching and learning to meet the diverse needs of learners

4 Be creative and innovative in selecting and adapting strategies to help learners to learn

Professional knowledge and understanding

7 Maintain and update knowledge of your subject and/or vocational area

12 Understand the teaching and professional role and your responsibilities

Professional skills

14 Plan and deliver effective learning programmes for diverse groups or individuals in a safe and inclusive environment

15 Promote the benefits of technology and support learners in its use

20 Contribute to organisational development and quality improvement through collaboration with others

6

Assessment

6.1 What is Chapter 6 about?

The formal and informal assessment of students is becoming a large part of the work of teachers throughout the Post-14 Education and Training sector. Although external awarding bodies may offer guidance and training with respect to assessment, and assessor awards aim to equip tutors with the ability to assess students taking a wider range of qualifications (see Section 6.5), it is the responsibility of tutors in their classrooms to assess and monitor student progress. This chapter aims to provide a basis for developing tutors' expertise in creating and using the range of assessment strategies necessary to do this.

Section 6.2 looks at our experience of being assessed, both inside and outside an educational context, emphasizing the significance of key events both to ourselves and to our students. Our negative experiences could have resulted from errors in the construction and use of the assessment concerned and there will be a consideration of the concepts of validity and reliability and the role they play in the structure and use of assessment. Crucial too is the type of referencing used and its relation to the aims and objectives of learning, and this is considered in Section 6.3. Section 6.4 will examine a range of assessment techniques and their suitability for particular learning strategies, while Section 6.5 looks particularly at the elements of evidence-based assessment. However, over the past few years, policy on evidence-based assessment has changed and this will affect GCSEs and A levels currently being taught and developed. There is a move away from evidence-based coursework-assessed approaches towards summative exam assessment and this development will be examined in Section 6.6. Section 6.7 considers how experience of assessment itself can form the basis of positive student learning. Finally, if assessment is to be of any enduring value in the learning process, it must be appropriately recorded and reported and Section 6.8 considers how most effectively the reviewing of student progress can be achieved.

6.2 Assessment: ourselves and our students

KEY ISSUES

How might assessment affect teachers and learners?

Why do we assess?

How might we improve the quality of assessment?

Just as many of us, consciously or unconsciously, tend to use those teaching strategies we experienced as learners, so our own experience of being assessed plays a key role in the development of our repertoire as a teacher.

Task 6.1: Our own experience

(a) Consider the experiences you have had of being assessed, either in an educational setting, such as the 11+, GCSE, A level or vocational exam, or outside, such as scout or guide badges, life-saving awards or job interviews. Choose one example of assessment which had a positive effect and one which had a negative effect.

(b) Share these with the group. Are there particular features common to the group regarding what was positive or negative in their experiences?

At the risk of stating the obvious, assessment which had a positive effect on you was more likely to be that which you were successful at. But, quite apart from the high quality of your performance, this could have been because you were aware of what was required or that the assessment itself was a fair test of your learning. Conversely, negative experiences could have been the result of misunderstanding the nature of the assessment or not having any feedback on your performance. Figure 6.1 presents a list of remarks made by a range of students in lifelong learning settings about the assessment of their work.

Task 6.2: Assessing your students

(a) Repeat Task 6.1, only this time choose three examples of assessment you have recently completed with your students. How do you think they felt about these experiences?

(b) Share your views with the rest of the group.

Under the pressure of day-to-day teaching and training it's easy to forget the power and significance of assessment for ourselves when setting assessment tasks for our students. We can also be tempted to include assessment automatically in our programme of work without considering its appropriateness or the way in which it will affect individual or group learning.

'When we have a test, I forget everything straight afterwards.'

'Our teacher takes so long to mark our work, we've forgotten what it was about by the time we get it back.'

'I'd like more constructive criticism from our art tutor. She just says "Great" all the time. When I challenge her, she claims she doesn't want to be too prescriptive.'

'I was delighted to get 85 per cent for my last essay . . . until I discovered everyone in the group got between 85 and 95 per cent.'

'Our lecturer only points out what you get wrong at the bottom of a piece of work . . . never how you could have got it right.'

'My mate's dad does all his assignments. My mate just word-processes them. It doesn't seem to matter.'

'Our "Introduction to Italian" tutor refuses to assess us. He says if we did badly we'd lose interest. But all of us want to know how we're doing.'

'Everybody in our group passes everything. We're getting a bit worried.'

'We have to write our own assessment of ourselves on our report forms. I never say I'm good at anything because it sounds like I'm showing off.'

'I understand all the work but I'm no good at getting it down on paper.'

'Our teacher sets our exam paper. But, of all the topics she revised, only one came up.'

'We do a lot of presentations, which I reckon is unfair as some people are more extrovert than others.'

'We took the exam at the end of the course, so, by the time the teacher discovered I hadn't understood a lot, it was too late.'

'My work experience supervisor resented having me foisted on him, so when my college tutor visited me and asked him how I was doing he dropped me in it.'

'I got confused by all the possible answers in the multiple choice test so I just started guessing.'

Figure 6.1 Reactions to assessment

Task 6.3: Why assess?

Choose one of the assessment examples from Task 6.2.

- Why did you assess at this particular moment? To check learning, because of awarding body requirements, the structure of the course (end of a module or unit), institutional demands?
- Why did you choose this form of assessment? Is it easy to use, prescribed by the awarding body?
- What feedback was there to students? How was it done? How will it help them to learn?
- What action will be taken as a result of assessment? Will you cover the same content in a different way? Will individual students get particular attention?

One reason for our positive and negative experiences could be that the assessment itself did not measure what it was intended to, or was invalid. So, a written exam is an invalid test of the ability to speak a language. A conversation with a native speaker would be more valid. More valid still, arguably, would be the ability to perform a range of oral tasks in a variety of contexts. Experienced drivers often claim the driving test to be an invalid means of assessing the ability to drive, suggesting the test is only a valid means of assessing the ability to pass the test itself. The introduction of a written test to supplement the practical driving test was criticized by some as an invalid method of assessing knowledge and awareness that is only demonstrable in real driving conditions. Those unfortunate enough to take a driving test on several occasions should, all things being equal, have the same chance of passing it each time, since the examiners base their judgements on a series of objectively demonstrated practical skills. The test, then, is reliable. It could be made more reliable if the same skills were required to be demonstrated on more than one occasion to several examiners, thus, for example, making examinees' nerves and any individual examiner's subjectivity less influential.

Task 6.4: Rating assessment methods

Table 6.1 shows a series of learning tasks and the method selected to assess each one. Decide, with a colleague, using a scale of 0–5, where 0 is low and 5 is high, how you would rate the methods in each case for both validity and reliability.

Table 6.1 Rating methods of assessment

Learning	Assessment method	Validity	Reliability
The causes of the First World War	Essay		
Empathizing with the emotional problems of 16-year-olds	Multiple choice test		
Memorizing chemical elements	Short answer questions		
Metaphor patterns in *Antony and Cleopatra*	Open book exam (text taken into exam and used for reference)		
Dribbling in football	Skills test		
Typical high-street shopping habits	Assignment/research task		
Knowledge of road signs	Written test		
Improving accent in a foreign language	Peer assessment		
Using 'Table' in Microsoft Word	Self-assessment		
Punctuation	Oral exam		
General receptionist duties	Discussion		
Dealing with customer complaints	Role play		
Domestic mobility for the physically disabled	Case study of physically disabled client		

Satterly (1990: 224, original emphasis) points out that validity and invalidity are not absolute qualities of assessment: '. . . one cannot meaningfully talk of an assessment or test being valid or invalid, but only of its *interpretation* as valid or invalid *for some specified purpose*'.

Task 6.5

Where validity or reliability was low in the examples above, how could you increase it, or what other method would be a more valid or reliable one?

A valid assessment method is one which tests whether the aims and objectives of a learning experience have been achieved. Discussion with a student would have a fairly low validity rating where general receptionist duties were concerned. Much more valid would be observation by a tutor in a real or simulated situation with a structured checklist or questionnaire relating to the skills and abilities speci-fied in aims and objectives such as handling phone calls and dealing with clients. Although an essay would have high validity in testing a student's grasp of the causes of the First World War, allowing discursive analysis of complicated pro-cesses, it could be relatively unreliable. A detailed marking scheme would increase reliability by ensuring that the same abilities and qualities were being credited for all students by all assessors.

6.3 Referencing

KEY ISSUES

The type of referencing we select will depend on the nature of our aims and objectives.

Criterion referencing is arguably the most effective at giving a picture of learning achievement.

To find out how effectively learning has taken place, we need to compare a per-formance, a demonstration of skill, knowledge or ability with something else as a way of characterizing it. This choice of a relation or correspondence is a choice of referencing type. Our selection of referencing type should follow from the aims and objectives we have set for student learning.

Should we wish to compare an individual student's achievement with that of the group they are a member of – whether that be a class, year group or national cohort – we would select *norm referencing*. The assumption here is that the per-formances of any group follow a normal curve of distribution – put simply, small percentages achieving high and low scores, with the majority achieving average marks. Raw scores are therefore adjusted to fit this normal curve and a picture given of any individual's performance in comparison with the group as a whole. This approach has drawn criticism from those claiming standards have fallen in public examinations. Norm referencing, they argue, bears no relation to absolute standards of achievement: should standards actually fall, grade distribution would mask this by remaining the same. Its defenders claim that it is fairer to assume a conformity of ability in successive year cohorts than exact conformity of question or overall exam paper level of difficulty. Those hostile to 11+ testing have argued that norm referencing allows authorities to select at random according to the resources they choose to allocate to selective education. A further argument against norm referencing challenges any claim it may make to tell us anything of value about an individual's learning achievement.

An approach that does do this, it is argued, is *criterion referencing*. Here the correspondence is between the performance and an objective standard or criterion. The difference between this and norm referencing can be seen in the following example: X may be regarded by all in her group as having by far the best singing voice, but measured against criteria relating to, say, enunciation, pitch, tone, interpretation and expressiveness, she may fare differently.

Task 6.6

(a) Reflect on your own experience of both norm and criterion referenced assessment.

(b) Compare your experiences with the rest of the group. How did they help or hinder your learning and overall educational achievement?

Criterion referencing may be combined with *grade referencing*, where criteria and levels of achievement relating to them are connected with points on a scale, literal or numerical. But they need not be and, as we shall see in Section 6.7, much recording of achievement in Post-14 Education and Training is descriptive of that achievement with little or no use of grades or marks.

Other types of referencing widely used in the sector include *comparisons with a scale of dependence* moving to independence, and *ipsative referencing*, where the comparison is with own previous performances. Both of these are prominent features of assessment of those with learning needs.

Task 6.7

(a) Choose two assessment tasks you have recently set. What type of referencing did you use in each case? Why did you choose them?

(b) Share this with the rest of the group. Were particular referencing types prominent in certain subject areas or on specific courses?

The selection of referencing type is, as we mentioned earlier, connected with your aims and objectives. If, for example, a central aim was about skill development, then ipsative referencing should be part of your overall assessment. And, as we shall now see, it is your aims and objectives which should also determine the assessment techniques and strategies you use.

6.4 Assessment techniques

KEY ISSUES

Assessment techniques are used in specific contexts.

These contexts may limit our freedom to use particular strategies.

Where possible, assessment strategies should be related to the aims and objectives of learning.

Before looking at particular assessment techniques or strategies, it is worth considering the contexts in which we intend to deploy them. Rowntree (1987) identifies a range of assessment features or modes. Assessment is variously formal or informal: at one extreme a degree finals paper, at the other, very generalized judgements made by a teacher as they observe an individual or group. It is formative or summative, its prime purpose being either to support student learning or, on the other hand, to gather information about it. It is continuous or terminal, taking place throughout a course of study or on its completion. It may focus on coursework or examinations, concern itself with process (the learning activities of students) or with product (something generated by that process, such as a drawing, an essay or a display, for example). The assessment may be internal, carried out by those within an institution or external (an examining body). Rowntree applies to assessment Hudson's (1966) distinction between convergent thinking, where students excel at a rational task with a single answer and divergent thinking, which thrives on open-ended tasks allowing creative freedom and imagination. And finally, he describes assessment as tending to be idiographic or nomothetic; that is, either concerned with characterizing or describing an individual's uniqueness, or more interested in comparing individuals with others in an attempt to arrive at a more general understanding of achievement.

Task 6.8

Consider the assessment you undertake as part of your teaching. Which of Rowntree's features can be accurately applied to it?

We will have more or less choice as to how we assess according to the context we work in. Our institution may, for example, prefer a particular examination board, require us to assess internally and continuously and report achievement terminally. But, where we do have choice, both the features of assessment and the particular strategies we use should be determined by the nature and purpose of learning, as expressed in our aims and objectives.

Task 6.9

Table 6.2 presents a set of aims with related objectives as well as a series of assessment strategies. Match the aims and objectives to the most suitable strategies.

Table 6.2 Choosing suitable assessment strategies

Aims		Objectives	Strategies
A	To exercise overall command of emergency services throughout a major incident	Maintain clear and accurate communications through changing circumstances	1 Objective/multiple choice test
B	To reflect on clinical practice	Evaluate positive and negative aspects of interactions with patients	2 Self-assessment
C	To handle TV interviews effectively	Demonstrate an ability to use appropriate body language on camera	3 Demonstration of skills/routine (e.g. resuscitation)
D	To be aware of a range of sources of information	Search the library catalogue by author, subject or title	4 Examination consisting of long essays
E	To develop and retain knowledge of costs of building materials	Know the costs of a variety of types of bricks	5 Role play
F	To understand the meaning of vocabulary	Define key words in a given passage	6 Interview
G	To bring about an awareness of health and safety matters	Indicate where fire exits are	7 Group discussion
H	To deal with major technical malfunctions	Describe action which would cancel or override malfunctions	8 Simulation exercise
I	To converse fluently in Spanish	Conduct a one-to-one conversation about everyday topics	9 Display
J	To identify major literary themes	Trace and describe ideas of kingship in Shakespeare's history plays	10 Short answer test

Table 6.2 *(Continued)*

Aims		*Objectives*	*Strategies*
K	To be able to support clients in expressing their emotions	Draw out clients' feelings about a traumatic incident	11 Seminar presentation
L	To monitor own progress	Aware of level of own achievement	12 Problem-solving exercise
M	To develop an argument and defend own views	Present an analysis of the causes of inflation and respond to questions from colleagues	13 Information-gathering exercise
N	To understand the structure of the British constitution	Describe broadly the functions of executive, legislature and judiciary	14 Peer assessment
O	To be able to give positive feedback	Appraise colleagues' work without giving rise to animosity	15 Audio/videotaping
P	To develop the capacity to work as a member of a team	Contribute ideas to a team project	16 Comprehension test
Q	To develop a sense of design	Able to use colour, shape and image to present a concept visually	17 Log/diary

A suggested matching for Table 6.2 is as follows:

A	8	G	3	M	11
B	17	H	12	N	10
C	15	I	6	O	14
D	13	J	4	P	7
E	1	K	5	Q	9
F	16	L	2		

Task 6.10

Now undertake a similar exercise with your own work. Consider the aims and objectives of a scheme of work, a series of sessions or of a single lesson. Look at the strategies you use to assess learning. How far do your strategies match your aims and objectives? Are there more suitable techniques you might use?

We have seen above that there can be at least two reasons for our use of some assessment strategies rather than others: a syllabus or our institution may require us to follow a particular pattern of assessment; or certain strategies may be more or less appropriate for the learning we wish our students to experience; that is, they fit our aims and objectives. But there are other reasons why teachers use particular assessment techniques and not others.

Task 6.11

Choose three assessment strategies you use frequently and three you never use. Apart from the two reasons specified above, are there further reasons for your using or not using those you have chosen?

When we conducted Task 6.11 with Diploma in Education and Training (DET) students, the following reasons came up most frequently. Time constraints often preclude the use of more elaborate assessment – teachers are often wary of allowing the assessment tail to wag the learning dog. Teachers themselves admit to lacking confidence in their skills to devise and use particular strategies, particularly more complex ones such as role play. Others doubt whether students themselves have the skills to deal with the demands of specific strategies, such as peer assessment. Many teachers feel they lack the resources to use certain techniques, for example, access to a video camera, a library or a PC. Teachers can be deterred by the comparative difficulty of some strategies – a log or diary are often cited – where they feel complex, often subjective judgements are required of them and there is the associated problem of reporting such achievement to third parties.

One of the reasons above mentions student skills. We saw in Chapter 3 how particular learning strategies suit some individuals rather more than others. Similarly, individuals find that particular assessment strategies allow them to perform to their maximum potential and differentiation in assessment, even when the same learning, the same knowledge or skills acquisition is being tested, offers them the flexibility to be able to do just this. Differentiation may mean selecting different assessment methods for different groups, or alternative tasks and questions within a given assessment exercise. Diploma in in Education and Training sector students have given the following examples of how they have used differentiation in their assessment:

- Men and women were placed in single-sex groups for a simulation exercise on a management course, after it was discovered that men in mixed-sex groups dominated the organization of the task, relegating the women to secondary roles.

- On a floristry course, some students with limited literary ability were examined for part of their assessment by oral interview.

- In a comprehension exercise, assessment material was provided using examples relating to students' ethnic or cultural background.

- Numeracy test papers were set in a student's first language.

> **Task 6.12**
>
> (a) Differentiation often raises the issue of equal opportunities. Discuss the examples above in your group. Do they give the students concerned a more equal opportunity of having their knowledge and skills properly assessed or an unfair advantage over others?
>
> (b) Do you use differentiation in your assessment? Do you now feel there are situations where you could and should use it?

6.5   Evidence-based and criterion referenced assessment

The use of evidence-based assessment, and particularly that relating to learning outcomes such as competences, has grown from changes in both work-related and vocational education and training as well as new programmes established by initiatives such as Curriculum 2000 and the Wolf Report (Wolf 2011). A range of education initiatives in the 1980s, such as the Certificate of Pre-vocational Education (CPVE) and the Technical and Vocational Education Initiative (TVEI), attempted to broaden the academic, subject-centred secondary and further education (FE) curricula to provide opportunities for learning and achievement for the many curricula excluded. Out of these initiatives grew the General National Vocational Qualification (GNVQ), but agreement on the nature and relationship of the general and vocational elements of Post-14 Education and Training is far from being reached (for a detailed treatment of 'vocationalism', see Chapter 1). However, such a broadening of the curriculum required assessment that was more flexible and equipped to measure a much wider range of demonstrated ability than previously. At the same time, new approaches to the assessment of work-based training were pioneered in the succession of initiatives launched to combat the spiralling youth unemployment of the early 1980s. As these developed, they became the template for a much broader range of work-based assessment strategies as the structural changes in the economy, such as the expansion of the service sector and the contraction of manufacturing, meant that a workforce was required which was more flexible and adaptable, equipped with generic, transferable skills rather than specific skills limited to a narrow occupational role. There was also disenchantment with the capacity of existing vocational qualifications to guarantee the ability to perform occupational tasks satisfactorily at work and to offer opportunities for development and progression. The review of the National Council for Vocational Qualifications (NCVQ) led to a framework of National Vocational Qualifications (NVQs) with occupational standards set by 'industry-led bodies'.

There are four major issues at the centre of the debate about competence-based assessment. The first concerns charges that it is unable to distinguish between levels of performance. Competences cannot be graded: you are either competent at something or you are not. You cannot be 'very', 'fairly' or 'just about' competent. Critics argue that motivation is therefore affected; there is simply no incentive for students to strive to do better, when a less thorough performance could be sufficient evidence to gain a 'competence'. Defenders of this approach to assessment point out that it is its avoidance of grading which is its strength; that individual achievement is related to performance criteria and underpinning knowledge rather than being compared to the achievement of other students or some absolute, unattainable standard.

The second issue concerns the extent to which competences focus on the performance or behavioural aspects of learning, rather than, say, cognitive aspects which are not so easily demonstrable publicly. While some may be happy with this focus for more obviously skill-based learning, it is argued that its application is inappropriate to professional contexts which require greater knowledge and understanding, such as nurse education, social work training, teacher education or police training. Many Diploma in Education and Training courses are now assessed using an evidence-based approach. The five competences shown in Figure 6.2 are examples from one such course.

Task 6.13: Sufficient evidence?

In pairs, specify the evidence you think would be sufficient for the demonstration of each of the five competences shown in Figure 6.2. As a group, to what extent was the public demonstration alone considered sufficient evidence?

Even though these five competences are concerned with classroom practice and therefore appear to be performance-oriented, it is likely that each needed supplementary evidence. We can observe (1) teaching approaches, methods and strategies but how do we judge if they are appropriate to learners' needs? Equally, we can observe a teacher establish and operate a rule (5), but how are we to know if they are themselves aware of the rule's significance in learning situations? The relationship between knowledge and performance has been considered in some detail (see Wolf and Black 1990) with some arguing that knowledge evidence waters down competence-based assessment, since assessing performance should

---

Core competence: demonstrate within a teaching programme practical presentation skills, flexible modes of delivery, awareness of social and cultural issues and skill in classroom management.

Specific competences:

1   can use a variety of teaching approaches, methods and strategies appropriate to learners' needs;
2   can manage a variety of learning environments to the optimum advantage of learners;
3   can demonstrate a range of communication skills and techniques which meet learners' needs (including non-verbal);
4   can demonstrate and create positive attitudes towards equal opportunities in a variety of learning situations;
5   can demonstrate an awareness of stereotyping, labelling and rule-making and their significance in learning situations.

Figure 6.2 Examples of competences used to assess a DET course

equally be an assessment of any knowledge underpinning it. On the other hand, three major inquiries into lifelong learning qualifications highlighted the importance of supplementing performance evidence with that from a range of other assessment strategies, particularly externally set and marked tests (Beaumont 1995; Capey 1995; Dearing 1996).

The third issue concerns the reliability of competence-based assessment. Although, on the surface, performance criteria can be spelled out in detail, assessors' interpretation of such criteria can vary. Systems of internal and external verification do, of course, help to minimize such variation but, as Wolf (1993: 17) points out:

> the [assessment] process is complex, incremental, and, above all, *judgemental*. The performance observed – directly, or in the form of artefacts – is *intrinsically* variable: one person's playing of a piano piece, one person's essay, is by definition not exactly the same as another's, and cannot be fitted mechanistically to either a written list of criteria or an exemplar.

Task 6.14: Acceptable evidence

If possible, this exercise should be carried out in curriculum groups, or in groups of closely allied subjects (e.g. hairdressing and health and beauty). Select a task which a student would be asked to perform as a part of their assessment. If you have a common framework such as an NVQ, agree a level at which such a task would be assessed. Now, individually, try to describe – *in your own language*, not that of a set of performance criteria, and in as much detail as possible – what you would accept as performance evidence for the successful completion of this task. Compare your accounts.

Finally, some argue that a competence-based system makes learning assessment-led. That is, for students at least, one eye is always on the competences that have yet to be awarded and the entire course of study then becomes skewed towards ticking off such competences. This can lead to extreme behaviour illustrated by the following (true) incident which occurred on a Diploma in Education and Training course some time ago. A college student had been knocked down by a vehicle on campus and (fortunately only slightly) injured. A Diploma in Education and Training student, a member of the college staff, had, being a first-aider, attended and dealt with the incident. Arriving late for his class, he explained the reason for his lateness. The tutor made a concerned inquiry about the injured student. 'He'll be OK,' was the reply, 'but what a stroke of luck! I've been waiting for something like this to come along for months to give me the evidence for that health and safety competence!'

Evidence-based assessment in action

Example 6.1 presents assessment material relating to a Level 2 NVQ Beauty Therapy programme, Example 6.2 presents material relating a BTEC Level 2 Health and Social Care 1st Diploma programme and Example 6.3 presents assessment relating to Functional Skills English Level 1. Familiarize yourself with these and then complete Task 6.15.

Example 6.1

Canterbury College Swale Campus Beauty Therapy Department

Unit 305 Summative Observation Tracking Sheet

Assessor .....Lily Mac Rew....,   Candidate Name: ....   Date: ....12.3.15.....

Start Time: ...10.55...   Finish Time: ....12.10....

Unit 305 – Provide body massage	Criteria	1 Mark	2 Marks	3 Marks	Comments	Score
Use suitable consultation techniques to identify treatment objectives	2	Basic consultation Example: uses open and closed questions, checks for contra-indications, identifies the treatment objectives correctly.	Good consultation Example: positive body language, uses open and closed questions to identify contra-indications, general health, lifestyle and expectations; identifies the treatment objectives and any factors that may limit or restrict the treatment.	Thorough consultation Example: positive body language , uses open and closed questions to identify contra-indications general health, lifestyle and expectations how client feels about their body and what improvement they would like to achieve; identifies the treatment objectives and any factors that may limit or restrict the treatment allows the client to ask any questions to confirm understanding. ✓	Good communication skills Contra-indications discussed previous treatments discussed Avoid varicose vein – legs discussed lifestyle, diet, water, objective – ease muscle tension.	③
Carry out a body analysis	3	Carries out a basic analysis, identifies	Carries out a good analysis,	Carries out a detailed analysis, identifies	Postural checks completed.	

Example 6.1 *(Continued)*

					Handwritten notes
		client's posture, records findings	client's posture and any figure faults, body type, records findings	client's posture and any figure faults, body type, and condition (ie soft fat, hard fat, cellulite), records findings	Sensory tests discussed skin type, body type etc
Provide clear recommendations to the client	5	A basic treatment plan is recommended Example: explains treatment procedure and any adaptations to meet client treatment needs	A good treatment plan is recommended Example: explains treatment procedure and any adaptations to meet client treatment needs based on factors identified during consultation (lifestyle, medication (if any), contra-indications, results of postural diagnosis), a choice of products to be used	A thorough treatment plan is recommended. Example: explains treatment procedure and any adaptations to meet client treatment needs based on factors identified during consultation (lifestyle, medication(if any), contra-indications, results of postural diagnosis), a choice of products to be used, adaptation of massage movements to suit client treatment needs, allows the client to ask questions about the treatment plan.	Explained movements to be used. Let client select oil Modification – varicose veins. Concentrate on shoulders. ③
Use and adapt massage techniques correctly to suit	10	Adapts the massage routine to suit client treatment objectives.	Adapts the massage routine to suit client treatment objectives,	Adapts the massage routine to suit client treatment objectives, muscle and fat type taking into account	Checked pressure and comfort throughout – Adapted according to ③

Example 6.1 *(Continued)*

client treatment needs.		Uses a variety of movements, movements are even and flowing, uses appropriate pressure for the client	muscle and fat type. Carries out massage movements correctly and fully with even flow showing variations in rate and rhythm according to treatment objectives, uses appropriate pressure for the client.	findings of the postural diagnosis. The whole routine flows throughout, uses appropriate pressure for the client, checks the client's comfort and wellbeing at appropriate times.	response from client
Complete the treatment to the satisfaction of the client	11	The treatment is completed within the agreed time and brought to a satisfactory close.	The treatment is completed within the agreed time, brought to a satisfactory close, excess massage medium is removed from the skin correctly.	The treatment is completed within the agreed time, brought to a satisfactory close, excess massage medium is removed from the skin correctly, the client is asked a feedback and is allowed sufficient time to get dressed.	1 hour 15 mins. feedback given. ③
Provide suitable aftercare advice	13	Basic aftercare advice. Example: how to deal with possible contra-actions, product(s) to use, importance of rest	Good level of aftercare advice Example: how to deal with possible contra-actions, product(s) to	Excellent aftercare advice Example: how to deal with possible contra-actions, product(s) to use, importance of rest and relaxation.	Allergy advice, tension – return once a week – Swedish massage, cause of treatments, avoid smoking, alcohol – expining water, diet, exercise, products-scrub ③

Example 6.1 *(Continued)*

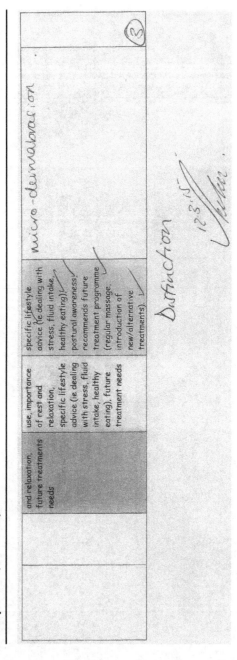

| | and relaxation, future treatments needs | use, importance of rest and relaxation, specific lifestyle advice (ie dealing with stress, fluid intake, healthy eating), future treatment needs | specific lifestyle advice (ie dealing with stress, fluid intake, healthy eating), postural awareness, recommends future treatment programme (regular massage, introduction of new/alternative treatments) | micro-dermabrasion |

Distinction

12.3.15

Example 6.2

Student Name	
Assignment Title and Number	Assignment 2: One-to-One And Group Interviews

Assignment criteria:

Unit No.		Pass						Merit				Distinction				
	Grading criteria assignment meets	P 3	P 4					M 2				D 1				
1	Grading criteria met by student	A	A					A				A				
	Grading criteria met by student															
	Grading criteria met by student															

Assessor Feedback:
Main Strengths

P3, P4, M2, D1 awarded
Unit grade Distinction

You have taken part in the one to one communication task in which you showed good use of appropriate language. You were also able to demonstrate good listening skills. You have been able to show and describe this very well . You have ensured that the reader of your essay would have a good understanding and knowledge of the topic you took part in and the barriers you faced. You have also described the strengths and weaknesses in this interaction; you again have ensured that the reader would fully understand these.

You have also taken part in the group communication task and you were able to contribute effectively to the conversation. Please see all the points above as you have also achieved them for this interaction.

Suggestions in how to improve

- Ensure you check all the criteria before submitting
- Please make sure you are getting someone to read through all of your written work before you hand it in
- Ensure that you use speech marks where you are actually quoting what others have said
- When talking about things you have done with others you need to use 'our' not 'are'
- Look at using the LRC for drop in sessions when someone will be able to proof read your assignments

General comments

Signed (Assessor)	G. Winder	Date	24/10/14
Signed (Assessor)		Date	
Signed (Assessor)		Date	
Signed (Assessor)		Date	

Example 6.3

Functional Skills English Level 1: Speaking, Listening and
Communication Assessment Record Sheet

Please complete the following information (a separate sheet for each learner).

Learner name:	Learner number:	Centre number:
	0117779	6B 70

plastic surgery

Activity: Formal	Date: 1 10 14	Activity: Informal	Date: 8/10/14
Please use the space below to note the context of the activity, how it was organised and any learner support.		Please use the space below to note the context of the activity, how it was organised and any learner support.	
Japan - excellent eye contact, fab info, great tone of voice, laid back - but appropriately so - excellent		great questioning techniques, excellent pictures, great tone of voice.	

Level 1: Take full part in formal and informal discussions and exchanges that include unfamiliar subjects.

The grid should be applied on a 'best fit' basis. To achieve a Level 1 overall a learner should have met each of the Level 1 standards at least once.

Just Below Level 1	✓	Achieved Level 1	✓
Makes some relevant contributions to discussion		Makes relevant and extended contributions to discussions	✓
Sometimes allows for and responds to others' input		Allows for and responds to others' input	✓
Some use made of preparation to the formal discussion of ideas and opinions		Preparation supports contribution to the formal discussion of ideas and opinions	✓
Makes some different kinds of contributions to discussions		Makes different kinds of contributions to discussions	✓
Some information/points of view presented clearly, with some use of appropriate language		Presents information/points of view clearly and in appropriate language	✓

Please tick the box if the learner has achieved Level 1:	
Centre summative comment:	
you research well, have an air of confidence and show commitment in every task you carry out.	

Assessor signature: *[signature]*   Date: 8/10/14

Please attach another page if you wish to make additional comments.

Task 6.15

What are the main similarities and differences between NVQ, BTEC and Functional Skills assessments?

Task 6.16

From the limited information available to you, how far does each piece of assessment answer criticisms of competence-based assessment that it:

- fails to distinguish levels of performance;
- focuses on performance/behaviour;
- can be unreliable;
- can be assessment-led?

It is likely that the professional skills required by teachers new to competence-based assessment are in two areas: first in devising and using strategies which produce the appropriate evidence to indicate competence and second in judging whether such evidence is acceptable.

Task 6.17: Devising assessment

In the same curriculum groups as Task 6.14, specify between two and five performance criteria. Now devise the strategies you would use which together could generate sufficient evidence to indicate competence with relation to all your criteria.

Some of the questions which frequently arise with regard to devising competence-based assessment and judging the acceptability of evidence are as follows.

- Are witness statements acceptable alone as third-party evidence or do they always need further verification?
- Should self-assessment be corroborated by supplementary evidence?
- How many times and in how many contexts should a skill be performed to establish a competence, bearing in mind that range statements and evidence indicators offered as guidance often specify content alone?
- How far is jointly authored/produced work acceptable as evidence?
- For how many competences can any one piece of evidence be acceptable?
- To what extent is a demonstration of competence dependent on the assessor's skill rather than the candidate's ability (in, say, a carefully managed review of progress)?

Task 6.18

How important were any of the above issues when you undertook Task 6.17? Were there any further issues which arose for your group?

6.6 Reform of GCSE and A level

Over the past few years, policy on evidence-based assessment has changed and this will affect GCSEs and A levels currently being taught and developed. There is a move away from evidence-based, coursework assessed approaches towards summative exam assessment. The 'new look' GCSEs have the following features.

1   A new grading scale of 9 to 1 will be used, with 9 being the top grade. This will allow greater differentiation between students and will help distinguish the new GCSEs from previous versions.

2   Assessment will be mainly by exam, with other types of assessment used only where they are needed to test essential skills.

3   There will be new, more demanding content, which has been developed by government and the exam boards.

4   Courses will be designed for two years of study – they will no longer be divided into different modules and students will take all their exams in one period at the end of their course.

5   Exams can only be split into 'foundation tier' and 'higher tier' if one exam paper does not give all students the opportunity to show their knowledge and abilities.

6   Resit opportunities will only be available each November in English language and maths.

For the new A levels:

1   Assessment will be mainly by exam, with other types of assessment used only where they are needed to test essential skills.

2   AS and A levels will be assessed at the end of the course. AS assessments will typically take place after one year's study and A levels after two. The courses will no longer be divided into modules and there will be no exams in January.

3   AS and A levels will be 'decoupled' – this means that AS results will no longer count towards an A level, in the way they do now.

4   AS levels can be designed by exam boards to be taught alongside the first year of A levels.

5   The content for the new A levels has been reviewed and updated. Universities played a greater role in this for the new qualifications than they did previously.

See www.gov.uk/government/publications/get-the-facts-gcse-and-a-level-reform for more information.

6.7 Assessment for learning

In their work with teachers, Paul Black, Dylan William and their colleagues (Black and William 1998; Black et al. 2002) found that:

> An assessment activity can help learning if it provides information to be used as feedback, by teachers, and by their pupils, in assessing

themselves and each other, to modify the teaching and learning activities in which they are engaged. Such assessment becomes 'formative assessment' when the evidence is actually used to adapt the teaching work to meet learning needs.

Their findings detail best practice of assessment for learning under four headings: questioning, feedback through marking, peer- and self-assessment and the formative use of summative tests.

Questioning

'Research has shown,' say Black et al., 'that many [teachers] leave less than one second after asking a question before, if no answer is forthcoming, asking another question, or answer their own question' (Rowe 1974, in Black et al. 2002: 5).

Task 6.19

In pairs, review one another's questioning practice. Consider the following points:

- Are you too hasty in asking a second question or answering the first yourself if no answer is forthcoming?
- For what purposes do you use questioning – to test learning and knowledge, to deepen understanding, to stimulate thinking and ideas, to establish a logical chain of thinking?
- Do you use mainly closed or open questions, those factual in nature, inviting one-word responses, with one right answer, or those wider in nature, capable of being answered in a variety of ways?
- Do you consider a number of student responses?
- Do you target and distribute questions or concentrate on students whom you know will give a (positive) response?

Feedback through marking

Black et al. (2002: 9) summarize the main ideas for improving written feedback to students as follows.

- Written tasks, alongside oral questioning, should encourage pupils to develop and show understanding of the key features of what they have learnt.
- Comments should identify what has been done well and what still needs improvement, and should give guidance on how to make that improvement.
- Opportunities for pupils to follow up comments should be planned as part of the overall learning process.

Task 6.20

The following written comments were made by different tutors as feedback on a BTEC Leisure and Tourism assignment. In pairs, consider which you think comprise effective feedback and which less effective?

'The assignment asks you to analyse/explain points but you have simply presented information.'

'You could have considered the following aspects of the company's operation – customer profiles, advertising, market research. Please write a paragraph on each and resubmit.'

'You need to work at your spelling, the grammatical structure of your sentences and your punctuation.'

'Although you have included sufficient information from your sources, your presentation of it is unclear and confused.'

'Read through the assignment and write down the following, indicating how they should be used and what they mean:

- Their, there, they're;
- Its, it's;
- Here, hear.'

'The following words were used in your assignment. Check in a dictionary whether you spelt them correctly: promosional, commercial, destination, inconsistent, somone, amenitys, consessionary.'

'You might want to try grouping your information in categories such as train routes, then fare structure, employees, marketing approaches.'

'Your account needs to be far more detailed than it is.'

'Pick out the following key points you present in the assignment and write down what the reasons for them are: the London–Manchester and London–Birmingham routes are the most popular; the company needs to reconsider its public image; there has been an overall loss from rail to bus and air services.'

'A good piece of work B+.'

Task 6.21

In pairs, swop four or five pieces of work you have recently marked. Assess your partner's feedback in each case. How effective was it? In cases where it might be improved, what could be amended or added?

Peer and self-assessment

Black et al. (2002: 12) make a strong case for this and feel classroom practice could be improved through:

- making transparent the criteria for evaluating learning achievements – to pupils to enable them to have a clear overview both of the aims of their work and of what it means to complete it successfully;

- teaching pupils the habits and skills of collaboration in peer assessment;
- encouraging pupils to keep in mind the aims of their work and to assess their own progress to meet these aims as they proceed.

Task 6.22

Task 6.21 was an example of peer assessment carried out by you and your partner. Reconsider your assessment of each other's feedback with the following points in mind:

- What were the criteria used for judging effective feedback?
- What advantages were there in peer assessment over assessment of your feedback by your tutor?

Formative use of summative tests

Black et al. (2002) consider that a creative and active approach to summative test revision can help students learn more effectively. Techniques here include students being 'asked to "traffic light" a list of key words or topics', flagging as green, amber or red, according to whether they have 'good, partial or little understanding'. Peer marking of tests is also recommended as is students generating and then answering their own questions.

Task 6.23

The following revision techniques have been used by teachers and students. Which of these have you used with your students and which do you know they use themselves? In pairs, share your experience and the effectiveness or otherwise of the techniques you have used. Which have led to the most effective student learning and why?

- students test each other;
- mind maps/spider diagrams;
- colour coding/highlighting points;
- timed answers to past paper questions;
- summarize key points;
- explaining work to someone who knows little about it (e.g., parent/friend);
- audio-taping key points;
- students setting own questions;
- use of revision guides/notes;
- putting notes onto postcards;
- others . . .?

6.8 Reviewing, recording and reporting achievement

The development of new courses involving a wider range of teaching and learning strategies is requiring teachers to be involved in much more complex assessment procedures. Typically, assessors are often now required, among other things, to:

- negotiate an assessment plan;
- discuss this plan;
- allow the candidate to express views/participate;
- document the process of evidence collection;
- give feedback which is specific, constructive and supportive;
- use questions which are open, clear and justifiable, not leading, probing or searching.

There is recognition here that assessment is more than an isolated judgement of a specific performance; that it should be integrated into a system of reviewing, recording and reporting achievement at the centre of which are the teacher and student.

Task 6.24

(a)   Working in pairs, choose a recent piece of assessable coursework each of you has completed. With one of you as the student and the other as the tutor, assess the work and record your interaction involving all the skills listed above. Then swap roles and repeat the exercise.

(b)   Which stage of the process proved the most difficult?

Many teachers find giving feedback the most problematic area of reviewing learning. This could be for a number of reasons: the tutor has the difficult task of bringing together a range of evidence of performance which they may not have assessed themselves; balancing feedback which is constructive and supportive but at the same time an accurate reflection of achievement is far from straightforward; negotiation assumes equality between participants when, in truth, the trainer rather than the candidate is finally empowered to make a decision about the acceptability of evidence. Francis and Young (1992), and others, have specified features which tend to characterize the giving of effective feedback. Good feedback is:

- clear and direct, whereby the reasons for assessment decisions are fully explained in language which is direct and unambiguous rather than vague or beating about the bush;
- constructive, because it is important to offer advice for further action which is in the student's capacity to take;

- descriptive of what the tutor has seen/observed/thinks rather than over-evaluative or judgemental;
- helpful and supportive on the tutor's part (this attitude must be fully communicated to the student);
- well timed, being given as soon as is practicable after evidence has been demonstrated and at a time when the student is receptive to feedback;
- fully understood by the student, with the tutor making every effort to ensure this, leaving no unresolved questions, misunderstandings or confusions;
- specific, being related to particular incidents or learning events.

Task 6.25

How far could the features above be applied to your pair work in Task 6.24?

The recording and reporting of achievement is usually based on records or profiles which vary in structure and style. Often, an awarding body will prescribe its own format but there may be institutional, departmental or curriculum area profile reports which are related to this or are freestanding. Most are variations of the four profile formats considered below.

The graded scale

These can take a variety of forms but their common feature is their placing of performance somewhere on a given scale. In Table 6.3 the assessor ticks a box on the continuum between one pole and another. In Table 6.4 the assessor inserts a number signifying a level of achievement for each assessment, where 1 equals good, 2 equals adequate and 3 equals poor.

Table 6.3 Polar graded scale for communication skills

Writes precisely, clearly with few errors Written accounts are comprehensive and coherent etc.						Expression is vague, difficult to understand with frequent errors Written accounts are brief and bitty etc.

Table 6.4 Numerical graded scale for communication skills

	1st assessment	2nd assessment	3rd assessment	4th assessment	5th assessment
Precision and clarity in writing					
Comprehensiveness of written accounts					
Etc.					

The strengths of the graded scale are:

- it is visually straightforward and easy to read;
- it can indicate progress when used formatively;
- it refers to specific skills/abilities.

Weaknesses include:

- the difficulty of representing precisely two ends of a real continuum by the descriptors at each pole;
- the absence of any criteria which might help the learner understand the basis of grading;
- a tendency to use ipsative referencing in the absence of assessment criteria.

Grid profiles

Grid profiles share a visual simplicity with graded scales but attempt to relate performance to assessment criteria, as shown in Table 6.5.

The advantages of grid profiles are:

- they are quick to complete;
- they specify what a student can do;
- they can be used formatively to plot development.

Table 6.5 Grid profile for communication skills

Written communications	Can express and reply to simple information	Can express and reply to simple information in a variety of contexts	Can express and reply to complex information	√	Can express and reply to complex information in a variety of contexts
Oral communications					

Disadvantages are:

- the descriptors may not do justice to learner achievement (a student who is outstanding at handling inquiries in reception might nevertheless have a tick only in the first box);
- grids are not tailored to individual students.

Open portrayals

This is essentially a blank sheet of paper on which an assessor is free to write what they choose to. In practice, some are more open than others. The NVQ comments on page 175, although representing an open portrayal, are closely related to a particular piece of work. A summative report at the end of a college year or course may offer a much wider portrayal.

The strengths of open portrayals are:

- they are highly dedicated to individual students;
- they are informative;
- they are comprehensive.

Weaknesses include:

- tutors have a habit of wanting to fill blank space if it exists;
- they can be unstructured;
- they can be time consuming both to write and to read.

Criterion-referenced competence statements

This is an approach now widely adopted in Post-14 Education and Training. The strengths of an approach using such statements are:

- they are positive, framed in 'can-do' terms;
- they lend themselves to negotiation and the reviewing of learning;
- they are related to learning/performance evidence.

Weaknesses include:

- relating evidence to competences can be complex and time consuming;
- there is no opportunity for levels of achievement to be acknowledged;
- learning outside the scope of particular competences is not credited.

Many teachers working in lifelong learning express two major anxieties about assessing their students: first, they are concerned about the increasing prominence of assessment and the time devoted to it, often at the expense, they feel, of student learning; second, they worry that much assessment they are required to carry out does not do justice to the richness of the learning experience they know their students have undergone. We hope this chapter has helped them to reflect on these matters and deal with them more effectively in practice.

Individual learning plans

The use of individual learning plans (ILPs) has become widespread across the sector in recognition that the more involved learners are in monitoring their own progress, the more effective it is going to be.

Task 6.26

Consider the ILP in Example 6.4 and the record of tutorial meeting. How do you think those who devised these expected them to be used? What features of learning and development does the ILP presuppose?

Example 6.4 Sample ILP

STUDENT INDIVIDUAL LEARNING PLAN

Your individual learning plan is a running record of action agreed between you and your personal tutor. Ownership of the plan is yours, but it will be of most use to you if you discuss and agree it with your course or personal tutor.

Use of an individual learning plan is designed to help you:
- plan the way forward rather than leaving things to chance;
- recognize your range of options;
- show others that you have a plan so that they can help you achieve it;
- record the advice and guidance you have received;
- make the right career decisions;
- set targets to reach your goals.

This plan summarizes your current position and identifies the goals you are aiming at; you will use it at your individual tutorial meetings when you will review your progress, agree actions and amend or confirm your goals.

NAME:	COURSE	YEAR
Georgina Hale	Diploma in Childcare Level 3	2010-11

TUTOR:
Alison Abrahams

FUNDING/WELFARE ADVICE IN PLACE?	STUDENT UNION CARD/LIBRARY ACCESS IN PLACE?
(YES) NO	(YES) NO

SECTION 1: WHERE AM I NOW?

EXISTING QUALIFICATIONS
List the qualifications you have gained so far:

GCSE: English C   Health and Social Care CC
      Maths C   Sociology B
      Science C   ICT   C
                        First Aid certificate

PREVIOUS EXPERIENCE

A. List your previous and current experience of work (including voluntary work):

Summer work in children's holiday club
Working at stables for friend's mum
Work experience in a primary school

B. List any training that you have undertaken (excluding those leading to a qualification):

First Aid

C. List your outside interests and activities:

Horses
Going to the cinema

D. What was the result of your initial assessment at college?

Literacy level 2, Maths Level 2

E. Have you got an up-to-date National Record of Achievement?

yes

Section 2: WHERE AM I GOING?

QUALIFICATION AIMS
A. programme of study (list all subjects/modules to be gained including key skills):
1. Working with babies & young children
2. The developing child
3. Health & Community care
4. Play & Early Learning
5. Working with Others Level 2
6. Improving own Learning & Performance Level 2

B. List any work experience you hope to gain while at college:

Experience of working in a nursery

C. List anything that might affect your ability to achieve (e.g. job domestic issues):

Saturday job in department store

Section 3: WHERE DO I WANT TO BE IN 5 YEARS TIME

> I do not know yet whether I want to go straight into employment working with children or go on to university to study a child and health related course or become a primary school teacher.

Section 4: WHAT DO I HAVE TO DO?

ACTION AGREED – between yourself and your tutor. These will indicate how you will achieve the targets you have set.

ACTION TO BE COMPLETED BY STUDENT
1. Full attendance and arrive for all sessions on time.
2. Bring all necessary equipment to classes.
3. Hand in work on time.
4. Show respect to others at all times.
5. Participate in sessions and complete necessary homework, reading etc.
6. Contact the college if unable to attend.

ACTION TO BE COMPLETED BY TUTOR
1. Arrange regular tutorials.
2. Monitor the learning and progress and give useful suggestions on how student can improve.
3. Set targets for the student to support them to achieve their qualifications with the best possible grade.

If you do not complete these actions you will find you have been placed on Academic Performance Review (please see your college diary). Meeting the actions agreed here are essential to making progress on your course

SIGNATURE OF STUDENT: Gina Hale	DATE: 22nd September 2010
SIGNATURE OF TUTOR: A. Abrahams	DATE: 2 2 . 9 . 2010

Links to the Professional Standards for Teachers and Trainers in Education and Training

Professional values and attributes

1 Reflect on what works best in your teaching and learning to meet the diverse needs of learners

4 Be creative and innovative in selecting and adapting strategies to help learners to learn

Professional knowledge and understanding

9 Apply theoretical understanding of effective practice in teaching, learning and assessment drawing on research and other evidence

Professional skills

17 Enable learners to share responsibility for their own learning and assessment, setting goals that stretch and challenge
18 Apply appropriate and fair methods of assessment and provide constructive and timely feedback to support progression and achievement

7

Exploring the curriculum

7.1 What is Chapter 7 about?

Why do our courses look the way they do? How have they developed over time to become the courses they are today? Can we understand our courses better in order to help improve the quality of our students' learning?

For many of us, working as busy teachers and trainers in a variety of organizations, scheduled to work with the maximum number of students in the minimum amount of time, the 'curriculum' is all too often simply whatever course we happen to be teaching at the time! This chapter provides an opportunity to pause and consider just what our courses are really about. Remember, unless we really know the answer to this question, that is, understand what it is we are meant to be doing and why, how can we be sure that what we are doing is the best for our students?

In order to understand how the chapter is organized, compare a course to a building. Consider what needs to be done before starting to build a new building or prior to adding an extension to an existing building. Sections 7.2, 7.3, 7.4 and 7.5 will pose some fundamental questions about the nature and organization of our courses in order to expose their foundations, rather as structural surveys and groundworks expose the fundamental state of the ground and dictate the foundations required to build a new structure or an extension.

Section 7.6 is the tea break, giving you some time to stop and consider your position in the light of all this new information before moving on to Chapter 8 which will help you to design, build and evaluate your new or revised course.

7.2 What is the curriculum?

KEY ISSUES

What is the curriculum and who dictates it?

Why is it continually changing?

Should it be continually changing?

As professionals working in the Post-14 Education and Training sector, we teach and train through many different courses covering a huge variety of subject matter and areas of skill development. However, one thing we have in common is that we all have some kind of curriculum through which we aim to help our students to learn.

Task 7.1: What is this notion of curriculum all about?

Drawing on your own experience and subject expertise, take a moment to think and then jot down a sentence explaining your own definition of 'curriculum'. Figure 7.1 shows some writers', teachers' and trainers' responses to this question.

Task 7.2: Comparing definitions

(a)   Which, if any, of the definitions presented in Figure 7.1 fits most closely with your own ideas?

(b)   What are the key differences and similarities when compared to your definition?

Figure 7.1 presents a diverse set of definitions but here is one view of the key similarities and differences. See how it compares with your responses to Task 7.2. Definitions 1 and 3 emphasize teacher and trainer planning while 10 mentions

---

1   The curriculum is what happens to students because of what teachers/trainers do

2   The curriculum is a formal course of study as at a college, university or training institution

3   The curriculum is a teacher's or trainer's intention or educational plan

4   The curriculum is a group of subjects and/or skills which make up a programme of study

5   The curriculum is a formal, timetabled programme of lessons

6   The curriculum is everything that happens to students at a college, university or training organization

7   The curriculum is an attempt to communicate the essential principles and features of an educational proposal

8   The curriculum describes the results of instruction

9   The curriculum lays down what is to be covered and to some extent the teaching and learning methods to be used

10   The curriculum is the organization's plan to guide learning towards pre-specified learning outcomes

11   The curriculum is a structured series of intended learning outcomes

12   The curriculum consists of every learning experience planned and provided by the organization to help pupils attain learning outcomes

13   The curriculum is the public form of attempting to put an educational idea into practice

14   The curriculum is a menu presented to students for consumption

---

Figure 7.1 Some definitions of curriculum

planning across an organization. Definitions 2, 5 and 12 also have an institutional emphasis but 4 is the only one which explicitly mentions subjects and skills, although these must be implicit in many of the others. Definitions 6 and 12 provide an interesting contrast in that 12 only mentions the planned curriculum whereas 6 includes the totality of a student's experience at an institution, the planned and the unplanned, recalling the notion of a hidden curriculum (Jackson 1968). Definitions 8, 10, 11 and 12 are similar in that all make particular mention of learning outcomes. Definition 9 alone seems to hint at ideas of curriculum content and process and 14 is unique in presenting learners as explicitly passive consumers of the curriculum. Finally, both 7 and 13 mention the notion of the curriculum as conveying a particular vision of learning while 13 emphasizes the public nature of a curriculum once it is in place.

From this, it is possible to identify what seem to be some key issues to consider in any definition of curriculum and these are shown in Figure 7.2.

This section has begun to expose and consider our own ideas about curriculum. What does some of the literature on curriculum tell us? Goodson (1994) makes the interesting point that, while curriculum development and implementation have been written about by many people, the more fundamental issues of curriculum definition, who constructs it, why and for whom have been more neglected. However, one writer who did address these questions was Stenhouse (1975), who starts by quoting the *Shorter Oxford English Dictionary* which defines curriculum as 'a course: especially a regular course of study as at a school or university'. Thus, curriculum may be viewed as the planned intentions of government and of teachers/trainers in their organizations. These plans often take the form of a public, written prescription detailing intended learning outcomes and Stenhouse goes on to mention that in many countries the curriculum is a state-controlled, legal requirement. For many of us, this resembles the National Curriculum, GCSE, BTEC, AS and A2 level specifications, NVQ specifications for vocational qualifications and the police and nurse training programmes, all of which can be viewed as public, published documents. Indeed, Higham et al. (1996) portray the 16–19 curriculum for schools and colleges as simply comprising the courses or qualifications (academic, vocational and core/key skills) for which students are studying.

- Evidence of planning (on a variety of scales) for student learning.
- Statements of what is to be learned.
- Indications of how it is to be learned.
- Pointers as to the outcomes of this learning.
- Statements on the role of learners in all this.
- Explanations about the vision behind the curriculum.
- Some dissemination or publication showing the public nature of the formal curriculum.

Figure 7.2 Some key issues in defining 'curriculum'

A second view of curriculum outlined by Stenhouse (1975) asks us to concentrate not just on the planned curriculum but on the reality of teaching and learning for teachers and students. Stenhouse challenges us to view the curriculum as what really happens in our classrooms and training areas. He also points out that the key reason teachers and trainers need to study the curriculum is to examine this balance between intentions and realities and use this information to improve their work and enhance students' learning.

Taylor and Richards (1985: 3), on the other hand, have little patience with any of the broader definitions of curriculum which try to include all the planned experiences, not just the formal things to be learned. They see these as the context within which the curriculum operates and which can affect the curriculum:

> . . . the course of study to be followed in becoming educated is in fact the oldest known meaning of the word [curriculum]. In contemporary writings, however, the phrase is frequently translated into 'the subjects to be studied' or 'the educational experiences to be provided' and not infrequently into 'the actual subject matter to be covered'.

Taylor and Richards argue that each of these definitions has its uses depending primarily on the context to which it is applied. Thus, an early years curriculum might be better viewed as educational experiences such as the sand tray; a school curriculum might consist largely of subjects, whereas in Post-14 Education and Training the curriculum is more closely associated with courses of study. The key issue, they say, is to choose whichever definition seems most appropriate and use this consistently and accurately.

So, bearing in mind Goodson's (1994) cautionary note, both Stenhouse (1975) and Taylor and Richards (1985) present notions of curriculum as public plans (often written) about what is to be learned, increasingly described as 'learning outcomes', and this is reflected by Higham et al.'s (1996) more recent contribution. However, Stenhouse adds a further idea, that of curriculum as the reality of learning for teacher and student. Whatever definition we choose to use, Taylor and Richards emphasize the need to be consistent and accurate in our use of the term 'curriculum'.

Task 7.3: Do you agree?

Set your original definition of curriculum against those above. Where do you stand now? Why do you believe this?

Having arrived at a working notion of curriculum, ask yourself a question. How much curriculum change has taken place in the last few years? The answer, of course, is that a tremendous amount has altered.

> **Task 7.4: Curriculum change in your work**
>
> In your own specialist area, note down the key changes you know about that have taken place in recent years. Include both the large-scale changes, often imposed by others, and the smaller-scale changes you, your colleagues or your organization have introduced.

Figure 7.3 presents a few examples of large-scale curriculum change. See if any of these figure in your list. These are curriculum developments on a national scale, but interestingly it is relatively easy to produce such a list without too much searching of the archives. The amount and rate of change in the last 25 years is remarkable. Of course, curriculum development has always taken place on a smaller scale. No doubt you will have been able to recall instances of specific course developments in your own work and organization. All this begs two key questions. Jot down your responses to Task 7.5 before reading on.

> **Task 7.5: What do you think?**
>
> (a)   Just why does the curriculum change?
> (b)   Should it be continually developing?

At this point, many teachers and trainers might well be tempted to mutter something about the government (or whichever agency is in overall charge of their area of work) never seeming to provide enough time or resources to do a proper job, never allowing enough time for any change to settle down before introducing yet more alterations and, perhaps, never really seeming to know what they really do

---

- Schools have had numerous versions of the National Curriculum to contend with since 1988 and achievement will now be assessed using the Progress 8 and Attainment 8 measures.
- Reform of GCSEs and AS and A levels from 2015.
- Changes to vocational qualifications and their relationship with academic qualifications arising from government policy influenced chiefly by the Wolf Report (Wolf 2011), including:
  - ➢   16–19 study programmes;
  - ➢   qualifications in the Technical Award category 14–16;
  - ➢   qualifications in Technical Certificate category at intermediate Level 2;
  - ➢   Tech Levels at Level 3;
  - ➢   Applied General Qualifications;
  - ➢   reform of apprenticeships.
- Establishment of the College of Policing and a Police National Curriculum following publication of the Neyroud Report.

Figure 7.3 Examples of large-scale curriculum change

want! In particular instances, this might well be true. Indeed, some writers such as Ahier and Ross (1995) talk about the curriculum being the result of a creative tension. Think of the haggling you can see taking place in many marketplaces abroad when you are on holiday. Seller and prospective buyer engage in a process of bargaining (arguing, debating, sometimes almost coming to blows!) until, if it works out, a compromise is reached. Each is out to get what they want. This is another form of creative tension and many curricula are the final outcome of argument, debate and conflict over different ideas about what should be taught and learned, how this should take place and the best means of assessing learning. Thus, all present curricula could be represented as simply the best compromise (hopefully) or the least bad compromise (more realistically) that can be achieved until new knowledge and ideas, together with evaluation data, make a revision necessary.

More cynically, the bargaining might be distorted by one of the hagglers threatening to use physical force whereupon the other calls their friends over to help! Thus, in this view, the curricula many of us have to deal with at present might simply be a dominant power group's position which will be replaced as soon as the balance of power shifts, with less importance being attached to the quality of education and training involved than to the political kudos attached to having produced change. The work of Ball (1987) and Goodson and Hargreaves (1996) largely on schools, and of Hyland (1994) on NVQs, all provide some fascinating insights into the politics of curriculum change but perhaps it might all be summarized by someone writing much earlier.

Taba (1962) was moved to use the term 'tinkering' when she portrayed curriculum as being the result of constant and ongoing modification. Think of 'tinkering' and imagine when you have been endlessly trying to get something, often some domestic gadget or part of a car, working properly. That is the image to hold in your mind and this helps us to avoid becoming too cynical.

Task 7.6: Which parts of the curriculum are you tinkering with?

(a)   Do you always teach the same thing in exactly the same way every time you teach it?

(b)   Should we teach students of science, of nursing, of motor vehicle maintenance, to exactly the same curriculum in the same ways and with the same assessment methods as we did 5, 10 or even 20 years ago?

We, the writers of this book, believe that the curriculum must develop continually. All of us will sometimes hanker for a supposed golden age of education and training lost somewhere in the mists of time, but it is deceptively easy to lose sight of the fact that, in every field, knowledge has progressed and the demands made on those educated and trained in that field have changed and intensified. All of this means that the curriculum must change.

However, remember your answers to Task 7.6 about your own everyday teaching and training. Most of us continually develop our teaching and training as we learn more about it over the years. The important thing is to ensure that the curriculum is changed – not to glorify an individual's or group's political position, but simply to improve the quality of student learning. To summarize, therefore, this section has begun a structural survey of the notion of curriculum by asking you to consider your notion of curriculum and to set it against those of other teachers and trainers and against ideas from the literature. It has examined some reasons for curriculum change and concluded that the key criterion of initiating such change should be the improved quality of student learning. The next section asks you to consider the nature of your own curriculum in more detail.

7.3 What are the key features of our courses?

KEY ISSUES

What are the key features of our courses?

How does your course look in relation to others?

What are the key models from the literature on curriculum?

What can curriculum models tell us about our courses?

This section helps us to identify, analyse and review the key characteristics of our courses in terms of purposes, what our students learn and how they learn. To help us to do this critically and rigorously, four curriculum models are used. This section continues the structural survey of curriculum begun in Section 7.2 and prepares us for a detailed analysis later. Figure 7.4 presents some teachers' and trainers' statements about how they view the key characteristics of learning in their courses. Notice how each of these statements conveys a sense of purpose and meaning about student learning. Thus, for instance, can you see how Sarah's aims and outcomes (purposes) include students learning the biology content well enough to achieve GCSE? However, Sarah also says that her students need to begin thinking as scientists, implying that her view of GCSE biology content is to teach students not simply a set of facts, but also a process of thinking, so that they can gain a better GCSE grade and use scientific thinking in their everyday lives.

Task 7.7: What are the key features of other people's courses?

Choose three of the statements in Figure 7.4 and identify what the teacher/trainer says or implies about:

- the aims and outcomes (purposes) of the course;
- the content of what is being learned;
- the process of that learning.

'Our aromatherapy course is about getting students to learn skills, acquire knowledge and to work with clients in a very special way.'

(*Suzanne and Nicole*)

'My art foundation course tries to help students to assume responsibility for developing and testing their own artistic knowledge, skills and understanding and to take control of their own careers as artists.'

(*Mathew*)

'My degree courses in different science specialisms all aim to produce practical, all-round scientists who are technically very knowledgeable, but who can also operate very effectively in practical situations and who can communicate and work closely with others.'

(*Sam*)

'My IT NVQ course gets students to learn how to use a piece of software as required in their workplaces.'

(*Angie*)

'My first aid course demands students learn basic procedures by heart but that they develop their common sense when dealing with emergency situations.'

(*John*)

'My bricklaying NVQ course means students need to learn the basic techniques but also need to be able to see how these will lead to a construction . . . see the potential their skills provide.'

(*Andy*)

'In their initial training on dangerous driving, my police trainees must know their law to the letter but they must also learn how to read a situation and to deal with the public in positive ways.'

(*Bob*)

'My GCSE biologists must know the biology syllabus content really well but they must also learn about thinking like scientists.'

(*Sarah*)

Figure 7.4 Teachers/trainers talking about their courses

Task 7.8: Key features of your course

Pause before reading on and try to summarize student learning in one of your own courses, or a part of it, in a sentence or so. Make sure you say something about the:

* purposes, often expressed as aims and outcomes;
* content;
* process of learning.

Keep your statement handy so that you can refer to it when attempting Task 7.9.

So far in this section we have concentrated on exposing the key features of other teachers' and trainers' courses and comparing them with our own. Let us test our thinking more fully by examining some of the literature on curriculum models. All these ideas can then be used to examine our own courses in more detail.

Interestingly, systematic approaches to developing the curriculum are relatively new, having first appeared in the USA in the 1940s before spreading to the UK in the 1960s. Four curriculum models appear consistently in the curriculum literature and these are summarized below.

The product or objectives model: a focus on *behavioural targets* for learning

This model has a behaviourist learning basis (see Chapter 3) and is interested in the product of a curriculum: just what does it equip a learner to do?

It is closely associated with Ralph Tyler (1971), was one of the earliest curriculum models and has become one of the most influential. Indeed, Tanner and Tanner (1980) argue that it is the dominant model of twentieth-century thought about curriculum design. Tyler organizes his model around four fundamental questions which, he claims, must be answered when developing any curriculum (Figure 7.5).

Tyler argues that each of these questions requires careful thinking including an element of needs analysis (of both students and others such as employers). Thus, aims and outcomes (the purposes of the curriculum) need to rest on the overall purposes (philosophy) of the relevant college, university or training organization, on the view of learning held by the curriculum developers and teachers/trainers, and on the subject matter itself. Once determined, these aims and outcomes must specify as clearly and unambiguously as possible what is to be learned. In turn, this will aid the selection and organization of the learning and assessment experiences and the evaluation procedures. All this, of course, links closely into the issues raised in Chapters 3, 5 and 9 of this book.

It is worth noting at this stage that Tyler concentrates on the how of curriculum-making not the what of the curriculum itself (Walker and Soltis 1997). Thus, it is possible to use his four questions to develop courses which will rest on very different notions of learning, teaching and assessment.

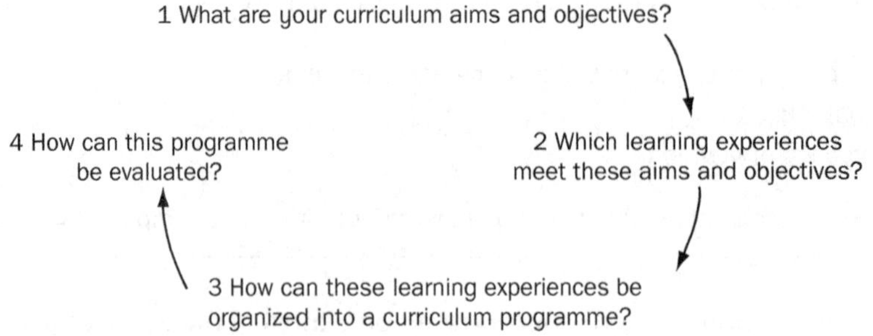

1 What are your curriculum aims and objectives?

4 How can this programme be evaluated?

2 Which learning experiences meet these aims and objectives?

3 How can these learning experiences be organized into a curriculum programme?

Figure 7.5 Tyler's model

However, in practice, this model is widely associated with behaviourist approaches to learning and the curriculum (see Chapter 3). Behavioural objectives are devised which pre-specify measurable learning outcomes. Learning and assessment experiences are then selected and organized to meet these outcomes and evaluation takes place to establish how well the course has enabled the specified behaviours to be learned. Students play a largely passive role in all this.

Nevertheless, the Tyler model remains probably the most influential of all and its clarity and simplicity mean that it is an accessible mechanism for curriculum design and development.

The content model: a focus on the *what* of learning

This is an approach to curriculum rooted in an instructivist view of learning (Reigeluth 1999) which is interested in the transmission of existing knowledge to new learners.

This curriculum model was developed in the 1950s and 1960s and rests on the work of, among others, Paul Hirst (1974). The emphasis is on the intellectual development of learners. Hirst believes that there are seven or eight forms of knowledge which represent the ways in which people experience and learn about the world. These are mathematics, physical science, knowledge of persons, literature and fine arts, morals, religion and philosophy. The curriculum is, therefore, designed to enable learners to develop their understanding of these areas which usually assume the form of curriculum subjects. Such a curriculum uses outcomes but of a broader kind than the purely behavioural type mentioned earlier. The prime aim of the curriculum is the transmission of wisdom – that is, knowledge already developed – often in the form of disciplines or subjects. It is this knowledge that becomes the chief factor influencing any curriculum decisions.

The process model: a focus on the *how* of learning

This is an approach to curriculum which is interested in the processes and procedures of learning so that the learner is able to use and develop the content, not simply receive it passively. In this it can be seen to have links to what we now see as the individual constructivist (Bruner 1990), social constructivist (Daniels 1996) and situated cognitivist (Lave and Wenger 1991) views of learning.

The model was explicitly developed by Lawrence Stenhouse (1975) as a response to the product or outcomes model described earlier. The emphasis is on defining content in cognitive terms as concepts and broad-based skills and this, in turn, defines the ways (processes and procedures) through which students need to learn. There is a reliance on teachers being relatively autonomous and possessing a high degree of professional ability since they must have a thorough understanding and judgement of the concepts, principles and criteria inherent in their own subjects (Taylor and Richards 1985).

Thus, teachers need to define the content of their course, define what constitutes a teaching procedure acceptable in subject terms and make clear the criteria by which students' work is to be judged (Stenhouse 1975). In this way, Stenhouse sees teachers as being able to plan rationally without using (behavioural) outcomes.

The situational model: a focus on the *cultural context* of learning

Dennis Lawton (1983) and Malcolm Skilbeck (1976) are linked to this approach which emphasizes the context in which the curriculum exists. This approach to curriculum seems now to echo some of the situated cognitivist (Lave and Wenger 1991) view of learning mentioned above.

In short, Lawton sees education as being about the transmission of the key elements of a society's culture to the new generation. His work sees culture as existing in eight subsystems such as economic, technological and aesthetic. The curriculum should then be organized in terms of the knowledge and experiences most appropriate for each subsystem. Skilbeck sees the culture of the college, university or training organization as a key factor in determining the eventual shape of the curriculum. He advocates what he terms 'situational analysis' – a review of the internal and external issues affecting the organization – as a precursor to using one of the other models. Thus, the situation in which the curriculum will operate becomes a key determinant of its eventual shape.

Task 7.9: What are these curriculum models all about?

Summarize the key aspects of each model (product/objectives, content, process and situational) in your own words. What are their key similarities and differences? Remember to refer back to the statement you made in response to Task 7.8.

At this point it is important to note that all these models are directive in that each lays down a prescription for carrying out the processes of curriculum design and development which allows different views on aims and objectives, content, learning, teaching and assessment to be combined so as to produce a curriculum. As such, theoretical models are useful in helping us to review an existing course or to design a new course since they also carry these proposed solutions to the problems of curriculum design and development.

Let us see if these models can help us in practice by enabling us to identify the key features of our courses. Remember, most of us teach on courses that others have designed even though we usually have some degree of freedom to interpret, sequence and manage the learning experiences of our students. This means that many of our courses are, in practice, a combination of different curriculum models.

For example, take the GCSE biology course mentioned in Figure 7.4. Sarah went on to describe her course as being 80 per cent content, product and situational and only 20 per cent process. That is, the curriculum seems most focused on getting students following a one-year retake course in a further education (FE) college department with a particular way of doing things (situational) to learn biology and to remember it for the examination (content) with the course itself being simply a passport to employment or higher-level courses (product), a view echoed by Sarah's students. The small proportion of process is Sarah trying hard within a tightly defined course and timescale to develop more scientific thinking and behaviour in her students.

In contrast, Andy described his NVQ bricklaying course as being 80 per cent product and 20 per cent content and process. He and his students see the NVQ as mainly a measure of their craft skills and as a means of obtaining and keeping employment. The content and process aspects simply refer to the basic knowledge required by the NVQ and the ways in which Andy helps his students to learn.

Finally, Suzanne and Nicole described their aromatherapy course as being one-third product, one-third content and one-third process and situational. This reflects the students' need for qualification in order to practise in many places (product), their need to know what they are doing (content) and the ways in which they must learn to work with clients in an often quite intimate fashion (process), something both Suzanne and Nicole felt to be particularly important in their profession (situational).

Task 7.10: Your course and the four models

Consider a course you teach in relation to the four curriculum models. Make a rough judgement about which of the models features in your course and in what proportions. What are the reasons for your answer?

There is a key lesson in all of this regarding how to treat theoretical models: use them not as a 'quick fix' but as tools to analyse the aims and outcomes (purpose), the selection and organization of learning and assessment activities and evaluation procedures.

Most teachers and trainers in Post-14 Education and Training find that their courses are a particular combination of product, content, process and situation. Each course will have its own points of emphasis. Take a teacher training programme for instance. It has a clear product emphasis, the outcome being that of a trained teacher/trainer with a national qualification and meeting the national standards (ETF 2014), a content dimension (the knowledge and understanding required of a fully trained professional) and process and situational aspects (the ways in which you learn and gain the qualification and the context in which the qualification is provided). While each of the four models seems to claim that it presents the correct way to develop a curriculum, in reality we need to balance a wide range of factors in order to arrive at a workable curriculum that can operate in practical situations. The value of curriculum models is that they can help us to be more thoughtful and professional in this process.

One further point is worth making. Although four models have been outlined and examined in this section, many of us have found that, in practice, we end up using the set of four questions posed by Tyler (1971: 201). This is certainly not because we are all behavioural outcomes enthusiasts but because the questions provide a straightforward framework for developing our courses. Indeed, many of our own students have pointed out that, in essence, the other models eventually arrive at a similar set of questions. The key thing is to ensure that, before you begin the curriculum development process, you have a clear idea about how you view learning and your subject matter. Then, Tyler's questions can help you build a practical curriculum.

To summarize, this section has continued the structural survey of curriculum by asking you to identify the aims and outcomes (purposes), content, process and context of your courses in relation to similar statements from other teachers and trainers. It has presented and examined four curriculum models and identified their key characteristics. You have set your own courses against the four models in order to clarify the precise nature of your courses. Finally, the section has provided advice on the use of theoretical models and has concluded that, in practice, all our courses contain elements of all the models, and it is the proportions that expose the differences. Bearing this in mind, Tyler's questions might be a useful framework provided we have already thought about our positions on learning and subject matter.

Having identified the key characteristics of our courses, the next section will ask why our courses possess these characteristics and investigate the assumptions, values and purposes that underpin them.

7.4 What ideologies (values, assumptions and purposes) underpin our courses?

KEY ISSUES

Why are courses organized so differently?

Why are there so many different curriculum models?

Should there be this variety in both theory and practice?

The previous section used practical and theoretical methods to help us to begin a review of our courses but it also showed the variety in curriculum theory (four different models) and practice – just look at the different responses of those teachers and trainers talking about their courses in Figure 7.4. This section asks why this variety exists, if it is necessary and, if so, why it is so important.

The 1980s saw the start of a concerted effort by government to reduce curriculum variety (see Chapter 1), and in particular since 1988 the compulsory education sector has seen the continuing evolution of the National Curriculum in an attempt to establish national benchmarks and raise standards. Meanwhile, lifelong learning has seen, among other changes, the ongoing development of NVQs to bring national standards to vocational training, the introduction of GNVQ (a supposed mix of academic education and vocational training) followed by the introduction of key skills, further revisions to GNVQ and, with Curriculum 2000, a wholesale revision of the A level and the ending of GNVQ with the introduction of Applied GCSE and AVCE, later called Applied A level.

These processes have continued apace. In 2002 the Green Paper *14–19: Extending Opportunities, Raising Standards* (DfES 2002a) envisaged, among other things, changes to the National Curriculum at Key Stage 4 (GCSE) and the introduction of a Matriculation Diploma. The Tomlinson Report (Working Group on 14–19 Reform 2004) revisited the whole area of 14–19 and the government response (the DfES White Paper on 14–19 *Education and Skills* 2005a) led to the development of 14–19 Diplomas. Higher education (HE) is also involved in wholesale curriculum change with the development of the Quality Assurance Agency Benchmarks and the HE National Qualifications Framework, as are a number of professions.

Recent years have also seen the complete reorganization of both the nurse and police training curricula to produce nurses and police officers with the knowledge, skills and abilities required for their rapidly changing roles in society. Meanwhile, do not forget the introduction and ongoing development of national standards for the training of teachers and others working in schools by the National College for Teaching and Leadership (NCTL), and by the Education and Training Foundation (ETF) for those working in the Post-14 sector, along with the establishment of the Higher Education Academy (HEA) for university lecturers.

However, even if the formal curriculum, the printed syllabus or specification is standardized, does that mean the curriculum in practice – as taught by lecturers, teachers and trainers, and experienced by learners – is standardized?

Task 7.11: Same course, same learning experience?

(a) When you were at school, did all the teachers of the same subject, say maths, teach in the same way? Explain your answer.

(b) In your own area of teaching/training, does every lecturer/teacher/trainer work in an identical way? Explain your answer.

(c) Do you think that the following groups of learners have identical learning experiences? Explain your answers.

 • All the first-year economics degree students in a university.

 • All NVQ Level 3 beauty therapy trainees in college or a workplace.

 • All police probationary constables in a training centre.

So, assuming that your answers above point towards some variation, however much the formal curriculum is standardized, the question remains as to why this variation exists. And we still have not answered the question about variation existing between the theoretical models and between curricula. For instance, why is NVQ different from the National Curriculum which is different from A level?

In short, the answer is that every curriculum represents a set of fundamental beliefs, assumptions and values, collectively termed 'ideologies', about the nature of education and training. As Barnes (1982: 60) says:

> No curriculum planning is neutral: every curriculum is imbued with values. These values embody a view of the kind of people we wish our pupils to become . . . and of the kind of society that such people could live in . . . As Eisner (1985) once wrote when discussing the idea of neutral curriculum planning, under the rug of technique, there lies an image of man.

We can cluster these beliefs about education and training into groups and call these 'educational ideologies'; that is, systems of meaning about education. In order to review and develop our own courses as teachers/trainers, we need to be able to identify these ideologies and hold our own considered position about them. This is important because these ideologies include assumptions about learning, teaching, the nature of subject knowledge and how education and training are linked to the wider economic, political, moral and social circumstances of the time. All this sets the context for making decisions about what to teach, how students should learn and how such learning should be assessed.

So, just what are these ideologies and how do they relate to education and training? Scrimshaw (1983) identifies five major educational ideologies which together represent over 2,000 years of thinking about the nature and meaning of education and training. They are now briefly described.

Classical humanism: maintaining a stable society by transmitting society's cultural heritage to students

Over 2,000 years ago in ancient Greece, Plato, in the *Meno*, developed a view of education as being a way of producing a just and harmonious society made up of rational and reflective individuals. His notions of just and harmonious were tied to a hierarchical society with the role of education being to train people to take up their proper roles. Thus, people at different levels in the hierarchy would require different curricula with only the rulers needing a full education in philosophy and the mathematical sciences because they were the only people who would need to develop wisdom.

Interestingly, around 1,000 years later, St Augustine devised a very similar proposal. He wanted a general education consisting of seven liberal arts to be provided to most pupils while a select few were to be given studies in philosophy and theology, ready to command a society dominated by the Christian Church.

Liberal humanism: the use of the intellectual disciplines in developing individuals and, thus, a fairer and more equal society

In the eighteenth century as, post-Renaissance, the thinkers of the Enlightenment period attempted to envisage a society beyond that controlled by hereditary monarchs, Rousseau (see Boyd 1956) advocated a view of society which assumed people to be naturally good but too often corrupted by their social environments.

For Rousseau, education was about providing structure, order and discipline to help learners develop into morally mature individuals. The curriculum would be developmental, take great account of individual differences and begin with everyday situations before moving on to a systematic study of the essential disciplines of literature, history, science, mathematics and so on (Taylor and Richards 1985). All this would, argued Rousseau, produce free thinking, responsible individuals able to play their full part in a free and democratic society.

Progressivism: meeting individuals' needs and aspirations so as to support their personal growth and strengthen a democratic society

In the early twentieth century in the USA, Dewey (1915) developed an approach which saw both the above ideologies as problematic. He saw classical humanism as too teacher-centred, too concerned with existing knowledge and with fitting people into an existing society. Liberal humanism, on the other hand, he considered too student-centred, ignoring the importance of the social contexts of learning and development. So, he developed a middle way between these two.

This involved Dewey's own vision of democracy as the best way for people in a society to live together and for individuals to grow and develop. He wanted schools that replicated democracy in an 'embryonic social community' in which students were encouraged to cooperate and work together and learn from each other as well as from their teachers (Walker and Soltis 1997). Education was to extend people's powers and possibilities as human beings. The curriculum would be based around active problem-solving in a variety of social contexts and be constructed of topics which interested and challenged students (learning from experience) with the aim that people would learn how to think for themselves, make decisions, cooperate and participate as makers of a democratic society.

Instrumentalism: a curriculum delivering a specific product such as the development of a skilled workforce

This ideology has become an increasingly important element in UK government policy since the Great Debate was initiated in 1976 and, given that the education policies of all major political parties in England, Scotland and Wales share this emphasis, shows every sign of remaining at the heart of government policy.

Instrumentalism, as it operates in the UK in the early years of the twenty-first century, sees the development of a highly educated workforce as essential in meeting growing international competition and values high levels of numeracy and literacy, subject areas covering aspects of science and technology and anything else seen as relevant to achieving this goal. Publications including the Foster Report (DfES 2005d), the DfES (2006b) White Paper *Further Education: Raising Skills, Improving Life Chances* and the Leitch Review of Skills (2006) all provide evidence of this.

The instrumental curriculum sees knowledge in factual terms and is clearly lecturer/teacher/trainer-led. Thus, through instrumentalist education and training, students are preparing themselves for their roles in the global workplace and in society as a whole.

Reconstructionism: education to change society

In stark contrast to the other ideologies, reconstructionism sees education as the means of moving society in a particular direction; in effect, as a tool of the state. In many developing countries, some degree of reconstructionism is, perhaps, necessary, as they seek to raise the living standards of their populations through a largely product-oriented curriculum.

However, totalitarian governments have always used education as a means of getting people to serve the interests of those in power and there are numerous past examples including Nazi Germany, the Soviet Union and, currently, China, where the purpose of education is described in Taylor and Richards (1985: 21) as being: 'to serve the ends of proletarian politics, not the pursuit of individual goals and aspirations'. Interestingly, by 2012, China is many years into a policy of using education as part of its attempt to move towards a more open, market-based economy while maintaining the political and social status quo. Clearly, China is now an increasing force in the global economy but time will tell if this use of education to support an economic, social and political balancing act will be successful.

Task 7.12: What are these five ideologies all about?

Summarize the key aspects of each educational ideology by commenting on the following:

- What is the historical origin of the ideology?
- How does it view the role of education and training?
- What kind of curriculum is advocated?
- What is the value given to individual learners?

Most courses in Post-14 Education and Training are influenced fairly clearly in their make-up by an ideology even if this is applied inconsistently, mixed with another and applied without universal agreement.

Task 7.13: Spot the ideology

Look at a course you teach and see if you can link it to a particular ideology. Explain your responses. Or, looking at the following courses, which ideology(ies) would you associate with any three of them? Explain your responses.

- NVQ.
- Nurse education.
- A level.
- Adult education (AE) courses in sugarcraft.
- MBA.
- Police training.
- GCSE and AS levels.
- University degrees in English and in travel and tourism.
- Skills for life and functional skills courses.

Having arrived at your responses to Tasks 7.12 and 7.13, consider one further issue. Are these fundamental assumptions, values and beliefs which underpin every course made explicit to teachers/trainers and learners? Is it simply assumed either that these are matters too obvious to be missed or that everyone else agrees and, therefore, no mention is necessary? What does your course documentation say about any of this? It is the unspoken and, all too often, the non-debated nature of ideologies in education that can cause difficulties for everyone.

In conclusion, this section has tackled the question as to why courses seem to vary so much both in theory and in practice. In essence, it is because course developers and those commissioning courses have their own assumptions, beliefs and values about the nature and purpose of education and training and these ideologies affect course design. In an age when courses seem likely to become more, rather than less, standardized, variation will still occur because teachers/trainers have their own ideologies and this will affect the ways they teach and train their students.

In terms of helping us with our own work, two issues need mentioning. First, as we review and develop our own courses, we must be explicit about our ideologies so that our colleagues, and other teachers/trainers, and students, will understand our intentions. Second, when we come to use other people's courses, we need to be able to identify the ideological underpinnings in order to arrive at how we will operate the course in practice.

7.5 The 14+ education reforms

KEY ISSUES

What are the major features of the 14+ reforms and strategies?

What is the impact of the 14–16, 16–18, 16–19 reforms on the curriculum?

What light does our discussion of curriculum models and ideologies shed on this reform?

The concept of 14–19 education can be traced back to the 1980s (Hodgson and Spours 2008) although the New Labour governments (1997–2010) undertook the first concrete steps to reform the 14–19 landscape. The 14–19 phase of education is crucial insofar as it tends to determine the path youngsters will take for future studies or employment. Although a range of 'Green' and 'White' Papers were issued (see Chapter 9) we can now see 14–19 initiatives as an overall attempt to reform the system through the introduction of the 14–19 Diplomas linked to employment sectors. These reforms were not successful overall and the issues remain the same. The gap between academic and vocational achievement and attainment is still too wide and the extensive reforms planned for 2015 onwards aim, in principle, to address some of these concerns. The timeline for these comprehensive reforms is from September 2015 through to 2019 for GCSEs. Table 7.1 gives an overview of the sheer numbers of papers, reports and reforms relating to Post-14 Education and Training.

The 14–19 education reforms under New Labour emerged as a result of concerns regarding the gap between academic and vocational programmes and the achievement of young students of that age who were either 'disengaged' or leaving education without an adequate qualification or necessary skills required for employment. There were also complaints from universities and employers that many youngsters were not ready to meet the challenges of HE or did not have appropriate skills for employment. It is important to underline that the 14–19 phase sits across distinct education phases, secondary and FE and is sometimes referred to as a 'hybrid' phase between the compulsory and the post-compulsory sectors. Distinct recognition of this phase is particularly evident in the establishment of the university technical colleges (UTCs) set up by the Baker Dearing Educational Trust. UTCs specialize in subjects in which there is a shortage of skills, such as Product Design, Digital Technologies and the Built Environment. By 2017, the number of UTCs will reach more than 55, offering specialisms in a specific technical area or industry and opportunities for young people to combine traditional GCSEs and A levels with technical qualifications related to the UTC's specialism. Funded by the government, these are designed to meet the skills required for the future, a twenty-first century model to meet what government calls 'the skills gap'. The aim of these UTCs is that the technical education on offer is supported by the

Table 7.1 14+ developments

Year	Paper/report/review	Focus	Main recommendations/outcome
1997	Green Paper: Qualifying for Success	16–19 Level 3 qualifications	• A levels split into AS and A2 to diversify studies and facilitate 'access' • GNVQ becomes a 'vocational A level' or AVCE • Key skills: the creation of a stand-alone award to address lack of generic skills (e.g. application of numbers, communication and information technology (CIT)).
Sept. 2000	Curriculum 2000	Application of Qualifying for Success: AS and A2 modular programmes and key skills are introduced, GNVQ is replaced by AVCE qualifications	• The General Certificate of Education (GCE) or A level programme becomes modular: 3 unit Advanced Subsidiary (AS) and 3 unit A2 levels • Offers greater flexibility, variety and broader AS subjects such as European studies, Communications, citizenship or critical thinking • The AS can be taken as stand-alone qualification or be continued at A2 level • The AVCE (6 units) also contains a 3-unit subsidiary level (ASVCE) mirroring A level programme but with vocational focus (e.g. business, information technology (IT) or health and social care) • Key skills
2002	Green Paper 14–19 Education: Extending Opportunities, Raising Standards	14–19 phase	• More flexibility of curriculum • Broader curriculum
2003	White Paper 14–19: Opportunity and Excellence	Builds on previous Green Paper	As above Reiterates the need to break down barriers between vocational and academic curriculum Cooperation between schools and colleges and vocational education and training • Sets up the 'Tomlinson' working group review of 14–19 education

Table 7.1 (Continued)

Year	Paper/report/review	Focus	Main recommendations/outcome
2004	Tomlinson Report 14–19: Curriculum and Qualifications Reform	14–19 education unified framework an English 'Diploma' or 'Baccalaureate'	A balanced 4-level (entry, foundation, intermediate and advanced) 14–19 curriculum allowing progression at own rate and a 'pick and mix' of vocational and/or academic subjects • general skills and knowledge • specialized learning, vocational or academic skills • employment of HE • supplementary learning with 'functional' maths, English and IT plus work experience, or involvement with community work, sports and arts grade for A grade at advanced level to stretch high achievers Diploma is 'named' after the age of 16 allowing for 'discovery' of subjects and paths pre-16 Apprenticeships to be integrated within the framework
2005	White Paper: Education and Skills	14–19 curriculum and assessment	Adopts some recommendations from Tomlinson but leaves out the unified approach GCSEs and A levels are 'strengthened' and stay as stand-alone qualifications 'Specialized' diplomas act as a bridge between vocational and academic studies Emphasis on functional skills Qualification does not depend on age any more but 'readiness' The Diploma is to be delivered in partnership with colleges, schools and employers Entitlement to all 14–19 to undertake any line of the Diploma by 2013 Work experience is encouraged

Table 7.1 (Continued)

Year	Paper/report/review	Focus	Main recommendations/outcome
2007	Green Paper *Raising Expectations*	Youth participation in education or training	Recommends a progressive increase of participation in education and training until age 17 by 2013 and to age 18 by 2015
2008	White Paper *Raising Expectations: Enabling the System to Deliver*	Application of Green Paper recommendations	Encourages 14–19 sub-regional grouping and the delivery of Foundation Tier and Diploma learning
2008	*Curriculum 2000 Review*	A levels	A levels modular system is simplified from 6 to 4 modules A grade A* is introduced as well as a stand-alone extended project
2008	Education and Skills Act	Youth learning participation	Raises the learning and training age to 18
2010	Schools White Paper	Introduces the English Baccalaureate	Leagues tables in schools show English and maths as part of the 5 good GCSEs (A*-C)
2011	Wolf Review	Review of vocational education in schools and FE	Reduces vocational qualifications by 3,000
2012	Ofqual consultation A level reform	A level standards	More rigorous assessment
2013	National Curriculum reforms published	Subject content and approval	Change in qualification performance measure in schools to point scores
2015	Education and Adoption Bill	Rapid academy conversions of failing schools	Imposing sponsors – closing legal loopholes

latest equipment from industry and UTCs work with local employers and a local university to develop and deliver the curriculum which focuses on problem-based learning. A criticism of this approach is that this is too narrow – often with only one specialism – for a generation which is preparing for many job roles across many sectors.

The concept of 14–25 education has emerged in recent times through the Coalition government of 2010–15 and the Conservative government of 2015, as a result of concerns about the attainment, progression and engagement of young people. Previously, the broad vision set out for 14–19 education and training included greater flexibility at Key Stage 4 and the inclusion of apprenticeships, along with increased collaboration across schools, colleges and work-based providers (DfES 2002a, 2003b). The 14–19 Diplomas have been largely discontinued which has meant that the door has opened for a wider set of reforms across the 14–19 landscape which some have argued will be the most significant since the Butler Act of 1944.

There have been shifts in opportunities for participation in education and training and expectations that young people will engage for longer. The establishment of academies, free schools and UTCs, for example, has meant that the landscape is facing rapid change in terms of existing provision in FE colleges, school sixth forms, sixth-form colleges and work-based learning providers. This is effectively establishing a system based on free market principles leading to commodification and consumer 'choice', which some might argue has displaced democracy. Free schools have been declared by the Secretary of State, Nicky Morgan, as the 'modern engines of social justice' helping 'break the cycle of disadvantage' and the government has reaffirmed its intention to open 500 new free schools during this parliament (DfE 2015a).

The retraction of the Aimhigher contracts across the country and the introduction of higher fees for HE have meant that fewer young people and adults are aspiring to progress to HE and alternative options are continuing to emerge. Given that these reforms are at the early stages of implementation, this section will outline many of the planned changes, including the 14+ curriculum and its new accountabilities.

A review of vocational education by Professor Alison Wolf in 2011 set out clear recommendations for 14–19 vocational qualifications and the 16–18 curriculum. It made recommendations for strengthening vocational education in schools, work experience, apprenticeships and for enrolling students in colleges before the age of 16. It made recommendations for lower attaining students at Key Stage 4 with a clear focus on the 'core academic skills' of English and Mathematics, and on work experience. It went further in that implementation of funding and performance measures mean that the focus is on these core areas and employment outcomes rather than on the accumulation of qualifications. Some 3,000 qualifications have been removed from performance tables as these were perceived to be of low value and not recognized by employers. There are also published lists of approved technical and vocational qualifications for 14–16- and 16–18-year-olds which will be reported in performance tables. Wolf set out expectations for the implementation of 16–19 study programmes, which are based on the prior attainment, education and employment goals of each learner. This review also enabled FE lecturers and professionals to teach in maintained schools through Qualified Teacher Learning and Skills status (QTLS) to strengthen vocational education in schools (Wolf 2011).

The issue of the curriculum has become even more complex. As Huddleston and Unwin point out, 'education providers are the servants of several masters: funding bodies, employers and learners, meaning there are increasing levels of influence from an employer driven curriculum' (2013: 52). Given the diverse nature of students attending FE colleges, which can now include 14–16-year-olds (in separated areas) opting to attend and, more importantly, not just those at risk of disengaging or disaffection, there has been a real shift of potential areas for growth and decline across education providers in Post-14 Education and Training. While the National Curriculum requirements in schools are driven through legislation and changes in accountabilities, the qualifications available in FE colleges structure much of what happens, which is often vocationally oriented, focusing on particular skills and knowledge related to a specific work sector and driven by an outcome-based approach through the design of the qualifications. FE has been the main provider of vocational education and prepares people for diverse destinations (Huddleston and Unwin 2013: 62). This can and does include progression to HE and employment. It is interesting to note the decline in A level provision across the FE sector and the increasing popularity of Access to Higher Education Diploma programmes offering 19 year + learners a second chance.   In fact, the then Secretary of State for Education stated:

> It is my view that the single most important purpose of A level qualifications is to prepare young people for further study at university, whether in the specific subject studied at A level or in a related subject area . . . Qualifications that command the confidence of our best universities will also command the confidence of teachers, parents, students and employers.
>
> (Gove, 2012 cited in Huddleston and Unwin, 2013: 54)

The aim of the DfE is to reduce modular assessment and introduce final exams at the end of a two-year A level (unless there is a need to test an essential skill) and schools and colleges are concerned about attainment and outcomes for learners and the effects this may have on life chances. It has been noted that the changes in AS and A levels may disadvantage students as schools and colleges prepare for changes. There are high levels of uncertainty in response to these reforms and worries about these stretching to 2020 as the changes are staged according to subjects.

> **Task 7.14: What kind of curriculum thinking should underpin the 14–19 phase of education?**
>
> Use what you have learned so far to consider the following: do you think the A level reforms are still needed or should we have moved to develop a wholly new integrated qualifications system?

There has also been rapid change to address what has been called 'a decline' in academic standards in schools with the introduction of the English Baccalaureate which sets out in the (Conservative) government's terms the 'social justice case for an academic curriculum in schools' (Gibb 2015). This measures only the attainment of those entering or achieving good (A*- C) GCSEs in English, Maths, Science, History or Geography, and a foreign language. The introduction of the EBacc as a performance measure has meant that many young people, compared to the first decade of the twenty-first century, have narrowed choices in terms of what they are able to study in schools, with Humanities and The Arts outside of the measure. There is potentially a more restricted choice if studying in a UTC designed to focus on a particular employment sector. Some UTCs and free schools do not offer humanities or arts subjects.

This is 'wholesale reform' and the previous attempts have been, according to Jephcote and Abbott (2005 cited in Huddleston and Unwin 2013), a 'tinkering' and 'tailoring' of the curriculum. The reform of qualifications is set to have a major impact for learners aged 14+ and as feared by the Nuffield Review in 2008 establishes:

> . . . a selective system, particularly post 16, casting a shadow over 'alternative' vocational provision, which is populated with 'refugees' from GCSEs and A levels. The focus on preparation for GCSE and A level examinations encourages mechanical and instrumental learning habits in young people and also fails to support a broad and coherent curriculum.
> (Huddleston and Unwin 2013: 56)

The two aims of the National Curriculum are:

> The national curriculum provides pupils with an introduction to the essential knowledge they need to be educated citizens. It introduces pupils to the best that has been thought and said, and helps engender an appreciation of human creativity and achievement.

> The national curriculum is just one element in the education of every child. There is time and space in the school day and in each week, term and year

to range beyond the national curriculum specifications. The national curriculum provides an outline of core knowledge around which teachers can develop exciting and stimulating lessons to promote the development of pupils' knowledge, understanding and skills as part of the wider school curriculum.

(DfE 2014a)

There are four key stages (KS) of the National Curriculum at which students follow programmes of study and will have individual targets for attainment. The 16–19 phase is often referred to as 'Key Stage 5' in school settings but not usually as this in FE. Students in schools and FE colleges will be on 16–19 study programmes tailored to individual aspirations in terms of career destinations but these may be based on what they have studied already and what type of impartial advice and guidance they have been given through career advisers or their teachers.

From 14–16, all learners in KS4 (or Years 10 and 11) are required compulsorily to study the following: English, Mathematics, Science, Citizenship, Computing and Physical Education. All schools are also required to teach Religious Education (KS1, 2, 3, 4) and in secondary schools, Sex and Relationship Education (SRE) (KS 3, 4). There is an entitlement in maintained schools for students to learn:

- the Arts, comprising Art and Design, Music, Dance, Drama and Media Arts;
- Design and Technology;
- the Humanities, Comprising History and Geography;
- Modern Foreign Languages (not compulsory National Curriculum subjects after age 14).

Students in maintained schools have a statutory entitlement to be able to study a subject in each of these four areas. Numeracy and Maths and Language and Literacy are expected to be developed where appropriate across subjects. (DfE 2014).

Performance measurement in maintained secondary schools, academies and free schools will change from September 2015 with the introduction of 'Progress 8' and 'Progress 8 Attainment', and pilots have been carried out to date with optional participation by schools. It is clear to see the push for EBacc subjects across the 'attainment buckets'. Progress 8 measures value added scores comparing pupils' results in secondary schools based on attainment levels in Key Stage 2 SATs. At Key Stage 4, Progress 8 measures a new accountability formula aimed at measuring the progress of secondary school pupils across a selected set of eight (best) subjects.

Table 7.2 The attainment buckets

The best 8 results across the formulae below		
Bucket 1	Bucket 2	Bucket 3
English* and Mathematics	EBacc	Other
	EBacc	Other
	EBacc	Other
One slot for English and one for maths – both double-weighted * *Higher score of English Language or English literature double-weighted if a student has taken both qualifications*	Three EBacc qualifications from: sciences, computer sciences, geography, history or languages	Three other slots: • any remaining Ebacc qualifications • GCSEs and any other approved academic, arts or vocational qualifications *No qualification can count for more than one GCSE, and no more than two approved high-value vocational qualifications can count in performance tables*

https://www.gov.uk/government/uploads/system/uploads/attachment_data/file/285990/ P8_factsheet.pdf

The Progress 8 score will always be determined by dividing the points total by 10 (the eight qualifications with English and mathematics counting double), regardless of how many qualifications the student sits or in which subjects. In addition to the above, there are new point scores for Level 1 and 2 qualifications, AS and double AS levels, graded music examinations, free-standing mathematics qualifications, BTEC First Awards and OCR Cambridge National Certificate depending on grades (DfE 2015b).

Task 7.15

(a) Which ideology and curriculum model underpin the EBacc?

(b) Some educationalists believe it is too narrow and not relevant to the twenty-first century. Do you agree with this belief?

16–19 reforms and the introduction of the study programmes in 2014

The 16–19 study programmes consist of the three elements set out in Figure 7.6 which sets out the rules of combination. [run on]

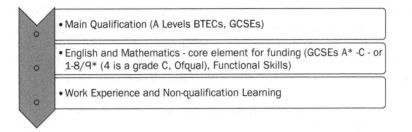

• Main Qualification (A Levels BTECs, GCSEs)

• English and Mathematics - core element for funding (GCSEs A* -C - or 1-8/9* (4 is a grade C, Ofqual), Functional Skills)

• Work Experience and Non-qualification Learning

Figure 7.6 Elements of 16–19 study programmes

These study programmes offer an opportunity for 16–19-year-olds to gain quali-fications and experience that employers are seeking in terms of addressing any skills gap. They consist of a main qualification alongside English and Maths, work experience and non-qualification learning components, offering students a comprehensive learning experience. Study programmes can be personalized to the individual learner, building on prior attainment and career aspirations. All 16–19 students are expected to follow a study programme along vocational or academic routes to support employment/HE progression opportunities. The work experience element is thought to have implicit benefits, including building con-fidence, teamwork skills, communication and time management skills which do on the surface resonate with the 'soft' or 'wider' key skills which have been part of many vocational-related programmes. The work experience element can also be problematic in that it can be difficult to secure quality placements in sectors relevant or related to learner aspirations, leaving this open to those who are best positioned in terms of contacts and links with employers. A range of options can fit here to products designed by awarding organizations. For example, AQA offer a baccalaureate consisting of A levels, skills, development activities and an addi-tional AS to provide breadth of study. Similarly, Pearson provides examples of how BTECs can fit with this structure.

For students who have not attained a good GCSE grade (i.e. A*-C) in English or Mathematics, funding is dependent on these being part of the study programme. However, the grading system for GCSEs is to change for 2015–16. The higher and lower tiers are to be replaced by a grading system of 1 to 9 with 9 being the high-est grade. These reforms are extensive and the process of reforming GCSEs, AS and A level qualifications has been continuing for some time. There have been changes to curriculum structure and the methods by which curricula are assessed. GCSEs are no longer modular and will be tested mostly through summative exam-ination at the end of two years. It is recognized that some subjects are much more difficult to assess through final examination and the shift away from coursework is not wholesale. For example, Drama and Design and Technology will require other forms of assessment.

The extent to which the new accountability measures for the 16–19 study programmes will reshape the FE marketplace is yet to impact. The DfE pub-lished its response to consultation in March 2015. This accountability culture is a move by government to drive up performance with measures across A level, tech level and applied general qualifications and will include progress, attainment, retention and destination as well as progress in Maths and English where applicable. The FE marketplace will shape the type of qualifications offered by schools and colleges and students will be able to 'choose' the type of provision in which to study. This is new to the FE sector as performance data is low on the list of factors which students consider when opting to attend courses (Russell 2014).

Task 7.16: What are the values and beliefs underpinning the 14+ reforms?

(a) Use the curriculum model or a combination of models from Section 7.3 to help you analyse the 16–19 study programmes. What kind of curriculum can you design?

(b) Which ideology or combination of ideologies from Section 7.4 might help you to analyse the core values and beliefs underpinning your examples?

Apprenticeships

Technical-level qualifications are designed to provide high quality vocational qualifications, with implementation from 2014. Some of these are recognized by employers, industry and professional bodies and HE, but not all. These qualifications identify a purpose which is declared. Technical-level qualifications, or 'Tech Levels' are for 16-year-old students who have a clear idea about the occupation they wish to pursue. They are vocational and equip students with the specialist knowledge they need to for a specific, recognized occupation, such as engineering, Computing, Accounting or Hospitality. To be recognized as a Tech Level and be compared to others in official performance tables, a qualification must:

- be a Level 3 qualification (the same level as A levels);
- lead to a recognized occupation;
- have public support from professional bodies or from five employers registered with Companies House.

Students who take one or more Tech Level, a Maths qualification at Level 3, and undertake an extended project, achieve the Technical Baccalaureate or 'TechBacc' standard. From September 2014 these Tech Levels were ready for teaching. They will be included in school and college performance tables from 2016, along with applied general qualifications and A levels (DBIS/DfE 2015). For up to date information on the TechBacc see the City & Guilds website, techbac.com.

There are published lists of accepted qualifications that meet specific criteria for 'Applied General, Technical Level', and 'Substantive Level 2' qualifications. These are included in the performance table reform and are part of league tables for 2016 onwards and 2016 school and college performance tables (to be published in early 2017). From 2016, 16–19 performance tables will report academic, tech level and applied general qualifications separately (DfE 2014b, 2015c; OCR 2015).

Raising of the participation age

The implementation of new legislation to introduce raising the participation age (RPA) to 17 by 2013 and 18 by 2015, gives the message to young people that this affects their progression and offers potential opportunities for them to engage with education and training. Under the (New Labour) government, which held office from 1997 to 2010, the involvement of young people in decision-making was increasingly evident in policy documentation, such as the Core Principles for the Involvement of Children and Young People for government departments (DfES, 2001), Every Child Matters (DfES 2004d) and the Children Act 2004, with the latter demanding that children be consulted where they are the subject of child protection inquiries or children in need assessments (Garnelas 2006). These policies were swiftly followed by the establishment of the Children and Youth Board to advise the Children's Minister (2004); the appointment of the Children's Commissioner for England (2005); the National Service Framework for Children (2004); Youth Matters (2005); the Childcare Act (2006); the Youth Opportunities Fund (2006); the Education and Inspections Bill (2006) and the Children's Plan (2007). These constituted a raft of support, guidance and legislation for the involvement of young people in decision-making about their education, care, health and leisure activities. In addition, from 2008, Ofsted began assessing local authorities' provision for young people's involvement in decisions about service provision (Garnelas 2006).

Focus groups conducted in 2012 with the first cohorts of young people affected by these changes in Medway schools found mixed results concerning students' awareness of the changes in participation to be implemented in 2013 and then 2015. The majority of students in Year 10 were aware that they could leave school at 16. Some were also aware that they would have to undertake some form of training or employment. On the subject of employment, students were unclear about how many hours they could work a week – this was more of an issue for students intending to stay on in school sixth forms.

There was also mixed feedback concerning subject options available to them in the sixth form. There was a broad spectrum of subjects (including work-related subjects) students thought they would like to study post 16. A few students mentioned apprenticeships but did not go into detail about specific work/sector routes. Students generally thought the new policy on RPA was a good thing.

Students did feel that they would like more information about progression from a variety of people and a few felt that their choices had been narrowed by recent government policy (EBacc) which restricted their choices in the longer term (i.e. Year 11 onwards). This was particularly so for the students achieving higher grades as they thought this would narrow their choices in terms of future careers (Cogger et al. 2012a).

There are issues with young people dropping out at 17 for many local authorities and Hodgson and Spours (2013) explore issues of middle attainers in sustained participation in upper secondary education in England who may be at risk of becoming the new 'NEETs' (not in employment, education or training). Given that the reforms of the New Labour government were unfinished and inconsistent, it has been argued that this generation of young people has been 'half served'; moreover, that these young people are now being 'overlooked' with their prospects worsened by recent Coalition policy because of its focus on high attaining students. Middle attainers have been defined here as those who reach Level 4 in KS2 SATs (Standard Attainment Tests) (Hodgson and Spours 2013). The participation statistical first release shows that there was a small rise in 16–18 NEETs in the period January 2015–March 2015 compared to the same period the previous year (0.3 per cent). The proportion of those not in education or training (NET) also rose slightly 16–18 and 19–24 (DfE 2015d).

Learners engaged in 14–16 education provision in FE colleges as a result of the Wolf Review are not to be confused with those learners who are attending alternative provision in schools or college settings, nor with those in Pupil Referral Units, nor those converting to alternative provision academies. Not all learners engage with education and for those at risk of or already disaffected there is provision for learners from 14 onwards. The type of alternative curriculum on offer varies enormously. Some examples include GCSEs in Maths, Science, English and Personal and Social Development programmes such as those provided by ASDAN. There is also Citizenship, Adult Basic Skills in Literacy and Numeracy, accredited enrichment programmes (e.g. AQA, ICT), functional skills, BTEC work skills and enterprise and work experience, including placements, young apprenticeships, Hairdressing, Animal Care, Beauty Therapy, BTEC Construction, Motor Vehicle programmes, Business and Administration, taster programmes and career guidance. These are provided at a range of levels from Entry to Level 2 (Cogger et al. 2012a).

The time spent accessing the alternative curriculum ranges from half a day per week to full-time learning. However, this provision aims to serve the complex needs of learners. There is such a variety of provision directed at such a range of needs that defining good alternative provision is more difficult than defining a good school (Taylor 2012: 5).

This system, undergoing extensive reforms, is likely to create even bigger divisions between vocational and academic learning. The choice for learners will inevitably be driven by school demands for EBacc subjects in order to make the most of the Attainment 8 data for the Progress 8 measure resulting potentially in an Ofsted inspection if targets are not met. Interestingly, exceeding targets can mean that Ofsted will not visit at all. At 14, in-school students will be placed on learning programmes which ought to suit their needs and aspirations. It might be better to enrol in a local college or UTC but students are often informed at the transition point from Year 6 to 7 that they will be in school until age 18 which may provide the wrong message and restrict opportunities. It is also pertinent to pinpoint the sociological argument advanced by some educationalists who suggest that the types of qualifications studied reinforce not only the learning divide between academic and vocational learning but also between social classes (Allen and Ainley 2007). Those from disadvantaged social classes tend to be less familiar with education programmes and orientations than their middle-class counterparts (Furlong 2005). Low achievers are also more likely to belong to lower social or disadvantaged classes (Cassen and Kingdon 2007). The EBacc may therefore ameliorate this and encourage more social mobility. It may also mean that more students will enrol in local FE colleges or on apprenticeships routes.

The main problem is that while lower achievers may be able to pass their GCSEs, an E–G grade (now 1, 2, 3) does very little for the learner in terms of certification, learning and confidence. It may sound more logical to engage learners with vocational learning at this stage instead of insisting they pursue a generic curriculum. But the school system does not seem prepared for such an alternative because of the nature of its curriculum and accountability measures. Indeed, Fordham (2015) takes this further and argues the case for the removal of applied and vocational subjects from the school curriculum with the idea that learning in schools should be abstract rather than work related.

Allen and Ainley (2007: 29) argue that education policies have been mainly ideological rather than technical, making workers more 'certified' than 'qualified':

> Rather than confirming the acquisition of genuine skills and aptitudes, educational credentials serve as screening devices for employers. They enable certain types of applicants with certain types of qualifications to proceed to particular positions . . . It is, however, ironic that, despite the criticism of academic qualification by their representatives, individual employers continue to recruit on the basis of success in qualifications that are considered to be the most academically prestigious.

So, while employers officially deprecate academic qualifications in favour of their vocational equivalents, most of them give their top jobs to applicants with traditional A levels or degrees from elite universities.

In terms of curriculum approach, it is becoming apparent that both the Coalition and now the Conservative government have been moving back to a more traditionalist approach to learning. This approach may take us further away from the concept of a unified 14–19 education curriculum.

7.6 Where do you stand so far?

KEY ISSUES

What is your working definition of curriculum?

How can the four curriculum models be of help?

Where do you stand in terms of educational ideology?

The purpose of this section is to provide an opportunity for us to pause a moment to review and record where we have got to in thinking about the theory and practice of curriculum matters. On the basis of this, we can then move forward to plan and develop a new, or revised, curriculum.

Task 7.17: Reporting on your review of curriculum

(a) What is your definition of curriculum?

(b) Why should the curriculum always be developing?

(c) Use the curriculum models to help analyse a course you teach on. What mixture of product, content, process and situation is it?

(d) What educational ideology do you feel most comfortable with? Why?

(e) What ideology lies behind a course you teach on? If it's different from your response to 7.17(d), does this raise any practical issues?

As practising teachers/trainers, this chapter has presented you with opportunities to consider your own work and that of other teachers/trainers. In order to help you, some of the theoretical work on curriculum has been introduced so that you can become more critical and thoughtful. However, have you noticed the different ways we can treat curriculum theory? The curriculum models are there to aid review and development and they provide ways of sorting out curriculum matters. So, in practice, our own courses often represent a particular combination of models.

Ideologies, however, are different. They represent our fundamental beliefs about the nature and purpose of a curriculum. Although some overlap of ideas is natural, we can only really embed the ideas of one ideology in any curriculum. So, having completed our structural survey of the curriculum, it's time to start planning and building. All this now means we can move on to Chapter 8 where we will begin to design and develop a new or revised curriculum, establish thorough evaluation mechanisms and be able to present and justify our new or revised course to others.

Links to the Professional Standards for Teachers and Trainers in Education and Training (with 2011 Teachers' Standards Mapped in Brackets)

Professional values and attributes

2 Evaluate and challenge your practice, values and beliefs (2, 8)

5 Value and promote social and cultural diversity, equality of opportunity and inclusion (1, 4, 5, 8)

Professional knowledge and understanding

7 Maintain and update knowledge of your subject and/or vocational area (3)

9 Apply theoretical understanding of effective practice in teaching, learning and assessment drawing on research and other evidence (5, 6, 8)

12 Understand the teaching and professional role and your responsibilities (8)

Professional skills

14 Plan and deliver effective learning programmes for diverse groups or individuals in a safe and inclusive environment (1, 4, 5)

19 Maintain and update your teaching and training expertise and vocational skills through collaboration with employers (3, 8)

20 Contribute to organisational development and quality improvement through collaboration with others (8)

8

Course design, development and evaluation

8.1 What is Chapter 8 about?

Given the increasing degree of central control over courses evident in recent years, we might be forgiven for assuming that, as teachers and trainers, we have little or no role to play in course design and development. This is far from true.

Even highly prescribed courses such as the National Vocational Qualification (NVQ), A level, or occupation-specific training programmes such as those for police officers or nurses still leave us, working as individuals or as part of a team, relatively free to interpret, sequence, resource and emphasize the various course elements in our own way, drawing on our own professional judgement to decide what will maximize opportunities for our students to learn. In this way we are able to design and develop the curriculum. This is a vital element in our work as teachers and trainers. Indeed, in examining curriculum design and development in some detail, this chapter views it as something which contributes to the overall aim of the book – to develop teachers' and trainers' professional abilities and to nourish their critical awareness.

This chapter focuses on the ways that we, as teachers and trainers, structure and organize students' learning. It challenges readers to examine the courses they teach. Sections 8.2 and 8.3 ask how a curriculum might be designed and developed, and how its effectiveness can be evaluated and judged. Section 8.4 examines how such new developments can be presented to colleges and training organizations so that they might be put into operation.

8.2 Designing and developing your course

KEY ISSUES

How can we develop or revise a course?

What is the role of ideology and curriculum models?

How can we identify what is needed in the new or revised course?

How can we specify course purposes?

How can we sequence and organize course content into learning and assessment experiences?

Sooner or later, as teachers or trainers, we all need to handle aspects of course design and development: for instance, starting a new job and planning our teaching, planning how we will put into practice a current NVQ/A level or GCSE specification by turning it into a practical course, revising a course that has been running for a while, or setting up a new course from scratch are all tasks that we need to be able to carry out professionally. The question is, how?

This section provides some practical answers based on a straightforward model derived from the theoretical and practical work described in Chapter 7. It makes no claims for being anything more than a practical framework by setting out a sequence of seven stages for curriculum developers to follow, shown in Figure 8.1.

This section covers Stages 1–6. That is, it will take you from identifying a manageable course development task through to selecting content, designing a full scheme of work and considering the place of your course in the curriculum of your institution overall. The final stage, that of course evaluation and feedback, will be tackled in the next section. This is to provide sufficient space for the important issue of evaluation, something which, all too often, is simply tacked on at the end of a course, seemingly as a bit of an afterthought.

Stage 1 Select a manageable course development task (it has got to be practical!).

Stage 2 Consider the ideological basis for the course, to identify the key values, beliefs and assumptions.

Stage 3 Conduct a needs analysis: if favourable, continue development work to ensure the proposed course really is worthwhile and practical.

Stage 4 Develop statements of purpose (aims and objectives) to set clear intentions and outcomes in the light of the above.

Stage 5 Specify content and sequence, then organize appropriate learning and assessment experiences to enable learners to achieve the intentions and purposes.

Stage 6 Consider how your proposed course fits into the curriculum offer of your institution.

Stage 7 Establish appropriate evaluation and feedback procedures, to review and improve the effectiveness of the course for learners.

Figure 8.1 A model for curriculum design and development

Stage 1: select a manageable course development task

The starting point is defining the kind of course that is needed – something that might be easier said than done. However, in order for you to gain the maximum benefit from the remainder of this chapter, you should have a curriculum development task to work on. Examples of courses developed by teacher training students in recent years are shown in Figure 8.2. Whatever you choose to focus on, try to make sure it is relevant to your work as a teacher/trainer and that it is something manageable.

Task 8.1: What curriculum to develop?

Select a course (or a part of it) you teach that you need to revise, or identify a syllabus, specification or subject you would like to teach (or that your organization has decided you should teach) but which needs developing into a practical course.

Once you have identified your curriculum development task, the next question for you to address is just what kind of course do you want it to be?

- Driving instructor training
- Brass band music for beginners
- Introductory sculpture
- Preparing for life at university
- Equal opportunities for special constables
- Outreach course for deprived youngsters
- Induction for early years workers
- NVQ information technology (IT) training
- Bricklaying for DIYers
- Students with special needs: a course for further education (FE) teachers
- How to have a good time and stay healthy
- LGV driver training
- Introductory reflexology
- Conflict management
- Introduction to a new IT system
- Minibus driver training

- Art and group therapy
- Various A level courses
- BA/BSc modules and units
- French for shopworkers
- NVQ customer care
- Health and safety at work
- Presentation skills
- Police promotion skills
- European art summer school
- Bereavement care for nurses
- Women's health and body care
- Applied GCSE and A level business units
- C&G gardening
- Suturing for nurses
- Applied GCSE health and social care

Figure 8.2 Examples of courses developed by teacher training students

Stage 2: consider the ideological basis for the course

> **Task 8.2: What kind of course and why?**
>
> Remember Chapter 7 and your own educational ideology that it helped you to define.
>
> (a)   What educational ideology (fundamental values, beliefs and assumptions) will you bring to the job of course design development?
>
> (b)   If you are revising an existing course, or developing a course from a pre-set syllabus or specification, what seems to be its underlying ideology?
>
> (c)   If your answers to (a) and (b) are different, can you balance the two? Explain how.

Your responses to Task 8.2 will act as a framework around which you can begin to develop your course. However, now that you have clarified the kind of course you want to develop, what needs must the course meet, and how are you to identify these, especially students' learning needs?

Stage 3: conduct a needs analysis

What needs must this course meet? Perhaps this is better rephrased to read *whose* needs? Quite naturally, this will depend on a whole range of factors including you, any of your colleagues who might be involved, the organization within which you are working, those who might use the course to make judgements (such as employers, colleges, universities) and, most important of all, the learners themselves.

> **Task 8.3: Whose needs and why?**
>
> List those with needs to be taken account of in planning your course. Why do you have to take their needs into account?

So, given these needs must be met, how are you to identify and analyse them? Just what is a 'needs analysis'? In short, it involves the collection and analysis of information from all those who will be involved and affected by the proposed course so that the planning stage can take account of as wide a range of needs as is practicable.

Obviously, this requires careful handling because every course demands a different level of needs analysis. For instance, if you are revising an existing course you should already have at least some basic information about needs which might simply need reviewing and extending in places. If, on the other hand, you are developing a brand new curriculum then a much more detailed needs analysis will be required before you make any further progress. Figure 8.3 provides a set of suggested questions, the answers to which would result in a full needs analysis report. If you are revising a course, choose whichever seem most appropriate. Having identified the kind of needs analysis you intend to carry out, you have

1 What are your organization's criteria for numbers, costs, accommodation, staffing and resources?
2 Is there any demand for the course?
3 How long is the demand estimated to last?
4 Are there any similar courses running in the area? If so, will there be sufficient demand for all to run?
5 What is the estimated size of the potential student population?
6 What would a profile of the prospective students show?
7 Will the course appear in league tables?
8 What costs will the course incur?
9 Will the course attract any funding?
10 For those courses attracting fee-paying students, what price will prospective students be willing to pay?
11 What does the assessment and evaluation data from previous cohorts contain?
12 How was any previous needs analysis carried out? What information does it contain?
13 Can other staff who have been involved provide you with any additional information?
14 Will your course meet the organization's criteria?

Figure 8.3 Questions for a needs analysis

then to decide how this information will be obtained. Figure 8.4 provides some suggestions. However, do not set up complicated surveys involving large numbers of people or feel obliged to cost everything to the last penny unless you are involved in a really large-scale development. Use your organization's support staff to help (e.g. if a technical costing is required) and be realistic. It is a matter of generating sufficient information on the basis of which you, your colleagues and your organization might make a professional judgement.

- *Meeting the organization's criteria*: liaise with others in the organization to clarify criteria and report back with information.
- *Judging demand size and longevity*: monitor any feeder routes for prospective students (e.g. conduct surveys of schools, employers, colleges, universities).
- *Identifying the competition*: survey other providers.
- *Profiling prospective students*: once you have identified feeder routes, survey these prospective students to identify their particular needs.
- *Costing*: *accurate* estimated costs of staffing, accommodation, resources, food/ drink, administration, examination and so on as appropriate.
- *Funding*: *checks* with organizations such as Skills Funding Agency (SFA), Higher Education Funding Council for England (HEFCE), local authorities, National Health Service (NHS) trusts, police forces and so on as appropriate.
- *Pricing*: survey of prospective students and of competition prices.
- *Learning from previous experience*: use existing assessment and evaluation data; liaise with other staff.

Figure 8.4 Possible strategies for needs analysis data collection

> **Task 8.4: Conducting a needs analysis**
>
> (a) Using Figures 8.3 and 8.4, conduct a needs analysis for your proposed course.
> (b) Summarize your findings in a report which will form part of your curriculum development documentation.

Having conducted and reported on the needs analysis, and assuming we are going ahead, the next stage is to specify or review the purposes of the course, often presented as aims and objectives.

Stage 4: develop statements of purpose (aims and objectives)

Course purposes are shaped by two key things. First, the ideology underpinning the course (already specified in Task 8.2). Second, the curriculum model, or combination of models, representing the key features of the intended course. For example, a progressive ideology and process curriculum model would lead to aims and objectives emphasizing individual learner development and growth whereas classical humanism and a product curriculum would aim for learners gaining specified kinds and quantities of knowledge in order to fulfil specified roles in society.

> **Task 8.5: Factors affecting course purposes**
>
> Consider what model or combination of curriculum models will best support the course you are developing. Take into account your own preferences and, if relevant, the emphasis apparent in the syllabus of specification.

There is another dimension to stating purposes. You may recall that Chapter 3 introduced several different approaches to learning which would have a clear effect on aims, which are broad statements of purpose, and, in particular, objectives, which are much more specific course or lesson targets and learning outcomes. For example, an expressly behavioural perspective on learning will lead to objectives very different to those generated from a purely cognitive approach. Figure 8.5, adapted from Cohen and Manion (1989: 32–41) presents some guidance on two different types of objective.

Task 8.6 provides some examples of behavioural and non-behavioural objectives from Diploma in Education and Training students' course development work.

> **Task 8.6: Examples of course objectives**
>
> From the list below, identify which objectives are behavioural and which are non-behavioural, and think about why.

The student will be able to:

- demonstrate how to grip the (golf) club correctly;
- demonstrate how to place a casualty into the recovery position;
- increase their understanding of the theories of loss and bereavement;
- appreciate the importance of taking responsibility for their own health;
- open a file, input data, save the data and exit from a database program;
- identify and meet necessary health and safety regulations;
- feel more confident about using the specialist equipment;
- understand the thinking behind a theoretical model in economics;
- become a more reflective and critical professional;
- drive a minibus to Driving Standards Agency standards.

Key characteristics of behavioural objectives:
- specify who is to perform the desired behaviour;
- specify this behaviour clearly and unambiguously;
- specify the conditions for the behaviour to be demonstrated;
- specify the standard used to determine success or failure.

Using behavioural objectives:
- requires great care because it defines learning in one particular way (behaviourally);
- requires teachers/trainers to be sure this is appropriate for the course and the intended learning;
- is better not done unless these conditions are met.

Key characteristics of non-behavioural objectives:
- may be more flexible and open-ended;
- still need expressing simply and linking to learning experiences;
- allow for broader notions of learning to be used, not just behaviour.

When to use each type of objective
- Behavioural objectives might well be most effective when the subject matter and intended learning is skill-based and can be demonstrated easily, or where overt writing or speaking can demonstrate appropriate levels of learning, or where learners need small, behavioural stages brought into the subject matter to provide clear, attainable targets.
- Non-behavioural objectives might be best used when the intended learning is more complex or less specific, is developmental and almost impossible to view in terms of behaviour without reducing the learning to an absurd level.

Source: Cohen and Manion (1989).

Figure 8.5 Defining, writing and using two types of objective

Having identified the main issues involved in expressing the purposes of a course through aims and objectives, there are two further points to make. First, when you come to write your course aims and objectives, keep them to the minimum necessary to specify the course intentions fully. Second, do not be afraid to mix behavioural and non-behavioural objectives provided you make it clear that you are doing this deliberately.

For example, in an NVQ healthcare assistants' course, your students will certainly need to meet the performance criteria which are, as with all NVQs, behavioural objectives and learning outcomes. However, you might also want to include in your practical operation of the course some more broadly based, non-behavioural objectives to cover the less obvious but very important aspects of working with patients on a busy ward. So, if your course intends learning of different kinds to take place, the objectives must recognize this. Just be honest and show you have been thoughtful about it.

All this means that we have reached the next stage, that of identifying and sequencing appropriate teaching/training and assessment experiences for our prospective students.

Stage 5: specify content and sequence, then organize appropriate learning and assessment experiences

For many of us, these are the tasks we immediately associate with the notion of course development. Indeed, we might well relish the work because it involves us in working out what we consider to be the programme through which students can learn our specialist subject most effectively.

However, it is not too long before a number of key questions arise. How is content chosen, or rejected? What makes for a correct sequence? How are learning and assessment experiences linked to all this? Is a detailed plan required for each session or will a scheme of work suffice? Just what level of detail is required at this stage in the development of a new or revised course? The remainder of this section will provide some practical answers to these questions.

How is content chosen? In many cases course content is already specified by a syllabus or course specification. In other cases, teachers/trainers might have a much freer choice. However, do not forget our earlier work in this chapter which indicated that, however tightly specified the course content might be, and no matter how well known and commonly covered it is, individual teachers/trainers will always provide their students with (however slightly) different experiences. We can take nothing for granted here. All of us need to consider the content we teach and the basis on which we have chosen it.

Task 8.7: Thinking about content and sequence

Choose one of the following contexts:

1 Ben, a 9-month-old baby, is with you in his bedroom playing. Please get him bathed and changed ready to go to sleep.

> 2   Jo, a learner driver, is going along a residential road at 25 m.p.h. and needs to turn the car round and drive back the way she has come. What does she need to do?
>
>   (a)   Using one of the above contexts what, in your opinion, is the best practice sequence in which the activity should be carried out?
>
>   (b)   What content do learner parents or drivers need to understand in order for them to achieve the objective of a (near) perfect performance?

Figure 8.6 presents two sets of responses from teacher training students to the first context in Task 8.7, bathing a baby. Note the differences. Is one of the sequences better? Why? What about the content involved? Would either or both sets of responses achieve the objective?

Group A explained that their objective was to achieve the bathing of the baby and that safety, hygiene and careful handling were the prime objectives and content to be used. In contrast, Group B stated that, for them, bathtime was

Group A response	Group B response
1 Warm baby clothes	1 Make sure baby is happily and safely playing in bedroom
2 Warm towel	2 Warm clothes, run water, test, put in bath toys and bubbles
3 Run bath	3 Bring in baby, start tape of bathtime songs and sing along
4 Take baby to bathroom	4 Remove soiled nappy and clean baby as needed while singing
5 Test water temperature	5 Place baby gently in bath, reassure using toys and music
6 Undress baby and remove nappy	6 Wash baby carefully, using different cloth for face, still singing and playing
7 Place baby carefully in bath	7 Carry on playing etc. as seems best
8 Wash carefully and hygienically	8 Gently remove baby from bath and wrap in warm towel
9 Remove baby from bath carefully	9 Dry baby carefully and apply cream/powder as appropriate
10 Wrap baby in towel and dry	10 Dress baby and begin playing going to bed game
11 Use cream etc. and put on fresh nappy	11 Turn off music, take baby to bedroom and lay him in cot
12 Take baby to bedroom	12 Play going to sleep game, read, play music etc. as appropriate
13 Dress baby	13 Bring game to an end and settle baby safely down to sleep
14 Lie baby safely in cot	14 Clean and tidy bathroom

Figure 8.6 How to bathe a baby

an important element in the baby's routine, in elementary learning about water and hygiene, but that it can be fun too and an aid in developing the child's relationship with its parent(s) and, thus, its overall development. It was also seen by one student as having been an enjoyable time for the parent too! In other words, ideologically and in terms of curriculum models, these groups had very different starting points which led, in turn, to different content and, to a lesser extent in this example, differences in sequence.

Task 8.8: Reviewing your sequence and content

Look back at your response to Task 8.7. How did you define the objective? Which ideology and curriculum model(s) influenced your sequence and content? Would you want to revise your response at all?

In order to identify the appropriate content and sequence for your proposed course, it is important to take account of two key factors. First, the syllabus or specification and its associated content, ideology and model(s). Second, your own educational ideology and what seems to you to be the most appropriate curriculum model(s), as expressed in your aims and objectives. You must strike a balance between the course as laid out and your own ideas if your content and sequence are to enable the students to achieve your aims and objectives.

Assuming you were about to teach parents to bathe their babies, what kinds of learning and assessment experiences would you use to help them learn? Again, the answer is linked to the balance struck between the course and your own ideas. Thus, to caricature Group A's position, they might be tempted to hire an expert to run a series of lectures entitled 'How to bathe a baby: the way to infant hygiene and safety', with slides, data on water temperature and accidents to babies in bathrooms. Worksheets might be used to enable learning facts and procedures by rote, there would be practice sessions with dolls and participants' performance might be assessed through observation of the practice and some written tests.

Being equally unfair to Group B, on the other hand, they might run a series of workshops entitled 'Hygiene and hugs: making bathtime an enriching experience for all – a holistic perspective'. These would involve parents, a health visitor and a child psychologist working with a facilitator who would start from everyone's own experiences. Through discussion, inputs and home visits by the professionals, some reflection (a reflective log?) and the use of students' own children (and bathrooms!) everything would be brought together. Assessment would be informal and based on participants' contributions, involvement and evidence of their reflection. Thus, your selection of learning and assessment experiences will emerge directly from all your previous work on developing the course. Assessment was handled fully in Chapter 6. It is mentioned here simply to emphasize its role in providing information to all those involved about what has and has not been learned.

One further question remains with regard to selecting content, sequence and learning and assessment experiences. As part of the process of course development or revision, is every session to be planned in detail? At this stage, the simple answer is no, unless what is being planned is a short event of some kind, say a one-day introduction to a new IT program. In this case, the full day's programme, resources and materials would be required.

In other cases, where longer and more involved courses are under development, what is needed is an outline scheme of work for the course and, usually, one short session (about an hour) which is planned and resourced to provide an indication of quality. As an illustration, Table 8.1 provides an example of part of a scheme of work.

Task 8.9: Selecting and sequencing content and deciding on learning and assessment experiences

Begin working on an outline scheme of work for your proposed course which will show how you intend students to achieve the aims and objectives specified earlier. Select and sequence your course content and, given practical limits to time and resources, decide on the kinds of learning and assessment experiences which will be most appropriate. Present them using the exemplar scheme of work layout in Table 8.1 or use one of your own.

Table 8.1 An extract 'from a scheme of work from a curriculum development proposal

BTEC National Diploma Level 3 Health and Social Care
Unit 8: Psychological Perspectives
Scheme of work
Guided learning hours (GLH): 30
Number of lessons: 24
Duration of lessons: 2 hour

Lesson	Unit content	Activities	Possible Resources	Links to other units
Learning outcome 1: Understand psychological perspectives (P1, M1)				
1	Introduction	**Teacher input** Introduce unit expectations Talk through assignments & hand out 1st assignment **Student input – class discussion** Psych starter activity – common sense or psychology **Student input – whole class activity** Memory game – one student reads story and have to pass that information onto a student who then passes it on etc.	• PowerPoint • Assignment brief • Common myths worksheet • Website handout • Memory game story	

Table 8.1 (Continued)

Lesson	Unit content	Activities	Possible Resources	Links to other units
2	Behaviourism – classical	**Teacher input** Explain CC & Pavlov's exp Hand out key words **Student Input – individual activity** Watch HP clip and have students use whiteboards to explain conditioning process using key terms **Student input** Activity on CC linked to H&SC **Teacher input** Little Albert experiment Activity on ethics from Little Albert **Student input** Strengths & weakness of approach	• PowerPoint • Worksheet on CC • Pavlov's dog exp video • Harry Potter dragon clip • Individual whiteboards • Key words worksheet • Studies handout	
3–4	Behaviourism – operant Write up behaviourism **(Assignment 1 – P1, M1)**	**Teacher input** Explain operant conditioning Big bang video & discussion **Student input – team activity** Create a reward & punishment scheme on flip chart paper **Student input – pair activity** Activity worksheet on OC & CC differences **Student input** Strengths & weakness of approach	• Activity worksheet on OC & CC • OC Big bang vid • Key words • Flipchart paper & pens	IE, TW, EP

Half term

| 5–6 | Social learning Write up SLT **(Assignment 1 – P1, M1)** | **Teacher input** Explain SLT & Bandura study Role models – good/bad – observe & copy – consequences **Student input** Think of a celeb describe them as a role model – are they good and bad? | • PowerPoint • Bandura video • Role model pictures • Key terms | EP, R, IE, SM |

Table 8.1 (Continued)

Lesson	Unit content	Activities	Possible Resources	Links to other units
7–8	Psycho-dynamic approach Write up psycho-dynamic **(Assignment 1 – P1, M1)**	**Teacher Input** Explain approach (Freud) – unconscious mind – key stages of development **Student Input** Personality test **Teacher input** Defence mechanisms **Student input** Activity on defence mechanisms **Teacher input** Explain the development of Erikson	• Personality questionnaire • Video on ID, ego & super ego • Scenario worksheet • Defence mechanisms worksheet • PowerPoint • Key terms	
9–10	Humanistic approach Write up humanistic **(Assignment 1 – P1, M1)**	**Teacher input** Explain hierarchy of needs with the class (Maslow) **Student input** Use computers to research what goes in each stage of the hierarchy to fill out hierarchy of needs template **Teacher input** Explain Rogers' development **Student input** Congruence test	• Hierarchy of needs picture (template for students) • ICT suite • Key terms • Congruence test	
11–12	Cognitive approach Write up cognitive **(Assignment 1 – P1, M1)**			

To summarize, therefore, this section has presented you with the challenge of developing or revising your own course. On the basis of the work presented in previous sections a seven-stage model for course design and development has been used and this section has taken you through six of these stages, to a point where your course is beginning to take practical shape. The importance of the definitions, ideologies and curriculum models handled in earlier sections has been stressed as a means of ensuring continuity and coherence of learning in your new course. The next section addresses the final stage of course development, that of devising effective and appropriate evaluation and feedback procedures.

8.3 Evaluating your course

KEY ISSUES

What is evaluation?

Why evaluate? For what purpose and for whom?

What are you going to evaluate?

How and when will you evaluate?

How can you ensure evaluation data feeds back into your course planning cycle?

Just as you thought you were safe! Having put time and effort into the processes of reviewing your existing course and then developing a new course or revising an existing one, you assumed that was that. A job well done. The course is ready to run and you are rightly proud of your work. But no! Here is one last stage to work your way through. Surely, you groan, evaluation is just about filling in a form (sometimes) at the end of a course and little or nothing being done afterwards?

So, just what is evaluation and why is it so important? Before going further, consider your responses to Task 8.11.

Task 8.11: Evaluation: your starting point

(a)   How regularly does evaluation take place?

(b)   How appropriate and user-friendly are your evaluation methods?

(c)   Do you let people use their own words at all?

(d)   Do you evaluate in ways other than end-of-course forms?

(e)   Do you evaluate against practically described learning purposes?

(f)   Do you discuss the results internally, externally, never?

(g)   Does anyone else get to know of the results?

(h)   Do you ever change anything afterwards?

Evaluation is all about finding out if our new course is working properly. This, of course, is what Ofsted means by 'self-evaluation' which lies at the heart of its inspection methodology. In general, therefore, evaluation involves generating data through a process of inquiry and then, on the basis of this, making judgements about the strengths and weaknesses and the overall effectiveness of the course, and making decisions about how to improve it further. As Cronbach (1980: 14) says: '. . . the history of social reform . . . is littered with examples of large-scale and costly catastrophes as well as more modest mistakes . . . evaluation offers to certify that a programme will live up to its advertising'.

There are people who use the words 'evaluation' and 'assessment' as if they were the same thing. Be careful. Assessment refers to information and judgements about individual students' learning. Evaluation is about gaining information and judgements about course effectiveness. It is important to see if our development work has succeeded and that our new course is meeting its aims and objectives. But there are others who are interested in our work and evaluation has to meet their needs too. So just who are these others?

Earlier sections of this chapter listed several groups who will be interested. As well as the course developers these include the students, the teachers/trainers, others such as managers in our organization together with employers, colleges and universities. We might well add funders, as many funding organizations such as the training and enterprise councils/technician education councils, organizations within the NHS or the police service, charitable trusts, research sponsors and private companies will insist on evaluation as part of their funding criteria. Finally, in a wider national and global sense, given the increasing climate of accountability, the community in general is often involved and interested in evaluation findings.

All this means that evaluation can become very complicated, an issue we deal with later in this section. However, in general, it means that any evaluation must specify its intended audience and then ensure it covers all their interests and not simply those of the course developer(s).

Task 8.12: Evaluation: what, why and for whom?

(a)   Provide a definition of evaluation and say why it is not assessment.

(b)   Why is evaluation an important part of course development?

(c)   For your course, who might be interested in an evaluation and why?

Having established the need for an evaluation, what is going to be evaluated? Partly, as was argued in Chapter 7, this will depend on the course ideology and curriculum model(s); that is, the kind of curriculum you have developed. However, you must also be clear about the main purpose of your evaluation. Is it to help course improvement, to establish its impact and outcomes or some combination of the two? And how much time and money is available, if any? Whatever you decide, ensure you are undertaking something which is practical. Considering these questions will help you to identify what you want to evaluate.

Even when you know the course well there may still be difficulties in deciding what to evaluate, or, as is often the case, what to leave out of an evaluation. Figure 8.7 presents two approaches to this question generated by groups of Diploma in Education and Training students. Which seems the most appropriate to you and why?

In general, Group B's approach is to be recommended simply because it maintains a tight focus on the evaluation work. Even if you have limitless time, money and other resources for evaluation, you still need to be clear about what you are evaluating.

Group A listed the main things that seem to happen in the course, e.g.:

- Are aims and objectives being achieved?
- Is it effective for the learners?
- What are the outcomes for the learners?
- What has been the impact on staff?
- Is there the right balance of process, content and product?
- Was there any evidence of enjoyment?
- What have the costs really been?
- What have the benefits really been?
- What do employers, colleges or universities think?

Group B identified broad areas for evaluation before generating specific questions, e.g.:

- the quality of classroom/training area experience;
- the organization of the course;
- levels of student motivation and attainment;
- the organizational context for the course.

Figure 8.7 Deciding what to evaluate: two approaches

Task 8.13: Deciding what to evaluate in your course

(a) What is/are the purpose(s) of your evaluation?
(b) What broad evaluation areas can you identify?
(c) Why have you decided on these?

Having established the purposes and focal points of the evaluation, what specific issues do you want information about under each of the broad headings and how will you gain this information? The close link between these two is, in reality, a reflection of your educational ideology and the theoretical basis of your course, and this will identify the practical methods of any evaluation. Figure 8.8 presents three theoretical evaluation models to show this. Remember, as with all theoretical models, including those discussed in Chapter 7, you need to use them to help you review and develop your own practice rather than allow them to dictate your approach.

As teachers/trainers, most of us need evaluation data on a range of course issues, both because we want to monitor and improve our work and because others require data for their own purposes. For example, every FE college must collect a wide range of statistical information for the Skills Funding Agency (SFA) about levels of recruitment, retention and attainment. This points clearly to you needing to employ a variety of evaluation methods (although very few people adopt the classical approach which is more suitable for a formal research project). This variety is certainly acceptable provided, as before, you acknowledge it openly in your course proposal to show you are aware of what you are doing.

1   *Scientific evaluation I: classical evaluation*

Features:

- views the course as an experiment or treatment to be administered to the students;
- solely interested in measuring course effectiveness defined by the intended outcomes;
- will have test group(s) following the course and control group(s) not following it;
- tests all the students before and after the course to judge course effectiveness and to compare the course with others;
- data and reports very statistical/quantitative.

2   *Scientific evaluation II: evaluation via behavioural objectives*

Features:

- still views the course as something of an experiment;
- draws on behavioural notions of learning and curriculum design;
- specifies the intended learning outcomes as behavioural objectives;
- records the proportion of students attaining/not attaining the specified behaviours;
- data and reports very statistical/quantitative.

This approach possesses all the advantages and disadvantages of behaviourist perspectives on education and training that were discussed in Chapter 3. For example, can all learning be expressed as behaviours? If not, then this reduces learning to a simplistic shadow of its true nature. However, there is an elegant simplicity to the approach which has seen it become ever more popular in a wide variety of education and training courses.

3   *Qualitative evaluation*

Features:

- views the course as a human, social activity, not as a scientific experiment;
- interested in a host of content and process issues but especially the course intentions and organization, the experience of the course in practice and the range of outcomes including the unintended;
- also interested in the perspectives of everyone involved, not just the course designer(s);
- uses methods such as observation, interviews and questionnaires as well as assessment and other data;
- reports more language-based than statistical.

This approach draws more on the arts and social sciences so that, rather than aiming for a simple rating of achievement, there is a more complex approach to the measurement of course effectiveness. This means that the aim is to present a holistic picture of the new course in operation which is designed to illuminate the reality of the course for all those involved. Thus, it is hoped, the various strengths and weaknesses might be identified.

Figure 8.8 Three models of evaluation

Task 8.14: In your own words

(a)   Summarize the main points about these three evaluation models.

(b)   Why, in practice, are a variety of approaches usually adopted?

Now you are in a position to identify what issues you want to evaluate within each of the broad evaluation areas identified in Task 8.13(b) and to specify how information about each could be collected. At this stage, just work through all the issues you would like to evaluate. To help you, Figure 8.9 shows how the same student Group B from Figure 8.7 turned their broad evaluation areas into a series of possible evaluation issues and strategies.

---

1   *The quality of classroom/training area experience*

Specific issues worth evaluating:

- Purpose
- Pace
- Clarity of teacher talk
- Quality of student activity
- Teaching/learning resources
- Tutor–student and student–student relationships
- Discipline
- Teacher subject knowledge etc.
- Quality of formative and summative assessment strategies

Suggested evaluation strategies/evidence sources (in no order):

- Teacher observation
  - by peer?
  - by outsider/manager?
  - by self?
- Ask the students
  - verbally?
  - in writing?
  - open or closed questions?
- Teacher qualifications
- Evidence of record-keeping/tracking and final success rates

2   *The organization of the course*

Specific issues worth evaluating:

- Planning – on the basis of any earlier evaluation?
- Resources
- Tutorials and support systems
- Staffing
- Monitoring and evaluation procedures

Suggested evaluation strategies/evidence sources (in no order):

- Evidence of schemes of work and resources available
- Course handbook on tutorial and support
- Evaluation data
- Staffing details
- Evidence of record-keeping/tracking and final success rates
- Ask the students
  - verbally?
  - in writing?
  - open or closed questions?

3   *Levels of student motivation and attainment*

Specific issues worth evaluating:

- Attendance
- Results
- Destinations

Suggested evaluation strategies/evidence sources (in no order):

- Registers
- Retention rates

Figure 8.9 Suggested evaluation issues and methods

- Are students' ideas valued?

- Formal results
- Teacher observation
  - by peer?
  - by outsider/manager?
- Ask the students and note student demeanour, non-verbal behaviour etc.
- Are there any indications of fun, enjoyment, humour etc. demonstrated by staff and students?
- Any earlier evaluation data?

4   *The organizational context for the course*

Specific issues worth evaluating:

- Accommodation
- Resourcing
- Staffing
- Library etc.
- Management and communication

Suggested evaluation strategies/evidence sources (in no order):

- Visit accommodation, view resources and library
- Ask the students
  - verbally?
  - in writing?
  - open or closed questions?
- Staffing details
- Formal question and answer systems
  - on paper
  - face to face

Figure 8.9 *(Continued)*

Task 8.15: Identifying specific evaluation issues and methods

Use the suggestions in Figure 8.9 to help your thinking about evaluation.

(a)   Select the specific issues you would want to evaluate in your course.
(b)   Select the evaluation strategies you think would give accurate data.
(c)   When would you collect the data? Why is the timing important?
(d)   Explain your choices. How practical do you think they are?
(e)   Revise your list of issues and strategies in the light of (d) so that you have a practical as well as an effective evaluation strategy.

Task 8.15(e) raises another major consideration, that of ensuring the evaluation you plan is able to operate in practice. Thus, your original choices in Task 8.15 might well have needed revising. Remember, a small scale, properly thought through and carried out evaluation will be far more useful than a large, impractical and poorly implemented version.

Finally, what will happen to the results of your evaluation? They will need analysing and presenting in a clear format so that the findings can be conveyed to whoever requires them and, more importantly, so that you can identify those

1	Identify the purpose(s) of the evaluation.
2	Identify the broad areas to be evaluated.
3	Consider the kind(s) of evaluation best suited to your needs.
4	Identify the specific issues to be evaluated and the methods.
5	Ensure the evaluation will be able to operate in practice.
6	Collect the data, analyse, and report to all involved.
7	Explain any proposed changes with reasons.
8	Build changes into next course planning cycle and evaluate.

Figure 8.10 Suggested sequence for developing a course evaluation

areas of the course that need improving and build these into your next course planning session (we should not forget that, in certain circumstances, there may well be a good case for not changing things). Whatever the situation, your report must explain the reasons for whatever action or non-action you propose to take.

To summarize, this section has defined course evaluation and has differentiated this from assessment. Evaluation has been presented as a means of judging course effectiveness for a range of interested parties and for a similar range of reasons. Advice has been provided about what to evaluate by suggesting the selection of a small number of key, broad areas as a starting point. Three theoretical models of evaluation have been used to explain the link between what is to be evaluated and how it can be evaluated, followed by an opportunity to make some of these links and to develop a practical and worthwhile evaluation programme. All this is presented as a sequence in Figure 8.10.

Note the final stage. Evaluation is a continuous process if it is to help you keep improving the quality of your course. Moreover, given the moves towards increased accountability in all areas of education and training, as Hopkins (1989) notes, evaluation now often leads to a public discussion and to subsequent action or judgement. There are league tables for almost every aspect of education and training. If we are to engage in evaluation for reasons other than simply our own professionalism, and it seems we must, then any evaluation we carry out must be of high quality in order to promote and develop high-quality education and training.

8.4 Scrutinizing your course

KEY ISSUES

Why not allow new and revised courses to operate as soon as they're worked out?

The scrutiny process: what is it all about?

How can a new or revised course be made ready for the scrutiny process?

What does a formal course proposal document contain?

What is involved in presenting a course and in scrutinizing other people's courses?

You might well ask, given all the hard work you have put in already, why you can not just run the course? There are two reasons. First, in line with the notions of increased efficiency and accountability mentioned frequently in this and other chapters, education and training organizations now expect new courses to be developed and presented to set criteria and then examined rigorously and, if necessary, revised, before being allowed to operate. In most colleges and universities, this is called the *scrutiny process*. National qualifications such as A level and NVQ are offered by awarding bodies and they have a similar process, as do the academic examining boards, for those who wish to develop new or amended versions of such courses.

Second, there is a professional development dimension. Given that we might well have spent time and energy on developing a new course and this might well have been a team effort, there is still a danger that, being so involved and committed to it, we will fail to spot all the flaws in our work. A scrutiny process helps by allowing the organization to take some responsibility for helping us avoid making mistakes. As will be seen later in the section, it also provides us, our colleagues in the organization and in other similar organizations with opportunities to learn about curriculum development by taking part in it. It is the scrutiny process which lies at the heart of this section.

What is the scrutiny process? It is a set of procedures designed to support staff in the development and revision of courses. It ensures that such courses meet the criteria set by the organization and other relevant bodies, are planned to the highest standards, are examined by experts (internal and external to the organization) and are only then allowed to operate.

In most cases, the organization will provide staff with guidelines and some support in the scrutiny process. In this instance, some guidelines are set out in Figure 8.11, while this section and the book as a whole act as support.

Phase 1: Course development or revision

1.1   The course development team plan what they consider to be an appropriate course following the appropriate framework (NVQ, degree, awarding organization rules, police/ nurse training regulations etc.).

1.2   The proposed course is organized into a course proposal document and distributed to the others involved in the scrutiny process.

Phase 2: Internal scrutiny

2.1   The course development team makes a formal presentation of their proposed course and document to an internal scrutiny panel composed of the organization's representatives and a number (three?) of staff colleagues acting as internal scrutineers.

2.2   The internal scrutineers use the course document to become familiar with the proposal, listen to the presentation, discuss it and pose searching but not unfriendly questions to the course development team on any issues of concern.

Figure 8.11 The scrutiny process

2.3 At the end of this meeting, the internal scrutiny panel must pass one of four judgements on the proposed course:

   1   Accept unreservedly in which case the proposal goes forward to Phase 4.

   2   Accept subject to minor changes in which case the proposal moves to Phase 3.

   3   Accept subject to major changes in which case the proposal moves to Phase 3.

   4   Reject, which means the proposal has no chance of becoming an approved course.

Phase 3: Revisions to original proposal

3.1 Depending on the scale of the changes imposed by the internal scrutiny panel, the course development team works to amend the course proposal in line with the panel's requirements and resubmits a revised course proposal document.

3.2 Once the organization can see that all the necessary changes have been made, the proposal proceeds to the next phase.

Phase 4: External scrutiny

4.1 The scrutiny panel will reconvene but this time with two or three external validators.

4.2 The external validators are specialists in the field but from other organizations. Their role is to carry out an expert and impartial critical scrutiny of the proposed course.

4.3 The course development team makes another formal presentation of their proposed course and document.

4.4 The panel listens to the presentation, discusses it and poses more questions to the course development team on any issues of concern.

4.5 At the end of this meeting, the external scrutiny panel must again pass one of four judgements:

   1   Accept unreservedly in which case the proposal goes forward to Phase 5.

   2   Accept subject to minor changes in which case the proposal moves to Phase 5 after these changes have been made.

   3   Accept subject to major changes in which case the proposal might well need further external scrutiny.

   4   Reject, which means that the proposal has lost its chance of becoming an approved course.

Phase 5: Course approved to operate

5.1 The organization will allow the course to be run for up to five years subject to satisfactory levels of recruitment, retention and student success and to satisfactory annual evaluation reports.

Figure 8.11 *(Continued)*

What does a course proposal document contain? Figure 8.12 shows the content normally required. In addition, such documents are always presented in as professional a manner as possible. After all, the document represents the quality of your proposed course to those on the scrutiny panels.

1   A brief rationale for the proposed course explaining why it is such an important development. Add information about student and market needs analysis. Add reasons for sizes of: recruitment targets; minimum and maximum numbers; staff/student ratios.

2   A statement of course aims.

3   An outline of course content expressed as objectives and outcomes.

4   A description of the course organization including: an outline scheme of work; one fully detailed session plan; a typical student's experiences; a typical student's attendance pattern.

5   Details of teaching and learning strategies to be employed.

6   An outline of the assessment framework to be used.

7   An outline of the evaluation framework to be used including sample materials.

8   An indication of any resource implications arising from the new course including accommodation, equipment and staffing (expertise and training as well as number).

9   A costs table including, if possible, hourly staffing costs, any other support costs, accommodation and equipment, recurrent costs, overheads etc. These are usually available from organizations' administrators.

10   An indication of revenue from the course showing sources and levels both short and (estimated) longer term together with some comment as to how certain and long-lasting the revenue might be.

Figure 8.12 Content of a course proposal document

Task 8.16: The scrutiny process: what is it all about?

(a)   Why shouldn't we just put our new courses straight into operation?

(b)   What are the purposes of a scrutiny process?

(c)   How does it work and what is the role of the course proposal document?

This all looks like a pretty large piece of work, and so it is. This is a full course proposal and getting a new or revised course off the ground is a serious business. So, how can you make what you have already produced in terms of your new or revised course into a formal course proposal ready to go forward to the scrutiny process? For quick reference, Table 8.2 links each task from Chapters 7 and 8 with sections in the course proposal document.

Task 8.17: Writing most of your course proposal document

(a)   Using Table 8.2 collect all your responses to earlier tasks together.

(b)   Write them up in full and arrange them under the 10 headings of a course proposal document, as outlined in Figure 8.12.

Proposal document content	Section	Task	Course development activity
1, 2, 3, 4, 5, 6, 7	7.6	7.15	Sharpen thinking on curriculum, ideology, curriculum models
1, 2, 3	8.2	8.1	Identify your curriculum development or revision task
1, 2, 3	8.2	8.2	Decide on the kind of course it will be
8, 9, 10	8.2	8.3	Identify the organization's criteria for costs, numbers etc.
2	8.2	8.4	Conduct a needs analysis
1, 2, 3	8.2	8.5	Decide on the broad purposes for the course
2, 3	8.2	8.6	Specify the course aims and objectives
4, 5, 6	8.2	8.7, 8.8, 8.9	Specify content, sequence, learning/ assessment experiences
7	8.3	8.11, 8.12, 8.13, 8.14, 8.15	Establish a set of evaluation procedures

Table 8.2 Tasks linked to creating a course proposal document

You should find that the only areas requiring further work are 8, 9 and 10 on resources, costs and revenue. Once again, do not worry. Even if you hate working with figures, Task 8.18 will show you how to tackle this area.

Task 8.18: Writing the rest of your course proposal document

Your own organization will have ready-made lists of costs for most kinds of course and will usually help refine these for your particular course. Ask for their standard costings and for additional advice if needed.

If you are hoping to run a self-financing course, hotels, conference centres and other venues all provide cost schedules on request. Just ask for them.

Revenue is more a matter of estimation. Work out what income you expect the course to generate and consider how certain you are of your figures and for how long you expect revenue to be earned. Write this up including the basis for your estimates. Ask your organization for help if you need it – they should be used to assisting their staff with this kind of issue.

(a)   Write up your work on these areas and add to your course proposal document.

(b)   Check through your document to ensure that every heading is complete and that the spelling, layout and general feel of the document is as professional (not flashy) as possible.

What is involved in being a presenter and a scrutineer at one of these scrutiny panel meetings? In order to gain for yourself the maximum quantity and quality of professional benefit from this chapter, you are strongly advised to work with at least one other person to reproduce a scrutiny process for yourself. If you are a member of a group, all the better. Several of you can work together to develop a proposal, perhaps starting with one person's idea or a real course development task someone has been given. Others can act as scrutineers of that group's proposal. Then you can reverse the roles.

In essence, what is being asked of you is to work from two perspectives: that of the curriculum developer and that of the scrutiny panel member. Things can often look different from someone else's perspective and you will learn a great deal by having your own course development scrutinized by someone else and by scrutinizing someone else's course proposal yourself. It will also be invaluable preparation for working on similar tasks in your teaching and training work. Indeed, a fair proportion of Diploma in Education and Training course proposals become real courses and go into operation very smoothly because of their careful planning and preparation. To help you to prepare for a scrutiny panel meeting, Figures 8.13 and 8.14 provide guidance on how to be a member of a scrutiny panel and how to be a course presenter. In order for scrutiny panel members to operate as effectively as possible, a sample checklist and form is provided in Figure 8.15.

The role of a scrutiny panel member is:

- to complete a comprehensive evaluation of the proposal focusing on the use of curriculum ideology and design model(s) as well as evaluating the proposal as set out in Figure 8.12;
- to help the course development team to make progress and suggest action points as needed (unless the proposal is a non-starter, in which case the organization should have stopped it earlier);
- harder than it might seem!

We must therefore be critical where necessary, award praise where appropriate and, above all, be positive. We are there to help another set of professionals with their work, not to turn it into our work!

Tasks of a scrutiny panel member:

- Before the scrutiny panel meeting to read the course proposal document thoroughly and draw up a checklist of questions and comments.
- During the scrutiny panel meeting to listen to the presentation and delete or add questions and comments to the checklist.
- Immediately following the presentation to ask questions of clarification.
- During the post-presentation discussion to ask questions, discuss and provide feedback in a critical and/or positive manner as appropriate, perhaps by always having a positive suggestion to make following any criticism. If changes are needed, the job is to help them be made, not simply point out the problem.

Figure 8.13 Being a scrutiny panel member

The role of a course presenter is:

- to provide as professional a proposal document as possible well in advance of the meeting;
- to provide evidence of depth of information and thinking through the presentation;
- harder than it might seem!

We must, therefore, plan and prepare for the presentation very carefully.

We are there to help other professionals to gain an accurate picture of our proposals, not to 'sock it to 'em'!

Tasks of a course presenter:

- Before the scrutiny panel meeting to supply sufficient copies of a high-quality course proposal document.
- To plan and deliver a professional presentation. There will usually be at least 20 minutes for your presentation and plenty of time for discussion and for the scrutineers' questions afterwards.
- To ensure that the style of the presentation reflects the course: give a sample of how students will experience it and use any techniques you feel are appropriate. Above all make it interesting (and fun!).
- During the scrutiny panel meeting to listen as well as talk, and not be too defensive.
- Immediately following the presentation to answer questions of clarification.
- During the post-presentation discussion to answer questions, discuss and respond to feedback as appropriate, avoiding defensiveness and always having a positive approach to the meeting. If need be, ask for positive action points to follow any criticism. Remember, if changes are needed, the job of the scrutiny panel is to help to develop the course.

Figure 8.14 Being a course presenter at a scrutiny panel

This would normally be printed over two sides of an A4 sheet and completed copies would be given to the presenters as well as to the organization's representatives.

Presenting team:

Course title and details:

Scrutiny panel criteria:

Use the following checklist to make brief notes here as needed.

1   Is there a brief rationale for the proposed course? Does it include:
  - a student and market needs analysis?
  - recruitment targets?
  - minimum and maximum numbers?
  - staff/student ratios?

2   Is there a statement of course aims and objectives? Are these appropriate to the needs of the client group? Do they specify the kinds of intended learning outcomes?

Figure 8.15 Suggestions for a scrutiny panel evaluation form

3   Is there an outline of course content which is linked to the intended aims/objectives/outcomes?

4   Is there a description of the course organization, an outline scheme of work and a session plan, outlines of staff/student ratios, and a typical student's experiences and attendance pattern?

5   Are there details of teaching and learning strategies/materials to be employed which seem to match the intended aims/objectives/outcomes?

6   Is the assessment framework to be used appropriate to the intended aims etc.?

7   Is the evaluation framework to be used appropriate to the intended aims etc.?

8   Is there evidence that the following have been considered?

   •   resource implications;

   •   costs;

   •   revenue.

General comments and any recommended revisions/additions:

Overall recommendation (delete as appropriate):

•   Accept now

•   Accept with minor/major revisions as specified above

•   Reject

Name of scrutineer:

Date:

Figure 8.15 *(Continued)*

Task 8.19: Preparing for a scrutiny panel

If you are able to attend a scrutiny panel meeting, either as a presenter or as a scrutineer, use Figures 8.13, 8.14 and 8.15 to help you prepare for the event.

To summarize, this section has examined the process through which most organizations now support and approve the development and revision of new courses. The scrutiny process has been explained and a framework provided for the new course to be presented as a single document. Furthermore, explicit links have been made between this final document and the tasks spread through this chapter so that readers are able to see how their work can contribute to a full course proposal.

Finally, the section has advised all readers to take part in the scrutiny process or something similar because of the tremendous amount of professional learning that will emerge from such an experience. To this end, guidance and advice have been provided covering both the roles of course presenter and scrutineer.

Links to the Professional Standards for Teachers and Trainers in Education and Training

Professional values and attributes

1 Reflect on what works best in your teaching and learning to meet the diverse needs of learners

2 Evaluate and challenge your practice, values and beliefs

5 Value and promote social and cultural diversity, equality of opportunity and inclusion

Professional knowledge and understanding

10 Evaluate your practice with others and assess its impact on learning

Professional skills

14 Plan and deliver effective learning programmes for diverse groups or individuals in a safe and inclusive environment

17 Enable learners to share responsibility for their own learning and assessment, setting goals that stretch and challenge

20 Contribute to organisational development and quality improvement through collaboration with others

9

Developments in Post-14 Education and Training

9.1 What is Chapter 9 about?

Teachers and trainers in Post-14 Education and Training may teach specialist subjects but they may also see themselves as educators or even educationalists and seek to become knowledgeable about the subject of education. This view is rather unpopular as teaching is seen more and more as a practical activity in which experience is valued over theoretical knowledge. The introduction of competence-based teacher training programmes means that teacher education programmes of the 1970s, built around the study of the subject of education, no longer exist. As we saw in Chapter 1, the new educational thought of that time resulted in ideas, theories and clear distinctions that are now thought to constitute an arid rationalism. It has been argued that too much had been lost in terms of theory, and that this had contributed to the current chaotic state of teaching in Post-14 Education and Training. As a way forward the focus was particularly on developing teachers' understanding of the various educational philosophies that influence their professional practice. These views were later related to well-known theories of learning and studies of the curriculum. As seen in Chapter 1, the new coalition government of 2010 seemed to be unaware of the shift to practice and away from theory over the last two decades and had a poor opinion of over-theoretical teacher training. This chapter complements Chapter 1 and other chapters in the book by providing teachers and trainers with the essential background to begin to examine the contemporary historical development of Post-14 Education and Training in order to understand the present.

There are pedagogical, professional and theoretical reasons why a chronology is both important and necessary and it may be useful to elaborate these at the outset to avoid any misunderstanding.

In pedagogical terms, a chronology provides a useful starting point for someone new to the study of education or of any subject. It is a pedagogical device.

Whatever the reason you want to understand a subject or topic, the essential first step is to develop a chronology of key events. Without this the process of serious study cannot begin. We would argue that if teachers do not have even a familiarity with the barest outline of the history of education, they have no real understanding of the subject. If you are a Post-14 Education and Training teacher, whatever your academic or vocational background, you should have such a basic knowledge of Post-14 Education and Training history and also of significant developments in lifelong learning and higher education (HE). Trainee teachers in Post-14 Education and Training and other sectors often see a chronology as just knowing dates and are uninterested. For very specific historical reasons a certain philistinism is now commonplace about historical events. Eric Hobsbawm has argued that this is because of the collapse of 'social mechanisms', such as the labour movement and trade unions, that linked people's experience to that of previous generations. The result of this collapse is that 'Most young men and women at the century's end grow up in a sort of permanent present lacking any organic relation to the public past of the times they live in' (Hobsbawm 1994: 3). In part, producing a chronology is an attempt to overcome this absence of a historical memory.

In professional terms, teachers sometimes like to think that their academic subject or their vocation is in some way independent of outside influences or broader trends in society. Nothing could be further from the truth. Any consideration of the nature of education or its translation into the sphere of policy is the result of a much more complex set of relations in society. This does not have to be a one-way street from broader social trends to education policy, nor is it a process devoid of contradiction. Serious thinking and passionately held beliefs about education will themselves have an impact on the way that society thinks about itself and there will often be a gap between intention and outcome. Nevertheless, the way education is viewed will say a great deal about society as a whole. This is because it is in the very nature of education that it will be emblematic of how society both would like itself to be and how it hopes and aspires to get there. In general then, it should be no surprise that discussion about education often preoccupies discussion about issues as apparently wide-ranging as economic performance and moral rectitude. The significance of the discussion for us is not at this level of generality but in the specific combination of political consensus and conflict, the identification of new problems and challenges and the shifts in policy with which we characterize the recent development of Post-14 Education and Training in Britain.

We would argue that any professional practitioner must have this 'historical' knowledge if they are to be purposeful and active participants in their own professional development and the development of their profession. Otherwise those that do have that knowledge will merely direct them without them having the benefit of the informed discussion and debate that is essential to the practice of education. Part of the rationale for this chronology is that we recognize that many teachers in Post-14 Education and Training will not have the background in educational history, social policy or related studies to give them a sufficient knowledge base to make a conscious contribution to debate. If approached studiously the chronology can, along with the associated activities, present opposing views and interpretations that, we believe, uncover the issues at the heart of contemporary debates and will provide clear critical guidelines for further discussion.

As far as theory is concerned, we can illustrate the possibilities of chronological thinking and show its importance by reference to the concept of the 'third way'. This new political idea has general application as well as a specific application to Post-14 Education and Training. In the late 1990s and early years of this century it was fashionable to talk of the 'third way' but hardly anyone asked what was the 'second way' or, indeed, the 'first way'? If we do not know the answer, the 'third way' is a meaningless label. Broadly, we can characterize the 'first way' as the period of political consensus after the Second World War that resulted in the welfare state. The 'second way' is the relatively short period of Thatcherism that undid this consensus as Thatcher set out to destroy what she saw as 'socialism', a process that was entirely negative in social terms. The 'third way' is an attempt to produce policies which do not return to the welfare state or the marketplace but allow government to have an impact through its policies on the global market to which 'there is no alternative' (TINA). There are various characterizations, of course, but most see the 'third way' as an attempt to find an alternative between the 'neoliberalism' of the Thatcherite sort and the 'social capitalism' adopted by those European governments that maintain a strong centralized welfare state (see Blair 1998; Giddens 1998; Hodgson and Spours 1999; Hayes and Hudson 2001). The 'third way' in Post-14 Education and Training, as in all policy-making arenas, is a contested road and all that can be predicted is frequent policy changes. One assessment of New Labour's first term in office concluded: 'Every day without a new education headline was regarded as a day wasted . . .' (Smithers 2001: 425). Some smart Post-14 Education and Training student teachers and trainers ask if there will be a 'fourth way' and the previous coalition government's promotion of the idea of the 'big society' once seemed to have been the beginning of a new era. But the concept never become popular as it was essentially another 'top-down' idea thought up by policy-makers and, because of this, was as fragile as other third way initiatives.

Reading the chronology, it will be easy to see the relevance of developments in Post-14 Education and Training to such a broad analysis. Since 2003, when the second edition of this book appeared, more and more reviews and reports have looked at the Post-14 Education and Training, and, in particular, the 14–19 phase (Working Group on 14–19 Curriculum Reform 2004; Foster 2005; Leitch 2006; DfES 2007a, 2007b; Wolf 2011; Richard 2012). It almost seems that any day without a new Post-14 Education and Training headline is a day wasted as far as policy-makers are concerned! We do not draw any conclusions or do the work of interpreting any aspect of this chronology for our readers. Our purpose is to encourage teachers and trainers to think for themselves about the history of Post-14 Education and Training and to develop their understanding of events. Suggestions and activities are given about how to think about the historical periods covered. We have also been involved in a small study of student responses to the chronology and some of the activities set out here that readers may find interesting (Hayes et al. 2007b).

As well as being important as a vehicle for developing our understanding, it is also true that a chronology is a very useful work of reference for all teachers. We even refer to it ourselves!

Section 9.2 introduces the chronology of Post-14 Education and Training in England, presented in Section 9.3, which gives the reader a broad survey of major developments. Even readers familiar with this history might like to skim-read the chronology.

9.2 The purpose of the chronology

What follows is an overview of major government reports, education Acts and important developments relating to Post-14 Education and Training which provide the essential historical background to the analysis of the issues discussed in previous chapters. Emphasis is given to developments in the post-Second World War period, although major developments relating to education since the Industrial Revolution are also summarized. The purpose is to provide the reader with basic factual information in a concise and accessible form. Authorial commentary and discussion has been largely omitted but the selection has a deliberate focus on developments in further education (FE) and youth training. We do not hide the fact that it is a central part of our argument that developments in this area have influenced education at all levels. Developments in the general educational sphere, in adult education (AE), HE and in special education are also listed if these are essential to the identification of educational trends.

Reading the chronology

A chronology is often seen as just a list of events in date order. We are using the term to describe a carefully selected list that gives the reader an overview of key events, reports, acts and writings in the history of Post-14 Education and Training. The best way to approach the chronology is to skim-read the dates and headings in bold. Then go back through the whole document reading complete sections or entries of interest. The tasks are in the form of questions to guide your thinking about historical periods.

Reflecting on the chronology

To make sense of the chronology we suggest two methods of reflection. The first is to think in terms of what different generations of young people and adults might have expected or experienced in terms of Post-14 Education and Training in any specific historical period. The second approach is to step back from the details of the particular discussion or development in Post-14 Education and Training and attempt to locate people's expectations in the wider context of social policy and political and economic events.

Boxes within the text contain relevant political and economic facts to remind the reader of the historical context of the events listed. The interaction between these three activities, getting familiar with particular events, imagining the expectations of generations of young people and adults, and locating these in a wider social context, are essential to understanding.

9.3 A chronology of Post-14 Education and Training

1563: Statute of Artificers This statute established the seven-year apprenticeship as the basic form of training in England. A further Act, the Poor Law of 1601, allowed for the forcible apprenticeship of pauper children. Craft apprenticeship was the form of technical training up to the time of the Industrial Revolution. Arguably, it remained the dominant form of work-related training up to the 1960s when the Industrial Training Act 1964 was passed.

1823: Mechanics' Institutes established Mechanics' Institutes were set up in Chester in 1810, Perth in 1814, Edinburgh in 1821 (actually a 'school of arts') and most famously in Glasgow in 1823. George Birkbeck taught at what was to become the Glasgow Mechanics' Institute but left to practise as a physician in London. He helped establish a similar institute there in 1823 which was to become Birkbeck College. The movement grew and had its own publication, *The Mechanics Magazine*. By 1826 there were 110 institutes and by 1850 some 600,000 people were attending classes in one of 610 institutes.

1846: pupil–teacher system introduced Bright pupils were apprenticed at 13 years of age to headteachers for a period of five years.

1856: Royal Society of Arts (RSA) founds first national examining board.

1856: Education Department formed Robert Lowe became vice-president in 1859 and introduced the system of 'payment by results' which lasted until 1900. Grants were given on the basis of school attendance, which was revealed to be low by the Newcastle Commission Report of 1861, and on the results of an examination in the 'three Rs'.

1864: Clarendon Commission Report The commission suggested that the classical curriculum of the public schools be supplemented by instruction in subjects such as mathematics and science.

1868: Taunton Commission Report The commission emphasized the importance of natural science as a subject because it was seen as of value in 'occupations'. The commissioners outlined various 'grades' of education ending respectively at 14 (Grade 3), 16 (Grade 2) and 18 (Grade 1), meeting the needs of the various social classes.

1870: Elementary Education Act (Forster Act) The Great Education Act introduced a national system of elementary education for children up to 13 years of age, replacing the previous system based on 'voluntary schools'. School boards became responsible for the running of the new 'Board Schools' and pupil attendance was at their discretion. Fees were charged. The Education Act of 1880 had to be passed to attempt to make elementary education compulsory by requiring school boards to enact by-laws to this effect. Employment of children under 10 was made illegal under the Factory and Workshops Act of 1878. Introducing the Act, Forster told the Commons: 'Upon the speedy provision of elementary education depends our industrial prosperity' (Maclure 1965: 104).

Task 9.1

Consider what sort of education a young person would receive at this time. Why should an educational debate about the suitability of an education based upon the classics or one extended to include more relevant subjects such as mathematics or science arise in the 1860s? Why should there be only an 'elementary' Education Act passed at this time and why one that provided an education which was neither universal nor free?

Education in context: 1868–1922

Prime ministers: 1868 Disraeli (Conservative); 1868–74 Gladstone (Liberal); 1874–80 Disraeli II (Conservative); 1880–5 Gladstone (Liberal); 1885–6 Gascoyne-Cecil, 3rd Marquis of Salisbury (Conservative); 1886 Gladstone (Liberal); 1886–92 Gascoyne-Cecil, 3rd Marquis of Salisbury (Conservative); 1892–4 Gladstone (Liberal); 1894–5 5th Earl of Rosebery (Liberal); 1895–1902 Gascoyne-Cecil, 3rd Marquis of Salisbury (Conservative); 1902–5 Balfour (Conservative); 1905–8 Campbell Bannerman (Liberal); 1908–16 Asquith (Liberal/Coalition); 1916–22 Lloyd George (Liberal/Coalition).

Presidents of the board of education: from April 1900, Spencer Cavendish, Duke of Devonshire; from August 1902, Charles Vane-Tempest-Stewart, Marquis of Londonderry; from December 1905, Augustine Birrell; from January 1907, Reginald McKenna; from April 1908, Walter Runciman; from October 1911, Joseph Albert Pease; from May 1915, Arthur Henderson; from August 1916, Robert Crewe-Milnes, Marquis of Crewe; from December 1916, Herbert Albert Laurens Fisher.

Key political and economic events: 1851 Great Exhibition; 1867 Paris Exhibition, Reform Act; 1868 Trades Union Congress formed; 1870–1 Franco-Prussian War; 1873 'Great Depression'; 1883 Depression, Fabian Society formed; 1887 Jubilee; 1889 first skyscraper in Chicago; 1897 Diamond Jubilee; 1898 Spanish American War, match girls strike; 1889 London dock strike; 1899–1902 Second Boer War; 1903 Ford Motor Company founded; 1914–18 First World War; 1917 Russian Revolution.

1879: the City & Guilds of London Institute (CGLI), founded in 1878, is given the responsibility for technical examining from the RSA.

1880: the famous Regent Street Polytechnic founded   One of many polytechnics that developed out of the Mechanics' Institutes in different parts of Britain.

1882–4: Samuelson Committee   The committee made recommendations about the need for scientific and technical instruction of the sort that was already available to workers in the USA and many European countries.

1889: Technical Instruction Act   This enabled the new counties and county councils to provide technical education. A transfer of tax reserves popularly known as 'whisky money' was used mostly to provide science education.

1890: day training colleges for teachers are introduced.

1902: Education Act (Balfour Act)   When introducing his bill in the house Balfour stressed the need for a sound general education. There was already a single supervisory body for education in existence at a national level. This was the Board of Education that had been formed by an Act of 1899. Actual provision of education at a local level became the responsibility of local education authorities (LEAs) which took over the powers of the school boards. They were required to form education committees. Pupils could now stay on in an elementary school up to 16 years of age and beyond. LEAs had powers to train teachers.

1903: the Association for the Higher Education of Working Men founded   It became the Workers' Educational Association (WEA) in 1905. By 1968 the WEA was catering for 150,000 students and had 85 full-time staff (WEA evidence to the Russell Report 1973).

1906: Haldane Committee Report on technical education   The report called for the establishment of a group of colleges of science and technology where the highest specialized instruction could be given. The result was the founding of Imperial College in 1907.

1907: Ruskin Hall (1899) became Ruskin College, Oxford   Its founding document states that the college is 'designed to equip the workers for the struggle against capitalism and capitalist ideology'.

Education in context: 1922–45

Prime ministers: 1922–3 Bonar Law (Conservative); 1923–4 Baldwin (Conservative); 1924 MacDonald (Labour); 1924–9 Baldwin (Conservative); 1929–35 MacDonald (Labour/coalition); 1935–7 Baldwin (national); 1937–40 Chamberlain (national); 1940–5 Churchill (coalition).

Presidents of the Board of Education: from October 1922, E.F.L. Wood; from January 1924, Charles Trevelyan; from November 1924, Lord Eustace Percy; from June 1929, Sir Charles Trevelyan; from March 1931, Hastings Lees-Smith; from August 1931, Sir Donald Maclean; from June 1932, Lord E.F.L. Wood, Baron Irwin (Viscount Halifax); from June 1935, Oliver Stanley; from May 1937, James Stanhope, The Earl Stanhope; from October 1938, Herbrand Sackville, The Earl De La Warr; from April 1940, Herwald Ramsbotham; from July 1941, R.A. Butler.

Ministers of education: from August 1944, R.A. Butler; from May 1945, Richard Law.

Key political and economic events: 1924 first Labour government; 1926 General Strike; 1929 Wall Street Crash, Depression; 1931 Empire State Building completed; 1933 Hitler becomes chancellor of Germany; 1936–9 Spanish Civil War; 1939–45 Second World War.

1917: School Certificate introduced.

1918: Education Act (Fisher Act)   This Act raised the school leaving age to 14 with most pupils staying in all-age elementary schools. Other key actions were: abolition of fees; the requirement that central government meet not less than half the costs of educational provision; and that young workers should have a right to day release. Many other things 'allowed' but not compelled by the Act fell when funding was cut by one-third in 1922 ('Geddes Axe'). Introducing his Education Bill on 10 August 1917, H.A.L. Fisher, the architect of the 1918 Act, argued that 'education is one of the good things of life' and that the 'principles upon which well-to-do parents proceed in the education of their families are valid; also *mutatis mutandis* for the families of the poor' (Maclure 1965: 175).

1922: R.H. Tawney's *Secondary Education for All* **published.**

1926: Evening Institutes established   The precursors of AE institutes and colleges, they, along with the technical schools, provided most of the technical education available in the inter-war period.

1926: Hadow Report *The Education of the Adolescent*   The Hadow Committee recommended a broad and balanced secondary school curriculum which prepared students for diverse occupational groups. It called for the establishment of 'modern' or 'central' schools and 'grammar' schools for pupils with different gifts. Hadow subsequently headed committees that reported on the primary school (1931) and the nursery and infant school (1933).

1938: Spens Report   The *Report of the Consultative Committee on Secondary Education* was strongly supportive of the idea of 'technical high schools' which would not be narrowly vocational but equal in status to grammar schools. The basis for the post-war tripartite system was now set. Spens also suggested changes to the curriculum, the School Certificate and the matriculation system.

1939–45: day release expands from 42,000 to 150,000 during the Second World War.

1940: the Department of Education publishes its 'Green Book' *Education after the War.*

1942: Beveridge Report   This set out plans for a comprehensive system of social security 'from the cradle to the grave'.

1943: Educational Reconstruction   This White Paper set out a vision of an educational system after the war which would provide for diversity while ensuring equality of educational opportunity.

1943: Norwood Report   In a report about examinations appeared proposals for a system of selection through intelligence testing for entry into a tripartite secondary education system made up of modern, technical and grammar secondary schools.

1944: McNair Report   McNair proposed three-year training courses for teachers. The report suggested that training for technical teachers should commence after, rather than before, they started to practise as teachers.

Task 9.2

This task should be in written form, either as short essays or as a group activity using flipcharts. Discuss the period from 1870–1945 with your fellow students. What would school leavers expect to receive in terms of Post-14 Education and Training during this period? Construct brief educational biographies of people who would have been in their late teens in, for example, 1880, 1910 and 1930. Having done this, identify the key characteristics of British education over the period from 1870 to 1913 and between the two world wars (1918–39). Comment on how you think this reflects the position of Britain in the world and its economic situation during the two periods. You might like to consider why 1870 is considered to be an economic turning point for Britain.

Education in context: 1945–51

Prime minister: 1945–51 Clement Atlee (Labour).

Ministers of education: from August 1945, Ellen Wilkinson; from February 1947, George Tomlinson.

Key political and economic events: 1945 United Nations established; 1947 European reconstruction (Marshall Plan); 1950–3 Korean War; 1950 Britain is the economic leader in Europe; 1951 Festival of Britain.

1944: Education Act (Butler Act)   This Act made provision of primary, secondary and FE a duty. A clause allowed for the possibility of compulsory (part-time) FE for all young people up to the age of 18. It was, however, only to become compulsory on a day to be decided. The school leaving age was to be raised to 15.

1945: Percy Report Higher Technological Education   The report looked at how universities were responding to the needs of industry.

Education in context: 1951–64

Prime ministers: 1951–5 Winston Churchill (Conservative); 1955–7 Sir Anthony Eden (Conservative); 1957–63 Harold Macmillan (Conservative); 1963–4 Sir Alec Douglas-Home (Conservative).

Ministers of education: from November 1951, Florence Horsbrugh; from October 1954, David Eccles; from January 1957, Viscount Hailsham; from September 1957, Geoffrey Lloyd; from October 1959, Sir David Eccles; from January 1957, Quintin Hogg, The Viscount Hailsham; from September 1957, Geoffrey Lloyd; from October 1959, David Eccles; from July 1962, Sir Edward Boyle. The Ministry of Education became the Department of Education and Science (DES) in April 1964 with Quintin Hogg (formerly Viscount Hailsham) as secretary of state for education and science.

Key political and economic events: the post-war economic boom; the Cold War; anticolonial struggles in the Third World; 1952 Mau Mau rebellion in Kenya; 1953 Organization of African Unity formed; 1956 Hungarian Revolution; 1956 Suez crisis, Vietnam War begins; 1957 Treaty of Rome, European Economic Community (EEC) formed; 1961 Berlin Wall; 1962 Cuban missile crisis.

1945: Emergency Training Scheme introduced   The aim of this scheme was to increase the supply of teachers in the aftermath of war. After much criticism, it ended in 1951.

1951: General Certificate of Education (GCE) introduced   The GCE replaced the much criticized School Certificate.

1956: White Paper *Technical Education.*

1957: Willis Jackson Report *The Training of Technical Teachers.*

1959: Crowther Report 15–18   The report looked at the different educational needs of a technological age. It noted that over 40 per cent of LEAs had no technical schools. For those who got 'incurably tired of school' the report argued for a 'fresh start in a technical college or some other quasi-adult institution' (HMSO 1959: 412). Specialization in-depth was necessary in the sixth form but not on the basis of vocational usefulness. Crowther recommended that the school leaving age be raised to 16. By 1980 it was hoped that half of 16–18-year-olds should be in full-time FE.

1960: the Further Education Staff College founded at Coombe Lodge, Blagdon, near Bristol.

1963: 'University of the Air' called for in a speech by Harold Wilson   Wilson told his biographer that this was what he wanted to be remembered for 'above almost anything else in his career' (Timmins 1996: 300).

1963: Robbins Report *Higher Education*   'Throughout our report we have assumed as an axiom that courses of higher education should be available for all who are qualified by ability and attainment to pursue them and who wish to do so' (Maclure 1965: 297). Robbins set out a vision of how HE could expand. He suggested an increase from 8 per cent of the school leaving population to 17 per cent by 1980. The report resulted in the setting up of the Council for National Academic Awards (CNAA) and made the training of teachers a responsibility of HE. Teacher training colleges were renamed colleges of education. Colleges of advanced technology (CATs) became university institutions.

Task 9.3

The 1960s was a decade of influential reports. Two others of note are the Newsom Report *Half Our Future* (1963) which suggested that schools should offer a more modern education relevant to the experiences of pupils of below average ability, and the Plowden Report *Children and their Primary Schools* (1967) which put the case for child-centred education. A reaction came at the end of the decade with the publication of the *Black Papers* on education in 1969 and 1975 which argued for a return to formal methods of teaching, grammar schooling and hard-working academic students at university level. Consider what education and training would be available to young people in the latter half of the decade. What is special about the 1960s that made it a decade of political and educational consensus?

Education in context: 1964–70

Prime minister: 1964–70 Harold Wilson (Labour).

Secretaries of state for education and science: from October 1964, Michael Stewart; from January 1965, Anthony Crosland; from August 1967, Patrick Gordon Walker; from April 1968, Edward Short.

> *Key political and economic events:* post-war political consensus: economic and indus-
> trial 'modernization' becomes a theme; The Beatles; Vietnam War; 1964 (USA) Civil
> Rights Bill; 1968 student protests, Organization of Arab Petroleum Exporting Countries
> (OAPEC) formed; 1969 first man on the moon.

1964: the Certificate of Secondary Education (CSE) introduced   CNAA
established.

1964: Industrial Training Boards (ITBs)   These boards were established by
the minister of labour as a consequence of the Industrial Training Act of the same
year. The ITBs were meant to improve the quality of training and thus tackle the
problem of real craft skill shortages. Administered by employers and trade union
representatives the ITBs covered most of the large industrial employment sectors.
Within seven years there were '27 ITBs covering employers with some 15 million
workers' (Finn 1987: 56).

1969: Open University founded.

> **Education in context: 1970–4**
>
> *Prime minister:* 1970–4 Edward Heath (Conservative).
>
> *Secretary of state for education and science:* from June 1970, Margaret Thatcher.
>
> *Key political and economic events:* 1971 collapse of the Bretton Woods agreement,
> President Nixon formally ended convertibility of gold 'on demand' with the dollar;
> 1973 miners' strike, oil crisis, three-day week, Britain joins the EEC; 1974–5 world
> economic recession.

1970: Education (Handicapped Children) Act   A hundred years after the
great Elementary Education Act, children categorized as 'severely subnormal' and
considered 'ineducable' were brought out of junior training schools and into the
education system.

1970: first tertiary college founded in Devon   The development of tertiary
colleges had been argued for by several influential figures, including Tessa
Blackstone.

1971: Open University enrolls its first students.

1972: James Report   This report suggested three stages of teacher training.
A two-year Diploma in Higher Education followed by a year of professional
studies based in school. This would lead to the award of the BA (Ed.).

1972: ROSLA The school leaving age was raised to 16 from September.

1972: *Training for the Future* (DE) This White Paper highlighted failures in the 1964 Industrial Training Act and called for the phasing out of the training levy and for a new role for ITBs. It set up the Training Opportunities Scheme (TOPS).

1973: Technician Education Council (TEC) and Business Education Council (BEC) set up This was as a result of the 1969 Haslegrave Report proposals to plan, coordinate and administer technical courses and examinations.

1973: Russell Report *Adult Education: A Plan for Development* As the title suggests, Russell argued for an expansion of non-vocational AE, particularly because of the unmet needs of 'school-leavers and young adults, older adults, the handicapped and "the disadvantaged"'. Russell set the tone for much of the subsequent debate about AE.

1973: Manpower Services Commission (MSC) The MSC was set up under the Employment and Training Act (1973) to supervise employment and with sufficient powers to plan training at national level. The MSC assumed its responsibilities on 1 January 1974.

1973: Haycocks Report (Haycocks I) on the training of full-time FE teachers This report made major recommendations for improved training. The government, in Circular 11/77, welcomed the proposals and supported the in-service training of 3 per cent of staff at any one time. The report was followed in March 1978 by Haycocks II on AE and part-time teachers and in August 1978 by Haycocks III on the training of FE teachers for 'education management'.

Education in context: 1974–9

Prime ministers: 1974–6 Harold Wilson (Labour); 1976–9 James Callaghan (Labour).

Secretaries of state for education and science: from March 1994, Reginald Prentice; from June 1975, Fred Mulley; from September 1976, Shirley Williams.

Key political and economic events: sterling crisis, International Monetary Fund (IMF) intervention, stagflation (inflation and high unemployment); 1975 Vietnam War ends, civil war in the Lebanon; 1978 Egypt and Israel sign the Camp David Treaty; 1979 Islamic Republic established in Iran; 'winter of discontent' in Britain.

1976: the Great Debate Prime Minister James Callaghan delivered a speech 'Towards a national debate' on 18 October 1976 at Ruskin College, Oxford. This speech has been described as 'a beacon in the history of post-war education. It brought education into the full light of public debate, giving education a position of prominence on public agendas where it has remained ever since' (Williams 1992: 1–2). One question that Callaghan was addressing had been set for him by Fred Mulley (secretary of state for education and science from June 1975): what was available for the 16–19-year-olds? One concern was the overspecialization at A level. In the speech the goal of education was said to be 'to equip children to the best of their ability for a lively constructive place in society and also to fit them to do a job of work'. Emphasis must be given to 'not one or the other, but both'. One passage is worth quoting as it could have been a statement made by any education minister, secretary of state for education, prime minister or member of the opposition since then:

> Let me repeat some of the fields that need study because they cause concern. There are the methods and aims of informal instruction: the strong case for the so-called 'core curriculum' of basic knowledge; next, what is the proper way of monitoring the use of resources in order to maintain a proper national standard of performance; then there is the role of the Inspectorate in relation to national standards; and there is the need to improve relations between industry and education.
>
> (Maclure 1988: 169)

The Great Debate itself centred around eight days of debate organized at a regional level and led by the DES. A White Paper *Education for Schools* published in 1977 summarized the debate.

Task 9.4

Claims about the importance of historical figures and their speeches are often made. To understand why Callaghan's speech is held to be exceptional the economic context must be examined. Some thinkers argue that the reasons for the revival of vocationalism since the 1970s are 'primarily economic' (Skilbeck et al. 1994: 1). Try to identify these economic factors. Begin by asking 'what educational opportunities would young people expect in the middle and late 1970s?'

1977: The Holland Report *Young People and Work* (MSC)   The Holland Report proposed 'building a better workforce more adapted to the needs of the eighties'. It proposed work experience and work preparation courses for unemployed young people. They would be paid a weekly allowance. It proposed the setting up of the Youth Opportunities Programmes (YOPs) which began in 1978.

1977: the Further Education Unit (FEU) set up as a curriculum development and dissemination body for FE   It was originally called the Further Education Curriculum Review and Development Unit. Although it was a quasi-autonomous body, the FEU was funded by the DES.

1978: The Warnock Report *Special Educational Needs*   Warnock abolished the various categories of handicap then in use and suggested a wider more individualized concept of special needs which was to be enshrined in the 1981 Education Act.

Education in context: 1979–90

Prime minister: 1979–90 Margaret Thatcher (Conservative).

Secretaries of state for education and science: from May 1979, Mark Carlisle; from September 1981, Sir Keith Joseph; from May 1986, Kenneth Baker; from July 1989, John MacGregor.

Key political and economic events: monetarism (controlling inflation by controlling the money supply); Thatcherism (the manifestation of this in the Thatcher government); privatization (denationalization of industry and government); 1982 Falklands War; 1984 miners' strike; 1987 stock market crash, 'There is no such thing as society' (Margaret Thatcher); 1989 fall of Berlin Wall, collapse of Communist regimes in Eastern Europe.

1979: *A Basis for Choice* **(FEU)**   This report emphasized the need for a 'common core' curriculum which emphasized transferable skills and flexibility through participating in 'learning experiences' rather than narrow skills-based teaching.

1981: *A New Training Initiative* **(NTI)**   The MSC produced two documents *A New Training Initiative: A Consultative Document* in May 1981 and later in December *A New Training Initiative: An Agenda for Action.* These documents set the training agenda for the decade. Skills training for young people and adults was covered.

1982: *17+ A New Qualification* **(DES)**   This document set out the basis for the introduction of the Certificate of Pre-vocational Education (CPVE) for students who had not yet chosen their vocation.

1983: Technical and Vocational Education Initiative (TVEI) starts   Announced by Mrs Thatcher in November 1982, TVEI was to be the largest curriculum intervention ever by a government. The scheme was under the control of the MSC. It was a broad and experimental scheme aimed at preparing 14–18-year-olds for the world of work and developing personal qualities such as enterprise and 'problem-solving' skills.

1983: Youth Training Scheme (YTS)   YTS replaced YOP. In 1988 there were over half a million contracted YTS places and an average of 370,000 students in training.

1983: Business and Technology Education Council (BTEC) formed through the merger of the Business Education Council (BEC) and Technology Education Council (TEC).

1984: *Training for Jobs*   This White Paper made clear the government's intention to make the MSC the 'national training authority'. Another report, *Competence and Competition* by the National Economic Development Office (NEDO)/MSC saw the competitive success of Japan, Germany and the USA as being related to their investment in education.

1984: the 'Great Training Robbery' begins   The lecturers' union the National Association of Teachers in Further and Higher Education (NATFHE) label for the way in which private agencies milked the cash cow of MSC money aimed at the new YTS initiative.

1985: Further Education Act   This Act allowed colleges to engage in commercial activities related to areas of expertise and generate more funding. Governors were made responsible for the college budgets.

1985: CPVE introduced   It was never successful, even with less able pupils, and take-up was poor.

1986: National Council for Vocational Qualifications (NCVQ) established on 1 October   Only 40 per cent of the workforce held relevant qualifications. Despite the 'tremendous expansion in training', this was still a much lower proportion than in other countries. The NCVQ's primary task was 'to reform and rationalise the provision of vocational qualifications through the creation of the National Vocational Qualification Framework' (NCVQ 1988: 1). The NCVQ introduced through the awarding bodies (RSA, CGLI etc.) competence-based NVQs that were based in the workplace and not just work-related.

1987: Enterprise in Higher Education Initiative (EHEI)   Seen as the HE equivalent of the TVEI this initiative had a budget of £100 million. The aim was to see every person in HE developing 'competences and aptitudes relevant to enterprise'.

1988: the General Certificate of Secondary Education (GCSE) replaces the GCE and CSE.

1988: Education Reform Act (ERA)   This Act, which followed from Kenneth Baker's so-called Great Education Reform Bill sought to revitalize the 'producer dominated' education system (Maclure 1988: iv). The ERA brought in the National Curriculum for schools with core subjects (English, mathematics, science and religious education) to be learned by all. Several cross-curriculum themes were also identified: environmental education; education for citizenship; careers education and guidance; health education; and economic and industrial understanding. It also had a strong emphasis on moral renewal seeking to promote 'the spiritual, moral, cultural, mental and physical development of pupils at the school and of society' (Maclure 1988: 1). The Act delegated financial responsibilities from local authorities to schools. It took polytechnics out of local authority control and replaced the National Advisory Body for Public Sector Higher Education with the Polytechnics and Colleges Funding Council. It required that half of the membership of the governing bodies of FE colleges represent employment interests.

1988: the MSC is absorbed into the Department of Employment (DoE), becoming the Training Commission for a short time and then the Training Agency.

1989: the Confederation of British Industry (CBI) publishes *Towards a Skills Revolution,* which advocated common learning outcomes for all students over 16. This document set out the employers' agenda for lifelong learning.

1989: In a speech at Lancaster University, Kenneth Baker calls for a doubling of the numbers of students entering HE The number of students attending should increase to 30 per cent. This was achieved by the mid-1990s.

1989: YTS replaced by Youth Training (YT).

Task 9.5

Discussions of the YTS and the role of the MSC dominated educational thought during the 1980s. Why was this? Again, it might be useful to construct an educational biography of a young person brought up in the time of the first Thatcher government.

Education in context: 1990–2001

Prime ministers: 1990–7 John Major (Conservative); 1997–2001 Tony Blair (New Labour).

Secretary of state for education and science: from November 1990, Kenneth Clarke.

Secretaries of state for education: from April 1992, John Patten; from July 1994, Gillian Shepherd.

Secretaries of state for education and employment: from July 1995, Gillian Shepherd; from May 1997, David Blunkett.

Secretaries of state for education and skills: from June 2001, Estelle Morris.

Key political and economic events: economic recession, Citizens' Charter, social authoritarianism, globalization, risk aversion; 1991 the Gulf War, civil war in Yugoslavia; 1992 United Nations (UN) intervention in Somalia and Bosnia; 31 August 1997, death of Diana, Princess of Wales; 15 January 2001, Wikipedia founded; 11 September 2001, World Trade Center twin towers destroyed by Al Qaeda terrorists.

1990: *Core Skills 16–19* **published by National Curriculum Council (NCC), after consultation with the FEU, School Examinations and Assessment Council (SEAC), NCVQ and the Training Agency (TA)**   It proposed six core skills in two groups:

- Group 1: 1. Communication; 2. Problem-solving; 3. Personal skills;
- Group 2: 4. Numeracy; 5. IT; 6. Competence in a modern language.

The first group was to be developed in all post-16 programmes and in every A- and AS-level syllabus. It also recommended the use of Individual Action Plans (IAPs) and the incorporation of National Curriculum themes in the post-16 curriculum with the addition of scientific and technological understanding and aesthetic and creative understanding.

1990: *A British Baccalaureate: Ending the Division Between Education and Training* **published by the Institute for Public Policy Research (IPPR)**   This proposed a unitary 'advanced diploma' delivered through a tertiary college system.

1991: Training and Enterprise Councils (TECs) established   There were 82 TECs. They were limited companies governed by local industrialists and are charged with identifying local training needs and organizing training to meet these needs and operated government training schemes such as YT. They were first announced by the government in 1988.

1991: *Education and Training for the 21st Century*   This White Paper was a review of the education and training system for 16–19-year-olds in which equal status was demanded for academic and vocational qualifications. Young people 'should not have their opportunities limited by out of date distinctions between qualifications and institutions' (DES 1991: 58). The DES argued that:

> Colleges lack the full freedom which we gave to the polytechnic and higher education colleges in 1989 to respond to the demands of students and the labour market. The Government intend to legislate to remove all colleges of further education . . . and sixth form colleges . . . from local authority control . . . Our policies over the last decade have not done much to enrich that preparation – for life and work.
>
> (DES 1991: 64–5)

1991: National Education and Training Targets (NETTs) set by the government but recommended by the CBI in *World Class Targets (1991)*   There was a major review of the targets in 1995 and another in 1998.

1992: Further and Higher Education Act   The polytechnics were granted university status and the 'binary division' was subsequently ended when polytechnics became universities in 1993. The Council for National Academic Awards (CNAA) was abolished and separate funding councils set up for FE and HE.

1992: Education (Schools) Act created the Office for Standards in Education (Ofsted).

1992: Colleges' Employers' Forum (CEF) was established It became the Association of Colleges (AoC) in 1996.

1992: GNVQs introduced Unlike NVQs, these qualifications would be based in schools and colleges rather than the workplace. Level 3 (later 'Advanced') General National Vocational Qualification (GNVQ) was to be 'equivalent' or 'comparable' to A levels. By 1997 students with GNVQs had a greater chance of obtaining a university place than A level students.

1993: the Department for Education's (DfE) *Charter for Further Education* The Charter set out rights and expectations and ended with information on how to complain about 'courses, qualifications and results' (pp. 24–9 gives 23 addresses and telephone numbers to complain to). All colleges were required to produce their own charters.

1993: incorporation of colleges The 1992 Further and Higher Education Act was implemented on 1 April. Colleges were taken out of the control of the LEAs and became independent business corporations. Some had turnovers which put them in the *Financial Times* list of big companies. One college had a turnover of almost £50 million.

1993: Modern Apprenticeships announced The first apprentices started on this initiative to revive apprenticeships. Modern Apprenticeships were based on specific occupations and developed by NTOs (National Training Organizations). They consisted of a minimum of an NVQ Level 3 qualification supplemented by GNVQ Core Skills qualifications and sometimes by qualifications outside of the scheme. They were open to both young men and young women aged between 16 and 24.

1994: *Competitiveness: Helping Business to Win* Michael Heseltine set out the theme of national competitiveness and calls for improved careers guidance for young people in this influential White Paper.

1994: Teacher Training Agency (TTA) The Agency was established in September under the directorship of chief executive Anthea Millett 'to improve the quality of teaching, to raise the standards of teacher education and training, and to promote teaching as a profession, in order to improve the standards of pupils' achievement and the quality of their learning' (TTA 1995: 7).

1994: new contracts dispute at its height   The FE colleges experienced over three years of action over the introduction of new contracts for lecturers and the abandonment of the so-called 'Silver Book' which set out conditions of service.

1994: report of the Commission on Social Justice   This report contains the genesis of what would become the 1997 Labour government's views on education and social policy for the 1990s and beyond.

1995: Further Education Development Agency (FEDA) formed   Launched on 7 April, FEDA inherited the staff of the FEU and the Further Education Staff College at Blagdon. Its main function was to 'help FE institutions provide what their student and other customers want and need'. As 'an independent body promoting quality in FE', FEDA intended 'not just to promote best practice but also embody it' (FEDA 1995: 1). Its key aims were to promote quality in teaching and learning, to provide leadership in curriculum design and development, and to ensure effective management.

1995: the Department for Education and Department of Employment merged in July to become the DfEE (Department for Education and Employment).

1996: Dearing's *Review of Qualifications for 16–19 Year Olds*   This is Dearing's second much publicized report (Dearing II). Dearing II went for stability and did not recommend a unified system to replace the three existing tertiary qualifications NVQs, GNVQs and A levels. It did suggest the incorporation of 'key skills' in all three qualifications and the relaunch of YT, modern apprenticeships and the National Record of Achievement. It also suggested that Advanced GNVQs be renamed applied A levels. Dearing's first report (Dearing I) *The National Curriculum and its Assessment* (1994) was a response to industrial action by teachers throughout the country concerned about the burden of assessment and the narrowness of the National Curriculum. Dearing I reduced time spent on the National Curriculum by 20 per cent and reduced the number of attainment targets and their related statements, Standard Assessment Tasks (SATs). It included a vocational option at Key Stage 4.

1996: the European 'Year of Lifelong Learning'.

1996: *Lifetime Learning* (DfEE)   A consultation document drawing on previously published work including *Competitiveness: Forging Ahead: Education and Training* (DfEE 1995a). The Labour Party published *Lifelong Learning*, a consultative document (1996).

1996: awarding bodies combine   In 1996, BTEC and London Examinations formed Edexcel. In 1998 C&G, The Associated Examining Board and the Northern

Examinations and Assessment Board formed the Assessment and Qualifications Alliance (AQA).

1996: *Inclusive Learning* (Tomlinson Report) This FEFC report called for colleges to embrace the idea of 'inclusive learning'. It wanted every member of staff to consider the individual needs of all learners rather than just those previously categorized as having 'special needs'.

1996: New Labour leader Tony Blair's 'education, education and education' speech to the Labour Party conference on 1 October, 20 years after Callaghan's Ruskin College speech The speech was published in the *Times Educational Supplement* of 4 October (p. 6) and some extracts follow.

> Ask me my three main priorities for Government, and I tell you: education, education and education . . . At every level we need radical improvement and reform. A teaching profession trained and able to stand alongside the best in the world and valued as such . . . There should be zero tolerance of failure in Britain's schools. The Age of Achievement will be built on new technology. Our aim is for every school to have access to the superhighway, the computers to deliver it and the education programmes to go on it. With the University for Industry for adult skills, this adds up to a national grid for learning for Britain. Britain the skill superpower of the world.

1996: Hello DOLLY.

> . . . what ought to matter most, in my view, to a learning prime minister is that there should be a powerful Whitehall department responsible for promoting learning across society. This department should be a great office of state on a par with the Foreign Office or the Home Office. If the learning society is to be a reality, nothing else will do. I would want to see the DfEE remain one department, but to change its name – symbolically but importantly – to the Department of Lifelong Learning. It could even be called DOLLY for short. Goodbye DfEE, as it were, Hello . . .
>
> (Barber 1996: 296)

Task 9.6

Lifelong or lifetime learning, the learning society; these phrases became pre-millennial buzzwords. Can we give them more than rhetorical substance? In what sense is lifelong learning going to be a reality for young people? What features of British society support the claim that we are, or are becoming a 'learning society' (see Field 2000: 35)?

1997: Report of Helena Kennedy's committee of inquiry into widening participation in education *Learning Works* Kennedy initially suggested redistributing resources and removing the bias towards undergraduates and school sixth forms. Seventy-five per cent of the 5 million students in England are supported by £3.5 billion of funding through the 'Cinderella' service of FE colleges, whereas the university sector with 25 per cent of the student population receives 75 per cent of the available funding. The shocking fact is that 'Sixty-four per cent of university students come from social classes 1 and 2. One per cent come from social class 5' (Kennedy 1997a). The general direction of the many recommendations of the report is a lifetime entitlement to education up to A level standard, with free teaching for people from deprived backgrounds or with no previous qualifications: 'The government should . . . give priority in public funding within post-16 learning to general education and transferable vocational learning, including key skills, at and leading to level 3: the costs of ensuring that all can succeed to (NVQ) level 3 must be recognised' (Kennedy 1997b: 43).

1997: publication of the Dearing Report *Higher Education in the Learning Society, National Committee Inquiry into Higher Education* One of the nine 'principles' governing the report (Dearing III, Dearing 1997) was that: 'Learning should be increasingly responsive to employment needs and include the development of general skills, widely valued in employment' (Summary Report, p. 5). Dearing III was hailed as the most comprehensive review of HE since the Robbins Report. Dearing III made 93 recommendations. These included: a system by which students pay fees covering up to 25 per cent of the cost of tuition (Chapter 20); the establishment of an Institute for Learning and Teaching (ILT) in higher education to accredit training programmes for HE staff and to look at computer-based learning (Chapter 8); the promotion of student learning as a high priority (Chapter 8); and a review of research which may allow some institutions to opt out of the competitive funding system based on the Research Assessment Exercise (RAE). In his introduction Dearing sees 'historic boundaries between vocational and academic education breaking down, with increasingly active partnerships between higher education institutions and the worlds of industry, commerce and public service' (Summary Report, p. 2).

1997: the government announced the abolition of student grants and the introduction of fee payments of up to £1000 per annum The power to do this is given through the Teaching and Higher Education Bill (see below).

1997: *Qualifying for Success: a Consultation Paper on the Future of Post-16 Qualifications* Key changes suggested in this paper were: new AS levels to encourage take-up of more subjects in the first year of study; modular A levels with synoptic testing at the end of all courses; upgraded and more flexible GNVQs; a new key skills qualification to enhance skills in communication, IT and number after the age of 16.

1997: NCVQ and the SCAA (Schools Curriculum and Assessment Authority) merge to form a new National Curriculum advisory body, the

Qualifications and Curriculum Authority (QCA) Its powers are a cause of concern to the awarding bodies.

1997: *Learning for the Twenty-First Century* In November, Professor Bob Fryer produced the report for the National Advisory Group for Continuing Education and Lifelong Learning (NAGCELL).This report consolidates much of the thinking about lifelong learning that appeared since the Report of the Commission on Social Justice.

1997: Teaching and Higher Education Bill This bill was the first of a series of responses by the government to Dearing III. It gave the secretary of state powers to interfere in university affairs and is seen by some as a major attack on academic autonomy.

1998: New Deal programme introduced in January as the flagship of the New Labour Government's 'Welfare to Work' strategy It required every young person between the ages of 18 and 24 who had been unemployed for more than six months to take a subsidized job, take up some form of education or training, take part in an Environmental Task Force, or do voluntary work. There was also a *25 Plus New Deal* that came on stream quickly due to the fall in numbers of the 18–24 age cohort.

1998: National Learning Targets for 2002 85 per cent of 19-year-olds to have (NVQ) Level 2 qualifications; 60 per cent of 21-year-olds to have (NVQ) Level 3; 50 per cent of adults to have the same level; and 28 per cent of adults to have (NVQ) Level 4 qualifications. They also sought a 7 per cent reduction in the number of non-learners.

1998: formation of a General Teaching Council (GTC) A GTC was established in Scotland as a result of the Wheatley Report (1963). A voluntary GTC (England and Wales) has been in existence since 1988 and has sought support from the various professional bodies and attempted to secure legislation. The Teaching and Higher Education Bill (1997) established a statutory GTC which will not be a teachers' GTC but will have a broad membership. Teachers in schools could now register with the GTC.

1998: *The Learning Age: A Renaissance for a New Britain* (DfEE) The expected White Paper on lifelong learning appeared as a Green Paper. It promised to bring learning into the home and workplace.

1998: *Higher Education for the Twenty-First Century: Response to the Dearing Report* This response set out the priority of reaching out to groups underrepresented in HE. It argued for a better balance between teaching, research and scholarship and for an Institute for Learning and Teaching in Higher Education (ILTHE) to be established to accredit programmes of training for HE teachers.

Work experience to become a feature of HE courses and the aim of employability stressed.

1998: Further Education National Training Organization (FENTO)   Approved to operate as a National Training Organization (NTO). One of its aims was to be held responsible for assessing the skill needs of all staff (employed) within the post-16 sector. Its first major project was to produce a set of national standards for supporting learning in further education in England and Wales (October 1998).

1998: a University for Industry (learndirect)   Established after discussions with 'learning organizations' such as Ford, Unipart and Anglian Water. This is not a physical but a virtual university, a network providing access to training.

1999: *A Fresh Start: Improving Literacy and Numeracy* (Moser Report)   Moser reported that one in five adults in the UK have significant literacy or numeracy problems and that 7 million people have no formal qualifications. One of the report's recommendations was that all basic skills teachers should have a basic skills teaching qualification.

1999: *Learning to Succeed: A New Framework for Post-16 Learning* (DfEE 1999)   This White Paper set out the case for and functions of the LSC. There are six reasons given: there is too much duplication, confusion and bureaucracy in the current system; too little money actually reaches learners and employers; there is an absence of effective coordination or strategic planning; the system has insufficient focus on skills and employer needs at national, regional and local levels; the system lacks innovation and flexibility; there is a need to exploit the potential of the new technology in the delivery and planning of provision (s2.11: 27). The report also announces the Connexions strategy 'for making sure that far more young people continue in education and training until they are at least 19' (s6.7: 50).

1999: *Bridging the Gap: New Opportunities for 16–18-Year-Olds not in Education, Employment or Training*   This report by the Social Exclusion Unit (1999) proposed that instead of a fragmented approach involving youth, careers and guidance workers, there should be a unified service with the task of 'Providing a network of Personal Advisors to provide a single point of contact for each young person and ensure that someone has an overview of each young person's ambitions and needs' (p. 81).

1999: *Curriculum Guidance for 2000: Implementing the Changes to 16–19 Qualifications* (QCA).

1999: ILT (The Institute for Learning Teaching in Higher Education) is launched   The ILT mission was to enhance the professionalism of teaching and the support for learning. It was absorbed into the Higher Education Academy (HEA) in 2004.

2000: Foundation degrees announced by David Blunkett, Secretary of State for Education and Employment, at the University of Greenwich New Campus on 15 February These degrees stress innovation in content and delivery and could be achieved, in part, through accrediting workplace learning. They would take two years full time rather than three. Flexible and part-time delivery was held to be very important. Foundation degrees were considered by some to be a move towards an American-style 'community college' system. By March 2002, 4,229 students had enrolled on work-based foundation degrees.

2000: *Connexions: The Best Start in Life for Every Young Person* This government strategy paper outlining their aim of ensuring that all young people have the opportunity to learn the skills they need to make a success of their adult lives. It was hoped that 50 per cent would later go to university. Personal advisers became a reality within the Connexions framework in April 2002.

2000: Curriculum 2000 begins in September It is announced by the DfEE as introducing 'the most significant changes to post-16 curriculum for 50 years'. These included the new AS qualification representing the first half of an A level; a choice of linear or modular assessment; the replacement of Advanced GNVQs with vocational A levels and the introduction of a new key skills qualification.

2000: New DfEE policy on qualifications and development for further education teachers and college principals The government issued a statement on 2 November introducing mandatory teaching qualifications for all new staff in FE from September 2001. New full-time staff will have two years to gain a Certificate in Education following appointment (for fractional and part-time staff a longer period is envisaged depending on the hours worked). The DfEE also made it a requirement that all courses leading to an FE teaching qualification be based on FENTO standards and be endorsed by FENTO as doing so. One of several estimates suggested that 43 per cent of part-time staff and 40 per cent of full-time staff have no 'high level' teaching qualification.

2000: the LSDA (Learning and Skills Development Agency) is launched on 27 November, replacing the FEDA It seeks a clearer focus on policy development and intends to play a leading role in research through the Learning and Skills Research Network (LSRN).

2001: an Institute for Learning (IfL) is launched Supported by various organizations, this is a complementary body to the GTC and ILT, and parallels their objectives by promoting the professional standing of FE teaching.

2001: the LSC (Learning and Skills Council) replaces the TECs and the FEFC on 1 April The LSC became responsible from that date for funding and planning all post-16 education and training except for HE. With a budget of £5.5 billion, the council operated through 47 local LSCs.

2001: the DfEE became the Department for Education and Skills (DfES) after the general election in June 2001   There was a pre-election consensus that 'A basic skills revolution will be at the heart of Labour's education policy if it wins a second term' (Crequer 2001).

2001: Individual Learning Accounts (ILAs) suspended from 7 December   The cornerstone of the government's lifelong learning strategy, ILAs were reportedly taken up by 2.5 million people. There were some 6,000 complaints about the scheme and 279 providers were thought to be suspect and many were investigated, some by the police.

Education In Context: 2001–2010

Prime ministers: 1997–2001, 2001–2005, 2005–2007 (resigned) Tony Blair (New Labour); 2007–2009 Gordon Brown (Labour).

Secretaries of state for education and skills: from June 2001, Estelle Morris; from October 2003, Charles Clarke; from December 2004, Ruth Kelly; from May 2005, Alan Johnston: from June 2007 Secretary of Sate for Children, Schools and Families, Ed Balls.

Ministers of state for lifelong learning, further and higher education: from September 2004, Kim Howells; from May 2005, Bill Rammell; minister of state for higher education and intellectual property (in Department for Innovation, Universities and Skills and subsequently Department for Business Innovation and Skills) from October 2008, David Lammy.

Key political and economic events: Invasion of Iraq, 20 March 2003; Human Genome Project completed 14 April 2003; Facebook launched, 2 February 2004; Climate change declared by Tony Blair, during his UK presidency of the G8, as 'probably, long-term the single most important issue we face as a global community', Gleneagles 6–8 July 2005; 7/7 bombings in London, 7 July 2005; Rise of China as a world economic super power with exports totaling over $1 trillion in 2007; Lehman Brothers investment bank files for bankruptcy and helps plunge the world into financial crisis, 15 September 2008; Barack Obama elected as the 44th and first black president of the USA, 5 November 2008.

2002: *14–19: Extending Opportunities, Raising Standards*   The key proposals of this controversial and 'very green Green Paper' were: to introduce a matriculation diploma that recognizes achievement at 19 across a range of disciplines; to free up the curriculum so that students aged 14 can follow relevant work-related courses; increased flexibility so that students can learn at a pace that is right for them, with a 'fast track to success' option for the more able; an individualized curriculum with all students having an individual learning plan (ILP) developed with the help of the personal adviser from the Connexions service. 'Vocational' as a term was also to be written out of qualification terminology in an attempt to challenge prejudice. Vocational A levels were just to be called

A levels. The Green Paper also proposed that the study of a modern foreign language should no longer be compulsory for the 14+. This ambitious programme of radical reform was aimed to be in place by 2006.

2002: the New Deal for Young People   The first National Audit Office report on the New Deal. The programme promised jobs for 250,000 young people but the study showed that it has resulted in increasing jobs by only 20,000 in its first two years of operation. The National Audit Office suggested that many of the young people on the programme would have found jobs anyway and those that did, did not stay in work for long. Government figures showed that 700,000 young people had participated in the programme and 339,000 had been helped to find jobs.

2002: the Sector Skills Development Agency (SSDA) takes responsibility for the new Sector Skills Councils (SSCs)   Along with all other NTOs, FENTO was scheduled to become part of a new SSC. The rationale for the changes was set out in a policy statement: *Meeting the Sector Skills and Productivity Challenge* (DfES 2001). Each SSC had the broad aim of tackling the skills and productivity needs of their sector throughout the UK. To do this they gave responsibility to employers to provide leadership for strategic targeted action to meet their sector's skills and business needs. The first SSDA director was Margaret Salmon, a non-executive director with Kingfisher plc. There were to be some 35 SSCs, less than half the number of NTOs.

2002: *Success for All*   This outlined the reform strategy of the Learning and Skills Council which aimed to bring the FE sector into the mainstream of the education system and to ensure that 14–19-year-old learners have 'greater choice and higher standards'.

2003: *21st Century Skills: Realising Our Potential*   This White Paper set out a 'skills strategy' from the DfES (2003a) (with the DTI and DWP) that sought to ensure that 'employers have the right skills to support the success of their businesses, and individuals have the skills they need to be both employable and personally fulfilled' (Summary: Paragraph 1). E-learning and information and communications technology (ICT) skills are stressed along with free learning for all adults to enable them to achieve a Level 2 qualification.

2003: first Ofsted and ALI inspections of FE colleges using their *Common Inspection Framework* (Ofsted/ALI 2000c).

2003: the IfL held its first AGM on 16 June 2003 as a nascent professional body for the sector.

2003: *Every Child Matters* (ECM)   The ECM report formed the basis of the Children Act 2004. It was produced in response to the Victoria Climbié Inquiry. The report puts child protection concerns central to the teacher's role.

2003: the Centre for Excellence in Leadership (CEL) launched in October   Its aim was to develop world-class leadership within the learning and skills sector. The CEL training programmes are for governors, principals and advanced teachers.

2003: *14–19 Opportunity and Excellence*, published in November, a year after Success for All   Proposed the creation of a more coherent 14–19 phase with greater flexibility and choice and an increase in vocational learning to tackle the number of learners leaving full-time education at 16 and create a parity of esteem between academic and vocational education.

2003: Ofsted's report, *The Initial Teacher Training of Further Education Teachers*   This was issued on 11 November, and declared FE teacher training to be unsatisfactory. The DfES response, which came out on the same day, *The Future of Initial Teacher Education for the Learning and Skills Sector*, set out an agenda for reform.

2004: the Higher Education Academy (HEA) formed in May   It absorbed the ILT (HE) and other professional and staff develop bodies in HE.

2004: *Children Act*   The *Children Act* focused the work of the teachers, and what soon became known as the 'wider workforce', including classroom assistants, social workers and police officers, on the ECM outcomes to improve children's well-being in five areas: (a) physical and mental health and emotional well-being; (b) protection from harm and neglect; (c) education, training and recreation; (d) the contribution made by them to society; (e) social and economic well-being.

2004: Tomlinson Report: *14–19 Curriculum and Qualifications Reform*   After a lengthy period of consultation, the working party on 14–19 Reform's much heralded final report appeared on 18 October. It proposed incorporating and ultimately replacing GCSEs and A levels in favour of a diploma as part of a continuous curriculum for 14–19-year-olds. Diplomas would cover both vocational and academic disciplines, combining them wherever appropriate to overcome the academic/vocational divide.

2004: QTLS   The award of 'Qualified Teacher Learning and Skills' was announced on 2 November 2004 by the Minister of State Kim Howells. It is described in *Equipping our Teachers for the Future: Reforming Initial Teacher Training for the Learning and Skills Sector* (DfES 2004c) which named the IfL as the professional body for the sector.

2005: *14–19 Education and Skills*   A White Paper, published in February, was the government's response to the Tomlinson Report of 2004. It proposed Vocational Diplomas, not the overarching diploma Tomlinson wanted, and aimed to ensure that every young person masters functional English and maths before they leave full-time education, that vocational options are improved, and that academic qualifications offer a suitable 'stretch' to motivate disengaged learners.

2005: Foster Review – *Realising the Potential: A Review of the Future Role of Further Education* Foster's Review, published on 15 November, argued the need for a clearly recognized and shared core purpose among FE colleges that focuses on the needs of both learners and business. The Review made it clear that the purpose of post-compulsory education (PCE) is directly linked to the needs of the economy but also describes as 'appalling' the number of young people who lack basic literacy and numeracy skills and which 'suggest great reservoirs of disappointment and poor self esteem' (Foster 2005: 9).

2005: *Youth Matters* This Green Paper proposed an overhaul of youth services on the basis of *Every Child Matters*. To many it implied that the days of informal work with young people were numbered.

2005: *Special Educational Needs: A New Look* Baroness Mary Warnock criticized the way inclusion was seen as being under the same roof rather than accessing a common curriculum. The statementing system was 'wasteful and bureaucratic' and 'must be abolished'.

2006: *Further Education: Raising Skills, Improving Life Chances* A White Paper proposing reforms in the skills and qualifications in post-16 education, for customized and individualized provision for learners, and diversification of education providers.

2006: University and College Union (UCU) Formed on 1 June from the merger of the Association of University Teachers (AUT) and NATFHE to become the largest post-compulsory union in the world.

2006: Lifelong Learning UK (LLUK) revised the teacher training standards for FE and consulted on Standards for Teacher Trainers in FE.

2006: Train to Gain (T2G) rolled out as a national project to fund adult training Colleges have to bid for up to three-quarters of their funding in competition with private providers.

2006: the Further Education and Training Bill The Bill proposed to streamline the LSC so it operates on a regional basis. It focused on learner and employee consultation. In a fundamental change to the FHE sector it announced that the Privy Council will be enabled to grant FE colleges the power to award foundation degrees.

2006: Leitch Review of Skills The final report of the Leitch Review was published on 5 December with the title *Prosperity for All in the Global Economy – World*

Class Skills. Lord Sandy Leitch's report aimed to 'Strengthen the Employer Voice' and increase employers' engagement and investment in skills. His recommendations included an employer 'Pledge' to commit to train, awareness programmes teaching people the value of skills, and a universal adult careers service.

2006: ALI released its final report before becoming part of Ofsted.

2006: the LSDA splits to form two new organizations The Quality Improvement Agency (QIA) (subsequently merged with CEL to form Learning and Skills Improvement Service (LSIS)) and the Learning and Skills Network (LSN).

2007: The '157 Group' of FE Colleges held its launch event on 15 January The 157 Group was named after paragraph 157 of the Foster Review that suggested that the most successful colleges have a bigger role in policy-making. It declared that it had 22 members at the time of its launch.

2007: *2020 Vision: Report of the Teaching and Learning in 2020 Review Group* This report, published on 4 January, from the review group headed by Christine Gilbert (Her Majesty's Chief Inspector for Schools) set out 'personalization' or 'personalized learning' as a central focus of education policy.

2007: ROSLA to 18? The Green Paper, *Raising Expectations: Staying in Education and Training Post-16*, launched on 22 March, proposed the introduction of measures that have the effect of raising the school leaving age to 18 by 2015. Any young person starting work must have training, and prison sentences are the ultimate deterrent for those refusing education and training.

2007: the IfL became the gatekeeper to QTLS The IfL, from September 2007, was to register all teachers in the learning and skills sector and seek to provide coherence across sectors. From that date, all new entrants to FE teaching must complete a 30-hour induction course leading to an Initial Teaching Award Learning and Skills (ITALS). A new system of registration of teachers through a 'Licence to Practise' was introduced. The IfL also took responsibility for overseeing the introduction and monitoring of mandatory continuing professional development (CPD) across the sector.

2007: PTLLS:CTLLS:DTLLS From 1 September all new entrants to FE will have to obtain: a 'Preparing to Teach in the Lifelong Learning Sector' (PTLLS) 'petals' award, which is a minimum threshold licence to teach for all in a teaching role and for those in a full teaching role a Diploma in Teaching in the Lifelong Learning Sector (DTLLS) 'details' at minimum Level 5 leading to Qualified Teacher Learning and Skills status (QTLS). The Certificate in Teaching in the Lifelong Learning Sector (CTLLS) 'kettles' is a specific programme for those associate teachers working to a prescribed curriculum.

2007: the Department for Children, Schools and Families (DCSF) created The term 'education' is removed from the title of the Department (28 June).

2007: Department for Innovation, Universities and Skills (DIUS) created (28 June).

2008: *NEET Toolkit* published To reduce the number of young people who are not in education, employment, or training (NEET) by 2 per cent by 2010 and to put in place support to enable all 17-year-olds to participate in learning in 2013 and for all 18-year-olds in 2015.

2008: 14–19 Diplomas introduced The first wave of five subjects to be taught from September: creative and media, IT, health and social care, construction and the built environment and engineering. The second wave to begin in 2009 and all to be available by 2013.

2008: Learning and Skills Improvement Service (LSIS) is created from the merger of CEL and the QIA (1 October 2008) The aim of the merger is to speed up quality improvement, increase participation and raise standards and achievement in the FE system in England.

2008: IfL membership rises from 4000 to 147,000 since registration became mandatory for new entrants to FE All employees working on LSC-funded programmes or contracts to register by 30 September 2008. Members have to record 30 hours of CPD every year and abide by the IfL Code of Professional Conduct.

2008: *Skills for Growth: The National Skills Strategy* A strategy to build a new 'technician class' by ensuring that three-quarters of people participate in HE or complete an advanced apprenticeship or equivalent technician level course by the age of 30. The paper also announced that by April 2010 the nine regional Learning and Skills Councils will cease to operate and that the IfL should be self-funding (from April 2011).

2008: LSC to be abolished Funding responsibilities for 16–19-year-old learners were to transfer to LEAs and the new Skills Funding Agency (SFA) was to distribute £4 billion of funding for adult learners in FE colleges. The Young People's Learning Agency (YPLA) was to coordinate and help make coherent local authority 14–19 provision (announced 17 March 2008, effective from 31 March 2010).

2008: Education and Skills Act For the first time in 30 years, the government legislated to raise the education leaving age to 18 in either full-time education or training, including school, college and home education, work-based learning, such as an apprenticeship, including traditional contracts of apprenticeship, or part-time education or training, if they are employed, self-employed or volunteering more than 20 hours a week.

2009: The Department for Business, Innovation and Skills (DBIS) Formed from the merger of the DIUS and the Department for Business, Enterprise and Regulatory Reform. The key role of the DBIS (or BIS) was to build Britain's capabilities to compete in the global economy, headed by Business Secretary Lord Mandelson. The DIUS was one of the shortest-lived ministries, being in existence for less than two years.

2009: *Investing in Potential*   A strategy paper to increase the porportion of 16–24-year-olds who are in education, employment and training.

Education in context 2010–present

Prime ministers: 2010–15 David Cameron (coalition, Conservative); *Deputy prime minister:* Nick Clegg (coalition, Liberal); 2015 David Cameron (Conservative).

Secretary of State for Education: from May 2010–July 2014, Michael Gove; from July 2014–15, 2015, Nicky Morgan.

Minister of state for further education, skills and lifelong learning (joint appointment with DBIS): from May 2010, John Hayes; from September 2012, Matthew Hancock (Parliamentary Under Secretary of State); from July 2014, Nick Boles; from May 2015, Nick Boles (Minister of State for Skills).

Minister of state for education and science (DBIS): from May 2010, David Willets; from July 2014, Greg Clark; from May 2015, Jo Johnson (Minister of State for Universities and Science).

Key political and economic events: recession, *The Economist* Global Public Debt Clock read $38 trillion and counting in January 2011; UK debt was $1.5 trillion (www.buttonwood.economist.com/content/gdc); European Union and the Euro under threat. A demonstration in Egypt is the first of many, leading to revolts across the Arab world, 25 January 2011; 'Arab Spring' turns to the 'Arab Winter' with a military coup in Egypt; civil war in Syria and the rise of the Islamic State of Iraq and the Levant (ISIL); Charlie Hebdo murders in Paris (7 January 2015).

2010: the Department for Education is created bringing the word 'education' back into the departmental title   The new website contains a note about departmental name changes: the DfE 'Replaced the Department for Children, Schools and Families (DCSF) in May 2010. Former names (DES, DfE, DfEE, DfES, DCSF) are retained in references to printed material issued before inception of the DfE and in other contexts as necessary'.

2010: free schools announced by Michael Gove, Secretary of State for Education. Free schools can be set up by groups of parents, teachers, charities, businesses, universities, trusts, religious or voluntary groups, but they are independent of local authorities and funded directly by central government. They are exempt from the national curriculum and have increased control over teachers' pay and conditions and the length of school terms and days. By May 2015 there were 400 free schools open or approved and the Conservative election manifesto pledged to open 500 more by 2020.

2010: first university technical college (UTC) opens The JCB Academy in Staffordshire, sponsored by Harper Adams University College, became the UK's first UTC. UTCs are 14–19 free schools led by a university, in partnership with local employers and sometimes an FE college. They focus on one or two technical specialisms for at least 40 per cent of school time and use the latest industrial equipment and technology. By 2015, 45 UTCs were approved or open but there were recognized problems with recruitment at 14 and some closures.

2010: the bonfire of the education quangos (14 October)   The DfE's arm's-length public bodies were to close or have some function brought in-house 'to improve accountability, transparency and efficiency'. They included the Teenage Pregnancy Independent Advisory Group (TPIAG); the Teachers TV Board of Governors; the British Educational Communications and Technology Agency (BECTA); the General Teaching Council for England (GTCE); the Qualifications and Curriculum Development Agency (QCDA). Culled at a later date were: the Training and Development Agency for Schools (TDA) (taken in-house); the School Support Staff Negotiating Body (SSSNB) and the Young People's Learning Agency (YPLA).

2010: *Towards a Strong Careers Profession* (The Silver Report)   This report makes the case for a stronger, more unified careers profession with common professional standards and a code of professional ethics (15 October 2010).

2010: Connexions service effectively abolished from 31 March 2011   A series of speeches by the Further Education Minister, John Hayes, set out the vision of a new all-age career service (Hayes 2010a, 2010b, 2010c).

2010: *Skills for Sustainable Growth: Strategy Document*   Aimed to address current failings in training by putting 'Apprenticeships . . . at the heart of the system that we will build' (16 November).

2010 *The Importance of Teaching: The Schools White Paper 2010*   Promises to 'transform the quality of initial training and continuing professional development'. Free schools on the Swedish model are introduced and teacher training by the charity Teach First is expanded (on 24 November 2011).

2010: Reform of the 14–19 Diplomas   The objective of the Reform is 'to make it easier to teach and award'. The entitlement was not enforced and schools and colleges could choose how many and what Diplomas they offered; DfE approval for new subjects was no longer required. The introduction of the final three Diplomas in humanities, science and languages was stopped; the extended Diploma was stopped and the Workforce Support Programme was ended in August 2010 to save £14 million. The Diploma initiative was effectively brought to an end (DfE *Reforming the Diploma* 30 November 2010).

2010: Lifelong Learning UK (LLUK) is not to be relicensed as the SSC for the lifelong learning sector after 31 March 2011 (DBIS 9 December 2010).

2010: the English Baccalaureate (EBacc)   Announced in the Schools White Paper 2010, the EBacc is a reformulation of the 2010 school league tables showing, for the first time, the proportion of pupils at school, local authority and national level achieving good GCSE grades (A*-C) in both English and maths, with science to be included from 2011.

2011: Education Maintenance Allowance (EMA) abolished (1 January 2011).

2011: Education Bill abolishes education quangos; abolishes the Diploma entitlement and allows the establishment of 16–19 academies (26 January 2011).

2011: *Review of Vocational Education* – the Wolf Report   There had been an 'explosion in vocationally related courses, from 1,882 in 2003/4 to 462,182 by 2010 but 'The staple offer for between a quarter and a third of the post-16 cohort is a diet of low-level vocational qualifications, most of which have little to no labour market value'. In this review, Professor Alison Wolf recommended a core academic curriculum up to 16 and stressed the importance of English and maths; that no more than 20 per cent of the Key Skills 4 curriculum time was to be spent on vocational subjects and that work experience should be post-16. She also argued that QTLS should be recognized in schools (Review announced 9 September 2010, published 3 March 2011).

2012: Common Inspection Framework for further education and skills (Ofsted). The focus of inspections will be on outcomes for learners; the quality of teaching, learning and assessment and the effectiveness of leadership and management.

2012: *Professionalism in Further Education* (The Lingfield Report) Lord Lingfield's report suggested that membership of the IfL become voluntary once again, ending a decade of dispute. Going further, it endorsed the creation of an FE Guild which would set professional standards and establish a refreshed relationship between employers and staff. The report proposed scrapping the lower-grade Level 3 and 4 teaching qualifications and removing the naming system of PTLLS, CTLLS and DTLLS, with their nicknames of 'petals, kettles and dettles' being unhelpful and confusing. There should be a mandatory basic induction qualification, followed by a Level 5 certificate in FE for most, with the option of a masters-level diploma for elite teachers. The qualifications required should be left to the discretion of employers (23 October).

2012: The Richard Review of Apprenticeships An independent review by Doug Richard published by DBIS. Recommendations included redefining apprenticeships, focusing with greater rigour on the outcome of an apprenticeship and using recognized industry standards to form the basis of every apprenticeship.

2013: the National College for Teaching and Leadership (NCTL)   Formed by the merger of the Teaching Agency and the National College for School Leadership (NCSL). This new single agency is to focus on promoting high-quality teaching and school leadership (1 April).

2013: *Rigour and Responsiveness in Skills* (DBIS/DfE policy paper) 'We need to put rigour and responsiveness at the heart of our skills system, to put employers and learners more directly in the driving seat . . .' (3 April).

2013: Career colleges launched in October by Lord Baker with the first three opening in September 2014 Career colleges are overseen by the Career Colleges Trust to take advantage of the government's decision to allow FE colleges to recruit at 14. The intention is to increase the range and choice of opportunities open to 14–19 year olds. They provide accelerated vocationally-focused programmes of study alongside core academic work, at colleges equipped to the highest standards and staffed by expert teachers in academic and vocational subjects. Career colleges are a 'college within a college' but, because student numbers are limited, each career college creates its own identity.

2013: *No More Neets: A plan for all young people to be learning or earning* (IPPR) 'There are over a million young people who are not in education, employment or training (NEET) in the UK, equivalent to almost a fifth (18 per cent) of all 18–24-year-olds.'

2014: the Research Excellence Framework (REF) 2014 This replaced the previous Research Assessment Exercise (RAE). The RAE had been used to measure the quality of research in HE in the UK in 2008, 2001, 1996, 1992 and 1989. One major change from the RAE was an emphasis on the 'impact' of research defined as 'an effect on, change or benefit to the economy, society, culture, public policy or services, health, the environment or quality of life, beyond academia'.

2014: *Future of Apprenticeships in England: guidance for trailblazers* 'Trailblazers' are groups of employers who are 'leading the way in carrying out the changes to apprenticeships. They have been working together to design apprenticeship standards and assessment approaches to make them world class'

(4 March). The apprenticeship standards created by the eight networks were launched as part of the seventh National Apprenticeship Week, 3–7 March 2014.

2014: 'Axe FE' said government officials According to Vince Cable, the Business Secretary, whose financially unprotected department cut the FE teaching budget by 25 per cent (£1.1bn).

2014: IfL ceases operation On Friday 31 October the IfL was no more, and its legacy and assets were passed to the Education and Training Foundation (ETF).

2015: *What Does Skills Policy Look Like Now the Money Has Run Out?* A report written by Ewart Keep of the University of Oxford's Centre on Skills, Knowledge and Organizational Performance (SCOPE) for the AoC. 'On current projections, and if nothing else changes, the overall reduction in the DBIS budget between 2010 and 2018 will be 42.5 per cent' with huge cuts being made to FE and skills training (5 January).

2015: Carter Review of Initial Teacher Training Sir Andrew Carter's Review held that 'partnership is the key' to successful training and neither schools nor universities could do it alone. However, he argued that the PGCE should become an optional qualification. The review also suggested that teachers needed a new professional body to be called the 'College of Teaching'(19 January).

2015: Skills Funding Letter (26 February) This announced a further cut to non-apprenticeship adult FE in England with funding decreasing by 25 per cent in 2015–16. Martin Doel, chief executive of the AoC, commented 'By 2020, if the next Government continues to cut at this rate, adult further education will be effectively a thing of the past'.

2015: 3 million apprenticeships to be created This according to a pledge in the Conservative Party election manifesto (15 April).

2015: the ETF launches the Society for Education and Training (SET) The SET is intended as a new membership organization for practitioners working in FE and training. Its aim is 'to promote the professionalism and status of those working in the post 16 education and training sector; ensuring our members gain wider recognition for their expertise and practice' (29 May).

2015: *Heading for the precipice: can further and higher education funding policies be sustained?* A Policy Institute at King's College/Gatsby Foundation 'Issues and Ideas' paper by Professor Baroness Alison Wolf concludes that 'In post-19 education, we are producing vanishingly small numbers of higher technician-level qualifications, while massively increasing the output of generalist bachelors degrees and low-level vocational qualifications' (24 June).

Task 9.7

'Third way' policies and practice in Post-14 Education and Training since the first election victory of New Labour in 1997 have been described as 'weak' because they are marked by a 'pervasive voluntarism' (Hodgson and Spours 1999: 146). 'Voluntarism' is held to be an inadequate basis for real change as it leaves too much up to individuals and institutions. Post-14 Education and Training policy-making can seem directionless and in need of a 'strong' approach requiring structural change through social partnerships, even if this means introducing an element of compulsion – for example, obliging employers to train. Volunteering, what critics label as 'compulsory volunteering' (Williams 2010), is a major theme in the new ideology of the 'big society'.

Others have argued that the 'third way', and this includes 'big society', policies of the 'weak' or 'strong' sort are inevitably fragile as they are often over-complex and bureaucratic ways of attempting to overcome the seeming disconnectedness and apathy of young people and adults, in what can be described as 'depoliticized' times, through strategies such as 'joined-up thinking' (Hayes and Hudson 2001: 63–8). The sudden dropping of the notion of the 'big society' is evidence for this. One response to this policy fragility is a shift towards a new 'strong' approach to disconnectedness in the form of a *moral* authoritarianism, telling young people what to think and how to behave (Hayes 2007).

Reviewing the policy initiatives and changes in the chronology since the mid-1990s, and from your own knowledge and experience of Post-14 Education and Training, consider what might constitute a 'third way' approach and whether it is successful in meeting what you would see as the educational aspirations of young people and adults. Remember that the key ideas in third way approaches are social inclusion, economic competitiveness, (local) community and (individual) choice.

Task 9.8

Having read the chronology, use your general knowledge of history, and the outlines given in the boxed sections, to connect major historical events with particular pieces of legislation and their associated developments in the educational sphere. If you do this, patterns emerge. For example, the three historical periods, 1870–1902, 1902–45, 1945–present, can be seen as illustrating an almost seamless development in which elementary, then secondary, then further or higher education (FHE) became a reality for many people. However, also taking 1870 as a starting point we can identify three historical periods: 1870–1914, 1914–39 and 1939–present that are sometimes seen as key periods in Britain's relative decline (Sked 1987; Gamble 1990; for Britain in recession, see Vaitilingham 2009).

Broad historical periods showing the general developments in Post-14 Education and Training can also be identified. Draw up a chart showing the broad changes in this area over the last 100 years. To do this, identify clearly the different forms of Post-14 Education and Training programmes that were provided, the social policy behind that provision and the relevant dates. This will be easier if the tasks of describing the education and training opportunities available to a young person at a given historical moment have been completed. Compare your chart with Table 9.1.

Table 9.1 Developments in Post-14 Education and Training

Period	Social policy	Educational provision
Nineteenth century	Little state intervention	Mechanics' Institutes
1900–45	Training through 'stop gap' measures	Evening institutes, technical schools
1945–76	Stop gap measures, social orientation, consensus	Day release, technical colleges
1976–97	Crisis, vocationalism, the new vocationalism	FE colleges, training schemes
1997–2009	The third way, social inclusion, therapeutic education	Expansion of FE and HE, new 14–19 provision
2010–present	The climax of the third way in the 'big society', recession, marketization of education	Academic curriculum; revival of apprenticeships – the end of FE?

Task 9.9

Draw up a brief chronology of key events and reports in your own area of subject or professional expertise. This need not be very detailed. How do key developments correlate with those outlined in the chronology?

Remember that your chronology is not fixed and should be kept up to date and extended. Indeed, we have changed this chronology in each edition of this book. Further historical details can be added or deleted as your interests, understanding and ideas develop. Add major events and developments as they occur.

Task 9.10: A note on further reading

It is useful to read texts written in different decades to get a flavour of the time. This runs counter to the fashionable desire to have only the most up-to-date texts in an academic reading list. The result is a loss of any sense of history. Here is a very limited selection.

For a historical review of government reports and acts, J. Stuart Maclure's *Educational Documents: England and Wales,* first published in 1965 is an excellent source. For the period up to 1945, H.C. Barnard's *A History of English Education* (1969) and W.H.G. Armytage's *Four Hundred Years of English Education* (1970) are full of detail. They need some supplementing, as they are general histories of education and education policy (see also Coffey 1992; Skilbeck et al. 1994: 156–62). A useful recent work is Frank Coffield et al.'s (2008) *Improving Learning, Skills and Inclusion: The Impact of Policy on Post-Compulsory Education.*

The key resources for government policy documents and commentaries is the Department for Education's website that has archived as well as recent documents, which can be downloaded free of charge at www.education.gov.uk.

Think-tanks increasingly produce up-to-date and challenging policy and research papers on education: the DEMOS (www.demos.co.uk), Civitas (www.civitas.org.uk) and Institute of Ideas (www.instituteofideas.com) websites are all worth visiting.

W.O. Lester Smith's *Education* (1957) provides some clear thinking and an interesting comparison with today's debates on education, industry and citizenship. It can often be found in most Oxfam and second-hand bookshops, and on Amazon.

For an understanding of how the new vocationalism was created and contested, Dan Finn's *Training Without Jobs* (1987) is good, as is Cynthia Cockburn's *Two Track Training* (1987) which looks at sex inequalities in the YTS.

For a more recent discussion of policy issues, Ann Hodgson and Ken Spours in *New Labour's Educational Agenda* (1999) provide a useful critical evaluation of government policy for 14+ education and they produce their own argument for a 'strong third way'.

Analysis of current developments requires reading professional journals and newspapers and the *Times Educational Supplement* (TES) is the key professional newspaper alongside its sister publication, the *Times Higher Education* (THE) magazine. The archive of TES articles online goes back to 1994 (www.tes.co.uk). The *Education Guardian* is a leading source of educational discussion in the daily papers. All articles are available free online at www.education.guardian.co.uk. *Adults Learning*, published by the National Institute of National and Continuing Education (NIACE), is useful for adult educators: www.niace.org.uk/Publications/Periodicals/AdultsLearning.

A sound critique of competence-based training is Terry Hyland's *Competence Education and NVQs: Dissenting Perspectives* (1994).

To start you thinking about issues such as postmodernism and globalization as they are believed to affect lifelong learning, a good book is James Avis et al.'s *Knowledge and Nationhood: Education, Politics and Work* (1996).

For a serious introduction to the debate about 'knowledge' in education, Michael Young's books *Knowledge and Control* (1971) and *Bringing Knowledge Back In* (2008) present the major issues through a seminal work and its devastating criticism by the same author three decades later.

Tom Bentley, former director of the think-tank DEMOS, has produced an original book: *Learning Beyond the Classroom: Education for a Changing World* (1998). Bentley examines the tension between decades-old educational infrastructures and the new institutions needed to respond to the challenges of lifelong learning. By contrast with Bentley's arguments for change is Melanie Phillips' book, *All Must Have Prizes* (1996), which 'charts the flight from literacy and knowledge that has taken place in Britain's education system'. Together they capture the ongoing education debate between traditionalists and modernizers.

For a readable account of the changing ideologies that lie behind the current interest in Post-14 Education and Training, we recommend John Field's *Lifelong Learning and the New Educational Order* (2000).

Those interested in further reading about contemporary issues in Post-14 Education and Training will find a stimulating set of papers in the companion to this book, John Lea et al.'s *Working in Post-Compulsory Education* (2003).

Finally, for students and lecturers with an interest in challenging fads and fashions, we recommend a book of essays on *New Philosophies of Learning* (2009), edited by Ruth Cigman and Andrew Davies for the Philosophy of Education Society of Great Britain, which explores some of the contemporary 'innovations' in approaches to learning, including neuroscience, the focus on learners' well-being and happiness and notions such as 'learning to learn'.

Links to the Professional Standards for Teachers and Trainers in Education and Training

Professional values and attributes

 2 Evaluate and challenge your practice, values and beliefs

Professional knowledge and understanding

 7 Maintain and update knowledge of your subject and/or vocational area

 8 Maintain and update your knowledge of educational research to develop evidence-based practice

 9 Apply theoretical understanding of effective practice in teaching, learning and assessment drawing on research and other evidence

12 Understand the teaching and professional role and your responsibilities

Professional skills

20 Contribute to organizational development and quality improvement through collaboration with others

BIBLIOGRAPHY

Adams, C. (2006) PowerPoint, habits of mind and classroom culture, *Journal of Curriculum Studies*, 38(4): 389–411.

Ahier, J. and Ross, A. (1995) *The Social Subjects Within the Curriculum*. London: Falmer Press.

Ainley, P. (1988) *From School to YTS: Education and Training in England and Wales 1944–1987*. Maidenhead: Open University Press.

Ainley, P. (1990) *Vocational Education and Training*. London: Cassell.

Ainley, P. (1993) *Class and Skill: Changing Divisions of Knowledge and Labour*. London: Cassell.

Ainley, P. (1994) *Degrees of Difference: Higher Education in the 1990s*. London: Lawrence & Wishart.

Ainley, P. (1999) *Learning Policy: Towards the Certified Society*. London: Macmillan.

Ainscow, M. and Tweddle, D. (1988) *Preventing Classroom Failure*. London: David Fulton Publishers Ltd.

Alexander, T. (1997) *Family Learning: Foundation of Effective Learning*. London: Demos.

Alexander, T. and Clyne, P. (1995) *Riches Beyond Price: Making the Most of Family Learning*. Leicester: NIACE.

Allen, M. and Ainley, P. (2007) *Education Make You Fick, Innit?* London: The Tufnell Press.

Anderson, J. (1980a) Socrates as educator, in D.Z. Phillips (ed.) *Education and Inquiry*. London: Basil Blackwell, pp. 64–80.

Anderson, J. (1980b) Lectures on the educational theories of Spencer and Dewey, in D.Z. Phillips (ed.) *Education and Inquiry*. London: Basil Blackwell, pp. 81–141.

Anderson, J. (1980c) Education and practicality, in D.Z. Phillips (ed.) *Education and Inquiry*. London: Basil Blackwell, pp. 153–8.

Annan, N. (1990) *Our Age: The Generation that Made Post-war Britain*. London: Fontana.

AoC (Association of Colleges) (2001) *The Teaching Pay Initiative Guidance*. London: AoC.

AQA (Assessment and Qualification Alliance) (2002) *Media: Communication and Production*. Guildford: AQA.

AQA (2005) *Teachers' Guide to GCSE AS and A Level in Health and Social Care*. Guildford: AQA.

Aristotle (1904) *The Politics, Book VIII*, trans. T.A. Sinclair. Harmondsworth: Penguin.

Armytage, W.H.G. (1970) *Four Hundred Years of English Education*. Cambridge: Cambridge University Press.

AUT (Association of University Teachers) (1997) *AUT Bulletin*, April.

Avis, J., Bloomer, M., Esland, G., Gleeson, D. and Hodkinson, P. (1996) *Knowledge and Nationhood: Education, Politics and Work*. London: Cassell.

Ball, S. (1987) *The Micro-politics of the School*. London: Methuen.

Ball, S.J., Maguire, M. and Macrae, S. (1998) *Choice Pathways and Transitions Post-16. New Youth, New Economies in the Global City*. London and New York: RoutledgeFalmer.

Bandura, A. (1977) *Social Learning Theory*. Englewood Cliffs, NJ: Prentice Hall.

Barber, M. (1996) *The Learning Game*. London: Victor Gollancz.

Barnard, H.C. (1969) *A History of English Education from 1760*, 2nd edn. London: University of London Press.

Barnes, D. (1982) *Practical Curriculum Study*. London: Routledge & Kegan Paul.

Barrow, R. (1984) *Giving Teaching Back to Teachers: A Critical Introduction to Curriculum Theory*. Brighton: Wheatsheaf.

Batchelor, S. and Norrish, P. (2005) Framework for the assessment of ICT pilot projects. Available at: http://www.infordev.org/en/publication.4.html.

BBC (2005) *Top GCSE Pass Rates Levelling Off*. Available at www.news.bbc.co.uk/1/hi/education/4202327.stm (accessed 17 December 2010).

Beaumont, G. (1995) *Review of 100 NVQs and SVQs*. London: DfEE.

BECTA (2006) *ICT and E-learning in FE*. Coventry: BECTA. Available at www. publications. becta.org.uk/display.cfm?resID=28534 (free download) (accessed 26 January 2007).

BECTA (2007) *ICT and E-learning in Further Education: Management, Learning and Improvement*. Available at www.webarchive.nationalarchives.gov.uk/20101102103654/publications.becta.org.uk//display.cfm?resID=28534 (accessed 1 February 2011).

BECTA (2009a) *The Impact of Digital Technology: A Review of the Evidence of the Impact of Digital Technologies on Formal Education*, November. Available at www. webarchive.nationalarchives.gov.uk/20101102103654/http://publications.becta.org.uk/display.cfm?resID=41343 (accessed 14 February 2011).

BECTA (2009b) *Harnessing Technology Review 2009: The Role of Technology in Education and Skills*. Available at www.publications.becta.org.uk/display.cfm?resID=41329&page=1835 (accessed 14 February 2011).

Bell, J. (2014) *Doing your Research Project*, 6th edn. Maidenhead: Open University Press.

Benn, C. and Chitty, C. (1997) *Thirty Years On: Is Comprehensive Education Alive and Well or Struggling to Survive?* Harmondsworth: Penguin.

Benn, C. and Fairley, J. (eds) (1986) *Challenging the MSC on Jobs, Training and Education*. London: Pluto Press.

Bennett, N. and McNamara, D. (1979) *Focus on Teaching*. London: Longman.

Bentley, T. (1998) *Learning Beyond the Classroom: Education for a Changing World*. London: Routledge/DEMOS.

Bills, D. (1988) Credentials and capacities: employers' perceptions of the acquisition of skill, *The Sociological Quarterly*, 29(3): 439–49.

Black, P. and William, D. (1998) *Inside the Black Box: Raising Standards Through Classroom Assessment*. London: School of Education, King's College.

Black, P., Harrison, C., Lee, C., Marshall, B. and William, D. (2002) *Working Inside the Black Box: Assessment for Learning in the Classroom*. London: NFER Nelson.

Blair, T. (1996) *Education, Education, Education*. Speech to the Labour Party Conference, *Times Educational Supplement*, p. 6.

Blair, T. (1998) *The Third Way: New Politics for the New Century*. London: Fabian Society.

Bloom, A. (1987) *The Closing of the American Mind: How Higher Education has Failed Democracy and Impoverished the Souls of Today's Students*. Harmondsworth: Penguin.

Bloom, A. (1991) Introduction, in J.J. Rousseau ([1762] 1991) *Émile*. Harmondsworth: Penguin.

Bloom, B.S. (1964) *Taxonomy of Educational Objectives: Handbook 1/CognitiveDomain*. London: Longman.

Bloomer, M. (1996) Education for studentship, in J. Avis et al. (eds) *Knowledge and Nationhood: Education, Politics and Work*. London: Cassell, pp. 140–63.

Bloomer, M. (1997) *Curriculum Making in Post-16 Education: The Social Conditions of Studentship*. London: Routledge.

Boden, M.A. (1994) *Piaget*. London: Fontana.

Bottery, M. (2000) *Education, Policy and Ethics*. London: Continuum.

Bourdieu, P. (1986) The forms of capital, in J.E. Richardson (ed.) *Handbook of Theory of Research for the Sociology of Education*. Westport, CT: Greenwood Press, pp. 241–58 (reprinted in A.H. Halsey, H. Lauder, P. Brown and A. Stuart Wells (1997) *Education: Culture, Economy and Society*. Oxford: Oxford University Press, pp. 46–58).

Boyd, W. (1956) *Émile for Today: The Émile of Jean-Jacques Rousseau*, selected, translated and interpreted by William Boyd. London: Heinemann.

Brookfield, S. (1986) *Understanding and Facilitating Learning*. Maidenhead: Open University Press.

Brookfield, S. (1995) *Becoming a Critically Reflective Teacher*. San Francisco, CA: Jossey-Bass.

Brooks, R. (1991) *Contemporary Debates in Education: An Historical Perspective*. London: Longman.

Brown, S., Jones, G. and Rawnsley, S. (eds) (1993) *Observing Teaching*. Birmingham: Staff and Educational Development Association.

Bruner, J. (1990) *Acts of Meaning*. London: Harvard University Press.

Bryan, J. (1998) Review of Reeves, F. (ed.) (1997) *Further Education as Economic Regeneration: The Starting Point*. Bilston: Bilston Community College and Education Now Books (pp. 99–101 in *Youth and Policy*, Issue 61, Autumn 1998).

Buchanan, S. (ed.) (1982) Introduction, in Plato (1956) *The Portable Plato*. Harmondsworth: Penguin.

Buckingham, D., Scanlon, M. and Sefton-Green, J. (2001) Selling the digital dream: marketing educational technology to teachers and parents, in A. Loveless and V. Ellis (eds) *Subject to Change: Literacy and Digital Technology*. London: Routledge.

Burkard, T. and Talbot Rice, S. (2009) *School Quangos: A Blueprint for Abolition and Reform*. London: Centre for Policy Studies.

Burnyeat, M. (1990) *The Theatetus of Plato*, trans. M.J. Levett. Cambridge: Hackett Publishing.

Butler, R. (1988) Enhancing and undermining intrinsic motivation: the effects of task-involving and ego-involving evaluation on interest and performance, *British Journal of Educational Psychology*, 58: 1–14.

Calderhead, J. (1987) *Exploring Teachers' Thinking*. London: Cassell.

Cameron, D. (2010) Big society speech, Liverpool, 19 July 2010. Available at www.number10.gov.uk/news/speeches-and-transcripts/2010/07/big-society-speech-53572.

Capey, J. (1995) *GNVQ Assessment Review: Final Report of the Review Group*. London: NCVQ.

Carr, W. and Kemmis, S. (2003) *Becoming Critical: Education, Knowledge and Action Research*. London: RoutledgeFalmer.

Carter, A. (2015) *Carter Review of Initial Teacher Training*. London: DfE.

Castle, E.B. (1961) *Ancient Education and Today*. Harmondsworth: Penguin.

Cassen, R. and Kingdon, G. (2007) *Tackling Low Educational Achievers*, Rowntree Foundation. Available at www.creativeite.org/resources/docs/reading/rowntree_report .pdf (accessed 11 February 2011).

CBI (Confederation of British Industry) (1991) *World Class Targets: A Joint Initiative to Achieve Britain's Skill Revolution*. London: CBI.

Chaiklin, S. (2011) Social scientific research and societal practice: action research and cultural-historical research in a methodological light from Kurt Lewin and Lev S. Vygotsky, *Mind, Culture, and Activity*, 18(2): 129–47. Available at: http://www. tandfonline.com/toc/hmca20/18/2 (accessed: 14 June 2015).

Chickering, A.W. and Havighurst, R. (1981) The life cycle, in A.W. Chickering (ed.) *The Modern American College*. San Francisco, CA: Jossey-Bass.

Child, D. (2007) *Psychology and the Teacher*. London: Cassell.

Cigman, R. and Davis, A. (2009) *New Philosophies of Learning – Journal of Philosophy of Education*. Oxford: Wiley-Blackwell.

CLA (Copyright Licensing Agency) (2011). Available at www.cla.co.uk/Licencesforeducation (accessed 12 February 2011).

Clarke, A. (2008) *e-Learning Skills*, 2nd edn, Palgrave Study Skills. Basingstoke: Palgrave Macmillan.

Cockburn, C. (1987) *Two Track Training: Sex Inequalities and the YTS*. London: Macmillan.

Coffey, D. (1992) *Schools and Work*. London: Cassell.

Coffield, F. (1997) Prophets of the true god, *Times Educational Supplement*, 24 January.

Coffield, F., Moseley, D., Hall, E. and Ecclestone, K. (2004) *Should We Be Using Learning Styles?* Learning and Skills Research Centre. Available at: www.lsrc.ac.uk, http://www. itslifejimbutnotasweknowit.org.uk/files/LSRC_LearningStyles.pdf.

Coffield, F., Edward, S., Finlay, I. and Hodgson, A. (2008) *Improving Learning Skills and Inclusion: The Impact of Post Compulsory Education*. London: Routledge.

Cogger, A., Goodhall, S. and Wennestrom, V. (2012a) *Medway RPA Project*. Canterbury: Canterbury Christ Church University and Kent and Medway Progression Federation.

Cogger, A., Goodhall, S. and Wennestrom,V. (2012b) *Report of the School Commissioned Alternative Curriculum in Medway*. Canterbury: Canterbury Christ Church University and Kent and Medway Progression Federation.

Cohen, L. and Manion, L. (1989) *Research Methods in Education*. London: Routledge.

Corbett, J. and Barton, L. (1992) *A Struggle for Choice*. London: Routledge.

Cornwall, J. (1996) *Choice, Opportunity and Learning*. London: Fulton.

Corson, D. (ed.) (1991) *Education for Work*. Clevedon: Multilingual Matters Ltd.

Cottrell, S. (2013) *The Study Skills Handbook*, 4th edn. Basingstoke: Macmillan.

Coulby, D. and Jones, C. (1995) *Postmodernity and European Education Systems*. Stoke-on-Trent: Trentham Books.

Cowen, N. (2008) *Swedish Lessons: How Schools with More Freedom can Deliver Better Education*. London: Civitas.

Crequer, N. (2001) Basic skills at the heart of Labour's future, *FE Focus, TES*, 23 February.

Cronbach, L.J. (1980) *Toward Reform of Program Evaluation*. San Francisco, CA: Jossey-Bass.

CSJ (Commission on Social Justice) (1994) *Social Justice: Strategies for National Renewal.* London: Vintage.

Cuban, L. (2001) *Oversold and Underused: Computers in the Classroom.* London: Harvard University Press.

Curzon, L.B. (ed.) (2003) *Teaching in Further Education,* 5th edn. London: Cassell.

Daniels, H. (1996) Introduction: psychology in the social world, in H. Daniels (ed.) *An Introduction to Vygotsky.* London: Routledge.

Daunt, P. (1991) *Meeting Disability: A European Response.* London: Cassell.

Davies, W.J.K. (1975) *Learning Resources.* London: Council for Educational Technology.

Dawn, T., Harkin, J. and Turner, G. (2000) *Teaching Young Adults: A Handbook for Teachers in Post-compulsory Education.* London: Routledge.

DBIS/DfE (2015) *2010 to 2015 Government Policy: Further Education and Training.* Available at: https://www.gov.uk/government/publications/2010-to-2015-government-policy-further-education-and-training/2010-to-2015-government-policy-further-education-and-training#appendix-3-technical-level-qualifications.

DCSF (Department for Children, Schools and Families) (2008) *Byron Review: Safer Children in a Digital World.* Available at: www.dcsf.gov.uk/byronreview (accessed 12 December 2010).

Deaney, R. and Hennessy, S. (2007) Sustainability, evolution and dissemination of information and communication technology: supported classroom practice, *Research Papers in Education,* 22(1): 65–94.

Dearing, R. (1994) *The National Curriculum and its Assessment* (Dearing I). London: SCAA.

Dearing, R. (1996) *Review of Qualifications for 16–19 Year Olds* (Dearing II). Hayes: SCAA.

Dearing, R. (1997) *Higher Education in the Learning Society: Report of the National Committee of Inquiry into Higher Education* (Dearing III). London: HMSO.

Department for Business, Innovation and Skills/Skills Funding Agency (2012) *Skills Funding Statement 2012–15.* London: DBIS/SFA.

DES (Department of Education and Science) (1991) *Education and Training for the 21st Century,* Cmnd. 1536. London: HMSO.

Dewey, J. (1915) *The School and Society.* Chicago, IL: University of Chicago Press.

Dewey, J. ([1916] 1966) *Democracy and Education.* New York: Macmillan/The Free Press.

Dewey, J. ([1938] 1971) *Experience and Education.* New York: Collier Books.

DfE (Department for Education) (2010a) *Academies Act 2010.* London: DfE. Available at: www.education.gov.uk/schools/leadership/typesofschools/academies/whatisanacademy/a0061222/academies-act-2010.

DfE (Department for Education) (2010b) *Reforming the Diploma.* London: DfE. Available at: www. education.gov.uk/schools/teachingandlearning/qualifications/diploma/a0064056/diplomaannouncements.

DfE (Department for Education) (2010c) *The Importance of Teaching: The Schools White Paper 2010.* London: DfE. Available at: www.education.gov.uk/b0068570/the-importance-of-teaching.

DfE (Department for Education) (2010d) *The Case for Change.* London: DfE. Available at: www.education.gov.uk/publications//eOrderingDownload/DFE-00564-2010.pdf.

DfE (Department for Education) (2011) *Education Bill 2011.* London: The Stationery Office. Available at: www.education.gov.uk/aboutdfe/departmentalinformation/educationbill/a0073748/educationbill.

DfE (Department for Education) (2014a) Available at: https://www.gov.uk/government/ publications/national-curriculum-in-england-framework-for-key-stages-1-to-4/ the-national-curriculum-in-england-framework-for-key-stages-1-to-4.

DfE (Department for Education) (2014b) Available at: https://www.gov.uk/government/ uploads/system/uploads/attachment_data/file/339942/2016_16_to_19_performance_ tables_inclusion_of_tech_levels.pdf.

DfE (Department for Education) (2015a) Available at: https://www.gov.uk/government/ news/free-schools-drive-social-justice-nicky-morgan.

DfE (Department for Education) (2015b) Available at: https://www.gov.uk/government/ uploads/system/uploads/attachment_data/file/415486/Progress_8_school_ performance_measure.pdf.

DfE (Department for Education) (2015c) Available at: https://www.gov.uk/further-education-courses.

DfE (Department for Education) (2015d) Available at: https://www.gov.uk/government/ uploads/system/uploads/attachment_data/file/428492/Quarterly_Brief_NEET_ Q1_2015_FINAL.pdf.

DfEE (Department for Education and Employment) (1995a) *Competitiveness: Forging Ahead, Education and Training.* London: HMSO.

DfEE (Department for Education and Employment) (1995b) *Lifetime Learning: A Consultation Document.* London: HMSO.

DfEE (Department for Education and Employment) (1997) *Qualifying for Success.* London: DfEE.

DfEE (Department for Education and Employment) (1998a) *Higher Education for the 21st Century: Response to the Dearing Report.* London: DfEE.

DfEE (Department for Education and Employment) (1998b) *The Learning Age: A Renaissance for a New Britain.* London: DfEE.

DfEE (Department for Education and Employment) (1999) *Learning to Succeed: A New Framework for Post-16 Learning* (White Paper). London: The Stationery Office.

DfES (Department for Education and Skills) (2001) *Meeting the Sector Skills and Productivity Challenge.* London: HMSO.

DfES (Department for Education and Skills) (2002a) *14–19: Extending Opportunities, Raising Standards.* London: The Stationery Office.

DfES (Department for Education and Skills) (2002b) *Success for All.* London: HMSO

DfES (Department for Education and Skills) (2003a) *21st Century Skills: Realising our Potential.* London: DfES.

DfES (Department for Education and Skills) (2003b) *14–19 Opportunities and Excellence.* London: DfES.

DfES (Department for Education and Skills) (2003c) *The Future of Initial Teacher Education for the Learning and Skills Sector.* Sheffield: Standards Unit.

DfES (Department for Education and Skills) (2004a) *Children Act 2004.* London: Stationery Office.

DfES (Department for Education and Skills) (2004b) *14–19 Curriculum and Qualifications Reform* (the Tomlinson Report). London: DfES.

DfES (Department for Education and Skills) (2004c) *Equipping our Teachers for the Future: Reforming Initial Teaching Training for the Learning and Skills Sector.* London: HMSO.

• DfES (Department for Education and Skills) (2004d) *Every Child Matters.* London: Stationery Office.

DfES (Department for Education and Skills) (2005a) *14–19 Education and Skills.* London: HMSO.

DfES (Department for Education and Skills) (2005b) *Harnessing Technology: Transforming Learning and Children's Services.* Available at: www.dfes.gov.uk/publications/e-strategy/ (accessed February 2007).

DfES (Department for Education and Skills) (2005c) *Youth Matters.* London: Stationery Office.

DfES (Department for Education and Skills) (2005d) *Realising the Potential: A Review of the Future Role of Further Education Colleges* (the Foster Review). Nottinghamshire: DfES.

DfES (Department for Education and Skills) (2006a) *Further Education and Training Bill [HL].* Norwich: DfES.

DfES (Department for Education and Skills) (2006b) *Further Education: Raising Skills, Improving Life Chances.* London: HMSO.

DfES (Department for Education and Skills) (2007a) *2020 Vision: Report of the Teaching and Learning in 2020 Review Group.* Nottingham: DfES. Available at: www.teachernet.gov.uk/docbank/index.cfm?id=10783.

DfES (Department for Education and Skills) (2007b) *Raising Expectations: Staying in Education and Training Post-16.* Available at: www.dfes.gov.uk/publications/raisingexpectations.

Dickinson, L. (1992) *Learner Autonomy.* Dublin: Authentik.

Digital Skills Committee (2015) *Make or Break: The UK's Digital Future Select Committee on Digital Skills Report of Session 2014–15.* Available at: http://www.publications.parliament.uk/pa/ld201415/ldselect/lddigital/111/111.pdf.

Dillenbourg, P. (2008) Integrating technologies into educational ecosystems. *Distance Education,* 29: 127–40.

DoH (Department of Health) (1999) *Making a Difference: Strengthening the Nursing, Midwifery and Health Visiting Contributions to Health and Healthcare.* London: DoH.

Donald, J. (1992) *Sentimental Education.* London: Verso.

Duckworth, V., Flanagan, K., McCormack, K. and Tummons, J. (2012) *Understanding Behaviour 14+.* Maidenhead: Open University Press.

Ecclestone, K. and Hayes, D. (2008) *The Dangerous Rise of Therapeutic Education.* London and New York: Routledge.

Education Forum (2010) *A Defence of Subject-based Education.* London: Institute of Ideas.

Egan, G. (1994) *The Skilled Helper.* Pacific Grove, CA: Brooks/Cole Publishing Co.

Eisner, E.W. (1985) *The Educational Imagination: On the Design and Evaluation of School Programs.* New York: Macmillan.

Ellington, H. and Race, P. (1993) *Producing Teaching Materials,* 2nd edn. London: Kogan Page.

Ellington, H., Percival, F. and Race, P. (1993) *Handbook of Educational Technology,* 3rd edn. London: Kogan Page.

Elliott, J. (1993) Introduction, in J. Elliott (ed.) *Reconstructing Teacher Education.* London: Falmer Press.

Engels, F. ([1878] 1975) *Anti-Duhring.* London: Lawrence & Wishart.

ETF (Education and Training Foundation) (2014) Available at: www.et-foundation.co.uk (accessed 26 June 2015).

Evershed, J. and Roper, J. (2010) *Teaching Information Technology 14+*. Maidenhead: Open University Press.

Farish, M., McPake, J., Powney, J. and Weiner, G. (1996) *Equal Opportunities in Colleges and Universities*. Buckingham: SRHE/Open University Press.

FEDA (Further Education Development Agency) (1995) Launch newsletter, May. London: FEDA.

FENTO (Further Education National Training Organization) (2001) *Governors and Clerks in Further Education Benchmark Standards*. London: FENTO.

FEU (Further Education Unit) (1987) *Marketing Adult and Continuing Education: A Project Report*. London: FEU.

Field, J. (2000) *Lifelong Learning and the New Educational Order*. Stoke-on-Trent: Trentham Books.

Finegold, D.N. and Soskice, D. (1988) The failure of training in Britain: analysis and prescription, *Oxford Review of Economic Policy*, 4(3): 21–53.

Finegold, D.N., Keep, E., Milliband, D., Raffe, D., Spours, K. and Young, M. (1990) *A British Baccalaureate*. London: IPPR.

Finlayson, H., Maxwell, B., Caillau, I. and Tomalin, J. (2006) *e-learning in Further Education: The Impact and End-point Outcomes*. Sheffield: Sheffield Hallam University School of Education and Education.

Finn, D. (1986) YTS: the jewel in the MSC's crown?, in C. Benn and J. Fairley (eds) *Challenging the MSC: On Jobs, Training and Education*. London: Pluto Press.

Finn, D. (1987) *Training Without Jobs: New Deals and Broken Promises*. London: Macmillan.

Fordham, M., (2015) Clio etcetera, blog, maf44@can.ac.uk.

Foster, A. (2005) *Realising the Potential: A Review of the Future Role of Further Education Colleges* (the Foster Report). London: DfES.

Francis, D. and Young, D. (1992) *Improving Working Groups: A Practical Manual for Team Building*. San Francisco, CA: Jossey-Bass/Pfeiffer.

Frey, B. and Birnbaum, D. (2002) Learners' perceptions on the value of PowerPoint in lectures, Pittsburgh University, ERIC ED467192.

Fryer, R.H. (1997) *Learning for the Twenty-First Century: First Report of the National Advisory Group for Continuing Education and Lifelong Learning*. London: NAGCELL.

Füredi, F. (1997) *Culture of Fear*. London: Cassell.

Füredi, F. (2004) *Therapy Culture: Cultivating Vulnerability in an Uncertain Age*. London and New York: Routledge

Füredi, F. (2009) *Wasted: Why Education isn't Educating*. London and New York: Continuum.

Furlong, A. (2005) Cultural dimensions of decisions about educational participation among 14–19 year-olds: the parts that Tomlinson doesn't reach, *Journal of Education Policy*, 20(3): 379–89.

Gagné, R. (1977) *Conditions of Learning*. New York: Holt, Rinehart & Winston.

Gamble, A. (1990) *Britain in Decline: Economic Policy, Political Strategy and the British State*, 3rd edn. London: Macmillan.

Gardner, H. (1983) *Frames of Mind: The Theory of Multiple Intelligences*. New York: Basic Books.

Gardner, H. (1993) *Multiple Intelligences*. New York: Basic Books.

Garnelas, C. (2006) *Youth Participation: Overview of Policy*. London: CRAE. Available at: www.sound-connections.org.uk/resources/CRAEfinal.ppt.

Gibb, N. (2015) Available at:

https://www.gov.uk/government/speeches/nick-gibb-the-social-justice-case-for-an-academic-curriculum.

Gibbs, G. and Habeshaw, T. (1989) *Preparing to Teach*. Bristol: Technical and Educational Services Ltd.

Gibbs, G. and Parsons, C. (1994) *Course Design for Resource Based Learning*. Oxford: Oxford Centre for Staff Development.

Gibbs, G., Habeshaw, S. and Habeshaw, T. (1988) *53 Interesting Ways to Appraise Your Teaching*. Bristol: Technical and Educational Services Ltd.

Giddens, A. (1998) *The Third Way: The Renewal of Social Democracy*. Cambridge: Polity Press.

Giddens, A. (1999) *Runaway World*. London: Profile Books.

Gilbert, C. et al. (2006) *2020 Vision: Report of the Teaching and Learning in 2020 Review Group*. London: DfES. Available at: www.teachernet.gov.uk/docbank/index.cfm?id=10783.

Gilroy, P. (1993) Reflections on Schön, in P. Gilroy and M. Smith (eds) *International Analyses of Teacher Education*. Abingdon: Carfax, *Journal of Education and Training* Papers 1.

Glennerster, N. (1995) *British Social Policy Since 1945*. London: Basil Blackwell.

Golden, S., McCrone, T., Walker, M. and Rudd, P. (2006) *Impact of E-learning in Further Education: Survey of Scale and Breadth*. London: DfES. Available at: www.webarchive.nationalarchives.gov.uk/20101102103654/http://foi.becta.org.uk//content_files/corporate/resources/foi/archived_publications/learning_21c_case_ht.pdf.

Goleman, D. (2005a) *Emotional Intelligence*. London: Bloomsbury.

Goleman, D. (2005b) *Working with Emotional Intelligence*: New York: Bantam Books.

Goodson, I.F. (1994) *Studying Curriculum: Cases and Methods*. Maidenhead: Open University Press.

Goodson, I.F. and Hargreaves, A. (eds) (1996) *Teachers' Professional Lives*. London: Falmer Press.

Gove, M. (2009) The democratic intellect – what do we need to succeed in the 21st century? Annual Lecture, Sir John Cass's Foundation. Available at: www.sirjohncass.org/LinkClick.aspx?link=Text+of+Michael+Gove+Lecture.pdf&tabid=464&mid=1453.

Gove, M. (2010a) Speech to the Westminster Academy, 6 September. Available at: www.education.gov.uk/inthenews/speeches/a0064281/michael-gove-to-westminster-academy.

Gove, M. (2010b) Speech to the Edge Foundation. Available at: www.education.gov.uk/inthenews/speeches/a0064364/michael-gove-to-the-edge-foundation.

Gravells, A. and Simpson, S. (2008) *Planning and Learning in the Lifelong Learning Sector*. Exeter: Learning Matters Ltd.

Grenfell, M. and James, D. (1998) *Bourdieu and Education: Acts of Practical Theory*. London: Falmer Press.

Hall, V. (1994) *Further Education in the UK*, 2nd edn. London and Bristol: Collins Educational and The Staff College.

Hamilton, D. (1976) *Curriculum Evaluation*. London: Open Books.

Hammond, M. et al. (2009) What happens as student teachers who made very good use of ICT during pre-service training enter their first year of teaching? *Teacher Development: An International Journal of Teachers' Professional Development*, 13(2): 93–106.

Hargreaves, A. (1994) *Changing Teachers, Changing Times: Teachers' Work and Culture in a Postmodern Age*. London: Cassell.

Harkin, J., Turner, G. and Dawn, T. (2001) *Teaching Young Adults: A Handbook for Teachers in Post-compulsory Education*. London: Routledge/Falmer.

Harris, R. (2009) Freedom of speech and philosophy of education, *British Journal of Educational Studies*, 57(2): 111–26.

Hayes, D. (2002a) Taking the hemlock: the new sophistry of teacher training for higher education, in D. Hayes and R. Wynyard (eds) *The McDonaldization of Higher Education*. Westport, CT: Bergin & Garvey.

Hayes, D. (2002b) New Labour: new professionalism. Paper presented at the 'Discourse, Power and Resistance in Post-Compulsory Education and Training' conference, Plymouth University, 12–14 April.

Hayes, D. (2003a) New Labour: new professionalism, in J. Satterthwaite E. Atkinson and K. Gale (eds) *Discourse, Power, Resistance: Challenging the Rhetoric of Contemporary Education*. Stoke-on-Trent: Trentham Books.

Hayes, D. (2003b) The changed nexus between education and work, in J. Lea, D. Hayes, A. Armitage, L. Lomas and S. Markless, *Working in Post-compulsory Education*. Maidenhead: Open University Press, pp. 43–55.

Hayes, D. (2003c) Managerialism and professionalism in post-compulsory education, in J. Lea, D. Hayes, A. Armitage, L. Lomas and S. Markless, *Working in Post-compulsory Education*. Maidenhead: Open University Press, pp. 87–100.

Hayes, D. (2004) The therapeutic turn in teacher education, in D. Hayes (ed.) *The Routledge Falmer Guide to Key Debates in Education*. London and New York: Routledge, pp. 180–5.

Hayes, D. (2005) Theoretically, how are you feeling? *FE Focus, TES*, 29 April.

Hayes, D. (2006) Rehumanising education, in D. Cummings (ed.) *Debating Humanism*. Exeter: Imprint Academic/Societas, pp. 84–92.

Hayes, D. (2007) Past caring about history, *FE Focus, TES*, 2 February.

Hayes, J. (2010a) 'The craft so long to lerne': skills and their place in modern Britain, speech to the Royal Society of Arts, London, 26 October. Available at: www.bis.gov.uk/news/speeches/john-hayes-skills-and-their-place.

Hayes, J. (2010b) New All Age Careers Service, speech to the Institute of Careers Guidance annual conference, Belfast, 4 November. Available at: www.bis.gov.uk/news/speeches/john-hayes-icg-conference.

Hayes, J. (2010c) Speech to the Association of Colleges Annual Conference, Birmingham, 17 November. Available at: www.bis.gov.uk/news/speeches/john-hayes-assoccolleges-speech.

Hayes, D. (2014) The 50 great books on education, *The Conversation*, 31 March. Available at: http://theconversation.com/the-50-great-books-on-education-24934 (accessed 24 June 2015).

Hayes, D. and Hudson, A. (2001) *Basildon: The Mood of the Nation*. London: Demos.

Hayes, D. and Marshall, T. (2015) *The Role of the Teacher Today*. London: Standing Committee for the Education and Training of Teachers.

Hayes, D. and Wynyard, R. (2002a) Resisting McUniversity, in D. Hayes and R.Wynyard (eds) *The McDonaldization of Higher Education*. Westport, CT, USA: Bergin & Garvey.

Hayes, D. and Wynyard, R. (2002b) Whimpering into the Good Night: resisting McUniversity, in G. Ritzer (ed.) *The McDonaldization Reader*. Thousand Oaks, CA: Sage.

Hayes, D., Marshall, T. and Turner, A. (2007a) *A Lecturer's Guide to Further Education*. Maidenhead: Open University Press.

Hayes, D., Browne, E. and Simmons, J. (2007b) *An Evaluation of the Pedagogical Uses and Cognitive Applications to Subject Specialism Teaching in Post-compulsory Education of the 'Chronological' Approach Described in the Bestselling Textbook Teaching and Training in Post-Compulsory Education.* Bristol: Escalate.

Hearnshaw, L.S. (1979) *Cyril Burt, Psychologist.* London: Hodder & Stoughton.

HEFCE (2005) *HEFCE strategy for E-Learning* 2005/12. Available at: www.hefce.ac.uk/pubs/hefce/2005/05_12/05_12.pdf (accessed January 2007).

Hennessy, S., Ruthven, K. and Brindley, S. (2005) Teacher perspectives on integrating ICT into subject teaching: commitment, constraints, caution, and change, *Journal of Curriculum Studies*, 37(2):155–92.

Hickox, M. (1995) Situating vocationalism, *British Journal of Sociology of Education*, 16(2): 153–62.

Higgins, S. (2009) *Interpreting the Evidence Base for the Impact of Digital Technologies on Learning.* Coventry: BECTA.

Higham, J., Sharp, P. and Yeomans, D. (1996) *The Emerging 16–19 Curriculum.* London: Fulton.

Hill, C. (2008) *Teaching with e-learning in the Lifelong Learning Sector*, 2nd edn. Exeter: Learning Matters Ltd.

Hillier, Y. (2005) *Reflective Teaching in Further and Adult Education*, 2nd edn. London: Continuum.

Hirst, P.H. ([1965] 1973) Liberal education and the nature of knowledge, in R.S. Peters (ed.) *The Philosophy of Education.* Oxford: Oxford University Press.

Hirst, P.H. (1974) *Knowledge and the Curriculum.* London: Routledge & Kegan Paul.

Hirst, P.H. (1993) Education, knowledge and practices, in R. Barrow and P. White (eds) *Beyond Liberal Education: Essays in Honour of Paul H. Hirst.* London: Routledge, pp. 184–99.

HMSO (Her Majesty's Stationery Office) (1959) *15–18: A Report of the Central Advisory Council for Education/England* (the Crowther Report). London: HMSO.

HMSO (1986) *The National Council for Vocational Qualifications: Its Purposes and Aims.* London: HMSO.

Hobsbawm, E. (1994) *Age of Extremes: The Short Twentieth Century 1914–1991.* London: Michael Joseph.

Hodgson, A. and Spours, K. (eds.) (1997) *Dearing and Beyond 14–19: Qualifications and Frameworks.* London: Kogan Page.

Hodgson, A. and Spours, K. (eds) (1999) *New Labour's Educational Agenda: Issues and Policies for Education and Training from 14.* London: Kogan Page.

Hodgson, A. and Spours, K. (2000) *Institutional Responses to Curriculum 2000.* London: Institute of Education.

Hodgson, A. and Spours, K. (2001) *Evaluating Stage 1 of the Hargreaves Review of Curriculum 2000.* London: Institute of Education.

Hodgson, A. and Spours, K. (2003) *Beyond A-levels: Curriculum 2000 and the Reform of 14–19 Qualifications.* London: RoutledgeFalmer.

Hodgson, A. and Spours, K. (2007) Specialised diplomas: transforming the 14–19 landscape in England? *Journal of Education Policy*, 22(6): 657–73.

Hodgson, A. and Spours, K. (2008) *Education and Training 14–19: Curriculum, Qualifications and Organization.* London: Sage Publications.

Hodgson, A. and Spours, K. (2010) Curriculum and qualifications under the coalition: turning back the clock? Paper presented at the 'Curriculum and Qualifications for Young People and Adults: A Changing Landscape' conference, London, Institute of Education, December.

Hodgson, A. and Spours, K. (2013) *Middle Attainers and 14–19 Progression in England: Half-served by New Labour and now Overlooked by the Coalition?* London: University of London, Institute of Education.

Hodgson, A., Savory, C. and Spours, K. (2001a) *Planning and Implementing Curriculum 2000: Different Institutional Approaches.* London: Institute of Education.

Hodgson, A., Savory, C. and Spours, K. (2001b) *Improving the 'Use' and 'Exchange' Value of Key Skills.* London: Institute of Education.

Hodgson, A., Spours, K. and Waring, M. (eds) (2011) *Post-compulsory Education and the Lifelong Learning Across the United Kingdom: Policy, Organization and Governance.* London: Bedford Way Papers.

Hoggart, R. (1996) *The Way We Live Now.* London: Pimlico.

Holland, R.F. (1980) *Against Empiricism: On Education, Epistemology and Value.* London: Basil Blackwell, pp. 2–25.

Hopkins, D. (1989) *Evaluation for School Development.* Maidenhead: Open University Press.

Houle, C.O. (1961) *The Enquiring Mind.* Madison, WI: University of Wisconsin Press.

Houle, C.O. (1972) *The Design of Education.* San Francisco, CA: Jossey-Bass.

Howard-Jones, P. (2007) *Neuroscience and Education: Issues and Opportunities.* Teaching and Learning Research Programme. Available at: http://www.tlrp.org/pub/documents/Neuroscience%20Commentary%20FINAL.pdf.

Huddleston, P. and Unwin, L. (2013) *Teaching and Learning in Further Education: Diversity and Change*, 4th edn. London: Routledge.

Hudson, A., Hayes, D. and Andrew, T. (1996) *Working Lives in the 1990s.* London: Global Futures.

Hudson, L. (1966) *Contrary Imaginations.* London: Methuen.

Hyland, T. (1994) *Competence, Education and NVQs: Dissenting Perspectives.* London: Cassell.

Hyland, T. (2005) Learning and therapy – oppositional or complementary processes? *Adults Learning*, 16(5): 16–17.

Hyland, T. (2006) Vocational education and training and the therapeutic turn, *Educational Studies*, 32(3): 299–306.

IfL (Institute for Learning) (2006a) *Towards a Code of Good Environmental Practice.* Available at: www.ifl.ac.uk/members_area/code_environ.html.

IfL (2006b) *Towards a Code of Professional Practice.* Available at: www.ifl.ac.uk/members_area/code_prof.html.

IfL (2006c) *Towards a Code of Ethics.* Available at: www.ifl.ac.uk/members_area/code_ethics.html.

Investors in People (IiP) UK (2006) *The Investors in People Standard*, 2nd edn. London: IiP.

Investors in People (2011) *Investors in People Framework.* Available at: www.investorsinpeople.co.uk/Documents/Branding2009/IIP_Framework09.pdf (accessed February 2011).

IRDAC (Industrial Research and Development Advisory Committee) (1990) *Skills Shortages in Europe.* Brussels: IRDAC.

Jackson, P.W. (1968) *Life in Classrooms*. New York: Holt, Rinehart & Winston.

Jarvis, P. (1995) *Adult and Continuing Education: Theory and Practice*. London: Routledge.

Jeffries, A., Thornton, M., Alltree, J. and Jones, I. (2004) Introducing web-based learning: an investigation into its impact on university lecturers and their pedagogy, *Journal of Information Technology Impact*, 4(2): 91–98. Available at: www.jiti.com/ (accessed March 2007).

JISC (2006) *Designing Spaces for Effective Learning*. Available at: www.jisc.ac.uk/uploadeddocuments/JISC%20learning%20spaces.acc.pdf (accessed 19 July 2010).

JISC (2007) *The Learner's Voice*. Available at: www.jisc.ac.uk/whatwedo/programmes/elearning_pedagogy/elp_learneroutcomes/elp_learnervoices.aspx (accessed March 2007).

Keep, E. (2015) *What Does Skills Policy Look Like Now the Money Has Run Out?* Oxford: SCOPE/AoC.

Kelly, G. (2010) We launched in 1910 in the throes of a schools revolution; 100 years on, another is on its way, Editorial, *TES*. Available at: www.tes.co.uk/article.aspx?storycode=6056909.

Kennedy, H. (1997a) *Guardian*, 27 May.

Kennedy, H. (1997b) *Learning Works: Widening Participation in Further Education*. Coventry: FEFC.

Knowles, M. (1984) *The Adult Learner, a Neglected Species*, 3rd edn. Houston, TX: Gulf Publishing Company.

Kolb, D. (1984) *Experiential Learning: Experience as a Source of Learning and Development*. New York: Prentice Hall.

Koller, D. (2012) *MOOCs on the Move: How Coursera Is Disrupting the Traditional Classroom*, podcast and video. Available at: http://knowledge.wharton.upenn.edu/article/moocs-on-the-move-how-coursera-is-disrupting-the-traditional-classroom.

Korndörffer, W. (1991) Vocational skills training in transition education, in D. Corson (ed.) *Education for Work*. Clevedon: Multilingual Matters Ltd, pp. 220–31.

Krol, E. (1994) *The Whole Internet*. Sebastopal, CA: O'Reilly and Associates.

Labour Party (1996) *Road to the Manifesto: Lifelong Learning*. London: Labour Party.

Langenbach, M. (1988) *Curriculum Models in Adult Education*. Malabar, FL: Krieger Publishing.

Langford, G. (1985) *Education, Persons and Society: A Philosophical Enquiry*. Basingstoke: Macmillan.

Laurillard, D. (2002) *Rethinking University Teaching: A Framework for the Effective Use of Educational Technology*, 2nd edn. London: Routledge.

Lave, J. and Wenger, E. (1991) *Situated Learning: Legitimate Peripheral Participation*. Cambridge: Cambridge University Press.

Lawton, D. (1983) *Curriculum Studies and Educational Planning*. London: Hodder & Stoughton.

Lea, J., Armitage, A., Hayes, D., Lomas, L. and Markless, S. (2003) *Working in Post-Compulsory Education*. Maidenhead: Open University Press.

Leadbeaver, C. (2004) *Personalisation through Participation*. London: Demos.

Learning and Skills Council (LSC) (2001) *Circular 01/02: Quality Improvement Standards Fund 2001/02*. Coventry: LSC.

Leicester, M. (1994) Competence, knowledge and education: reply to Hyland, *Journal of Philosophy of Education*, 28(1): 113–18.

Leitch Review of Skills (2006) *Prosperity for All in the Global Economy – World Class Skills* (final report). London: HM Treasury. Available at: www.dfes.gov.uk/skillsstrategy/uploads/documents/Leitch%20Review.pdf.

Lester Smith, W.O. (1957) *Education*. Harmondsworth: Penguin.

Lewis, T. (1991) Difficulties attending the new vocationalism in the USA, *Journal of the Philosophy of Education*, 25(1): 95–108.

Lewis, T. (1997) Towards a liberal education, *Journal of the Philosophy of Education*, 3(3): 477–90.

Lewin, K. (1946). Action research and minority problems. *Journal of Social Issues*, 2(4), pp. 34–46.

Lingfield, R. (2012a) *Professionalism in Further Education: Interim Report* (March). London: DBIS

Lingfield, R. (2012b) *Professionalism in Further Education: Final Report* (October). London: DBIS.

Livingstone, S. (2012) Critical reflections on the benefits of ICT in education, *Oxford Review of Education*, 38(1): 9–24.

LLUK/FENTO (2005) *E-learning Standards for E-Learning Context – Application of ICT to Teaching and Supporting Learning*. London: LLUK.

LLUK (2007a) *New Overarching Professional Standards for Teachers, Tutors and Trainers in the Lifelong Learning Sector*. London: LLUK. Available at: www.lluk.org/wpcontent/uploads/2010/11/new-overarching-professional-standards-for-teachers-tutorsand-trainers-in-wales.pdf (accessed 8 October 2010).

LLUK (2007b) *Using the MSC Leadership and Management Standards in the Lifelong Learning Sector*. London: LLUK. Available at: www.lluk.org/4561.htm.

Locke, J. ([1693] 1989) *Some Thoughts Concerning Education*. Oxford: Clarendon Press.

Lovell, R.B. (1980) *Adult Learning*. London: Croom Helm.

LSN (Learning and Skills Network) (2008) *Measuring e-Maturity in the FE Sector: A Research Report Prepared by the Learning and Skills Network*. Coventry: BECTA. Available at: www.becta.org.uk/research/reports/measuringmaturityfe08 (accessed 15December 2010).

Lukás, G. (1968) *History and Class Consciousness*. London: Merlin Press.

Lumby, J. and Foskett, N. (2005) *14–19 Education, Policy, Leadership & Learning*. London: Sage Publications.

Maclure, J.S. (1965) *Educational Documents: England and Wales*. London: Chapman and Hall (reprinted by Methuen, London and New York).

Maclure, S. (1988) *Education Reformed: A Guide to the Education Reform Act*. London: Hodder & Stoughton.

Malik, K. (2001) *What Is It To Be Human?* London: The Institute of Ideas.

Martinez, P. (1999) *Learning from Continuing Professional Development*. London: FEDA.

Marx, K. ([1867] 1974) *Capital*, Vol. 1. London: Lawrence & Wishart.

Marx, K. ([1875] 1968) Critique of the Gotha Programme, in K. Marx and F. Engels (eds) *Selected Works*. London: Lawrence & Wishart.

Maslow, A.H. (1970) *Motivation and Personality*. New York: Harper & Row.

Maynard, T. and Furlong, J. (1993) Learning to teach and models of mentoring, in D. McIntyre, H. Hagger and M. Wilkin (eds) *Mentoring: Perspectives on School-based Teacher Education*. London: Kogan Page.

McCulloch, G. (2002) Disciplines contributing to education? Educational studies and the disciplines, *British Journal of Educational Studies*, 50(1): 100–19.

McGivney, V. (1990) *Access to Education for Non-Participating Adults*. Leicester: NIACE.

McIntyre, D., Hagger, H. and Wilkin, M. (eds) (1993) *Mentoring: Perspectives on School-based Teacher Education*. London: Kogan Page.

McNamara, B. (1979) *Focus on Teaching*. London: Longman.

McNiff, J. (2003) How do we develop a twenty-first century knowledge base for the teaching profession in South Africa? How do we communicate our passion for learning? Available online at www.jeanmcniff.com/21.html.

McNiff, J. with Whitehead, J. (2002) *Action Research: Principles and Practice*, 2nd edn. London: RoutledgeFalmer.

McNiff, J. and Whitehead, J. (2006) *All You Need to Know About Action Research*. London: Sage.

Millerson, G. (1964) *The Qualifying Associations: A Study in Professionalism*. London: Routledge.

Moon, J. (2004) *Reflection in Learning and Practice* Abingdon: RoutledgeFalmer

Moore, M. (1983) On a theory of independent study, in D. Sewart, D. Keegan and B. Holmberg (eds) *Distance Education: International Perspectives*. London: Croom Helm, pp. 68–94.

Mortiboys, A. (2005) *Teaching with Emotional Intelligence: A Step-by-step Guide for Further and Higher Education Professionals*. London and New York: RoutledgeFalmer.

Mullan, P. (2001) *The Imaginary Time Bomb: Why an Ageing Population is not a Social Problem*. London: IB Tauris.

Muttona, T., Mills, B.G. and McNicholls, J. (2006) Mentor skills in a new context: working with trainee teachers to develop the use of information and communications technology in their subject teaching, *Technology, Pedagogy and Education*, 15(3): 337–52.

Napier, R.W. and Gershenfeld, M.K. (1989) *Groups, Theory and Experience*, 4th edn. Boston, MA: Houghton Mifflin.

NCVQ (National Council for Vocational Qualifications) (1988) Information Leaflet Number 1. London: NCVQ.

Nolan, J.L. (1998) *The Therapeutic State: Justifying Government at Century's End*. New York: New York University Press.

Nuttall, L. (1988) Transmitted, caught or taught? A whole school approach to personal and social education, *Pastoral Care*, March.

OCR (2015) Available at: http://www.ocr.org.uk/qualifications/by-type/vocational-education-and-skills/16-19-performance-table-reform/.

Ofsted (Office for Standards in Education) (2001a) *Handbook for Inspecting Colleges*. London: Ofsted Publications.

Ofsted (Office for Standards in Education) (2001b) *Curriculum 2000: The First Year of Implementation*. London: Ofsted.

Ofsted (2003) *The Initial Training of Further Education Teachers: A Survey*. HMI 1762. Available at: www.ofsted.gov.uk/publications/index.cfm?fuseaction=pubs .summary&id=3425.

Ofsted (Office for Standards in Education) (2010) *Handbook for the Inspection of Further Education and Skills*. London: Ofsted.

Ofsted (Office for Standards in Education) (2014) *Teaching, Learning and Assessment in Further Education and Skills – What Works and Why*. Available at: www.ofsted.gov .uk/resources/140138 (accessed 2 June 2015).

Ofsted (Office for Standards in Education)/ALI (Adult Learning Inspectorate) (2001) *A Common Inspection Framework for Post-16 Education and Training*. London: HMSO.

Passmore, J. (1973) On teaching to be critical, in R.S. Peters (ed.) *The Concept of Education*. London: Routledge & Kegan Paul, pp. 192–211.

Pemberton, C. (2006) *Coaching to Solutions: A Manager's Tool Kit for Performance Delivery*. Abingdon: Taylor & Francis.

Perks, D. (2004) The shattered mirror: a critique of multiple intelligences theory, in D. Hayes (ed.) *The Routledge Falmer Guide to Key Debates in Education*. London and New York: Routledge, pp. 122–6.

Perks, D. (2007) *What Neuroscience Cannot Tell Us About Humanity*. Battles in Print. Available at: www.battleofideas.org.uk/2010/battles/1070.

Perkinson, H.J. (1980) *Since Socrates: Studies in the History of Western Educational Thought*. London: Longman.

Peters, J.M. (1994), Instructors as researchers and theorists: faculty development in a community college, in R. Benn and R. Fieldhouse (eds) *Training and Professional Development in Adult and Community Education*. Exeter: CRCE.

Peters, R.S. ([1963] 1980) Education as initiation, in P. Gordon (ed.) *The Study of Education*, Vol. 1. London: Woburn, pp. 273–99.

Petty, G. (2014) *Teaching Today: A Practical Guide*, 5th edn. Oxford: Oxford University Press.

Phillips, M. (1996) *All Must Have Prizes*. London: Little, Brown & Company.

Plato (1956) *Protagoras and Meno*, trans. W.K.C. Guthrie. Harmondsworth: Penguin.

Plato (1993) *The Apology*, in H. Tarrant (ed.) *The Last Days of Socrates*. Harmondsworth: Penguin.

Plato (1982) *Republic*. In *The Portable Plato*, edited with an introduction by Scott Buchanan. Harmondsworth: Penguin.

Pollard, A. and James, M. (eds) (2004) *Personalised Learning: A Commentary by the Teaching and Learning Research Programme*. London: ESRC.

Powell, S. and Tummons, J. (2011) *Inclusive Practice in the Lifelong Learning Sector* Exeter: Learning Matters.

Poynter, G. (2000) *Restructuring in the Service Industries*. London: Mansell.

Preedy, M. (1989) *Approaches to Curriculum Management*. Maidenhead: Open University Press.

Prensky, M. (2001) Digital natives, in *On the Horizon*, NCB University Press, 9(5), October 2001. Chapter PDF available at: www.marcprensky.com/writing/Prensky%20-%20Digital%20Natives,%20Digital%20Immigrants%20-%20Part1.pdf (accessed February 2007).

Priestley, M. (2003) Curriculum 2000: a broader view of A levels? *Cambridge Journal of Education*, 33(2): 237–55.

Pring, R. (1992) Liberal education and vocational preparation, in M. Williams, R. Daugherty and F. Banks (eds) *Continuing the Education Debate*. London: Cassell, pp. 54–64.

Pring, R. (1993) Liberal education and vocational preparation, in R. Barrow and P. White (eds) *Beyond Liberal Education: Essays in Honour of Paul H. Hirst*. London: Routledge, pp. 49–78.

Pring, R. (1995) *Closing the Gap: Liberal Education and Vocational Preparation*. London: Hodder & Stoughton.

Pring, R., Hayward, G., Hodgson, A., Johnson, J., Keep, E., Oancea, A., Rees, G., Spours, K. and Wilde. S. (2009) *Education for All: The Future of Education and Training for the 14–19 Year Olds*. Abingdon: Routledge.

QCA (Qualifications and Curriculum Authority) (2001a) *Review of Curriculum 2000: Report on Phase 1*. London: QCA.

QCA (Qualifications and Curriculum Authority) (2001b) *Review of Curriculum 2000: Report on Phase 2*. London: QCA.

Quality Assurance Agency (1999) *Guidelines on the Quality Assurance of Higher Education*. Gloucester: QAA.

Race, P. (1992) *53 Interesting Ways to Write Open Learning Materials*. Bristol: Technical and Educational Services Ltd.

Raffe, D. (2005) Learning From 'Home International' Comparisons: 14–19 Curriculum and Qualifications Reform In England, Scotland and Wales. Joint Seminar of Education and Youth Transitions Project and Nuffield Review, 15 March 2005. Available at: www.nuffield14-19review.org.uk/cgi/documents/documents.cgi?a=117&t=template.htm.

Raggatt, P., Edwards, R. and Small, N. (eds) (1966) *The Learning Society, Challenges and Trends*. London: Routledge in association with the Open University.

Reece, I. and Walker, S. (2003) *A Practical Guide to Teaching, Training and Learning*, 3rd edn. Sunderland: Business Education Publishing.

Reeves, F. (ed.) (1997) *Further Education as Economic Regeneration: The Starting Point*. Bilston: Bilston Community College and Education Now Books.

Reigeluth, C. M. (1999) *Instructional-design Theories and Models*. Mahwah, NJ: Lawrence Erlbaum Associates, Inc.

Richard, D. (2012) The Richard Review of Apprenticeships. London: DBIS.

Riley, P. (1985) *Discourse and Learning*. London: Longman.

Robbins, Lord L.C. (1963) *Higher Education: Report of the Committee on Higher Education*, Cmnd 2154. London: HMSO.

Roberts, K., Blunden, G. and Ruseborough, G. (1994) Review symposium: class and skill, *British Journal of Sociology of Education*, 15(1): 119–27.

Robertson, J. (1989) *Effective Classroom Control*. London: Hodder & Stoughton.

Rodriguez, P., Nussbaum, M., and Dombrovskaia, L. (2012) ICT for education: a conceptual framework for the sustainable adoption of technology-enhanced learning environments in schools, *Technology, Pedagogy and Education*, 21(3): 291–315.

Rogers, A. (1996) *Teaching Adults*. Maidenhead: Open University Press.

Rogers, C. (1983) *Freedom to Learn for the '80s*. Columbus, OH: Merrill.

Rousseau, J.J. ([1762] 1991) *Émile*. Harmondsworth: Penguin.

Rowell, L., Yu Polush, E., Riel M. and Brewer, A. (2015) Action researchers' perspectives about the distinguishing characteristics of action research: a Delphi and learning circles mixed-methods study, *Educational Action Research*, 23(2): 243–70. Available at: http://www.tandfonline.com/doi/abs/10.1080/09650792.2014.990987 (accessed 17 June 2015).

Rowe, M.B. (1974) Wait time and rewards as instructional variables, their influences on language, logic and fate control, *Journal of Research in Science Teaching*, 11: 81–4.

Rowntree, D. (1987) *Assessing Students: How Shall We Know Them?* London: Kogan Page.

Russell, B. ([1959] 1989) *Wisdom of the West*. London: Bloomsbury.

Russell, D. (2014) *Times Educational Supplement*, 10 July.

Ryan, A. (1995) *John Dewey and the High Tide of American Liberalism*. New York: W.W. Norton.

Ryle, G. (1973) Teaching and training, in R.S. Peters (ed.) *The Concept of Education*. London: Routledge & Kegan Paul, pp. 105–19.

Salmon, G. (2002) *E-tivities: The Key to Active Online Learning.* London: Kogan Page.

Satterly, D. (1990) *Assessment in Schools.* London: Basil Blackwell.

Scales, P. (2011) *Teaching in the Lifelong Learning Sector,* 2nd edn. Maidenhead: Open University Press.

SCETT (2011) *In Defence of Teacher Education.* Worcester: Standing Committee for the Education and Training of Teachers.

Schön, D.A. (1983) *The Reflective Practitioner: How Professionals Think in Action.* London: Temple Smith.

Scrimshaw, P. (1983) *Purpose and Planning in the Classroom.* Maidenhead: Open University Press.

Seghal-Cuthbert, A. (2015) Neuroscience and education – an incompatible relationship, *Sociology Compass,* 9(1): 49–61.

Selwyn, N. (2011) *Schools and Schooling in the Digital Age: A Critical Analysis.* Abingdon: Routledge.

SEND (2014) *Code of Practice.* Available at: https://www.gov.uk/government.../send-code-of-practice-0-to-25.

Sennett, R. (2008) *The Craftsman.* London: Allen Lane.

Silver, R. (2010) *Towards a Strong Careers Profession: Report of the Careers Progression Task Force* (the Silver Report). London: DfE.

Simon, B. (1985) Marx and the crisis in education, in *Does Education Matter?* London: Lawrence & Wishart, pp. 173–96.

Sked, A. (1987) *Britain's Decline: Problems and Perspectives.* London: Basil Blackwell.

Skilbeck, M. (1976) *Curriculum Design and Development.* Maidenhead: Open University Press.

Skilbeck, M., Connell, H., Lowe, N. and Tait, K. (1994) *The Vocational Quest: New Directions in Education and Training.* London: Routledge.

Skinner, B.F. (1938) *The Behaviour of Organisms: An Experimental Analysis.* New York: Appleton-Century-Crofts.

Skuse, P. (1997) Evidence from Turner's Syndrome of an imprinted X-linked locus affecting cognitive functioning, *Nature,* 387: 705–8.

Smith, P., Rudd, P. and Coghlan, M. (NFER) (2008) *Harnessing Technology: Schools Survey 2008. Report 1: Analysis.* Coventry, BECTA. Available at: www.partners.becta.org.uk/index.php?section=rh&catcode=_re_rp_02&rid=15952 (accessed 15 January 2011).

Smithers, A. (2001) Education policy, in A. Seldon (ed.) *The Blair Effect.* London: Little, Brown & Company, pp. 405–26.

Smyth, J. (1989) Developing and sustaining critical reflection in teacher education, *Journal of Teacher Education,* 40(2): 2–9.

Social Exclusion Unit (1999) *Bridging the Gap: New Opportunities for 16–18 Year-Olds not in Education, Employment or Training.* London: The Stationery Office.

Stanton, G. (2005) *The Proposals for a New System of Specialist (Vocational) Diplomas,* Nuffield Review of 14–19 Education and Training Working Paper 32. Available at: www.nuffield14-19review.org.uk/cgi/documents/documents.cgi?a=117&t=template.htm.

Stenhouse, L. (1975) *An Introduction to Curriculum Research and Development.* London: Heinemann.

Stothart, C. (2006) Do the iPod shuffle, but don't miss the lecture, *Times Higher Education Supplement.* Available at: www.timeshighereducation.co.uk,story.asp? sectioncode=26&storycode=203333 (accessed 21 February 2011).

Sutcliffe, J. (1990) *Adults with Learning Difficulties*. Leicester: NIACE.

Taba, H. (1962) *Curriculum Development: Theory and Practice*. New York: Harcourt Brace.

Tanner, D. and Tanner, L.M. (1980) *Curriculum Development: Theory Into Practice*. New York: Macmillan.

Tarrant, H. (ed.) (1993) *The Last Days of Socrates*. Harmondsworth: Penguin.

Tawney, R.H. (1922) *Secondary Education for All* (reprinted 1988). London: The Hambledon Press.

Taylor, P.H. and Richards, C.M. (1985) *An Introduction to Curriculum Studies*. Windsor: NFER Nelson.

Teacher Training Agency (TTA) (1995) *Corporate Plan 1995: Promoting High Quality Teaching and Teacher Education*. London: TTA.

Tennant, M. (2002) *Learning and Change in the Adult Years: A Developmental Perspective*. San Francisco, CA: Jossey-Bass.

Tennant, M. (2005) *Psychology and Adult Learning*. London: Routledge.

The Economist (1996) Training and jobs: what works?, 6 April.

The Leitch Review of Skills (2006) *(The Leitch Report) Prosperity for All in the Global Economy – World Class Skills*. London: HMSO.

Therborn, G. (1978) The Frankfurt School, in *New Left Review* (ed.) *Western Marxism: A Critical Reader*. London: Verso, pp. 83–139.

Thomson, A. (2009) Why the professor called 14–19 diplomas a vocational 'tease', *FE Focus*, *TES*, 20 February.

Thorndike, E.L. (1912) *Education: A First Book*. New York: Macmillan.

Tight, M. (ed.) (2003a) *Adult Learning and Education*. London: Routledge.

Tight, M. (2003b) *Key Concepts in Adult Education and Training*. London: Routledge.

Timmins, N. (1996) *The Five Giants: A Biography of the Welfare State*. London: Fontana.

Tomlinson, S. (2001) *Education in a Post-welfare Society*. Maidenhead: Open University Press.

Tough, A. (1979) *The Adult's Learning Projects: A Fresh Approach to Theory and Practice in Adult Learning*. Toronto: Ontario Institute for Studies in Education.

Tufte, E.R. (2003) PowerPoint is evil, *Wired*, 11(09), September. Available at: www.wired .com/wired/archive/11.09/ppt2.html (accessed 12 December 2010).

Tyler, R. (1971) *Basic Principles for Curriculum and Instruction*. Chicago, IL: University of Chicago Press.

Usher, R. and Edwards, R. (1994) *Postmodernism and Education*. London: Routledge.

Vaitilingham, R. (2009) *Recession Britain: Findings from Economic and Social Research*. London: Economic and Social Research Council.

Vygotsky, L.S. (1978) *Mind in Society*. Cambridge, MA: Harvard University Press.

Wake, G. (2005) *Functional Mathematics: More Than 'Back to Basics'*, Nuffield Review of 14–19 Education and Training Aims, Learning and Curriculum Series, Discussion Paper 17. Available at: www.nuffield14-19review.org.uk/cgi/ documents/documents. cgi?a=117&t=template.htm.

Walker, D.F. and Soltis, J.F. (1997) *Curriculum and Aims*. London: Teachers College Press.

Walklin, L. (1990) *Teaching and Learning in Further Education*. Cheltenham: Stanley Thornes.

Wallace, S. (2013) *Managing Behaviour in Further and Adult Education*, 3rd edn. Exeter: Sage.

Warnock, M. (2005) *Special Educational Needs: A New Look.* Impact No. 11, Philosophy of Education Society of Great Britain.

Waugh, C. (2000) Learning policy: a powerful indictment – but what role has the working class to play? *General Educator,* 62: 13–16.

Wheeler, B. (2014) Officials wanted to axe FE Colleges – Vince Cable, *BBC News,* 6 October. Available at: http://www.bbc.co.uk/news/uk-politics-29496475 (accessed 24 June 2015).

Williams, A. (2010) 'The Big Society' (or 'compulsory voluntarism'). Paper presented at the Muslim Institute summer conference, Cardiff, 24 July 2010, *Culture Wars,* 26 August 2010. Available at: http://www.culturewars.org.uk/index.php/site/article/the_big_society_or_compulsory_voluntarism/.

Williams, K. (1994) Vocationalism and liberal education: exploring the tensions, *Journal of Philosophy of Education,* 28(1): 89–100.

Williams, M. (1992) Ruskin in context, in M. Williams, R. Daugherty and F. Burns (eds) *Continuing the Education Debate.* London: Cassell.

Williams, M., Daugherty, R. and Burns, F. (eds) (1992) *Continuing the Education Debate.* London: Cassell.

Willis, P. (1987) Foreword, in D. Finn (ed.) *Training Without Jobs: New Deals and Broken Promises.* London: Macmillan.

Winch, C. (2003) *Some Philosophical and Policy Considerations Concerning Vocational and Prevocational Education,* Nuffield Review of 14–19 Education and Training Working Paper 1. Available at: www.nuffield14-19review.org.uk/cgi/documents/documents.cgi?a=117&t=template.htm.

Wolf, A. (1993) *Assessment Issues and Problems in a Criterion-based System.* London: FEU.

Wolf, A. (1995) *Comperence-based Assessment:* Maidenhead: Open University Press.

Wolf, A. (2002) *Does Education Matter? Myths about Education and Economic Growth.* Harmondsworth: Penguin.

Wolf, A. (2005) 'Alison Wolf,' *Times Higher Education Supplement (THES),* 18 March. Available at: www.timeshighereducation.co.uk/story.asp?storyCode=194802&sectioncode=26.

Wolf, A. (2009) *An Adult Approach to Further Education: How to Avoid the Destruction of Adult and Vocational Education.* London: Institute of Economic Affairs.

Wolf, A. (2011) *Review of 14–19 Vocational Education* (the Wolf Report). London: DfE.

Wolf, A. (2015) *Heading for the Precipice: Can Further and Higher Education Funding Policies be Sustained?* London: Policy Institute at King's College/Gatsby Foundation.

Wolf, A. and Black, H. (1990) *Knowledge and Competence: Current Issues in Training and Education.* Sheffield: Careers and Occupational Information Centre.

Woods, J. and Hine, J. (eds) (2009) *Work with Young People: Theory and Policy for Practice.* London: Sage.

Working Group on 14–19 Curriculum Reform (2004) *The Final Report on 14–19 Curriculum and Qualifications Reform* (the Tomlinson Report). London: Working Group on 14–19 Reform.

Woudhuysen, J. (1997) Before we rush to declare a new era, in G. Mulgan (ed.) *Life After Politics.* London: Fontana, pp. 352–9.

Wragg, E. C. (1999) *An Introduction to Classroom Observation,* 2nd edn. London: Routledge.

Yaffe, D. (1978) *The State and the Capitalist Crisis.* London: Mimeo.

Young, M.F.D. (1971) *Knowledge and Control: New Directions for the Sociology of Education.* London: Collier-Macmillan.

Young, M.F.D. (1998) *The Curriculum of the Future: From the New Sociology of Education to a Critical Theory of Learning.* London: Falmer Press.

Young, M.F.D. (2008) *Bringing Knowledge Back In.* London: Routledge.

Young, T. (2014) *Prisoners of the Blob: Why Most Education Experts are Wrong About Nearly Everything.* London: Civitas.

Youngman, M.B. (1986) *Analysing Questionnaires.* Nottingham: University of Nottingham School of Education/Trentham Books.

Youngman, M.B. (1994) Designing and using questionaires, in W. Bennett, B. Glatter and R. Levačić (eds) *Improving Educational Management through Research and Consultancy.* London: Paul Chapman Publishing in association with the Open University.

Zuber-Skerritt, O. (1996) 'Emancipatory action research for organisational change and management development'. In Zuber-Skerritt, O. (ed.) *New Directions in Action Research.* London: Falmer Press, pp. 83–104.

INDEX

Page numbers in *italics* refer to tables.